Managing Disruptive Behaviors in the Schools

A Schoolwide, Classroom, and Individualized Social Learning Approach

Ronald C. Martella

Eastern Washington University

J. Ron Nelson

University of Nebraska–Lincoln

Nancy E. Marchand-Martella

Eastern Washington University

Boston   New York   San Francisco
Mexico City   Montreal   Toronto   London   Madrid   Munich   Paris
Hong Kong   Singapore   Tokyo   Cape Town   Sydney

Series Editor: *Arnis E. Burvikovs*
Editorial Assistant: *Matt Forster*
Production Editor: *Michelle Limoges*
Marketing Manager: *Tara Whorf*
Editorial-Production Service: *Omegatype Typography, Inc.*
Manufacturing Buyer: *JoAnne Sweeney*
Composition and Prepress Buyer: *Linda Cox*
Cover Administrator: *Kristina Mose-Libon*
Electronic Composition: *Omegatype Typography, Inc.*

For related titles and support materials, visit our online catalog at www.ablongman.com.

Between the time website information is gathered and published, some sites may have closed. Also, the transcription of URLs can result in typographical errors. The publisher would appreciate notification where these occur so that they may be corrected in subsequent editions.

Library of Congress Cataloging-in-Publication Data
Martella, Ronald C.
     Managing disruptive behaviors in the schools: a schoolwide, classroom, and individualized
     social learning approach / Ronald C. Martella, J. Ron Nelson, Nancy E. Marchand-Martella.
          p.   cm.
     Includes bibliographical references and index.
     ISBN 0-205-31839-8
     1. Classroom management.   2. Behavior modification.   I. Nelson, Ron (J. Ron)
II. Marchand-Martella, Nancy E.   III. Title.

LB3013 .M35 2003
371.102'4—dc21   2002016388

Printed in the United States of America
10   9   8   7   6   5   4   3   2   1   07   06   05   04   03   02

Contents

PART THREE • *Classroom Organizational Systems*   132

6   *Managing Behavior within the Classroom*
Preliminary Considerations   132

7   *Managing Behavior within the Classroom*
Instructional Variables   157

8   *Managing Behavior within the Classroom*
The Think Time Strategy   **188**

PART FOUR   •   *Individualized Organizational Systems*   215

9   *Managing Individualized Behavior*
Pinpointing and Tracking a Behavior Problem   **215**

10 *Managing Individualized Behavior*

Functional Behavioral Assessments **248**

11 *Managing Individualized Behavior*

Increasing Desirable Behaviors **283**

12   *Managing Individualized Behavior*
Decreasing Undesirable Behaviors   **314**

Preface

One of the most critical issues facing teachers is behavior management. Teachers consistently rate behavior management as their most concerning issue. Unfortunately, most teachers do not think they are equipped to deal with the multitude of behavior problems they face daily. Behavior management is not typically well planned; behavior management procedures are usually used more on an as-needed basis. In other words, many teachers fly by the seat of their pants when dealing with behavior issues in the classroom or in other locations around the school. There are several problems with approaching management in this way. First, behavior management procedures are less successful at stopping the behavior when they are not planned beforehand. Second, there are no assurances that behavior change will maintain over time and generalize to other settings. Third, the use of aversive-based management approaches may be more likely in the classroom. Finally, there is ultimately less time for instruction because there are increases in behavior problems in the classroom.

Therefore, teachers and other school-related personnel must look at behavior management as they do instruction. Teachers do not typically enter into instruction without some advanced planning or development of lesson plans. For reading, teachers must decide how best to teach their students, such as through a meaning emphasis approach, a code-based approach, or a combination of the two. Many teachers, however, enter into behavior management without doing the same thing. Teachers and other school-related personnel should plan for behavior management. To do so, they must determine how best to approach management issues. Teachers and other school-related personnel must decide on what they see as the motivating factors for misbehavior, such as for some inner need for control or due to some environmental event taking place. In making this decision, it is critical for teachers to consider the scientific evidence supporting one approach or the other. Several theories and models are available to teachers to improve the behavior of students. Many do not have any support whatsoever.

Thus, it is not enough to simply pick a management technique. Teachers and other school-related personnel must understand why techniques work or, more importantly, why they may not work. This understanding must come from what is known about the theories, models, or techniques gained through empirical scientific research. Therefore, as with instructional methods, teachers must be aware of the research support for behavior management methods.

Managing Disruptive Behaviors in the Schools: A Schoolwide, Classroom, and Individualized Social Learning Approach is designed differently from other management texts. We designed this text to aid teachers and other school-related personnel in the problem solving that must occur when preventing or responding to behavior management issues. We see this problem-solving approach as having three levels: schoolwide management, classroom management, and individualized management. Other texts do not provide the balanced coverage of each area, as is done here. For example, many texts provide extensive coverage of classroom management techniques but provide little if any coverage of schoolwide and individualized management techniques. Other texts provide extensive coverage of individualized management techniques but provide little if any coverage of schoolwide and classroom techniques. Therefore, our goal is to provide the most extensive coverage possible of all three critical levels of behavior management so that teachers and other school-related personnel can plan for and respond to behavior management issues effectively.

Contents

Part I is an introduction to behavior management. In Chapter 1, different behavior management models are described and assessed, common misconceptions of effective behavior management models are explained, and the right to effective behavioral treatment is discussed. Chapter 2 provides the social learning foundations on which the text is based. Understanding these foundations is critical if one is to become an effective behavior manager.

Part II describes schoolwide organizational systems. A discussion of school violence is provided in Chapter 3. Topics covered include the safety of schools, misconceptions about school safety, and how to conduct a fact-based threat assessment. Chapter 4 provides a description of an empirically validated schoolwide planning system (SPBIS). This system can be used to plan for the school climate, discipline and attendance procedures, and security issues. Chapter 5 provides a more in-depth description of a schoolwide system, including how to plan, select, implement, and evaluate evidence-based interventions and programs.

Part III describes classroom organizational systems. Preliminary systems covered in Chapter 6 include seating arrangements, nonverbal communication, rules, routines, precorrection strategies, social skill development, and group contingencies. Instructional variables are discussed in Chapter 7. These instructional variables include the use of time, curriculum and lesson plans, transitions, and the use of evidence-based instructional methods. Chapter 8 provides a detailed description of the Think Time strategy. This strategy is extensively field-tested and research validated. A step-by-step description on the use of Think Time is provided.

Part IV provides individualized organizational system information. Chapter 9 discusses how to pinpoint and track a behavior problem. Data-based decision making is highlighted in the chapter. Functional behavioral assessments are covered in detail in Chapter 10. The types of functional behavioral assessments are described as well as how to use information from these assessments to write an effective behavior management plan. Intervention methods for increasing desirable behaviors are covered in Chapter 11. These procedures include both antecedent manipulation procedures as well as positive reinforcement-based consequential procedures. Finally, Chapter 12 provides a description of interventions aimed at decreasing undesirable behaviors. These interventions are arranged within the chapter from the least restrictive and intrusive to the most restrictive and intrusive.

Each chapter opens and closes with a vignette relating to the chapter's content. In addition, chapter-opening objectives as well as end-of-chapter discussion questions are included. Another feature is a list of web resources for readers interested in further investigation of issues discussed in this text. This can be found in Appendix B. We trust the reader will find this valuable for obtaining additional information on evidence-based practices. Our collective professional goals have been to bring about the development of effective management procedures used in the schools. We hope that this book will further this important cause.

We recommend that the book be used in its current sequence, by school psychologists, administrators, general educators, counselors, and other related service providers. Special educators, however, may wish to follow a sequence of Part I, Part IV, Part II, and Part III, because these educators typically deal with students who exhibit severe behavior problems after other school and classroom management systems have failed.

Acknowledgments

We dedicate this book to our children, Ame'dee and Dominic (RCM and NEM-M) and Carly (JRN). In addition, we would like to acknowledge the individuals who have affected our careers. First and foremost, we wish to thank our families for their support. Also, to all the faculty who spent countless hours teaching us about what works in behavior management, we thank you. We would also like to thank those individuals who have meant a great deal to us—our colleagues. Specifically, we would like to thank Drs. Marion Tso, Kathleen Waldron-Soler, Flint Simonsen, Mike Epstein, Hill Walker, and George Sugai.

Several individuals were involved in completing this text. We would like to thank everyone at Allyn and Bacon for their continued support in this project, especially Mr. Paul Smith and Mr. Arnis Burvikovs, without whom this project would not have come to fruition. To the students who helped with tasks associated with the production of this text—Steve Lavigne, Greg Maddigan, and Cheryl Schieffer—we extend our sincere thanks. Finally, we wish to thank the reviewers who provided invaluable feedback and suggestions to help us produce a better book: Belva C. Collins, University of Kentucky; J'Anne Ellsworth, Northern Arizona University; Lawrence Lyman, Emporia State University; Darcy Miller, Washington State University; Barba Patton, University of Houston–Victoria; Jack V. Powell, University of Georgia; Bruce Smith, Henderson State University.

1

Behavior Management Models

Chapter Objectives

After studying this chapter, you should be able to:

- Explain how assertive discipline is implemented.
- Define logical consequences.
- Illustrate how to implement Glasser's model.
- Specify the approach of love and logic.
- Characterize the Kounin model.
- Depict the Jones model.
- Describe the Ginott model.
- Characterize the pros and cons of each of these models.
- Explain why there are misunderstandings of effective behavior management approaches.
- Specify the right to effective behavioral treatment.

VIGNETTE

MS. JACKSON HAS A STUDENT in her seventh-grade classroom who is having difficulty due to his angry outbursts. Ms. Jackson has tried a variety of techniques to decrease José's outbursts, all without success. She has tried telling him how his actions affect others. She has also tried to help him manage his anger by counting to 10 before he speaks. As a last resort, Ms. Jackson has been sending José to the office, where he talks about his anger with a school counselor.

Ms. Jackson does not know what to do. She has discussed the problem with other teachers and has tried their suggestions. She has asked Jose's parents to help her by talking with José and by not allowing him to play video games after school if he has a difficult day.

Ms. Jackson recently learned that José had been assessed 2 years previously for a suspected behavior disorder. The assessment team, however, determined that he did not meet the criteria for such a disability. She also learned that José has had counseling services over the last few years but to no avail. Most teachers believe that José is simply a student who has difficulty controlling his anger and that the best way to prevent his angry outbursts is to stay away from him and not to make many demands when he is in a bad mood.

Ms. Jackson believes that not making demands on José to prevent outbursts is not a viable option. She believes that doing so is not really helping her or José. She also believes that her job is to teach José how to act appropriately while he is in her classroom. Therefore, Ms. Jackson decides to journey into the world of behavior management approaches to see what has been found to work in situations such as hers.

Overview

The topic of how to manage student behavior in schools has been around as long as there have been schools. Behavior management has been and still is the chief concern of educators across the country (American Educator, 1996; Elam, Rose, & Gallup, 1996). When students misbehave, they learn less and keep their peers from learning (Schloss & Smith, 1994). Classroom behavior problems take up teachers' time and disrupt the classroom and school. Unfortunately, widespread use of effective management programs by teachers has not been instituted to solve management problems (Bailey, 1991).

Over the years, many management methods are tried, and many fail badly. Every year, "new and improved" behavior management methods hit the schools only to be thrown out by the end of the year. There are at least four possible causes for this cycle. First, preservice teachers may not be trained well in behavior management methods. Typically, a single classroom management class that provides a superficial view of behavior management is offered. Second, teachers may not be trained to analyze research on behavior management methods. We tend to flock to the "flavor or the month" procedures without a great deal of regard for what has been shown to work. Third, there is no unified theory of behavior management. Because the causes of behavior problems are often not agreed on, teachers may become confused about the causes of student behavior. Finally, behavior management is often viewed as a reactive approach to behavior problems and is either classroom or individually based.

We view behavior management from a three-tiered perspective. Figure 1.1 shows behavior management as a funnel. The largest number of students is exposed to a schoolwide approach so as to prevent and respond to behavior difficulties. Next, behavior management is handled from a classroom perspective. Finally, behavior management may be seen as individualized, in which the most troubled students are handled. Unfortunately, behavior management is rarely taught as schoolwide, classroom, and individualized approaches that can be used both to prevent and to respond to behavior problems. Behavior management is typically a response to the misbehavior. Educators should focus on treating behavior problems as they do academic problems. Prevention of behavior difficulties should be the goal; prevention, however, takes a great deal of planning at the building, classroom, and individual student levels.

Throughout this textbook, we overcome many of these weaknesses in behavior management training. This chapter covers different approaches that have been or are used to manage classroom behavior. Different philosophical perspectives of behavior management as well as the misunderstandings of effective behavior management approaches are also discussed.

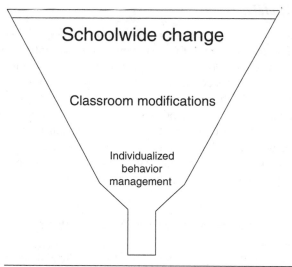

FIGURE 1.1 *Comprehensive behavior management model.*

What Is Discipline?

Over the years, **discipline** has been equated with punishment, specifically corporal punishment. Punishment and discipline, however, are not the same thing. Discipline involves teaching others right from wrong. The following are common definitions of the word *discipline* found in most dictionaries: training to act in accordance with rules, instruction and exercise designed to train proper conduct or action, behavior in accordance with rules of conduct, and set or system of rules and regulations. As seen in these definitions, discipline is about teaching students how to behave appropriately in different situations. Discipline is not punishment, although punishment is one possible way toward discipline. The question becomes, Are there other ways of teaching discipline to students?

What Are Alternative Behavior Management Approaches Used in Schools?

With the changing attitudes toward the use of punitive management procedures, schools have looked for alternative methods of student discipline. These approaches were and are aimed at developing and maintaining appropriate student behavior. The authors of these approaches attempt to describe why these approaches work. Unfortunately, many of the authors have overlooked some fundamentals in their approaches; that is, they ignore the effects on the student and fail to use scientific functional definitions for their approaches. Following are brief descriptions of various behavior management approaches used in schools. (These models are not exhaustive of all possible models, but they are representative of models used in the United States.)

Assertive Discipline Model

Lee Canter and associates developed the **Assertive Discipline** model, originally based on six major assumptions of student behavior. First, students should comply with rules. Second, students cannot be expected to determine appropriate classroom rules and follow them. Third, punishment will cause students to avoid bad behavior and engage in good classroom behavior. Fourth, good behavior can also be encouraged through rewards. Fifth, for proper classroom management, parents and school administrators must help enforce rules. Finally, better control will be demonstrated in the classroom if teachers learn to become assertive. In other words, teachers should communicate the ideas that their needs come first, that students will not be allowed to take advantage of teachers, and that teachers mean what they say and say what they mean. In their book *Assertive Discipline,* Canter and Canter (1976) stated the following:

1. Teachers have the right to determine the environmental structure, rules, and routines that will facilitate learning.
2. Teachers have the right to insist that students conform to their standards.
3. Teachers should prepare a discipline plan in advance, including statements of their expectations, rules, and routines and the type of discipline method to be used if and when students misbehave.
4. Students do not have the right to interfere with others' learning.
5. When students do not behave in a manner consistent with the teacher's expectations, teachers can respond one of three ways: nonassertively by surrendering to their students, hostilely by showing anger, or assertively by calmly insisting and assuming that students will fulfill their expectations.
6. Students choose to misbehave, and teachers should not accept their excuses for such misbehavior.
7. Teachers should use positive and negative consequences to convince students that it is to their benefit to behave appropriately.
8. Teachers should not feel badly when forced to use harshly negative consequences when necessary because students want teachers to help them control themselves.
9. Teachers have the right to ask for help from parents and school administrators when handling student misbehavior.

Canter and associates have modified assertive discipline over the years (Charles, 1996). Originally, Canter tried to get teachers to be strong leaders in the classroom. Therefore, his focus was on getting and keeping teachers in charge. In more recent times, however, Canter emphasizes the importance of focusing on student needs by talking with students more and teaching them how to behave appropriately. Therefore, Canter modified his model to make it more focused on positive discipline methods rather than on the use of force and **coercion.**

Steps to Assertive Discipline.   Canter and Canter (1992) describe the following five steps to Assertive Discipline.

Teachers Recognize and Remove Roadblocks to Assertive Discipline.   A major roadblock that must be removed is teachers' *negative expectations* about their ability to change the behavior of disruptive students. Indicating that students behave in a certain manner and cannot be changed due to their upbringing in a dysfunctional home is one example. Indicating that no one has been successful with these students in the past and probably will not be successful in the future is another roadblock. Teachers must acknowledge that they can and do affect student behavior. Therefore, if students are misbehaving, it is due to a lack of attempt to change the students' behavior or a lack of skill in doing so.

Another roadblock is teachers' assumed *lack of positive influence* on student behavior. Therefore, if teachers wish to remove this roadblock, they must do three things. First, teachers must acknowledge that all students need limits and have high expectations for appropriate behavior placed on them. Because it is the teachers' responsibility for setting limits and expectations, they should not make excuses for doing so. Second, Canter suggests that students admire and respect teachers who set high expectations and set limits for them; these limits and expectations, however, should be managed in a humane manner. Finally, teachers who have a laissez-faire approach to management will not be respected by their students. Therefore, teachers must take control over student behavior and be responsible for behavior change.

A final roadblock is an assumed *lack of support* from administrators, parents, and other school personnel. Teachers have a right to request and receive support from these individuals when dealing with management issues.

Practicing the Use of Assertive Response Styles.   Teachers must realize that their response styles set the tone for their classroom. All teachers can learn to display an **assertive response style,** which is the most effective style teachers can have. Canter suggests that there are three general response styles: nonassertive, hostile, and assertive. **Nonassertive response styles** do not place strong demands on students. When demands are placed on students, they are passive. For example, stating to a student who is disrupting the class, "Please stop talking during this assignment," and then not addressing the continued disrupting behavior again reflect a nonassertive style. A **hostile response** style is one in which teachers make threats and sarcasm in response to student misbehavior. For example, stating to a student that he or she will regret talking back to the teacher is hostile. Hostile teachers are aggressive toward students. Unfortunately, these teachers may see student misbehavior cease because students may stop misbehaving out of fear of the teacher. Students who are exposed to such a style may become more likely to lash out against the teacher whenever there is an opportunity. Finally, an assertive response style is one in which teachers set the rules, and if students break the rules, teachers follow through with the discipline procedure, such as placing a check mark besides a student's name.

Make a Discipline Plan That Contains Good Rules and Clear, Effective Consequences.   The development of good discipline includes three components: rules, positive recognition, and consequences. Rules should state what the students should do in observable terms. For example, stating that students should keep their hands to themselves is better than stating that students should be respectful of others. Positive recognition involves providing attention to students who behave appropriately; doing so encourages good behavior in the future, improves self-esteem, and fosters a positive classroom climate. Finally, consequences involve implementing penalties when students misbehave. Canter recommends a discipline hierarchy as follows: (1) a verbal warning for the first disruption (e.g., "Sam, the rule is to keep your hands to yourself, and this is a warning"); (2) a time out for the second and third disruptions (e.g., "Sam, you continue to choose to touch other students, so you need to go to time out for 5 minutes"); (3) a phone call to parents for the fourth infraction ("Sam, you continue to touch others, so you have chosen to have your parents called"); (4) a trip to the principal's office for the fifth infraction ("Sam, you touched another student again, so you have chosen for me to send you to the office to discuss your behavior with the principal"); and (5) an immediate trip to the principal's office for the first infraction if the behavior is so severe that the hierarchy is disregarded (called a severe clause) (e.g., "Sam, punching another student is not tolerated, and you have chosen to go to the principal's office immediately").

Teach the Discipline Plan to the Students.   Canter highlights the need to teach students the discipline plan to make it work effectively. This teaching must be done explicitly and involves an explanation of why the rules are needed, instruction on the classroom rules, making sure the students understand the rules, an explanation of how students who follow rules will be rewarded, an explanation of why consequences are needed, instruction on what the consequences for rule infractions will be, and making sure students understand the discipline plan.

Teach Students How to Behave Responsibly.   A critical aspect of Assertive Discipline is teaching students how to behave appropriately. This instruction involves three components. First, students should be taught how to follow specific directions by giving directions just prior to an activity and then having the students act out the expectations. Second, positive recognition, especially **praise,** should be used when students are on task and following rules. Finally, when students engage in minor behaviors that are not disruptive, they should be redirected through the use of "the look," physical proximity, the student's name, and proximity praise.

Difficult Students.   Canter indicates that approximately 5% to 10% of students will continue to misbehave. Therefore, three approaches are used to work with these difficult students. First, a one-on-one problem-solving conference is scheduled in which the student and teacher attempt to gain insight into the student's behavior. The purpose is not to punish the student but to provide guidance. Second, relationships are built from the use of positive support. Teachers should show these students that they care about them as people and should make an attempt to get to know them on a more personal basis. These students must feel that the teachers truly care about them. Finally, an individualized behavior plan should be developed. These students need an intervention plan that is more specialized to their needs than to those of other students.

Analysis.   Assertive Discipline is based on the assumptions that teachers are the leaders of the classroom and that they should use punishment to bring control to the classroom, if needed. A major positive aspect of Assertive Discipline is the assumption that the behavior in a classroom results from what the teachers do in the classroom. Also, Canter has attempted to add more proactive methods of preventing management problems through teaching students about rules and expectations. Unfortunately, Assertive Discipline has several major weaknesses. An operational definition of punishment (see Chapter 2) is not used. In other words, punishment is assumed to be in effect with Assertive Discipline. Second, there is an inadequate database to suggest that the approach works. Much of the reported data on Assertive Discipline includes teacher testimonials. Although testimonials are important to consider, other important data sources are missing, such as does Assertive Discipline decrease the level of student misbehavior in the classroom as measured by direct observations and does Assertive Discipline decrease the level of office referrals? A third problem is the reliance on threats, warnings, and a discipline hierarchy. Research evidence suggests that threats and warnings tend to escalate the problem behaviors in a classroom (Nelson, 1996b). In other words, when teachers use threats and warnings, students are more likely to become aggressive than when threats and warnings are not used. Finally, Canter misuses the term *consequence* to suggest that it refers to punishment. Consequences, however, are anything that occurs, such as reinforcers, after behaviors are emitted. Therefore, Canter continues to misinform teachers by suggesting that consequences are restricted to certain events that occur after behaviors occur.

Assertive Discipline seems to be a behavior reduction method that can work under certain circumstances. Unfortunately, if Assertive Discipline does work to suppress unwanted behavior, it does so in a manner that may well make the long-term problem of disruptive behavior worse. The use of threats and warnings along with a lack of reinforcement for appropriate behavior seriously compromise the efficacy of this approach.

Logical Consequences Model

Rudolf Dreikurs (1968) developed the **Logical Consequences** model, built on the belief that we learn through our interaction with our environment. In doing so, behaviors are exposed to three types of negative consequences: natural, arbitrary, and logical (Clarizio, 1986). Clearly, natural consequences are usually the most effective form of negative consequences in stopping unwanted behavior. A natural consequence for touching a hot stove is getting burned. A natural consequence for fighting is to get hurt. A natural consequence for abusing toys is for the toys to break. A natural consequence for a student who lies is that no one believes that person. A natural consequence for calling others names is to be ignored by peers. A problem with natural consequences is that they may either be too minor to have an effect, such as a broken toy when other toys are available, or that we must prevent the outcomes of these consequences, such as not allowing one to become injured. Another difficulty with relying on natural consequences is that they may not appear. For example, there are no real natural consequences for temper tantrums or drawing on one's desk.

If we cannot rely on natural consequences under all circumstances, we have a choice as educators as to the type of consequences we can use. **Arbitrary consequences** are artificial in that they usually do not occur in all classroom environments. An arbitrary consequence for fighting is to send the student to the principal's office. An arbitrary consequence for abusing toys is to reprimand the student. An arbitrary consequence for a student who lies is that the student loses computer time. An arbitrary consequence for calling others names is to send the student to time out. For those consequences that do not have natural consequences, arbitrary consequences could involve sending the student to in-school suspension for a temper tantrum or taking away free time for drawing on one's desk.

The second option for teachers to use rather than arbitrary consequences is logical consequences, those consequences that are connected in some manner with the offense. A logical consequence for fighting during recess is to prevent the student from going to recess for a week. A logical consequence for abusing toys is for the toys to be removed for the rest of the day. A logical consequence for a student who lies is for the teacher to tell the student that he or she is not believable. A logical consequence for calling others names is to require the student to be seated alone and away from the other students. For temper tantrums, a logical consequence is to remove the student from class until he or she calms down. As a logical consequence for writing on a desk, the teacher could require the student to wash it.

When teachers have the option of using arbitrary or logical consequences, logical consequences should be chosen. Dreikurs (1968) and Dreikurs, Grunwald, and Pepper (1982), among others, have suggested the use of logical consequences because they "fit the crime" and are understandable to students. In addition, logical consequences, they argue, produce fewer negative side effects such as power struggles because they appear to result from students' behavior rather than be arbitrarily selected by teachers. Finally, logical consequences are said to be less harsh when compared with arbitrary punishers.

Assumptions of Logical Consequences.   There are six assumptions of the Logical Consequences model (Dreikurs, 1968). First, inappropriate behavior is motivated by unconscious needs to gain attention, exercise power, exact revenge, or display inadequacy. It is the teachers' responsibility to determine and aid students in determining the motivation for their misbehavior. Once the motivation is determined, teachers can take steps to decrease the motivation. If the motivation is attention, teachers should refrain from providing attention. If the motivation is to exercise power, teachers should avoid involving themselves in power struggles. If the motivation is revenge, teachers should treat students in a manner that avoids the need for them to seek revenge, such as having students who were disrespectful to other students apologize. If the motivation is to display inadequacies, teachers should seek to build student self-confidence.

Second, if the motive for attention is satisfied, inappropriate behavior associated with other motives will not be manifested. Therefore, attention is a primary driving force for unwanted classroom behavior. By knowing that, teachers can put more focus on the types of attention students are receiving for the misbehavior.

Third, students can learn to understand their own motives and eliminate misbehavior by having teachers help them explore why they behave as they do. In this way, teachers aid students in becoming aware of why they are doing certain things and in developing self-control.

Fourth, students behave more appropriately when they suffer the logical consequences for the misbehavior. Logical consequences function to provide information to students that the unwanted behavior is not appropriate and will not be accepted in the classroom. Therefore, logical consequences allow students to begin to take more responsibility for their own actions.

Fifth, presenting students with a choice between two choices offers a sufficient basis on which they can learn to be responsible. When students have a hand in what they will be doing at any point in time, they will feel less controlled and will be more likely to behave appropriately.

Finally, students react to life based on their birth order. Therefore, the experiences children have in their families will be reflected in their behavior.

Analysis.   The basic assumption made in the Logical Consequences model that the motivation for classroom behavior is due to attention might be correct. Much of student motivation is to gain attention from teachers or peers. Whether this motivation is conscious or unconscious, however, is difficult to demonstrate. It seems adequate to determine if the motivation is or is not attention. Unfortunately, the other motivational areas (i.e., exercise power, exact revenge, display inadequacy) are all inferences that cannot be substantiated through direct observation. In other words, to suggest that students are misbehaving in a classroom due to an attempt to exercise power is based on what the students are receiving in return for the behavior (e.g., to gain a tangible item). This return for the behavior is then inferred to be a need for power. The major difficulty with this line of thought is that the focus is on the student as the cause for the behavior rather than on what the teachers do in response to student behavior.

The assumption that students behave more appropriately when they suffer logical consequences is also problematic. Although it is true that if logical consequences are effective the unwanted behavior will be less likely to continue, it does not mean that appropriate behavior will follow. What is needed, then, are logical consequences for appropriate behavior as well.

Another difficulty is that proponents of the Logical Consequences model equate arbitrary consequences with punishment. Logical consequences, however, can also function as punishment. In addition, what is an arbitrary consequence in one instance (e.g., sending the student to a part of the room away from peers for work refusal) may be a logical consequence in another context (e.g., sending the student away from peers for hitting another student). Therefore, what makes something an arbitrary or logical consequence is not the consequence in and of itself but the context in which it is presented. In other words, arbitrary and logical consequences can be the same things. Both types of consequences are provided to eliminate the behavior; thus, they are both meant to be punishers. Unfortunately, logical consequences may not be severe enough to overcome the reinforcement of the students' actions.

The assumptions that students can learn to understand their own motives and that they should be provided with choices are adequate. Teaching students to determine why they emit certain behaviors is an important skill. Also, providing a choice of activities to students has been shown to increase the likelihood that students will complete the chosen activity (Dunlap et al., 1994; Vaughn & Horner, 1997). Thus allowing student choices should be part of a management program implemented in a classroom.

The Logical Consequences model can be an effective method of behavior management if implemented without the inferences of various motivations. The research base for this model, however, is limited (Grossman, 1995). Therefore, before the Logical Consequences model is used, we should make sure that the approach has been determined to be effective through research.

Glasser's Model

William Glasser (1965) developed control theory. Glasser's basic premise was that students are in control of their own behavior and choose whether to behave appropriately or not. Classroom management should be designed to help students make better choices. Activities such as class meetings conducted weekly or more often can provide students feedback on how their behavior affects others. In addition, these meetings provide students with a variety of ideas for improved behavior in the future and provide support from peers to make behavior changes. Consequences for unwanted behaviors may or may not be used with students. The key to this approach is getting students to realize how their choices of behavior affect others.

Glasser outlines several assumptions. First, students are self-regulating and can learn to manage their own behavior. Second, students learn responsible behavior by examining a full range of consequences for their behavior and making value judgments about their behavior and its consequences. Third, avoiding an exploration of motives will help students accept responsibility. Fourth, student behavior consists of an effort to satisfy personal needs for love, power, freedom, and fun. Fifth, students have a unique way of satisfying their own needs. Finally, students cannot be forced to change what they believe about how best to satisfy their needs.

Glasser made changes in his earlier theory after 1986. The most obvious change was that the name of the theory was changed from "control" to "choice" because the term *control* is misleading and difficult to accept (Glasser, 1998a). He believed that the change to the term *choice* would be more acceptable to teachers and their students. A more significant change is Glasser's focus from looking only at the types of choices students make to approaches teachers can use to motivate students to participate willingly. Glasser realized that approaches used to force students to behave properly would ultimately fail. Schools must be redesigned to be quality schools that produce quality schoolwork.

Concepts.   **Glasser's model** rests on the assumption that human beings have five basic needs: survival, belonging and love, freedom, fun, and power. Choice theory explains behavior as a result of choosing what is most satisfying at the time. Therefore, what we do is not a result of what is going on in our external environment; instead, what we do is determined by what is most satisfying at the time. In other words, external control is a falsehood; internal control (i.e., act as best we can to satisfy a need) is where motivation is seated. Therefore, students do not come to class on time because teachers have set rules about coming to class. Students come to class on time if they view what is going on in the class as meaningful to them and can satisfy a basic need such as having fun or gaining power over what is to be learned.

Need for Survival.   Students' need for survival involves the need for food, shelter, and freedom from harm. Freedom from harm is important in that teachers can have a direct effect on how students feel in the classroom. Teachers can aid students in their satisfaction of this need by helping them feel safe in the classroom and by not using coercion to try to control behavior.

Need for Belonging and Love.   The need for belonging and love involves feeling comfortable and secure and having legitimate membership in the group. Teachers can aid in this need by creating a classroom environment in which students work together on meaningful activities, are included in class discussions, and receive attention from the teacher and others.

Need for Freedom. The need for freedom involves the ability to make choices, demonstrate responsibility, and be self-directed. Teachers should allow students to make choices regarding what they will study, how they will study it, and how they will demonstrate their execution. Also, teachers should use cooperative learning to allow students to investigate a topic of their choosing.

Need for Fun. Students have a need for fun that involves having a good time. To meet this need, teachers should become involved in interesting activities and be able to share their accomplishments with other students. In this context, fun refers to both emotional and intellectual enjoyment.

The Need for Power. Students have a need to feel important. Glasser calls this need "power." He believes that the struggle for power in every aspect in our lives is a uniquely human **trait**. According to Glasser, power is neither good nor bad because someone can use power to help those who are more powerless or to take advantage of the powerless. Students' need for power can be used by teachers by involving students in class decisions and responsibilities, such as taking roll or taking care of audiovisual equipment. Therefore, teachers can help students meet their need for power by giving them responsibilities. Students who do not have their need for power met will seek other avenues to gain power.

What Teachers Can Do. Glasser indicates that if schools are to survive, they must redesign themselves to emphasize quality in all student work. Clearly, a critical aspect of this change involves creating quality conditions in which fewer teachers and students are frustrated. Students must be helped to feel that they belong and have a certain amount of power. At the same time, students should have fun while learning and should feel free to choose what they learn in the process. Therefore, Glasser believes that schools must change. This change needs to be toward quality, which can be accomplished by encouraging, supporting, and helping students to produce quality work.

Conditions of Quality. Glasser (1998b) outlines six conditions of quality. First, there must be a warm, supportive classroom environment. Coercion should never be used in schools to control student behavior. If coercion is used, mistrust will prevail. Students must believe that teachers and administrators have their best interest in mind for them to produce quality work. Second, students should be asked to do only useful work. Useless material, such as memorizing useless facts, will soon be forgotten. If teachers expect useful work, students will be motivated to put forth the effort to learn. Third, students need to be asked to do the best they can. Students must be given the necessary time to complete assignments in a quality fashion. Fourth, students need to be asked to evaluate their own work and to improve upon it. All work can be improved; teachers need to help students understand how. Fifth, quality work needs to feel good. When students work hard to learn something, they should come out of the experience with a feeling of satisfaction. Finally, quality work can never be destructive. The type of effort students put forth should be to improve themselves or their environment. Work should not be to achieve good feelings through drugs, by harming other people or other living things, or by destroying property or the environment.

Setting Rules.   Glasser believes that rules should be developed in the class. Students, however, only need to learn the importance of courtesy. Therefore, rules should reflect courteous behavior without the need for other types of rules. For example, the rules "be kind to others" and "do our best work" should be sufficient. Students should aid in the development of rules and provide reasons why rules are needed and important. Also, when rules are broken, student feedback should be solicited on what should occur, and teachers should aid in determining why the rules are being broken and what can be done to avoid broken rules in the future.

If rules are broken, Glasser suggests that teachers stop the misbehavior in a nonpunitive manner and refocus the students on their work. If students are upset, teachers should tell them that help will not be provided until they are calm. Teachers should not speak in an emotional manner. If students do not calm down after 20 seconds, teachers should give them a time out from the lesson and discuss the situation with the students later. The critical aspect of the intervention is to treat students with respect and courtesy, not punish them. Students will then improve their behavior and the quality of their work.

Analysis.   Glasser's model has a number of positive attributes. For example, getting students involved in developing classroom procedures is positive. Also, who would not agree that making learning fun and exciting is an admirable goal? Glasser has also contributed to the overall change in behavior management perspectives that students' behaviors are affected by what teachers do in the classroom and that management methods should be positively based rather than coercive.

The basic premise that students are motivated by an effort to satisfy needs for love, power, freedom, and fun is difficult to substantiate, however. In other words, these things are inferences based on what we see students doing. For example, if a student is attempting to gain attention from the teacher, we may be tempted to infer that the student is seeking love. Likewise, if a student refuses to follow a teacher's instructions, we may be tempted to infer that the student is seeking power. These inferences, however, are based on what the student is doing and what the student receives in exchange for the behavior. Therefore, the inferences are not necessarily correct. We can simply stop at the point of saying that the student receives attention for the behavior or the student is able to get out of a task when she refuses to complete a task. Also, assuming that students choose their behavior in the way Glasser suggests puts the focus of responsibility on the students. Students do not have free choice in the classroom because the teacher sets up limits to behavior. Therefore, any choices students make are largely dependent on what the teachers do in the classroom. The focus, then, should be on what the teachers do that affects student behavior. Further, Glasser notes that student motivation comes from inside while also saying that teachers can set up the environment to improve motivation by meeting the needs of the students. If teachers can help meet student needs, the control does not come from within the students but, ultimately, from what the teachers do, which is external. Therefore, Glasser's model is inconsistent with its basic premise of motivation and what teachers can do to affect this motivation. A final problem with Glasser's model is that there is a paucity of research documenting its effectiveness especially because a cause- (i.e., satisfying needs) and-effect (i.e., improved student behavior) relationship cannot be demonstrated. This relationship cannot be shown because internal needs (1) are not directly observable and (2) cannot be directly controlled or manipulated.

Love and Logic Model

Jim Fay (1981) at the Cline/Fay Institute developed the **love and logic model,** which rests on four basic principles. First, students' self-concept is always a prime consideration. Therefore, teachers should always attempt to bolster students' self-esteem, even when disciplining them. The belief is that before students' behavior can be changed, their self-concept must be changed. Second, students should always be left feeling as if they have some control. Thus, alternatives should be provided to students so that they can make choices. Third, an equal balance of consequences and empathy should replace punishment whenever possible. Thus, teachers should allow natural consequences for students' behaviors to take place. When teachers impose sanctions on students, students tend to think about the anger expressed by the teachers rather than focusing on their own inappropriate actions and poor decisions. Fourth, students should be required to do more thinking than the adults do. In other words, students are required to make decisions with regard to their behavior and to live with the consequences of those decisions.

According to Fay (1981), there are three types of teaching and parenting styles: helicopters, drill sergeants, and consultants. Helicopters tend to hover over students to rescue them from the hostile world. These teachers/parents make excuses for students, take on the responsibilities of students, make decisions for students, and use guilt to get students to behave in a certain manner. The implied message sent to students is, "You are unable," which creates dependent students. Drill sergeants command students and direct their lives. These teachers/parents tell students how they should feel and handle responsibility. They have many demands and provide absolutes. They also provide threats and orders and use punishment, including the infliction of pain and humiliation. The implied message to the student is, "You are too dumb," which creates rebellious students. Consultants provide guidance and consultant services for students. These individuals provide messages of self-worth and strength, share personal feelings about something, provide and help students explore alternatives, and then allow students to make their own decisions. These teachers/parents aid students in experiencing natural consequences for their actions and aid students in exploring solutions to problems. The **implicit** message students receive from these teachers/parents is, "You can," which creates students who are thinking and responsible individuals.

Clearly, teachers should focus on being consultants to their students. The types of consequences used are logical, as described previously. In addition, consultants should go through a problem-solving process with their students. This process includes the following five steps. First, show empathy with statements, such as, "If that happened to me, I think I would feel…" Second, send power messages showing that teachers have confidence in students. A question such as, "How are you going to solve that problem?" would be appropriate. Third, gain permission to share alternatives by asking students if they would like to hear what others have tried. Fourth, aid students in looking at the consequences by saying something like, "What would you think would happen if…" Finally, give students permission for solving the problem or not solving it by stating something like, "I will support your decision in how you approach this problem."

When students are resistant to the teachers' guidance, several things should be attempted. For resistant behavior, teachers should catch students doing something good, interpret the resistant behavior, try to understand why the students are doing it, and provide qualified positive regard by telling students what teachers liked. When students are disruptive, the teachers should ignore the behavior, catch it early before it escalates, talk it over with students, and if needed, isolate students from others. Praise should be used, but it should be specific, directed toward the task, and given sparingly.

Overall, love and logic can be reduced to two rules (Fay, 1996). First, adults should set firm limits in loving ways without anger, lectures, or threats. Second, when students cause a problem, teachers should hand it back in loving ways. In other words, teachers hold students accountable for solving their problems in a manner that does not make a problem for others. Students are offered choices with limits imposed by the teachers. Teachers use enforceable statements and provide delayed or extended consequences; these consequences, however, are delivered with empathy.

Analysis.   Being concerned with how students feel about themselves is an important role of teachers. Also, decreasing the use of punishment is an important goal for all educators. Leading students through a problem-solving process can be an effective means of changing students' behavior, and providing choices to students can aid in their development as responsible individuals. The avoidance of threats and warnings and holding students accountable are positive aspects of the model. Also, catching the behavior early is an effective technique.

There is no **systematic method** of determining why students do what they do, though. It is not always true that if students feel loved and are provided with choices, they will become more responsible. At times, catching students being good and ignoring unwanted behavior is not enough. Teachers need more guidelines to prevent and respond to unwanted behavior. Talking it over with students can be a positive technique, yet *when* the talking occurs is important. Talking it out immediately after the behavior occurs may make the problem worse over the long run (Sulzer-Azaroff & Mayer, 1991). In addition, isolation of students for disruptions is an attempted punishment technique and should be acknowledged as such.

Overall, love and logic has many positive features. Unfortunately, the model provides many poorly defined procedures. Also, research demonstrating the overall effectiveness of the model is lacking, possibly due to the problem of not having precisely defined procedures and techniques.

The Kounin Model

Jacob Kounin (1970) developed the **Kounin model.** Kounin wanted to investigate the difference between effective and ineffective teachers with regard to management skills. This model has five assumptions. First, negative or positive moves by teachers toward students radiate out (the **ripple effect**) and influence others. Second, students need to be controlled by their teachers. Third, control can be improved by increasing the clarity and firmness of

desists (i.e., remarks intended to stop misbehavior). Fourth, teachers can improve control by displaying **"withitness"** (i.e., being aware of what is going on around them). Finally, when students have been appropriately identified as problem students and when the teachers' moves are properly timed, greater control of students' behavior is possible (Fay, 1996).

Principal Concepts.   To achieve meaningful behavior change, the Kounin model suggests the following concepts: the ripple effect, withitness, momentum, smoothness, group alerting, student accountability, overlapping, satiation, valence and challenge arousal, and seatwork variety and challenge (Charles, 1996).

The Ripple Effect.   The ripple effect involves the tendency for primary-aged students to react to teachers' actions when those actions are aimed at other students. For example, reprimanding one student for misbehavior tends to result in better behavior from the other students. The ripple effect, however, is not only seen with negative statements. Positive statements also have a ripple effect with young students, such as praising a student for on-task behavior resulting in improved on-task behavior of other students. Kounin found that older students seemed to be much more influenced by their liking of teachers (i.e., students behave better for the teachers they like).

Withitness.   One of the most powerful concepts Kounin found in reducing misbehavior in the classroom is withitness, which is simply being aware of what is going on in the classroom. Kounin believed so strongly in withitness that a major distinction between effective and ineffective teachers was whether they had it or not. Withitness is an important concept in that it allows teachers to catch student behavior early, before it escalates or generalizes to other students in the classroom. Also, students who believe that teachers are aware of their actions are less likely to misbehave in the first place.

Momentum.   Kounin believed that effective teachers begin lessons immediately after the start of class, keep lessons moving ahead with little down time, bring the lessons to a close, and make efficient **transitions** from one lesson to another. Momentum requires teachers to be well organized so that lesson pacing is not compromised.

Smoothness.   Smoothness is being able to conduct a lesson without undue interference or changes that disrupt the students. There are several obstacles to smoothness, such as getting off task during a lesson or spending too much time on one concept. As with momentum, smoothness involves teacher organization.

Group Alerting.   Kounin believed that it was important to gain students' attention to inform them what is expected. Group alerting involves making sure students are paying attention and then providing them with specific instruction on what they are supposed to do at any one time.

Student Accountability.   Student accountability involves keeping students involved in the lesson. Teachers can help with student involvement by making them active learners and asking them to answer questions, demonstrate concepts, or explain how something is done.

Overlapping.   Effective teachers can seemingly do several things at once. One example is a teacher who can provide a lesson to a group of students while answering questions from someone else in the classroom. Kounin called this skill "overlapping" in that several activities overlap and the teacher can control or have an influence over each of them.

Satiation.   Effective teachers attempt to avoid students becoming bored and frustrated. Therefore, these teachers try to make learning interesting and try to make students successful. When students are bored or frustrated, they tend to become less than interested in a topic. Kounin called this lack of interest "satiation." Satiation becomes evident in students' classroom behaviors. Students who are satiated on a lesson become disengaged from the lesson and turn to other less acceptable behaviors for relief, such as talking, moving about the classroom, and annoying others.

Valence and Challenge Arousal.   Kounin believed that teachers could delay satiation by making instructional activities more enjoyable and challenging. Teachers should be concerned with whether students have positive or negative reactions to a lesson. If students have negative reactions, teachers should find ways to change the students' **"valence"** (i.e., students' positive or negative reaction to a lesson) so their reaction to a lesson is positive. Kounin believed that teachers must show enthusiasm and use a variety of activities when teaching students so that they have a positive reaction to a lesson. Also, teachers can use media such as films, demonstrations, and props to make topics more interesting and meaningful to the students.

Seatwork Variety and Challenge.   Seatwork variety and challenge is similar to valence and challenge arousal except that rather than focusing on making instruction enjoyable, teachers should make seatwork interesting to students. Seatwork should also challenge students to prevent satiation of the topic.

Analysis.   The use of desists can stop behavior problems from continuing. The use of the Kounin model can be effective for low-level misbehavior. All teachers should learn how to use desists and withitness to control student behavior. In fact, much of Kounin's influence is seen in Chapters 5 and 6. The problem with the model, however, is that it is not complete. It does not suggest what to do with those students who continue to misbehave even for effective teachers. A comprehensive management system may involve components of the Kounin model but also needs many more components to be effective for most students.

The Jones Model

Frederic H. Jones (1987) developed the **Jones model,** which rests on three assumptions: children need to be controlled to behave properly, teachers can achieve control through nonverbal cues and movements calculated to bring them physically closer and closer to the students, and parents and administrators can be used to gain control over student behaviors. The main emphasis of this model is on overall group behavior.

Skill Clusters.   Jones proposed three clusters of teacher skills that keep students engaged in learning by preventing misbehavior or responding effectively to misbehavior: body language, incentive system, and provision of efficient help (Charles, 1996).

Body Language.   Jones indicated that 90% of effective discipline involves body language. Body language involves eye contact (e.g., looking directly into the students' eyes when communicating), physical proximity (e.g., moving next to misbehaving students), body carriage (e.g., strong movement and erect body stance), facial expressions (e.g., smiles when pleased with student behavior and frowns when displeased), and gestures (e.g., palm out to indicate to students to stop or thumbs up to indicate pleasure with their behavior).

Incentive Systems.   Jones believed that incentives are an important part of effective classroom management. He believed that effective teachers use incentives systematically. Unfortunately, the types of incentives many teachers use (e.g., points, stars) are available to only the top performers. Jones believed that incentives should be available to all students. He advocated five types of incentives. First, "genuine incentives" should be provided. These incentives, such as watching films or having free time to pursue personal interests, are group based. Jones believed that these incentives should be available to all students. He does not view tangible items (e.g., awards, certificates) to be viable incentives because they can be costly, are difficult to give, and may have little educational value.

Second, Jones advocated using "Grandma's rule." Teachers should provide an incentive to finish an assignment so that students earn something they want. Teachers may desire to provide the reward first, before the assignment is complete. The reward must be contingent on the completion of the assignment, however.

Third, incentives should be of "educational value." Having parties or engaging in noneducational rewards is difficult to condone. Therefore, Jones advocates using incentives that are somehow tied to academic content, such as reading, music, or physical education time.

Fourth, all students should be allowed to participate in the incentive. Thus, Jones advocated the use of group-oriented contingencies, which he called "group concern." In other words, all students can earn the incentives together.

Finally, "ease of implementation" is critical. The incentives should be easy to implement. Jones indicated that the following should be done: establish and explain the system, allow the class to vote periodically on teacher-approved incentives they wish to earn, use a stopwatch to determine the amount of time left over for preferred activities, and use low-preference activities during the time students lost from the time allotted for their preferred activity.

Provision of Efficient Help.   Jones found that teachers use their time inefficiently when students are involved in seatwork activities. He found that teachers spend about 4 minutes per student answering questions and helping. Jones believed that the optimum amount of time for such help is less than 20 seconds, with a goal of 10 seconds. Therefore, he proposes teachers do the following. First, organize student seating so that students are easy to reach. Second, use graphic reminders that provide examples and instructions. Third, once teachers arrive at the side of the students, quickly praise them for doing something correctly, provide a straightforward suggestion that will get them going, and then leave immediately.

Main Elements.   Jones (1987) defined four main elements involved in classroom management: classroom structure, **limit setting, responsibility training,** and backup systems.

Classroom Structure.   **Classroom structure** involves the seating arrangements, rules, and routines present in the classroom. Teachers should make sure that the seating arrangements maximize learning and that the rules and routines have been taught to students and parents. In terms of the seating arrangements, teachers should use assigned seats and arrange the class so that students face the chalkboard and not each other. The teacher's desk should be at the back of the room.

Limit Setting.   Limit setting involves sending a message to students through body language. Physical demeanor that communicates to students that teachers are in charge is important. Jones believes that body language is the language of emotion and intentions, both conscious and unconscious. There are two keys to understanding limit setting: first, effective discipline begins at the emotional level; second, calm is strength and upset is weakness. Thus, Jones recommends the following for limit setting: (1) terminate instruction when a student misbehaves; (2) turn completely around if one's back is facing the target student and look the student in the eye; (3) move to the edge of the desk and continue to maintain eye contact; (4) lean over the student and ask for compliance, saying thank you for compliance if exhibited; (5) lean over at the waist, placing one palm on the student's desk and telling the student what needs to be done, saying thank you if he does it; (6) if using the palms does not work, rest on elbows and repeat the verbal prompt while maintaining eye contact and composure, saying thank you if the student complies; and (7) if another student goes to the rescue of the student, bend over to the first student's level and repeat, being sure to be located between the two students. This procedure is repeated with the student who came to the rescue.

Responsibility Training.   Responsibility training involves building patterns of cooperation. This training involves getting students to behave appropriately in a voluntary manner. Responsibility training could be conducted by using the praise, prompt, and leave strategy. This strategy involves praising students (e.g., "You are off to a good start"), **prompting** them (explaining what they need to do), and leaving them (e.g., "Now it's your turn to do this independently"). In addition, a **preferred activity time (PAT)** procedure can be used. Preferred activities are those things that students enjoy but that are an extension of the academic content. For example, painting murals related to a unit on the *Mayflower* landing or developing plays based on historical events could be preferred activities. The PAT procedure goes as follows. Predetermine a reward that can be given to the whole class. Students retain this preferred activity time with responsible behavior and earn it at the end of the predetermined time interval (e.g., at the end of the week). If a student misbehaves, start a timer and subtract the length of time the student was off task from the total PAT. If a student is consistently off task or disruptive, omission training, which involves removing the student from the PAT system, can be used. In the place of the PAT, the student earns points for the class for being on task a certain number of minutes.

Backup Systems.   Backup systems are needed when students continue to test the teacher. If all else fails, use warnings, remembering to be relaxed and to maintain eye contact when talking. If warnings do not work, the teacher can "pull a card." Card pulling involves taking an index card out of a file box so that it is in plain view of the student. The card has the parent's phone number on it. If this method does not work, use the "letter home on desk technique." This technique involves writing a letter home to the parents. The teacher then walks back to the student and tells her that the letter will be sent if she repeats the misbehavior within one week. The letter is taped to the student's or teacher's desk in plain view. The teacher allows the student to tear up the letter after the week is over if the misbehavior is not exhibited.

Analysis.   The Jones model shows that preventative measures can be used in behavior management. Certainly body language is important when attempting to communicate with students. In addition, approaching discipline in a calm manner is supported by research in behavior management. Also, the use of incentives as outlined by Jones is an effective method of reinforcing students.

The PAT system, however, is an example of a poorly designed token economy system (see Chapter 11). When using an incentive system such as a token economy, the process should be one of earning the incentives rather than working to avoid losing the incentives. With the PAT system, there is a response cost system (see Chapter 12), which is a punishment-based system. The PAT system functions by motivating students to behave appropriately to avoid the loss of time from the total time provided at the beginning. A more positive system is to motivate students to behave appropriately to *earn* the time: the better students are, the more time they earn.

Also, the use of incentives as outlined by Jones assumes that these incentives will function as reinforcers (see Chapter 2). These incentives, however, will not function in a way that will motivate all students to behave appropriately. Teachers need a workable solution when these incentives fail to produce the desired results.

Along these lines, the Jones model is limited in that it relies on threats and warnings when students continue to misbehave. The use of cards and letters is an attempt to get students to behave to avoid these things. Research has shown that threats and warnings tend to make behavior problems escalate and get worse (Nelson, 1996b). It is in the best interests of teachers and students to avoid such aversive techniques. A final problem with the Jones model is that there is a lack of research validation of this model.

The Ginott Model

Haim Ginott (1971) developed the **Ginott model.** Ginott believed that teachers were the essential element in classroom management. Ginott's model is based on eight assumptions. First, students' behavior can be improved if teachers interact with them more effectively, treating them with understanding, kindness, and respect. Second, positive communication by teachers improves the self-concept of students, which produces better classroom discipline. Third, students can learn to be responsible and **autonomous.** Fourth, accepting and clarifying students' feelings will improve their classroom behavior. Fifth, the improper use of praise encourages dependency of students on teachers. Sixth, punishment encourages student misconduct. Seventh, insulting students causes them to rebel. Finally, promoting cooperation increases good discipline. Overall, teachers should view learning as occurring in the present. Therefore, teachers should not prejudge students based on what they know or think they know about them. In addition, teachers should not hold grudges based on what occurred in their past interactions with the students. The focus must be on what is going on now.

Congruent Communication.   Ginott's model rests on congruent communication as its central element (Charles, 1996). Congruent communication rests on the belief that students cannot think right if they do not feel right. Teachers can make students feel right by improving their relationships with them by ending their language of rejection (e.g., blaming, preaching, bossing, ordering, threatening) and using a language of acceptance (e.g., Ginott, 1972). A language of acceptance involves seven aspects. First, teachers should use "sane messages." These messages are those statements that address situations rather than students' character (e.g., "It is time to be working" rather than "Either you begin to work or else"). Second, teachers should invite students to cooperate rather than demand that a behavior occur (e.g., "You have a choice of watching the film quietly or beginning your reading seatwork" rather than "Pay attention to the film now"). Third, teachers should provide acceptance and acknowledgment for student behavior (e.g., "I know it is difficult to be ignored by other students, so how can I help you?" rather than "I am sure the other students did not mean to ignore you"). Fourth, teachers should confer dignity upon the students (e.g., "I realize that you forgot to do your homework last night. Coming to me to tell me was a very mature thing to do" rather than "How could you have forgotten to do your homework? I reminded you to do it at the end of class yesterday"). Fifth, teachers should express anger with "I messages" versus "you messages" (e.g., "I am disappointed that you two got into a fight. I was afraid that someone would get hurt" rather than "You two know better than to fight. You both could have gotten hurt"). Sixth, teachers should use laconic language, using succinct language rather than over talking (e.g., "It is hard to learn with so much noise" rather than "The rule is not to talk out in class. Doing so disturbs other students"). Finally, teachers should provide appreciative praise where the students' behaviors are described versus describing the students' abilities (e.g., "I enjoyed reading your paper" rather than "You are a great writer").

Teachers at Their Best and Worst.   Ginott believed that effective alternatives to punishment should be found because students learn from how teachers respond to problems. Therefore, teachers who show self-discipline are able to show their students (even those who misbehave) how to deal with problem situations. According to Ginott, teachers with a lack of self-discipline lose their tempers, call students names, insult students, behave rudely, overreact, show cruelty, punish everyone for another's actions, threaten, give long lectures, back students into a corner, and make arbitrary rules without student input. Teachers who show self-discipline are those who recognize student feelings; describe the situation; invite cooperation; are brief; do not argue with students; model appropriate behavior; discourage physical violence; do not criticize, call names, or insult students; focus on solutions; allow face-saving exits for students; allow students to help set standards; are helpful; and de-escalate conflict.

Series of Small Victories.   Ginott attempted to inform teachers that they have an option in the way they discipline their students. First, they can use threats and punishment to bring about behavior change, or they can use more positive techniques. The problem with using threats and punishment is that students will grow resentful of their teachers and become less willing to cooperate. Positive methods as advocated by Ginott can bring about self-direction, responsibility, and concern for others on the part of the students. Teachers must be aware, however, that changes in student behavior will not occur overnight. Rather, small changes will take place over a period of time. Teachers cannot rush this change. Therefore, they must look for a series of small victories.

Analysis. The use of cooperation is a positive aspect of this model; another is being concerned with how students feel themselves. Also, all teachers should adhere to avoiding the use of blame, shame, insults, and intimidation. Anything teachers can do to make the learning environment more pleasant should be done. Students function more favorably in a classroom where positive disciplinary methods, rather than a reliance on punishment procedures, are used. Punishment procedures can, as Ginott observed, result in negative side effects, leaving students, and the classroom, worse off. Therefore, Ginott's stance on the use of positive procedures is important for teachers to follow.

Assuming that increased self-concept improves classroom behavior and performance by itself, however, is not supported by the research (Scheirer & Kraut, 1979; Sulzer-Azaroff & Mayer, 1991). In fact, data obtained by Seligman (1995) indicate that many individuals with higher than normal levels of self-esteem have higher levels of disruptive behavior. In addition, the use of praise is positive if that praise is used judiciously and made specific. Also, assuming that praise can lead to dependency does not preclude the use of praise. Stating that punishment encourages misconduct is an indication that a technical definition of punishment (see Chapter 2) is not being used. Another problem is that although many of the procedures used in this model are considered to be good practice (e.g., congruent messages, allowing choices), there is no mechanism built in for those students who continue to misbehave, nor is there any assessment to determine why students misbehave. Finally, there is a lack of research validating this approach.

Conclusion

The aforementioned management methods all have some positive attributes. Some aspects of the methods, such as getting students involved in the behavior management programs and treating students with respect, can and should be used by teachers Any model that aids students in becoming more self-sufficient should be strongly considered. For behavior management approaches to be successful, however, they must be well defined and able to be replicated. Also, teachers should be able to explain not only why a management method worked but also why it failed to determine what the next step in solving the management problem should be. This explanation requires a consistent manner in viewing and interpreting the outcomes of different approaches.

Unfortunately, none of the described approaches have a solid philosophical and research base on which to make these explanations. In addition, an adequate behavior management approach must have built-in assessment and evaluation techniques to determine what management procedures are most appropriate and whether the procedures are working. None of the aforementioned models has systematic assessment and evaluation techniques developed.

All the aforementioned models have one thing in common: they all rest on some form of consequences for misbehavior, although many argue against external control. Whenever we praise a positive behavior or use logical consequences for an unwanted behavior, the consequences come from the environment. To suggest that one model is superior to another because it does not use external control methods is simply incorrect. Once it is agreed upon that all management methods use some form of external control, it must be determined which method works the best. This analysis is what is missing from these models. None of the models sets out to determine systematically which external management method (1) works best for each student and (2) has the fewest negative side effects. The approach discussed in this book attempts to do just that, to determine which method works best for each student and the possible side effects of the methods.

Another problem with the aforementioned methods are the claims many of them make that students are free to choose their behavior and that the facilitation of this choice is critical in their development. Choices, however, are always limited. In fact, to affect their students' behavior, teachers rely on a lack of free choice. If students had free choice, nothing teachers do would affect their behavior. Teachers are constantly attempting methods of directing the choice of students. Therefore, we must admit that we are attempting to influence student behavior and thus take steps to do so in appropriate manners. To suggest that students should be allowed to take control over their behavior by having teachers allow them to choose their behavior and suffer or take responsibility of their actions is false and misleading.

Another area of concern with the aforementioned models is the scientific support each has. Ultimately, teachers must consider if the method works or not. What should determine the form of disciplinary method to use in the classroom is the research support of the procedures used. Anyone can claim that their method is effective, and most do. It is far different to demonstrate over time that a method actually leads to meaningful behavior change. Therefore, teachers must determine what in the research literature has been shown to work. A major weakness of these approaches is that systematic observation and behavior tracking methods are not built into the methods. To implement a behavior management procedure effectively, we have to not only implement the procedure but also establish formative measures to track the effectiveness of the procedure.

What Are the Misunderstandings of Effective Behavior Management Approaches?

Unfortunately, two major misconceptions prevent professionals from using some of the more effective behavior management procedures available today: **intrinsic** versus **extrinsic reinforcers** and the issue of control.

Intrinsic versus Extrinsic Reinforcers

Several individuals have made statements regarding the use of external control procedures, indicating that they harm students. For example, Deci and Ryan (1985) have written that the use of extrinsic rewards tends to undermine intrinsic interest in subjects. In other words, when we reward students for reading, they may become less interested in reading for pleasure and will not read unless external rewards are attached. Kohn (1992) has also discussed the negative effects of extrinsic rewards on the intrinsic motivation of children. There are, however, several difficulties with the conclusions of these authors. First, when Deci and Ryan (1985) and Kohn (1992) speak of rewards, they are not speaking of reinforcers. (The differences are discussed in Chapter 2.) Second, there is no agreed upon definition of an extrinsic reward. For example, is praise from a teacher extrinsic? What about discussing what a student has learned after she just finishes reading? Essentially, we can define virtually anything that goes on in the classroom environment as extrinsic. Third, the critics do not distinguish between behaviors that are reinforced on a continuous basis and those that are reinforced intermittently. In other words, if we see a behavior occur in the absence of an extrinsic reinforcer, is the behavior occurring due to intrinsic interest, or have we simply not seen the extrinsic reinforcer take place? (Schedules of reinforcement are discussed in Chapter 2). Fourth, the critics have also forgotten that they are extrinsically reinforced for their views. It is probably a safe bet that the critics are paid for what they do and most likely would not continue to give workshops or teach for the sheer enjoyment of doing so. In other words, we are all extrinsically reinforced for what we do without the negative effects about which we have been warned.

Fifth, the critics have failed to make distinctions in regard to how the extrinsic reinforcers are provided. Chance (1992) wrote an interesting review of the research on the effects of extrinsic reinforcers on intrinsic motivation. According to Chance, there are three ways we can provide extrinsic reinforcers: task contingent, performance contingent, and success contingent. In **task contingent,** we reinforce students for simply engaging in a task for some period of time. There is no requirement in regard to the quality of the task. The main goal is to get students to do something. According to Chance, task contingent reinforcers tend to decrease the likelihood that students will do the task in the future in the absence of any external contingencies. Thus, Chance indicated that this decrease in performing the task would support what Deci and Ryan (1985) and Kohn (1992) warned us about. Interestingly, the research cited by Deci and Ryan (1985) and others have relied on task completion rewards. The second method of providing extrinsic reinforcers involves performance contingent. **Performance contingent** means that external reinforcers are provided if students have met a predetermined performance criterion. According to Chance (1992), performance contingent reinforcers will increase intrinsic interest in a subject if students make the performance criterion. Those students who do not meet the performance criteria, however, will experience a decrease in their intrinsic interest in the subject. Finally, **success contingent** reinforcers reinforce students for meeting a predetermined criterion as in the performance contingent example, but students are also reinforced along the way. In other words, the task is broken into smaller subtasks, and students are reinforced for their progression to the final performance criterion. According to Chance, success contingent reinforcers tend to increase intrinsic interest in a subject. Therefore, it is not appropriate to make a general statement that extrinsic rewards should not be used with students. It is appropriate to state that we must make sure we are using reinforcers and not rewards and that we are using success contingent reinforcers rather than task completion reinforcers.

A final problem with the critic's assertion that we should not use external control procedures is that there is no distinction between artificial and natural reinforcers. **Artificial**

reinforcers are those reinforcers not typically used in a particular setting, such as paying students for good behavior. Natural reinforcers are those reinforcers typically used in certain environments, such as providing grades for good performance. Rather than debating about intrinsic versus extrinsic reinforcers, it seems much more worthwhile to discuss artificial versus natural reinforcers. It is hard to imagine a world devoid of external contingencies. Laws in society are tied to external contingencies; imagine a society without any laws. Thus, we must acknowledge that external reinforcers (and punishers) are always present. Once acknowledged, we can take steps to decrease the need for the use of punishers and increase our use of natural reinforcers. Natural reinforcers, then, are those reinforcers typically present in certain contexts. What may be natural in one context (e.g., getting paid for work, getting grades in school) may be artificial in another context (e.g., getting paid in school, getting grades at work). The point is not to say that we should never use artificial reinforcers, only that our goal is to use natural reinforcers. At times, we must use more artificial reinforcers to gain influence over a behavior. Once this influence is achieved, we must move to more natural reinforcers. (This concept is discussed more in depth in later chapters.)

Issues of Control

One often misunderstood concept is that of **control.** When the term *control* is used, people think of being manipulated and being made to do things against their will. Therefore, when we speak of controlling a behavior, we may become the objects of criticism. Control, however, is not always what it seems. In a sense, everything we do is under some form of control. We usually pay our taxes on time to avoid the penalty of not doing so. We typically slow down when going over the speed limit if we see a police officer. That you are reading this book is likely due to some "control" placed on you by a professor (who requires the book for a class) or due to your motivation to learn more about behavior management to make your professional or personal life better. If we think of control in this way, whatever we do with a child, adolescent, or adult will involve some sort of control. Telling a child to be quiet, giving an adolescent a curfew, or asking another adult to hand you the newspaper will involve consequences (either positive or negative). Having a student go through a Glasser's problem-solving process is an attempt at control in that the teacher is trying to get the student to behave appropriately as a result of the problem-solving process. Making a school task more enjoyable and meaningful to students is an act of control because the teacher is attempting to increase the likelihood that students will be motivated to learn.

Therefore, when many professionals speak of control, they are not talking of using techniques similar to what may be used in a prisoner-of-war camp. What they are talking about are techniques that we all use every day of our lives; for example, tipping a waitress for good service may make it more likely for the waitress to continue to provide good service in the future.

Conclusion

There are misunderstandings of effective behavior management approaches. These misunderstandings can have a profound impact on whether we are successful or unsuccessful in managing students' classroom behaviors. If we are going to improve our behavior management skills and become more adept at the prevention of and the response to student misbehavior, we must use what has been shown to work in the short term as well as over time. Therefore, it is critical to have a knowledge base developed through research (See Martella, Nelson, & Marchand-Martella, 1999, for an in-depth discussion of research methodology.)

What Is the Right to Effective Behavioral Treatment?

Van Houten et al. (1988) outline six rights that individuals have with regard to effective behavioral interventions. First, individuals have a right to a therapeutic environment. In other words, we must have "a physical and social environment that is safe, humane and responsive to individual needs" (p. 381). Second, the overriding goal in behavior management is to provide services that ensure personal welfare. Thus, we must provide students with skills that promote their independence. Third, students have a right to have behavior management plans developed and implemented by individuals who are competent. An individual's competence comes from having adequate training and experiences in behavior management. Fourth, we must teach functional skills. This right involves providing students with skills that allow them to function effectively and fully now and in the future. Fifth, we must provide an assessment and ongoing evaluation. Assessment involves conducting a functional behavioral assessment and developing a behavior plan based on the results (see Chapter 10), whereas ongoing evaluation involves taking data (see Chapter 9) to determine if the behavior management plan is having an effect. Finally, students have a right to the most effective interventions available. Effective interventions are those that have been scientifically validated. The use of behavioral interventions that have not been scientifically validated is not considered an ethical practice and may result in the use of abusive techniques that violate the basic rights and freedoms of students. Therefore, educators who develop and use behavior management procedures must be informed about the procedures that have an adequate research base. This information can be found in the professional research literature.

Summary

Student behavior is one of the most critical concerns in schools today. We are faced with misbehavior in our schools on a daily basis and need effective methods of preventing and responding to misbehavior. Several methods have been advocated over the years. Unfortunately, few of these methods have demonstrated their effectiveness scientifically. We continue to use ineffective management methods even in the face of evidence that they do not work as claimed or that those claims have not been validated. Fortunately, we know what does and does not work.

The results of an extensive review of the literature commissioned by the National Institute of Justice, Office of Justice Programs, U.S. Department of Justice, Office of Juvenile Justice Delinquency Prevention, and U.S. Department of Education on school-based prevention efforts revealed six findings (Gottfredson et al., 2000). First, it appears that minor forms of problem behaviors are common in school, whereas school violence (e.g., shootings, fighting, weapons) is relatively rare (see Chapter 3). Furthermore, the level of problem behaviors in schools varies widely.

Second, schools use a wide range and variety of activities or programs to reduce or prevent problem behavior. These activities include, for example, discipline policies and practices, curriculum and instructional practices, counseling, mentoring, family involvement, and staff development for faculty. Few, if any, of the activities or programs have been validated.

Third, schools generally fail to use a full range of reinforcement strategies and sanctions. Rather, schools tend to rely on rules and severe consequences for a range of problem behaviors. For example, responses to misconduct such as community service, peer mediation, student courts, and even detention are not used much relative to suspension. Furthermore, reinforcement strategies for appropriate behavior are used infrequently.

Fourth, a majority of the school-based activities designed to prevent problem behaviors are of such poor quality that they have little effect on the levels of problem behavior. For example, only 10% of schools have established adequate discipline policies and practices. Even efforts aimed at the individual are implemented so poorly that they produce no measurable difference on student outcomes.

Fifth, organizational support for implementation of school-based prevention activities predicts their relative effect. Localized planning and responsibility for initiating prevention activities also predicts their relative treatment effect. Localized planning leads to the integration of the prevention activities into the regular part of the school program, increasing their sustainability (see Chapter 4). Validated prevention programs not only have higher technical quality, but also are used more extensively than locally developed programs (see Chapter 5). Furthermore, consistent with the focus of this book, validated prevention programs are based on behavioral or behavioral/cognitive techniques.

Finally, organizational capacity predicts the extent of use and student exposure to prevention activities. Faculty morale, organizational focus on clear goals, perceived amenability to program implementation, open identification of problems, and open teacher-principal communication greatly affect the use of and exposure of students to prevention activities. The principal plays a key role in the development of the school's organizational capacity.

Our children are much too important to continue to use management methods that are suspect and have only philosophical support rather than scientific support. The remainder of this book discusses several of these evidence-based management methods.

VIGNETTE • *Revisited*

Finding the past management attempts to be less than successful but also wishing to help José with his problem, Ms. Jackson reflected on the situation at hand. She thought that there surely must be other professionals who have had similar problems. There must be others who had found effective management procedures to use with students like José, but where could she find this information?

Ms. Jackson decided that she needed to find evidence-based practices. That is, she wanted to find management procedures that have been found to be successful with students like José.

Ms. Jackson found that there was a long list of such evidence-based practice articles and that the procedures that have been found to be most effective are the behavioral and behavioral/cognitive ones. She also learned that there were several negative side effects to the use of punishment techniques and that most professionals in behavior management encourage teachers to attempt more positively based management systems. Finally, Ms. Jackson learned that by implementing these evidence-based procedures she could indeed improve José's behavior.

Now Ms. Jackson's goal is to learn more about these procedures and their underlying assumptions before designing a behavior management program. The information she learned is presented in the following chapters.

Discussion Questions

1. What are the possible reasons for the lack of use of evidence-based management procedures?

2. What was your definition of discipline before reading this chapter? What is it now?

3. What are the different models used for behavior management as described in this book?

4. How are each of these models used?

5. What are the strengths of each of the models described in questions 3 and 4 above?

6. What are the weaknesses of each of the models described in questions 3 and 4 above?

7. What are the misunderstandings related to intrinsic versus extrinsic reinforcers?

8. What are the misunderstandings related to the issue of control?

9. How can we overcome these misunderstandings?

10. Why are scientifically validated management approaches important?

11. What does the right to effective behavioral treatment mean?

2

Social Learning Foundations

Chapter Objectives _____

After studying this chapter, you should be able to:

- Illustrate the differences between cognitive and social learning views of learning.
- Describe the A-B-C's of learning.
- Characterize the role of observational learning.
- Explain what reinforcement means.
- Depict the concept of extinction.
- Illustrate what punishment means.
- Describe how we can distinguish between reinforcers and punishers.
- Depict the conditioning of stimuli to be reinforcers or punishers.
- Specify the concepts of deprivation and satiation and explain how they affect reinforcers.
- Describe the process of stimulus control.
- Explain how shaping takes place.
- Illustrate the different methods of chaining.
- Describe the schedules of reinforcement and how these schedules affect student performance.

VIGNETTE

MR. HUANG HAS A FIRST-GRADE CLASSROOM in an inner-city school. He has several students who refuse to follow his directions. Two boys in particular cause the majority of the difficulties in the classroom. Mr. Huang has met with each boy's parents to explain his concerns with their behavior and how their behavior affects other students. The parents of the two boys seemed to be annoyed at Mr. Huang's suggestion that their children could even cause such disturbance. They also seemed to become angry toward the boys as well.

Mr. Huang believes that the boys are likely emotionally or physically abused at home. He has never seen any identifying marks on them; his belief is simply speculation based on his observations of the boys' reactions when he told them he was going to talk to their parents. The boys told Mr. Huang that they were afraid that their parents would get angry and yell. They did not, however, provide any other information. Given Mr. Huang's belief that the boys come from homes in which some form of abuse may be present, he believes that their problem behaviors are caused by their emotional instability. Mr. Huang discusses this possibility with the school counselor, who also sees the emotional aspects of the boys' home lives as being the cause of their problem behaviors.

Not knowing what to do about the behavior of these boys, Mr. Huang approaches the school's behavior specialist. He provides the aforementioned information to this specialist and is surprised to hear what the specialist has to say about the two boys. The specialist states that the boys' emotions are not the causes of the problem behavior. She states that emotions do not cause behavior to occur but are, in themselves, behaviors. Therefore, Mr. Huang should find out what is the cause of the boys' emotional behavior. The specialist does not believe the assumption that the boys' behavior problems have resulted from their emotional issues. Rather, their behavior problems have resulted from their reinforcement in the classroom in some manner and/or from appropriate behavior being punished. Mr. Huang argues that he does not use punishment with his students, and he certainly would not reward unwanted behavior. The behavior specialist encourages Mr. Huang to learn more about social learning foundations because the manner in which he is using the terms *reinforcement* and *punishment* may not be accurate. She also suggests to Mr. Huang that he find out about how unwanted behaviors can be shaped in the classroom environment.

Having the motivation to solve these behavior problems, Mr. Huang sets out to learn more about these social learning foundations.

Overview

Perhaps the most important aspect of behavior management is learning the foundations upon which management methods are based. One mistake is to think of behavior management as a set of procedures that can be used to solve problems. Thinking of behavior management only as a set of "tricks we pull from a bag" is a mistake because it does not allow for problem solving to occur if we fail in our attempt to solve the behavior problem. Imagine for a moment that a teacher used a certain intervention to reduce students' problem behaviors in the classroom and that the intervention had the intended effects. The reasons for this success are not likely to be a major concern for the teacher because the goal of reducing the problem behavior has been achieved. The teacher may not have the time to reflect on the reasons for this success and will probably move to address other issues in the classroom. Suppose, however, that the intervention was not successful. No change was evident in the behavior. What then? What typically occurs is that the teacher tries another intervention and another intervention until she finds an effective one. Unfortunately, for a few students, the teacher may run out of "tricks in her bag." Even if she found the intervention that was effective, a great deal of time has been lost through an almost hit-and-miss approach to behavior management.

Now suppose that the teacher considered why the intervention she used failed. If the reasons for this failure can be determined, she would most likely be able to determine the next step to solving the problem. To figure out why a particular intervention has failed, we must understand the conceptual and technical aspects of the interventions or procedures used. Techniques work or fail for reasons, and these reasons are critical to understand especially if one fails in one's attempt to solve a problem behavior.

Determining why an intervention works or does not work requires a conceptual system. In other words, we can interpret successes or failures from a cognitive, **behavioral,** humanistic, constructivist, psychoanalytic, or another **perspective.** The perspective we use to interpret the reasons for successes or failures will be critical in determining future successes. This book approaches behavior management from a **social learning theory** perspective. We use this perspective to understand why our interventions work or fail. The social learning perspective assumes that human behavior is determined by a person's interaction with his or her environment, which includes the physical setting such as the home, school, and classroom and the social surroundings such as peers, teachers, and parents. This perspective is a firmly grounded scientific approach.

How Is Human Behavior Learned?

There are several theories of learning. Many of these theories seem solid conceptually, but there are some critical differences between and among these theories that must be learned.

The Difference between Cognitive and Social Learning Theories

Cognitive Theory.   If we compared the two general theories of learning—cognitive and social learning—we would see that there are major similarities and few differences. These differences, however, could have a large effect on how we view student behavior and how we respond to the behavior. As shown in Figure 2.1a, the basic cognitive model can be described as having four critical areas related to learning: environmental antecedents, cognitive processes, behavioral output, and environmental consequences. Antecedents are those things that occur just prior to the behavior, whereas consequences are those things that occur just following the behavior. In between the antecedent and the behavior are cognitive processes. These processes can be shown through several cognitive theories. Consider the following **cognitive theory** for illustrative purposes. Suppose that we have a particular antecedent, such as telling a student to sit in his seat. This antecedent enters into the student's head and into his sensory registers. Note that there are an infinite number of antecedent stimuli—such as other classroom sounds, lighting, and movement and tactile and kinesthetic stimuli such as the feel of the chair and the position of the student's body—entering the sensory registers. Thus, the antecedent stimuli have several competing antecedent stimuli. All these stimuli enter into the sensory registers. A student's attention to and perception of a particular antecedent stimulus will allow the stimulus to enter into the working memory or short-term memory. This memory system is what you are using when reading this book. The way the student perceives your instruction to sit down is dependent on her experiences in the past and present and her expectations of the future. Therefore, if you have had a good relationship with the student in the past and the student is favorable toward you, you will be more likely to get compliance and the student will take her seat.

(a) Cognitive interpretation

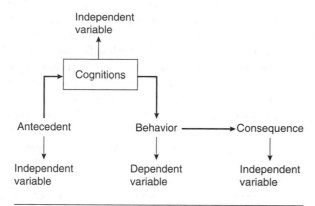

(b) Social learning interpretation

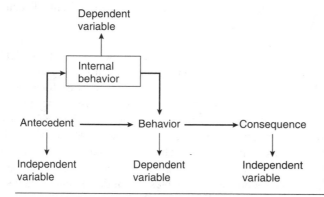

FIGURE 2.1 *Models for cognitive and behavioral interpretations of behavior causes.*

On the other hand, if the student sees you as being manipulative and not respectful of her needs, you may see noncompliant behavior or failure to sit down.

Assume that the student followed directions and sat down. You praise her for sitting down. How the student views the praise will affect whether she follows rules in the future. Your praise and the student's reaction to it will likely be placed in the student's long-term memory until a later time when you provide another instruction to the student. Therefore, a student's behavior is dependent not only on your instructions (environmental antecedent) and how you respond to her compliant or noncompliant behavior (environmental consequence) but also on how she processes these antecedents, interprets past consequences, and has expectations for future consequences. As shown in Figure 2.1a, a student's behavior, both positive and negative, is affected by three things, called *independent variables.* These variables have an effect on the student. Your reading of this book is an independent variable. The student's behavior is a dependent variable. The behavior is affected by the independent variable. We hope your understanding of behavior management will be affected by reading this book.

The environmental antecedents and consequences are labeled as "secondary" independent variables because they are important but are not the main focus. Of course, how you provide an instruction and what you do after the student responds are important, but how the student perceives the instruction and consequence is critical here. Therefore, the cognitive processes are the "primary" Independent Variables. So, where would an intervention be focused based on this theory? An intervention would focus not only on the antecedents and consequences of a behavior but also on how a student perceives or processes the information she received from the antecedents and consequences.

For example, if we had a student who was aggressive after he was provided a work assignment to be completed independently, we may focus on the assignment. What type of assignment was it? Was it too hard? Was the student given adequate feedback in the past on his performance? In addition, we would try to "fix" the inner difficulty. That is, we would attempt to change how the student goes through the cognitive process that leads to the aggressive episodes. To do so, we may provide the student with some other way to process the information. We may teach him to control his anger by talking to himself to calm down. We may also wish to have him visualize something soothing such as walking through a park. In other words, we teach him how to deal with the anger he is feeling because it is his anger that causes his aggressive acts to occur.

Social Learning Theory.   As shown in Figure 2.1b, the social learning model is similar to the cognitive one in that there are three environmental events: antecedents, behaviors, and consequences. (This model, like the cognitive one, is simplified for illustrative purposes.) The antecedents and consequences, however, are considered to be "primary" Independent Variables, whereas the cognitive position is that the antecedents and consequences are "secondary" independent variables. The behavior in the social learning model is the dependent variable, as it is in the cognitive model. The major difference is when we consider the role of inner cognitions or behaviors. From the social learning perspective, inner behaviors are behaviors. They are dependent variables, not independent variables. In other words, what goes on inside the head is affected by what is occurring in the world around us. These inner behaviors are not causes of outward behavior independent of environmental events, but they are behaviors.

So, what would we do differently from a social learning perspective as opposed to a cognitive perspective? We would take the inner behaviors such as feelings and thoughts into consideration, but we would assume that these inner behaviors were caused by what is occurring in the student's world. For example, take the student who became aggressive when he was provided work to do. The anger felt by the student is important information for us to consider. He was angry and became aggressive. The anger and aggressiveness are assumed to come from the same source: assigned work. The cause of the student's aggressive behavior comes from the assigned work, not from his anger. From a social learning perspective, we would not focus specifically on the student's anger; we would instead focus on the antecedents (e.g., providing the work) and the consequences (e.g., the type of feedback the student gets when doing and finally completing the work). We may find that the work is too hard or that the student does not have the prerequisite skills to complete it adequately. We may find that the student is fatigued and does not have the skill to ask for help. We may find that there is little praise for his efforts and only ridicule from others. If we can find what is causing the aggressive acts to occur, we can also determine what is causing the anger to occur.

Interestingly, we may also want to provide other skills that would interfere with anger or prevent it from occurring, such as thinking about something that is soothing, going for a walk in the park, counting to 10 before acting, or practicing relaxation techniques. The difference between the cognitive and social learning perspectives, then, is how we interpret the interventions. Effective interventions are effective interventions no matter if they are designed and used by cognitivists, humanists, constructivists, or behaviorists. The *interpretation* of why these things work or do not work is what makes them different, which explains why having a conceptual system is so critical. The conceptual system will allow us to make interpretations of what we see. From a social learning perspective, everything we do to change the cognitive processes is an environmental manipulation. Therefore, how we respond to what a student does can be viewed as attempts to change the environment in some manner to lead to changes in the person's overt as well as inner behavior.

A person's overt behavior will tell us to a certain extent what is going on inside the individual. These overt behaviors may come in the form of "body language"; for example, when we are depressed, we may slump over in our chair. Facial expressions such as when we are happy we may smile, physical acts such as punching others when we are angry, and verbal behavior such as saying that we feel sad are other examples. All these adjectives are labels of inferences we see or hear coming from others. These labels do not cause behavior to occur but are behaviors that tell us something about particular individuals' environmental history.

The unifying aspect of any behavior management system should be determining if what is done actually works. If we—cognitivists, behaviorists, humanists, or constructivists—rely on the student's behavior to tell us if what we are doing is working or not and we take this information into consideration in the future, we all should end up in the same place. It is our position that the model that will lead to this place of success sooner will be by using the social learning perspective to interpret why a particular behavior is occurring. As we see later, assessments that are required by law for students with disabilities (called functional behavioral assessments) when unwanted behaviors are demonstrated are dependent on the assumptions of the social learning model. Therefore, the social learning model is used throughout this book to interpret why misbehaviors (actually all behaviors, positive as well as negative) are occurring.

The A-B-Cs of Learning

The simplest model to explain behavior is the **three-term contingency,** which is made up of the antecedent, behavior, and consequence (Cooper, Heron, & Heward, 1987; Malott, Malott, & Trojan, 2000; Miltenberger, 2001; Skinner, 1953). These three aspects of behavior work together to determine if a behavior will be performed now and at a later time. For example, suppose that a student hits another student when called a name. The name-calling would be the antecedent, and the aggressive act would be the behavior. Once the act is committed, there will be a consequence of some sort. The person who was hit may cry. The consequence, if it is a reinforcer (defined later), will make it more likely that the behavior is repeated in the future under similar circumstances, with similar antecedents. Thus, the three terms work in unison. To understand why people behave as they do, we must understand what the antecedents, behaviors, and consequences are.

Realize that this model is simple when first seen, yet it is actually quite complex when we consider all the possible antecedents, behaviors, and consequences we are exposed to every day. In addition, the three-term contingency can be expanded to four, five, or more terms. Once we get past four terms, though, we need computer models to track the possibilities. Some of the most extensive work on moving past the three-term contingency has been conducted by Patterson (1982a) in terms of coercive family processes.

Consider what could happen when we move to a **four-term contingency.** The first term in the four-term contingency can be called a *setting event.* The setting event changes the dynamics in the other three parts: antecedent, behavior, and consequence. For example, consider Figure 2.2. As shown in Figure 2.2a, we have a student in class who is given an assignment (antecedent). We see that the behavior is a refusal to complete the work (behavior), and the student receives a reprimand from the teacher (consequence). If we move to a fourth-term contingency as shown in Figure 2.2b, we see that a setting event may be the teacher who gives the assignment. In the first case, the assignment is given by Teacher A. When Teacher A gives the assignment, the student refuses to complete the work and receives the reprimand. When Teacher B gives the assignment, the student complies and the teacher praises her. Setting events change the dynamics of the other three terms. Therefore, to understand the causes of a student's behavior, it may not be sufficient to consider only the three-term relationship but to go to a fourth term.

(a)		Antecedent	Behavior	Consequence
		Teacher gives student assignment	Student refuses to work	Teacher provides reprimand

(b)	Contextual Stimulus	Antecedent	Behavior	Consequence
	Teacher A	Teacher gives student assignment	Student refuses to work	Teacher provides reprimand
	Teacher B	Teacher gives student assignment	Student completes work	Teacher provides praise

FIGURE 2.2 *Example of a teaching interaction with and without considering a contextual stimulus.*

What Is the Role of Observational Learning?

Modeling

Modeling is an important concept in the understanding of human behavior. One definition is that "a model is any antecedent stimulus that is topographically identical to the behavior the trainer wants imitated" (Cooper et al., 1987, p. 366). According to Cooper et al., models can be actual demonstrations, or they can be done symbolically. Actual demonstrations might involve showing a student how to hold a pencil and then asking the student to imitate you. Actual demonstrations also occur for unwanted behaviors, such as when a student sees another student escape from having to do a task by swearing at the teacher and being sent out of the classroom. In this case, the student could imitate the behavior of the other student when faced with a task she does not want to do.

Symbolic models are presented in sources other than in the student's actual environment. Examples include models in books, movies, and television. A major concern today is with such media. When students view models of aggression and violence, they may become more likely to do the same thing. This tendency is especially true if the person displaying the model has similar characteristics to the student (e.g., another teenager). Therefore, it is crucial that appropriate models are shown in the classroom and imitation is reinforced; conversely, inappropriate models should be prevented and/or not allowed to continue, and imitative behaviors should not be reinforced.

Modeling, then, is a possible reason for the display of many behaviors in school (Alberto & Troutman, 1999; Zirpoli & Melloy, 2001). Students are faced with a multitude of models, both good and bad. Once an imitative behavior is displayed, however, if must be reinforced in some manner for the behavior—either wanted or unwanted—to continue. Therefore, it is important to know what reinforcement is and how to use it to strengthen wanted behaviors.

What Is Reinforcement?

Over the years, there has been great misunderstanding of what **reinforcement** is and what it is not (see Kohn, 1992, for an example). We hope to clear up these misunderstandings so that terminology will be used appropriately. Reinforcement can be categorized into two areas: positive and negative.

Positive Reinforcement

When one thinks of **positive reinforcement,** one may think of something that is given to a student. The "something" given to a student, however, is a **reward.** Rewards and reinforcers are not the same things. We give rewards, but they may not effect behavior. On the other hand, positive reinforcers do have an effect on behavior. The definition of positive reinforcement has three components (Skinner, 1953). First, positive reinforcement requires a stimulus to be added to the environment. This stimulus can be virtually anything. Providing praise, reprimands, spankings, good grades, and a surprised look may all be positive reinforcement.

Second, positive reinforcement requires that the presentation of the stimulus be contingent on the behavior. In other words, the behavior must occur for the stimulus to be presented. When we behave, we change our environments in some manner. This change may be the presentation of something into our environments. As can be seen in this second component to the definition of positive reinforcement, we do not reinforce people; instead, we reinforce behaviors. Third, positive reinforcement requires an increase in the future probability of the behavior. This statement does not mean that the behavior has to increase more in the future, only that the behavior is more likely to be repeated due to the presentation of the stimulus.

Thus, a reinforcer is different from a reward. Rewards do not require the increased likelihood of the behavior. If a reward is provided to a student and the behavior is more likely to occur again in the future, the reward becomes a reinforcer. The two are not the same thing. Therefore, if a teacher indicates that she gave a student a reinforcer but nothing happened, she most likely gave a reward. Reinforcers, by definition, must work.

Another mistake frequently made when discussing positive reinforcement is indicating that a student behaves in a certain manner to get a reinforcer. The correct way to look at this scenario is that a student behaves in certain way because he was reinforced under similar circumstances in the past. Remember that reinforcers require an increase in the future probability of the behavior. Thus, positive reinforcers are defined by what is presented in the past and how this affects what occurs in the future (Cooper et al., 1987). The reason this point is so important is that if a student is displaying a behavior (either positive or negative), it can be assumed that the behavior is occurring due to reinforcers that were presented in the past under similar circumstances. If we can determine what those similar circumstances were and what the stimulus was that resulted from the behavior, we have gone a long way in finding the cause of the behavior. Once a likely cause is determined, it is a short step to designing an effective management system. Assessments designed to find these causes are functional assessments and are discussed in Chapter 10.

Note that positive reinforcers do not only increase desirable behaviors, but they can also increase undesirable ones. One mistake we make is to reinforce unwanted behavior inadvertently by doing something such as providing attention to the misbehavior. If we do provide attention to misbehavior and the attention serves as a reinforcer for the student, the misbehavior will increase.

Negative Reinforcement

Negative reinforcement is frequently mistaken for punishment. Negative reinforcement actually makes a behavior more likely to occur. The definition of negative reinforcement has three parts (Skinner, 1953). First, negative reinforcement requires the removal of an aversive stimulus, which is anything that evokes or occasions an **escape** or **avoidance response.** In other words, anything that a student attempts to avoid or escape, such as a test, is probably an aversive stimulus. Second, the removal of a stimulus must be contingent on the behavior. That is, for the aversive stimulus to be terminated, the behavior must occur. Third, there must be an increase in the future probability of the behavior.

At first, it seems difficult to generate examples of negative reinforcement. If we look around, though, we will see them everywhere. For example, what do we normally do when we see a police officer on the highway and we are driving faster than the speed limit? We probably slow down. There is an ongoing aversive stimulus in this example. The ongoing aversive stimulus is the threat or possibility of a ticket if we continue to speed. Slowing down is an attempt to avoid a ticket. Therefore, when we do not get stopped, our slowing down behavior is probably reinforced. We will be more likely to slow down again when we see a police officer. The ongoing aversive stimulus is represented by the police. Slowing down removes the threat of a ticket. The threat of a ticket is the negative reinforcer. Another example of a negative reinforcer is an alarm clock. When it goes off in the morning, we probably get out of bed to turn it off. To increase their effectiveness, we use the most obnoxious sound we can and place it as far away from the bed as possible. Paying our rent or mortgage on time is another example. We probably would incur a penalty for any bill we pay late. Late charges are potential negative reinforcers. Paying our taxes on time is another behavior that most of us do to avoid fines. Finally, some cars are equipped with buzzers that terminate only when seat belts are worn. The buzzer is designed to serve as a negative reinforcer to get us to put on our seat belts.

Many times we attempt to get others around us to do things they may not wish to do by using negative reinforcement. If we nag another person to take out the trash, that person may take out the trash to stop our nagging. The nagging, then, is functioning as a negative reinforcer. In the classroom, we frequently use negative reinforcement to get students to do things. We may warn students that if they do not study, they will fail their test. Students would then study so as to avoid failing. We may warn students that if they continue to misbehave, they will lose recess. Again, the students may behave well to avoid missing recess. Threats and warnings are used as negative reinforcers.

Although negative reinforcement can be effective in getting students to perform as we would like, there are several problems with their use (Sulzer-Azaroff & Mayer, 1991). First, negative reinforcement requires an ongoing **aversive stimulus,** which is something that evokes or occasions an escape or avoidance response. Aversive stimuli are those things we would try to avoid. Therefore, the threat of a bad grade unless we study may be an aversive stimulus if it is something that we attempt to avoid by actually studying. Second, negative reinforcement may occasion negative side effects. These side effects, including those listed in Table 2.1, occur due to the presence of an aversive stimulus. Finally, negative reinforcement may make it more difficult to learn. According to Catania (1998), it may take longer for an organism to learn a skill if negative reinforcement is used as the motivational

TABLE 2.1 *Negative Side Effects of the Use of Aversive Stimuli*

- Can make student avoid person providing aversive stimulus
- Can make student fearful of the person providing the aversive stimulus
- May stop other student behavior/provokes withdrawal
- Models the use of aversive stimuli
- Promotes negative self-esteem
- Promotes aggression toward the person providing aversive stimulus
- Is negatively reinforcing to the person providing aversive stimulus
- Is overused

technique. Catania discusses research with lower animals such as rats because human experimentation would probably be considered unethical, but examples can be seen every day in our lives. The model proposed by Catania to show why learning is more difficult with negative reinforcement is shown in Figures 2.3 and 2.4. Figure 2.3a shows an instance of a behavior. The flat line indicates no behavior, and the vertical line indicates a behavioral event. In this example, the behavioral event may be answering a question correctly. Figure 2.3b shows the behavioral event with a representation of positive reinforcement (in this case, verbal praise from the teacher). When a student is verbally praised, she may emit other behaviors (e.g., thinking about how smart she is) that can temporarily interfere with further responses, which is shown in Figure 2.3c. When this interfering behavior occurs, it tends to delay further learning even for a very short period.

Figure 2.4 shows an instance of negative reinforcement. The behavior in this example—answering a question correctly—is the same as that shown in Figure 2.3a. As with the positive reinforcement example, the flat line indicates no behavior. Figure 2.3b shows the ongoing aversive stimulus—in this example, the threat of a bad grade if the question is not answered correctly—before the response. As with positive reinforcement, the reinforcer occasions behaviors that may interfere with learning, even for a short period. Figure 2.3c demonstrates this problem. Interfering behaviors such as getting nervous, thinking negatively (e.g., "I'm going to fail"), and so on are going on before the question is answered. These behaviors slow learning. Everyday examples of the effects, such as when students display test anxiety, react with aggression to an assignment, or get emotional when an assignment is given, can be seen in the classroom. When these interfering behaviors occur, negative reinforcement may be present in the classroom.

How does negative reinforcement affect classroom management? For one thing, the use of negative reinforcement is possibly used more often by teachers and other professionals than other behavior management procedures. Unfortunately, most teachers and other pro-

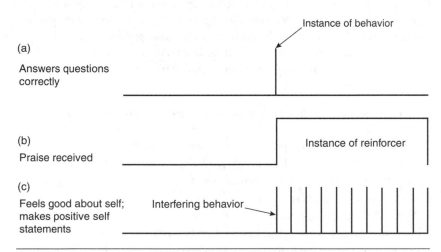

FIGURE 2.3 *Example of learning through a positive reinforcement paradigm. (Adapted from Catania, 1998.)*

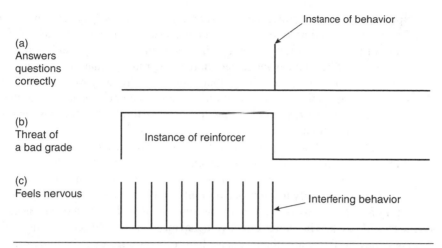

FIGURE 2.4 *Example of learning through a negative reinforcement paradigm. (Adapted from Catania, 1998.)*

fessionals are unaware that they are using negative reinforcement to get the students to work. Behavior management systems that require warnings and threats are examples. If these threats and warnings are aversive stimuli to students, they will evoke behaviors that may interfere with learning. Examples include: telling students that if they do not study, they will fail; that if they do not come to class on time, they will be sent to the principal's office; and that if they continue to misbehave, their parents will be called or they will be sent to time-out.

Sidman (1989) warned of the use of negative reinforcers. He indicated:

> Negative reinforcement is the first of two major categories of control that I define as coercive. (The second category…is punishment.) Both positive and negative reinforcers control our behavior, but I do not call positive reinforcement coercion. When we produce things or events that we usually consider useful, informative, or enjoyable for their own sake, we are under the control of positive consequences. But when we get rid of, diminish, escape, or avoid annoying, harmful, or threatening events, negative reinforcers are in control; with that kind of control, I speak of coercion. The distinction is not arbitrary.… Negative reinforcement…engenders side effects, often unintended, that poison our everyday social and institutional relationships.…
>
> A person who is largely sustained by positive reinforcement, frequently producing "good things," will feel quite differently about life than will a person who comes into contact most often with negative reinforcement, frequently having to escape from or prevent "bad things." (pp. 36–37)

The alternative to the use of negative reinforcement seems obvious: use positive reinforcement whenever possible. Instead of using threats and warnings, tell the students what good things will come from studying for a test, coming to class on time, or displaying positive behavior in the classroom. This change is a difficult one to make because we are all exposed to negative reinforcement every day of our lives (pay rent on time or enact a penalty, pay taxes on time or enact a fine, go the speed limit or get a ticket). We are experts in the use of negative reinforcement; it is ingrained in our society. Yet it is not the most effective manner of behavior management in the long run. Ultimately, we want our students to behave well due to the good things that come from doing so rather than the bad things that come from not doing so. We want our students to come to learn due to the positively reinforcing aspects that result rather than the negative things that occur when one does not perform in a certain manner.

Now, the reply that frequently comes about is, "Students should not always expect to get things in return." In addition, statements such as "motivation to learn comes from within the student" are common. When we state this question and make these statements, however, we are probably using negative reinforcement to get students to perform. Simply expecting a behavior to occur usually means that if it does not occur, negative consequences will result. Therefore, effective behavior management requires us to think about human behavior differently than we have before. It requires us to be more effective in our planning and implementation of behavior management programs. It requires us to be teachers rather than taskmasters.

What Is Extinction?

To implement effective behavior management systems, **extinction** is an important concept for us to learn. We know that if a behavior is reinforced (positively or negatively), it will continue in the future (Chance, 1999). We also know that if a behavior is not reinforced, it will cease to exist. According to Chance, extinction is the process in which a behavior ceases to exist due to a lack of reinforcement. **Extinction** is the permanent removal of the source of reinforcement for a behavior (Pierce & Epling, 1995). Consider our own behavior. If we were not paid for work any longer, work behavior would probably cease, for that particular job at least. If our friend stopped talking to us, we probably would not have that friend for very long. If pushing on the gas pedal of our car no longer made it go forward, we probably would stop driving that car. In all these examples, when reinforcement is removed, we stop emitting the behavior for that particular job, with that particular friend, or in that particular car. Student behavior is the same as ours. If a student did not receive good grades for hard work, hard work would cease, if good grades functioned as reinforcers for working hard. If a student no longer received our attention for asking a question properly, asking questions properly would decrease if our attention functioned as the reinforcer. In addition, if a student's misbehavior ceased to bring about our anger, the misbehavior may cease to exist if our anger functioned as the reinforcer for the misbehavior.

Extinction is critical in that it can be used to decrease unwanted behavior. Extinction has four problems, however. First, extinction requires us to know what the reinforcer(s) is (are). If the source of reinforcement cannot be determined, extinction will not work. Determining the source of reinforcement is covered in Chapter 10. Teachers may claim that extinction does not work, saying, "I ignored the student's misbehavior, and it continued to occur." Unfortunately, extinction was not being used. Extinction by definition works.

Therefore, the teacher in the example is making a mistake in assuming that his attention functions as a reinforcer. It is likely that the reinforcement is coming from another source, such as other students.

The second problem with extinction is that it is frequently accompanied by an increase in some aspect of the behavior (Pierce & Epling, 1995). This increase is called an **extinction burst,** a rapid increase in the frequency, duration, or intensity of the behavior. These bursts, which we have all experienced, are often difficult to live through. Take an infant who will not sleep through the night. Once the child is fed, changed, and warm, we may choose to ignore the crying to teach her to sleep through the night. We keep track of the behavior and are likely to see an increase in the loudness and duration of the crying. This behavior is an extinction burst. What happens to our behavior when a friend or partner ignores us? We will probably see a burst in our own behavior. We may get louder when trying to talk to our friend or partner, we may speak faster, or we may tap the person on the shoulder and say, "Please listen to me!" When an extinction burst occurs, it is safe to assume that we have removed the source of reinforcement. Removing the source of reinforcement is aversive to the individual, doing so may bring along the negative side effects of aversives (see Table 2.1). The burst does, however, tell us that we are on the right track and to continue on if, and only if, the burst is not dangerous to the person or to others and we can live through the burst of behavior. If we see the burst causing more harm than good, extinction should cease. Similarly, if we do not think that we can live through the extinction burst, we should not attempt extinction in the first place. The problem with beginning extinction and then ceasing its use because we cannot tolerate the burst is that it will most likely reinforce the individual's outburst. Thus, nontechnically speaking, what we do by stopping an extinction program because we cannot live through the burst is to teach the individual that when we do something you do not like, all you have to do is increase the frequency, duration, and/or intensity of the behavior and we will stop doing the program. Therefore, although extinction can be a very important tool to use to decrease a behavior problem, there are side effects to its use. If we cannot deal with the side effects of extinction, it should not be used.

Third, even when the behavior seems to be eliminated, it can come back at various times. This phenomenon is called **spontaneous recovery** (Chance, 1999). There are several theories why spontaneous recovery takes place, but a discussion of these theories is beyond the purpose of this book. The important things to know about spontaneous recovery are that it can happen and that it can be stopped. When a behavior spontaneously presents itself, the extinction program must remain in place. If the behavior is inadvertently reinforced, it will strengthen and become a problem again. Thus, we believe that the behavior is gone, but it comes back and surprises us, it catches us off guard. We usually describe spontaneous recovery in lay terms by saying that the child is testing us. If we are able to keep the extinction program in place, the behavior will again be eliminated. The next time that there is spontaneous recovery, it should be at a lower level than before and take less time to eliminate. Figure 2.5 shows a model of this phenomenon for tantrum behavior. It is important to remember to refrain from inadvertently reinforcing this recovery of behavior.

A fourth problem with extinction is that it does not teach a desirable behavior; instead, it only eliminates an unwanted one. Therefore, if we were to use extinction, we

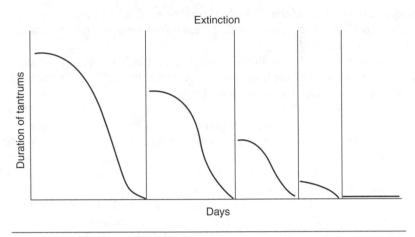

Extinction

Duration of tantrums

Days

FIGURE 2.5   *Example of spontaneous recovery for tantrum behavior.*

should always incorporate a positive reinforcement program for a wanted behavior to take the place of the unwanted one. This point is discussed in more depth in Chapter 12.

What Is Punishment?

Although professionals differ at times in terms of defining **punishment** (see Catania, 1998; Michael, 1993a; Sidman, 1989; Skinner, 1953), we define punishment using the more commonly accepted definition. Similar to reinforcement, punishment can be separated into two categories: positive and negative.

Positive Punishment

The definition of **positive punishment** has three parts (Miltenberger, 2001). First, positive punishment requires the presentation of a stimulus. In this case, the stimulus is an aversive one. Second, positive punishment requires the stimulus presentation to be contingent on the behavior. Finally, positive punishment requires a decrease in the future probability of the behavior. If there is no decrease in likelihood of the behavior being repeated again in the future, there is no punishment. Therefore, punishment is essentially the opposite of reinforcement. Remember that reinforcement results in an increase in the future probability of the behavior, whereas punishment requires a decrease.

This definition requires us to view what happens to the behavior once the stimulus is presented. Therefore, assuming that a spanking functions as a punisher is a mistake. A spanking may function not as a punisher but as a reinforcer (we describe why later). Punishers, like reinforcers, cannot be defined beforehand. Again, this view is foreign to the way we have been taught over the ages. We are taught that punishers are what we do not like, whereas reinforcers are what we like. What we like or do not like, however, is not always the same for all individuals. Saying that we would not like to be reprimanded by a teacher but we would like to achieve good grades is not true for others just because it is true for ourselves.

Although it is true that punishment decreases the likelihood that the behavior will be repeated in the future, there are several problems with its use. In fact, many professionals in the field dissuade others from using punishment techniques (see Sidman, 1989, for his discussion on the use of coercion). Some professionals indicate that punishment does not work. We must ask, however, Work for what? Punishment does work in reducing the probability of the behavior. On the other hand, punishment may not result in long-term changes. In other words, once punishment is withdrawn, the changes that come about may not last. The same is true of reinforcement. Another, and perhaps most critical, disadvantage of positive punishment is that it requires the presentation of an aversive stimulus. The same negative side effects of negative reinforcement come into play here. The problems with the use of aversive stimuli as shown in Table 2.1 are true of positive punishment procedures. Therefore, we should attempt to avoid the use of positive punishment and use it only as a last resort.

Negative Punishment

Negative punishment also decreases the likelihood of a behavior being repeated in the future. Unlike positive punishment, which requires the presentation of an aversive stimulus, negative punishment requires the removal of a reinforcing stimulus contingent on a response (Miltenberger, 2001). Negative punishment works based on extinction principles. Recall that once a source of reinforcement is removed from a behavior, the behavior will extinguish. With negative punishment, if the source of reinforcement is removed from the behavior for even a short period, the behavior will less likely occur in the future.

As with negative reinforcement and positive punishment, negative punishment has negative side effects. The removal of a reinforcer can be said to be aversive. Therefore, several of the side effects of the use of aversive stimuli are present with negative reinforcement (see Table 2.1). The main advantage negative punishment has over positive punishment and negative reinforcement is that negative punishment is not an active presentation of an ongoing aversive stimulus. Thus, negative punishment can be seen as a more desirable method of behavior management than the other two (positive punishment or negative reinforcement), whereas positive reinforcement is the most desirable of the four (positive reinforcement, negative reinforcement, positive punishment, and negative punishment).

How Do We Distinguish between Reinforcers and Punishers?

As shown in Table 2.2, we can determine what type of reinforcer or punisher is in effect for a particular behavior. If a stimulus is ever presented, we have a "positive" something. If a stimulus is removed, we have a "negative" something. In addition, if the probability of the behavior increases in the future, we have a reinforcer, and if the probability of the behavior decreases in the future, we have a punisher.

TABLE 2.2 *Reinforcement and Punishment Grid*

	Presentation of a stimulus contingent on response	*Removal of stimulus contingent on response*
Probability of future behavior increases	Positive reinforcer	Negative reinforcer
Probability of future behavior decreases	Positive punisher	Negative punisher

How Are Reinforcers and Punishers Learned?

Typically, we do not think of how something becomes reinforcing or aversive to us. Our reinforcers and punishers likely change over our lifetime. Reinforcers and punishers can be categorized into two areas: primary or secondary.

Primary and Secondary Positive Reinforcers

Primary Positive Reinforcers. **Primary positive reinforcers** are those things that we do not learn (Miltenberger, 2001). They are inborn. Therefore, primary reinforcers are also called unconditioned reinforcers. These reinforcers are those things that allow for the survival of the species. Primary reinforcers include food, water, warmth, and sex. For example, when we are hungry (i.e., it has been a long time since we have eaten), we will behave in some manner because doing so resulted in food in the past under similar circumstances.

Secondary Positive Reinforcers. **Secondary positive reinforcers** are those things that are learned (Miltenberger, 2001). These reinforcers are also called conditioned reinforcers. If we look around, we will see virtually an unlimited number of secondary reinforcers: the type of clothes we wear, the type of car we drive, the type of televisions we have are all examples of secondary reinforcers. Two of the most used secondary reinforcers (if they increase the future probability of the behavior) are money and praise. Praise is probably the most used secondary reinforcer in schools. Money is probably the most used reinforcer in work. Other examples of secondary reinforcers in schools are grades, points, and awards.

Secondary reinforcers are learned. We are not born with an appreciation for money or praise. Many students in school still do not have an appreciation for good grades. Still others react to praise as if we ridiculed them. Why do these stimuli function as reinforcers for some and punishers for others? The reason is an individual's conditioning history.

Conditioning of Secondary Positive Reinforcers. When we are born, we have a limited number of reinforcers. Those reinforcers are limited to those that are primary. When we provide a primary reinforcer such as food to a baby, however, we are also providing other stimuli such as attention, the sound of our voice, the look of our face, and the way we hold

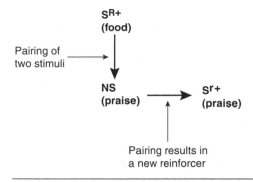

FIGURE 2.6 *Conditioning of new secondary reinforcer via pairing with a primary reinforcer. S = Stimulus, NS = Neutral stimulus, S^{R+} = Primary positive reinforcer, and S^{r+} = Secondary positive reinforcer.*

the baby. All these "neutral" stimuli are paired with the primary reinforcer (e.g., food). Through this pairing, these neutral stimuli will take on reinforcing properties. In this model, shown in Figure 2.6, the pairing of the stimuli is critical in the conditioning of secondary reinforcers. Figure 2.7 also shows conditioning taking place, but this conditioning is slightly different from that shown in Figure 2.6. In this example, the neutral stimulus is paired with a previously conditioned stimulus. Therefore, the conditioning of stimuli to be reinforcing can grow exponentially. One potential problem with conditioned reinforcers is that they will lose their reinforcing properties unless they are intermittently paired with other "backup" (i.e., paired) reinforcers.

At some point in time, we will begin to pair stimuli with stimuli different from those that were paired initially. When we have the type of multiple pairings as shown in Figure 2.8, we have what is called a generalized reinforcer, a stimulus that is not dependent on any one backup stimulus such as that shown in Figure 2.6 or 2.7. The best example of a backup reinforcer is money. Money can buy not only food but also other primary reinforcers and secondary reinforcers such as expensive cars. The advantage of generalized reinforcers is that when one backup reinforcer is removed, it will still be a reinforcer. Therefore, if money could no longer buy food, money would still be reinforcing because it can buy shelter and other reinforcers.

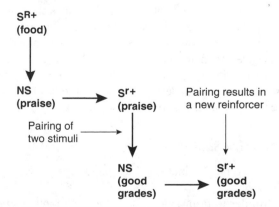

FIGURE 2.7 *Conditioning of new secondary reinforcer via pairing with an established secondary reinforcer. (See Figure 2.6 for notation.)*

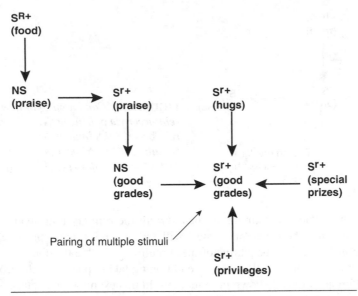

FIGURE 2.8 *Generalized conditioning of a secondary reinforcer via pairing with several reinforcers. (See Figure 2.6 for notation.)*

To see this conditioning occur in an explicit manner, watch an expert work with a student with severe or profound mental retardation. A student's response might be reinforced with an edible such as candy because food is a primary reinforcer. The teacher may provide the candy and see what else the student does. The teacher will also provide verbal praise when the candy is being provided. What the teacher is doing is not only teaching a particular response but also teaching praise to be a reinforcer. What will occur is that the candy will gradually be faded out and the praise faded in to take the place of the candy as a reinforcer.

In the typical world, we do not condition reinforcers in an **explicit** manner. The conditioning process occurs naturally. Here is what makes us all different from one another in terms of motivators. We all have different learning histories or life experiences that teach us that some things are reinforcers and others are not. The reason grades are reinforcing for some and not for others has to do with past experiences with grades. Students who are reinforced for good grades likely have parents who pair good grades with other reinforcers such as praise, or these students have had their good grades paired with reinforcers in some other manner in the past. Another possibility is that bad grades have been paired with punishers; therefore, the students avoid the bad grades by getting good ones. In this case, bad grades have undergone conditioning of another sort, described below.

Primary and Secondary Aversive Stimuli

There are two major categories of aversive stimuli—primary and secondary.

Primary Aversive Stimuli.   Similar to primary reinforcers are **primary aversive stimuli.** These stimuli are ones that evoke an escape or avoidance response without any learning taking place beforehand (Kazdin, 2001). In other words, primary aversive stimuli are stimuli that are aversive from the time we are born. Examples are electric shock, nauseating smells and tastes, and pain. Avoiding these stimuli will generally allow for the continuation of our species.

Secondary Aversive Stimuli. **Secondary aversive stimuli** are those stimuli that are learned (Kazdin, 2001). These stimuli are not aversive from the time we are born. Examples of these stimuli are reprimands, praise, poor grades, good grades, and some people. These stimuli were originally neutral to us but took on conditioned aversive properties in the past. For example, we are not born trying to escape another's reprimand. Poor grades are not something that we consider to be a bad thing unless we learn that they are not good. We must learn that what is unwanted in an educational setting should not be desired. How, though, does this learning occur?

Conditioning of Secondary Aversive Stimuli. The conditioning process of secondary aversive stimuli is the same as that for secondary positive reinforcers. Initially, a primary aversive stimulus such as pain is paired with a neutral stimulus, such as the word *no*. The word *no* will take on conditioned aversive properties through time (Dorsey, Iwata, Ong, & McSween, 1980). For example, if an infant approaches a hot stove and we yell "no" to that infant just before she touches the stove and the infant gets burned thereafter, the "no" is likely to take on aversive properties. Similarly, if reprimands are paired with spankings, reprimands are likely to take on aversive properties. Therefore, if we watch a student attempt to avoid something or someone, it is highly probable that this something or person has been paired with an aversive stimulus. In the same manner as with secondary positive reinforcers, secondary aversive stimuli can result from a neutral stimulus being paired with a previously conditioned secondary aversive stimulus. For example, we could pair bad grades (neutral stimulus) with a reprimand (previously conditioned secondary aversive stimulus) and condition bad grades to be aversive.

Advantage and Disadvantage of Conditioning of Positive Reinforcers and Aversive Stimuli. The major advantage with all this conditioning is that we function much more successfully in a culture or society through conditioning. Most of us ultimately learn the boundaries by which we must live in our culture through this conditioning. If we think of a classroom as a culture, we can see how critical it is for our students to learn what the accepted reinforcers and punishers are and respond accordingly. Therefore, we learn that good grades are reinforcing and that misbehavior in the classroom will result in a reprimand (aversive stimulus).

Unfortunately, conditioning can go the other way as well. Conditioning is not subjective, but objective. In other words, we do not only condition "desirable" things to be positive reinforcers and "undesirable" things to be aversive. We can inadvertently do just the opposite. For example, consider a student who has learned that attention is a reinforcer. This student will behave in some manner because doing so has resulted in attention in the past under similar circumstances. Now suppose that the only time this student gets attention (a conditioned positive reinforcer) is when he misbehaves. When the student misbehaves, he is reprimanded. Reprimands are always paired with attention. Therefore, reprimands can take on reinforcing properties (Van Houten, Nau, MacKenzie-Keating, Sameoto, & Colavecchia,

1982). Essentially, if the attention the student can get is negative attention, he will perform accordingly.

Not only can we condition social stimuli to be reinforcing, but we can condition what should be primary aversive stimuli such as spankings as secondary positive reinforcers (Martin & Pear, 1999). One of the authors had an experience once in another country while teaching a class in behavior management. During the class, a father asked why his 3-year-old daughter hit her baby brother. The father was asked what happened to the girl when she hit the baby, and the father indicated that he spanked her. He was confused about why she would continue to hit her brother when he would punish her. The first thing that should come to mind is that because the behavior persisted, spankings were not functioning as punishers. The father was asked how much attention he gave his daughter. He indicated that she did not get much attention from him because most of his time was spent taking care of the baby. If we consider the conditioning of reinforcers, we can set up a causal model for the father. First, we know that the spankings were probably primary aversive stimuli because they usually brought about pain. Second, we can assume that attention for this little girl was a reinforcer. Before the baby was born, she received her father's full attention. Third, we can assume that spankings were paired with attention because for the father to spank the girl, he had to provide her with his undivided attention. Therefore, we can see that we can take a primary aversive stimulus, pair it with a secondary positive reinforcer, and condition the aversive stimulus to be a secondary positive reinforcer. In this case, the spankings were actually functioning as positive reinforcers.

This example shows how something we would probably deem to be a punisher actually functions as a reinforcer. Although this fact seems counterintuitive, it occurs frequently and can be seen all around us. Therefore, the critical thing we can learn from these instances is to not define a reinforcer or punisher beforehand but to determine if something is a reinforcer or punisher after viewing what happens to the behavior when the consequence is provided.

Deprivation and Satiation States

The effectiveness of any one stimulus as a reinforcer depends on whether or not there is a **deprivation** state present (Martin & Pear, 1999). In other words, what is reinforcing now may not be an hour from now due to some event occurring. This event may be termed an **establishing operation** (Michael, 1993b). An establishing operation is defined as "an antecedent event or change in the environment that alters the effectiveness of the reinforcer and the rates of the responses that have produced that reinforcer previously" (Sulzer-Azaroff & Mayer, 1991, p. 589). For example, suppose that we just came home from college for a holiday and our mother gave us a rather large meal. After the meal, she told us that if we clear the table, she will give us more to eat. The likelihood that more food will motivate us to clear the table is probably low. We may clear the table for other reasons, but not for more food. In this case, we have been satiated by the food. Therefore, **satiation** is a decrease in reinforcer effectiveness of a stimulus due to receiving "a lot" of that stimulus, usually in a short period. On the other hand, if it has been a long time since we have eaten a good home-cooked meal (and we are "starving") and our mother asks us to set the table so that we can eat, the likelihood that we will set the table quickly increases due to our being deprived of the stimulus of food. Therefore, deprivation can be defined as an increase in the reinforcer effectiveness of a stimulus due to a lack of that stimulus.

The critical point here is that what is reinforcing for a student can change throughout the week, day, or hour depending on deprivation and satiation states. Thus, teachers should continuously monitor the effects of stimuli used as reinforcers and vary the types of reinforcers used.

What Is Stimulus Control?

Stimulus control is a term used to depict the probability of a response occurring after a stimulus (antecedent) has been presented (Sulzer-Azaroff & Mayer, 1991). If we have stimulus control over a particular behavior (e.g., student sitting down), a particular stimulus from the teacher (e.g., telling the student to sit down) will be more likely to occasion the student's behavior (e.g., sitting down) than when that stimulus is not present. When we have a lack of stimulus control we are not able to get a behavior to occur at all or not on a consistent basis when we present a particular antecedent.

Stimulus control is all around us. When you come to a stop sign (stimulus), you usually stop (behavior). This stimulus, called a **discriminative stimulus,** is symbolized by: S^D. Thus, stop signs are S^D's for stopping. Green lights at corners are S^D's for going through. A discriminative stimulus is essentially a signal that indicates that a response in its presence was reinforced in the past and will likely result in a reinforcer in the future. In the classroom, teachers who flick the lights to indicate that it is time to get to work are using a stimulus control method. The flickering lights are "hoped" to be S^D's for getting into one's seat and getting ready to work. Classroom rules are set up to be S^D's for appropriate behaviors.

We can further this concept by showing that there are two categories of discriminative stimuli. The first involves S^{D+} and S^{D-}. An S^{D+} is an indication that a behavior that occurred in the presence of this stimulus was reinforced in the past. For example, if we provide good citizen awards to a student who followed directions (S^{D+}), we will make it more likely that the behavior will occur again under similar circumstances in the future (assuming that good citizen awards are reinforcers). An S^{D-} is an indication that a behavior (escape or avoidance) that occurred in the presence of this stimulus was negatively reinforced in the past. Another way to look at the S^{D-} is an indication of punishment if an escape or avoidance response is not made. For example, Mr. Yuck labels on medicine bottles are attempts at gaining stimulus control over not consuming bottle contents. The labels can be interpreted as indications that consuming the contents will result in sickness or not consuming the contents (avoiding them) will result in not becoming sick. Similarly, if one is speeding, seeing a police officer on the highway is an S^{D-} for slowing down to avoid a ticket. The second category of discriminative stimulus is an **S-delta,** or S^Δ. The S^Δ is an indication that a behavior in its presence will not be reinforced. Faculty who put up "do not disturb" signs on their doors are attempting to control behavior by indicating that the probability of reinforcement for knocking (i.e., opening the door) will not result.

The way we gain stimulus control over a response is to reinforce the response in the presence of a particular stimulus but not in the presence of another stimulus (Cooper et al., 1987). Red stoplights generally gain control over stopping behavior because going through the red light may result in negative consequences, whereas stopping at the red light generally allows you to avoid these negative consequences. Going through a green light generally is reinforcing because it allows us to avoid getting yelled at from those behind us if we were to stop and allows us to get to our destination more quickly. Telling the students to line up at the door will gain stimulus control if we reinforce them every time they line up at the door appropriately but do not reinforce them when they do not. Reinforcing in the presence of one stimulus (the S^D) while not reinforcing in the presence of another stimulus (S^Δ) is called differential reinforcement. (Differential reinforcement is used in another manner below.)

What Is Shaping?

Shaping is the reinforcement of successive approximations of behavior (Skinner, 1953). In other words, we reinforce when the behavior gets closer to the ultimate goal behavior. Think of behavior as a lump of clay at the beginning. Our goal is to mold this clay into a bowl. At the start the clay looks nothing like a bowl. As we gradually mold the clay, it begins to look more and more like a bowl until it becomes a bowl. Human behavior is much the same, especially in schools. When we begin to teach a student to write a paper, rarely is a paper publishable. There are usually spelling errors, grammatical errors, and content errors. If we were to grade a student on our ideal of a well-written paper from the beginning, most students would fail. What we can do is gradually change the paper over time until it meets with our ideal. We do so by having steps along the way. Because our criterion is set at a lower level for the first draft, the initial paper may look nothing like the final version. Each successive version should become cleaner and cleaner until the final product is acceptable.

Therefore, much of our teaching is shaping the skills of our students. Shaping works by reinforcing successive approximations of a behavior (Skinner, 1953). Although the first instance of the behavior is acceptable now, it will not be later. A poor paper that was acceptable earlier is not reinforced now. The criteria change and become more stringent when the student can meet the criteria. We also see this with children when they begin to talk. We get excited when we hear our young child say "mmm." We hug the child and make a big deal about it. After a while of hearing "mmm," we begin to lose interest until the child says, "mmmo." We again get excited until the child says, "mmmooom." Notice that the new sounds are reinforced while the older ones are ignored. Essentially, the child's saying "mommy" is being shaped. This shaping, then, is achieved through differential reinforcement. One behavior is not reinforced while another one is.

Shaping may or may not be planned. We typically do not systematically implement a "Say *mommy*" program. Shaping, however, occurs naturally as we interact with our environments. Thus, not only can positive or appropriate behaviors be shaped, so can inappropriate or unwanted ones. Unfortunately, we shape unwanted behaviors of our children too often. Take, for example, when a child is not sleeping through the night. Many people will tell you to let the child cry to sleep as long as he is dry, fed, and warm, but that is very difficult for parents to do. With good intentions, parents will start by trying to ignore the crying child. At some point, the crying will get to the parents, and one or both parents will go to the child's room, pick him up, and cradle him in their arms. The next time the parents attempt to ignore the crying, they may wait for a longer period of time. At some point, though, they may break down and go the child's room. This cycle will continue, thereby shaping the duration and intensity of the child's crying. In the classroom, a similar phenomenon occurs. A teacher may attempt to ignore minor inappropriate behavior until the behavior reaches a point where it cannot be ignored. When this attention is provided, if it is a reinforcer, the more serious behavior will occur more rapidly until attention is gained. Therefore, we can shape unwanted behaviors up to a point where they are serious obstacles to learning.

While this shaping is going on, parents and teachers will usually be unaware of what is happening. They may not ever see the increasing duration, frequency, or magnitude of the behavior. It is similar to when parents know that their children are growing physically but cannot notice this growth from day to day. Thus, it is crucial to understand that unwanted behavior can be unknowingly shaped by inadvertently reinforcing increased levels of the behavior.

What Is Chaining?

Chaining is a concept wherein individual behaviors in an individual's repertoire are put together to form a longer behavior (Skinner, 1953). These individual behaviors are called links. Each link serves a dual purpose, called the dual stimulus function (Sulzer-Azaroff & Mayer, 1991). Therefore, chaining requires the identification of a task analysis—a task broken down into several steps. Figure 2.9 shows such a **task analysis** for the completion of a research paper. (The links are rather large and could be further broken down into subbehaviors.) As shown in the figure, the first link in a chain acts as an S^D for the next link. In other words, completion of the first link sets the occasion for the second. The second link serves as a conditioned reinforcer for the first link because being able to emit the second link can occur only after the first link is completed. The completion of the second link is also an S^D for the next link, and so on. The final link is a conditioned reinforcer for the previous link only. Therefore, each step serves as an S^D for the following step and as a conditioned reinforcer for the previous step. This dual function of all the steps except the first and last steps is called dual stimulus function. Of course, the completion of the final link is reinforced by the end product. As shown, the grade for the paper is the reinforcer for turning it in.

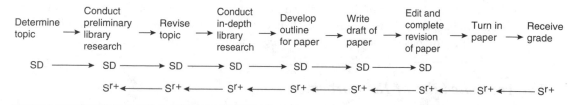

FIGURE 2.9 *Task analysis for writing a research paper. Figure shows the dual stimulus function of each behavior. SD = Discriminative stimulus and S^r+ = Secondary positive reinforcing stimulus*

If you think of it, virtually everything we do, we do in a chain. For example, driving a car requires behaviors that must be put together to drive such as getting into the car, putting on the seat belt, putting the key into the ignition, and so on. Putting together a child's toy on her birthday also requires a chain of behavior. In fact, if we think about the instructions, they show what the chain of behaviors is to put the toy together. There are three ways to teach through the use of chaining; forward, backward, and total task or whole task chaining. Because this book is oriented toward preventing or responding to behavior difficulties, only a brief discussion of each of the chaining methods is presented; these methods are ones of teaching behaviors, either academic or adaptive. The concept of chaining can also be used to decrease the probability of a behavior occurring. This approach to chaining is covered in Chapter 12.

Total or Whole Task Chaining

Total or **whole task** (Sulzer-Azaroff & Mayer, 1991) **chaining** involves teaching the chain of behaviors at once. Thus, the steps to completing a research paper would be taught together. Most of us learn a chain of behaviors through this approach.

Forward Chaining

Forward chaining involves teaching the first step first until it is mastered by the student (Cooper et al., 1987). Once the student can independently complete the first step, the first and second steps are taught together. Once the student can complete the first two steps independently, the first three steps are taught together, and so on until all the steps have been taught and are mastered. Forward chaining is frequently used with students who have mild to moderate developmental disabilities (Sulzer-Azaroff & Mayer, 1991).

Backward Chaining

Backward chaining is an approach that involves teaching the student to complete the final step of the chain until it is mastered (Delbert & Harmon, 1972). Once the last step is mastered, the next-to-last step and last step are taught until mastered, and so on. In this way, the teacher teaches the task by beginning with the last behavior or link and working back up the chain. Backward chaining may be considered appropriate for students with more severe developmental disabilities (Sulzer-Azaroff & Mayer, 1991) because these students may need more explicit instruction to make each step a conditioned reinforcer; the last step is paired with the result of the completed product (the reinforcer), which conditions the last step to be a conditioned reinforcer. Then, the next-to-last step is paired with the final step, which conditions the next-to-last step to be a conditioned reinforcer, and so on.

What Are Schedules of Reinforcement?

What reinforcement is and what it is not have already been discussed. Reinforcement occurs every day, yet reinforcement for each and every behavior does not necessarily occur. How often a behavior is reinforced will partially determine how difficult it will be to extinguish the behavior. Therefore, to work successfully with behavior problems, we must know the basic reinforcement schedules (Ferster & Skinner, 1957) (see Table 2.3).

Continuous Reinforcement Schedule

A **continuous reinforcement schedule** (also called a fixed ratio one, or FR-1) is when each behavior a student emits is reinforced. For example, if a student talks out three times in a class and is given attention each of those three times, she is on a continuous reinforcement schedule (assuming that attention is a reinforcer for her). Because a continuous reinforcement schedule strengthens a behavior, continuous reinforcement schedules should be used when we are attempting to teach a behavior (Sulzer-Azaroff & Mayer, 1991). Unfortunately, continuous reinforcement schedules not only strengthen positive behavior but also strengthen unwanted ones.

In terms of unwanted behaviors, continuous reinforcement schedules have one positive attribute: behaviors that are reinforced on continuous reinforcement schedules tend to extinguish rather quickly. An extinction burst may still occur, but generally it takes a short amount of time for the behavior to cease compared with behaviors that are on intermittent reinforcement schedules.

Intermittent Reinforcement Schedule

When an individual's behavior is reinforced, the reinforcement may not occur after each occasion of the behavior. Reinforcement may be intermittent. There are four basic intermittent schedules of reinforcement: fixed interval, variable interval, fixed ratio, and variable ratio.

Fixed-Interval Schedule.   A **fixed-interval schedule of reinforcement** is defined as reinforcement of the first response after a set time has elapsed. Note that the definition does not say that reinforcement occurs after a set amount of time has elapsed. A response is critical to the definition. For example, suppose that our mail came at the exact same time of day, say 2:00 P.M. (signified FI-2:00 P.M.). Also suppose that we are expecting some important mail to come, but we do not know which day. At first, we may not go to the mailbox during the early part of the day, but the number of times we go to the mailbox begins to

TABLE 2.3 *Definitions of the Four Basic Schedules of Reinforcement (Fixed Interval, Variable Interval, Fixed Ratio, and Variable Ratio)*

- *Fixed interval (FI):* Reinforcement is delivered for the *first* appropriate response occurring after a specified period of time.
- *Variable interval (VI):* Reinforcement is delivered for *first* appropriate response occurring after an average period of time.
- *Fixed ratio (FR):* Reinforcement is delivered after a specified number of correct responses.
- *Variable ratio (VR):* Reinforcement is delivered after an average number of correct responses.

increase as it approaches 2:00 P.M. As 2:00 P.M. approaches, the rate of our response looks similar to that shown in Figure 2.10a. This response pattern will be repeated on successive days. This pattern is called a fixed-interval scallop. The first response after the mail comes is reinforced. In other words, it does not matter how many times you go to the mailbox during the day; only one response will be reinforced, and that is the response that occurs after the mail has come. Therefore, a fixed-interval schedule of reinforcement produces a lower rate of response, because only one response is required for reinforcement and a non-continuous response rate (i.e., the rate is low and then increases as the time gets nearer).

Another example of a fixed-interval schedule of reinforcement is telling students that they must wait for 30 minutes before going to the computer (FI-30 minutes). Their "going to the computer" behavior will not be allowed until the 30 minutes has elapsed. They will not get to use the computer until they go to it. Therefore, going to the computer will not be reinforced until the time has elapsed.

Variable-Interval Schedule. A **variable-interval schedule of reinforcement** involves reinforcement of the first response after an average amount of time has elapsed. For example, suppose that the mail in the above example does not come at 2:00 P.M. every day, but

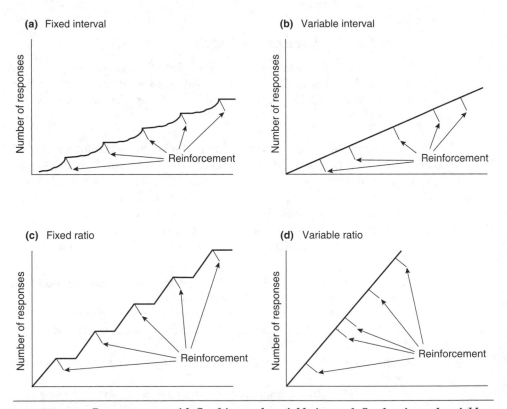

FIGURE 2.10 *Response rates with fixed-interval, variable-interval, fixed-ratio, and variable-ratio schedules of reinforcement.*

on average it comes at 2:00 P.M. (signified as VI-2:00 P.M.). Sometimes the mail comes at 10:00 A.M., sometimes at 4:00 P.M., and sometimes at 2:00 P.M., but you will never know when the mail will come. Therefore, your response rate may look more like that in Figure 2.10b. You cannot anticipate when the reinforcement (e.g., mail) will come. Therefore, you continue to go to the mailbox.

Another example is making a phone call. When you call someone, you may get a busy signal. Now suppose that you knew exactly when the other person would get off of the phone. The person you are trying to call will spend some length of time on the phone (say 30 minutes, signified FI-30 minutes). Your response of calling would probably look more like that in Figure 2.10a. Usually, however, we do not have this information. Therefore, watch the response pattern. We will probably hit the redial button several times quickly until our rate of response decreases and we space out our calling. After a while, our rate is similar to that in Figure 2.10b (VI-30 minutes). The rate will be low to moderate (because the number of calls does not increase the probability of someone getting off the phone, but how long we wait until we place our next call does), and the responses will be continuous (because we do not know if the next call will be answered.

A final example similar to a variable internal schedule of reinforcement is providing pop quizzes. Here we are trying to get students to study at a consistent pace throughout the week. We do not want the students to cram before a big test. Therefore, we provide unannounced quizzes on average every 2 days (VI-2 days). The quiz could come tomorrow, the next day, or 4 days from now, though. Because the students do not know when the quiz will come, they are more likely to study on a more consistent pattern.

Fixed-Ratio Schedule. A **fixed-ratio schedule of reinforcement** is reinforcement of a certain number of responses. Technically, what is reinforced is the last response in a series of responses. For example, if we required students to complete 20 math problems each day (signified FR-20) before they could go out for recess, we would have a fixed ratio of reinforcement. The 20th response is reinforced each day. Note that it does not matter how long it takes the students to complete the 20 responses, only that they complete them. The response pattern seen with a fixed-ratio schedule is found in Figure 2.10c. As seen in the figure, the response rate would be high in that students will try to get their work done quickly to go outside (if going outside is a reinforcer). Also notice that the response rate is noncontinuous because once the 20th problem is completed, the students will wait a while before beginning a new set of 20 problems.

Variable-Ratio Schedule. The **variable-ratio schedule of reinforcement** may be the most frequently used schedule of reinforcement in today's classrooms. Teachers rarely plan to reinforce particular student behavior at a set time, but they will reinforce behaviors on an almost random schedule. A variable-ratio schedule of reinforcement is one in which an average number of responses will result in reinforcement (again, technically, the last response in an average number of responses is reinforced). For example, when students are working on a problem, teachers may go over and praise the students after they complete one or two problems at one time and 10 problems the next. The average number could be something like 5 problems (signified as VR-5). The number of problems needed to be completed for reinforcement to take place is not the same each time.

Misbehavior is frequently on a variable-ratio schedule of reinforcement. Teachers usually do not attend to each and every misbehavior but will attend to misbehavior at various points in time, say after 2 misbehaviors, or 10, or 20. On average, some number of misbehaviors will be reinforced. The response pattern seen with a variable-ratio schedule of reinforcement is seen in Figure 2.10d. As shown, the response rate is high (because reinforcement depends on the number of responses) and steady (because the individual cannot predict if the next response will be reinforced).

Extinction

As with the response rates, the effects of extinction will depend on the type of schedule of reinforcement in place. Essentially, extinction takes less time when using a continuous reinforcement schedule compared with an intermittent one (Chance, 1999). Consider the reason for this difference. If we received a reinforcer for every instance of a behavior and then that reinforcement was suddenly removed, we would probably detect this difference. Thus, we would likely stop responding very soon thereafter. On the other hand, if we received a reinforcer every so often and then the reinforcer was suddenly removed from the behavior, it would be more difficult to detect this change. We would continue to respond for some period because the next response may be reinforced.

In terms of differences in extinction while a behavior is on one of the intermittent schedules, variable schedules are more resistant to extinction (Chance, 1999). In other words, it takes longer for a behavior to extinguish when using a variable reinforcement schedule than a fixed one. If we were getting reinforced for every fifth response and then the reinforcer was removed, we would soon know that we were not reinforced when we should have been. Therefore, we would be more likely to stop behaving as we did. If, on the other hand, we received a reinforcer after every fifth response on average and then the reinforcer was removed, we would have a more difficult time determining if we missed the reinforcer. Nontechnically, with fixed schedules we can anticipate when the reinforcer should come; with a variable schedule, we would not be able to anticipate when the reinforcer is to come. Therefore, we continue to respond for some time because the next response may be reinforced; we just do not know. As the variable schedule is thinned out (say from a VR-5 to a VR-50), the behavior becomes more and more difficult to extinguish. If we take a person who is "addicted" to slot machines, she may be on a VR-1,000. How long would it take for the behavior to extinguish? It would take a very long time.

When working with students who have a long history of misbehavior, we can be fairly confident that the misbehavior is on some form of variable schedule of reinforcement. Knowing that should lead us to understand that it may take a great deal of time to extinguish a behavior.

Summary

Understanding the role that our environments have in shaping our behaviors is critical in understanding why we behave as we do. It is not adequate to blame students for their unwanted behavior. The blame never gets us anywhere. When students display unwanted behaviors, an opportunity is opened for us. This opportunity is an educational one, because unwanted behavior is an indication that learning an unwanted behavior has taken place and that new learning must occur. Therefore, the educator's job is to determine what learning must take place to reduce the unwanted behavior.

If we are to place blame for unwanted behavior, we must place it where we can have the most control. We cannot control a student's home life or culture; we cannot control a student's physiology. We can, however, control or change a student's school and classroom environments to bring about changes in behavior. Although the school and classroom environments are not the whole story behind the student's unwanted behavior, the school and classroom environments are the only sources of behavior in which we can have an effect.

The remaining chapters in this book discuss ways to determine what in the school or classroom is affecting student behavior (both wanted and unwanted). In addition, ways to make changes in the student's immediate environment are discussed.

VIGNETTE • *Revisited*

After studying the causes of behavior problems, Mr. Huang concluded that it is better to look at what is going on in his classroom to explain why the students are behaving as they are rather than to assume that the cause resides in some uncontrollable variable such as in the home. Mr. Huang began to understand that even students who came from difficult home environments could learn to behave acceptably. What is needed is an effective reinforcement system that strengthens their positive behavior and ignores their unwanted behavior.

Mr. Huang also realized that what he thought was punishment—removing the students from the classroom—could actually be working as a reinforcer. In other words, Mr. Huang's response to the students' unwanted behaviors may be having the exact opposite impact that he had expected. He also realized that on many of the occasions when he tried to ignore the students' minor misbehaviors, he would attend to them if they reached an unacceptable level. In other words, Mr. Huang was making the problem behaviors worse by shaping them to a more disruptive level. Mr. Huang is interested in learning more about how to use this information to prevent future behavior problems.

Discussion Questions

1. What is the difference between the cognitive and social learning views of learning?

2. How can human behavior can be viewed from these perspectives?

3. How can the cause of student behavior be viewed as a relationship among antecedents, behaviors, and consequences? Provide an original example.

4. How are reinforcers different from rewards? For the following, describe how each is similar and different from the other: (a) positive and negative reinforcers; (b) positive and negative punishers; (c) positive reinforcers and positive punishers; (d) negative reinforcers and negative punishers.

5. How can stimuli that do not function as reinforcers or punishers take on reinforcing or aversive properties?

6. How do deprivation and satiation states affect a stimulus as a reinforcer?

7. How can teachers improve the classroom behavior of students by acquiring stimulus control over student behavior? Provide an example of a teacher programming for stimulus control.

8. How can a teacher get a student who is rarely on task become on task for long periods of time by using shaping?

9. Why is knowing about the concept of chaining important for teachers? Provide an example of how each of the three methods of chaining can be used to teach a student to sit down and begin working soon after she enters the room.

10. Why is it more difficult to decrease a behavior that is intermittently reinforced than one that is continuously reinforced? If a behavior was on an intermittent schedule, which schedule or schedules would provide the least resistance to extinction?

3

Managing the School Environment

School Violence

VIGNETTE

MS. SALINIS HAS BEEN RIVETED by the images of school shootings reported by the national news media. The magnified coverage describes the school shootings as "an all-too-familiar story" or "another in a recent trend." Experts interviewed after each of these shootings indicate that the students exhibited behavioral patterns that school officials had overlooked.

Ms. Salinis has been teaching literature at an urban high school for 15 years. During this time, she has taught many youth who exhibited problematic behavioral patterns. Until the magnified national coverage of school shootings, she had not thought a great deal about whether school violence is a problem or if such students are at risk for committing violence. Her principal handed out copies of *Early Warning, Timely Response: A Guide to Safe Schools* (Dwyer, Osher, & Warger, 1998) and encouraged staff to read it. The principal informed staff about the possibility of installing metal detectors to ensure that "a school shooting would not happen here." Parents also began to talk to Ms. Salinis about their fears that a school shooting might occur at school. As one parent put it, "It scares me to death that I'm sending my child to school to get an education and that I may end up burying her."

Ms. Salinis decided to look at the school violence problem more closely. She was interested in finding out whether school violence was a problem and whether she could detect students at risk of committing violent acts.

Overview

Although violence in schools has been declining, policy makers and parents are still concerned about the safety of children in today's schools. The decline in school violence may be affected by an expansion of problematic policies across the United States. For example, it is not uncommon for students to be expelled for minor acts under the guise of improving school safety. In 1997, 3.1 million students were suspended from school, most for nonviolent, noncriminal acts (Brooks, Schiraldi, & Ziedenberg, 2000). Students face greater risks of dropping out permanently and becoming entangled in the courts when they are excluded from school. Minority students and students with disabilities are bearing the brunt of these new exclusion policies. African American, Latino, and students with disabilities are suspended from school at several times the rate of white students.

The larger threat comes not from school shootings but from the policies and practices that are being implemented in our schools. These failed policies will cause schools to neglect the development and implementation of schoolwide positive behavioral intervention and support programs. As Americans soberly reflect on the needless loss of life that occurred in places such as Paducah, Kentucky, and at high schools such as Santana High and Columbine High, there is a need to take a closer look at school safety. The focus of this chapter is on school safety. A description of school safety is followed by a discussion of the consequences of misconceptions of school safety. This discussion is followed by a description of how to conduct a fact-based assessment of threats of violence.

Are Schools Safe?

In this section, the extent to which school are safe is examined. We use comprehensive reviews of school safety conducted by the Justice Policy Institute (Brooks et al., 2000; Donohue, Schiraldi, & Ziedenberg, 1998) and look at several areas to provide a comprehensive look at school safety. The areas include school-related violent deaths; fights and gun possession in schools; school crime; and student, teacher, and public perceptions of school safety.

School-Related Violent Deaths

One would think that it would be relatively straightforward to determine the rate of **school-related violent deaths** occurring in any given year. Unfortunately, no reliable, scientific counts are maintained regarding the true number of children killed in schools in the United States each year (Donohue et al., 1998). The best data on the rate of school-associated violence occurring each year are compiled annually by the National School Safety Center. It is important to note, however, that there are two primary methodological flaws to consider when interpreting the true number of students killed in schools and whether there is a trend over time.

First, the National School Safety Center uses a broad definition of school-associated violent deaths. The center records any deaths that occur on school property, including suicides and deaths of adults or children, caused by adults or children in, near, or on the way to school. Thus, some of the deaths are included in the count simply because they occurred on school property. For example, a speech diagnostician was shot and killed in a high school parking lot by her boyfriend, who then turned the gun on himself. A similar killing and suicide of two adults on school grounds occurred in Hoboken High School in New Jersey. As such, of the 40 "school-related violent deaths" that occurred in the 1997–1998 school year, these 4 adult deaths counted as 10% of the total.

Second, the center relies on newspaper clippings as its data source for school-related violent deaths. Thus, the number of school-related violent deaths may be dependent on the extent to which it is on the media's "radar screen" from year to year. For example, although homicides in the United States dropped by 13% between 1990 and 1995, coverage of homicides on ABC, CBS, and NBC evening news programs increased by 240% (Donohue et al., 1998). As a result, the center may be counting a change in reporting of school-related violence rather than a change in the number of incidents themselves.

The number of school-related violent deaths from the 1992–1993 to 1998–1999 school years is presented in Figure 3.1. To reiterate the discussion above, these numbers also include suicides and deaths of adults or children, caused by adults or children in, near, or on the way to school. Thus, the relatively low numbers of school-related violent deaths are inflated. Inspection of Figure 3.1 reveals that not only is the relative number of school-related violent deaths low, but it has consistently declined over the years. For example, during the 1998–1999 school year (which included the Columbine shooting), the center reported 26 deaths. This represented a 40% decline from the previous year and was 26% below the average for the previous 6 years (Brooks et al., 2000).

Fights and Gun Possession in Schools

The Centers for Disease Control (CDC) reported in the *Journal of the American Medical Association* (cited in Brooks et al., 2000) the results of the CDC's Youth Risk Behavior Survey. The purpose of the study was to compare responses in student-reported risk factors from the 1997 surveys with those reported in 1991 and 1993. The results showed a continued decline in student-reported risk factors between 1993 and 1997 (results are summarized below). With regard to violence-related risk factors, there was a decline in the number of students who carried a weapon or were involved or injured in a fight in school between 1991 and 1993. There was also a decline in the number of students who carried a

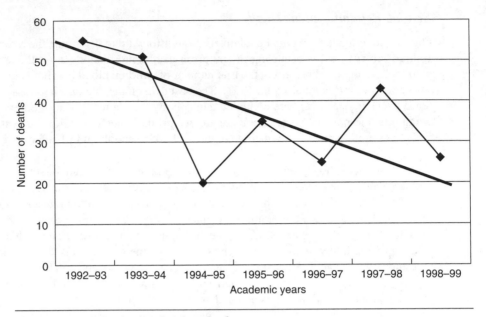

FIGURE 3.1 *School-related violent deaths.*

weapon, fought, or were injured in a physical fight in school between 1991 and 1993. A summary of the primary results follows:

1. There was a 14% decrease in student reports of physical fights on and off school grounds (42.5% to 36.6%) and a 9% decrease in students who reported being in a physical fight on school grounds (16.2% to 14.8%).
2. There was a 20% decrease in student reports of being injured in a physical fight on and off school grounds (4.4% to 3.5%).
3. There was a 30% decrease in student self-reports of carrying a weapon in the previous 30 days (26.1% to 18%).
4. There was a 25% decrease in students who reported carrying a gun to school in the previous 30 days (7.9% to 5.9%).
5. There was no statistically significant increase in the number of students who reported feeling too unsafe to go to school.
6. There was no statistically significant change in the rates of student reporting property being stolen or damaged.

School Crime

The Bureau of Justice Statistics (BJS) and the National Center for Education Statistics (NCES) conducted a joint study on changes in students' perceptions of student crime between 1993 and 1999 (cited in Brooks et al., 2000). The results were consistent with the

CDC's study on fights and gun possessions in school. Using statistics gathered under the National Crime Victimization Surveys, BJS/NCES found a decline in nonfatal crimes against students aged 12 to 18 occurring at school or going to or from school between 1993 and 1997. A summary of the primary findings follows:

1. There was a 29% decrease in the number of reported school crimes (3,795,200 to 2,721,200).
2. There was a 34% decrease in the number of serious violent crimes (306,700 to 201,800).
3. There was a 27% decrease in the total number of violent crimes (1,438,200 to 1,055,200).
4. There was a 29% decrease in reported thefts (2,357,000 to 1,666,000).

Student, Teacher, and Public Perceptions of School Safety

Students.   A *New York Times*/CBS telephone poll of 1,038 teenagers (aged 13–17) done in October 1999 found that the percentage of youths who said that they were being victimized inside or outside a school had dropped from 40% to 24% between 1994 and 1999 (cited in Brooks et al., 2000). Furthermore, 87% of students reported that they believed that their schools were safe. Although 52% of students reported that they thought an attack like the shooting at Columbine High School could happen in their school, they believed that such an event did not concern them much. The results of a semiannual telephone survey conducted by Metropolitan Life Insurance support the conclusion that students generally feel safe at school (cited in Brooks et al., 2000). Comparison of student responses between 1993 and 1998 showed that students believe their schools are safe. Finally, the National Education Longitudinal Study (1998) revealed that only 8% of 10th graders reported that they felt unsafe.

Teachers.   In addition to surveying students, the Metropolitan Life Insurance semiannual telephone survey included a sample of teachers. This survey found that teachers believed that their schools were relatively free from nonfatal violence. The 1998 survey conducted just 6 months after a string of five highly publicized school shootings revealed that 86% of teachers said that their schools were more or as safe as their schools were the year before. Furthermore, nearly twice as many teachers (11% to 21%) reported that the level of violence in their schools had declined from the previous year, and fewer teachers reported an increase in violence from the previous year. Finally, only 1% of teachers reported that they were worried or very worried about being physically attacked in and around their schools.

Public.   In contrast to students and teachers, the public at large has misconceptions about the safety of schools. National news media coverage of violent events—Santee, California; Pearl, Mississippi; West Paducah, Kentucky; Jonesboro, Arkansas; Edinboro, Pennsylvania; Springfield, Oregon; and Littleton, Colorado—has heightened fears that schools are unsafe. Studies by the Bureau of Justice Statistics, the National Center for Education Statistics, and various other sources found violent crime was relatively rare in schools and not on the increase (Brooks et al., 2000). There is a less than a one in a million chance of a school-aged youth dying or committing suicide on school grounds or on the way to school.

Despite the 40% decline in school-associated violent deaths between the 1997–1998 and 1998–1999 academic years (43 to 26), there was almost a 50% increase in the number of Americans who were fearful of their schools (Brooks et al., 2000). School board members, parents, and the public at large continue to believe that schools are unsafe. Although many policy makers note the rareness of these tragic events, somehow the message that our schools are safe places for our children has been lost on the public. Telephone polls and surveys consistently find that adults believe that schools are unsafe. For example, a *USA Today* poll done the day after the Littleton, Colorado, shooting found that 68% of Americans thought it likely that a shooting could happen in their town or city (cited in Brooks et al., 2000). In addition, 49% of respondents reported that they were more likely to be fearful of their schools than in the previous year, and 80% expected more school shootings.

Although we might expect the fears of adults to be heightened after a school shooting, the passage of time appears to do little to ease their fears around school safety. For example, in May 1999, 1 month after the Littleton, Colorado, shooting, a Gallup poll found that 52% of parents feared for their children's safety at school. Even 5 months later, nearly half of parents (47%) still worried about their children's safety in the classroom (cited in Brooks et al., 2000). Furthermore, a telephone poll on future election issues conducted in November 1999 by the *Washington Post* found that the second most frequently given answer was that "children in America are no longer safe at their own schools" (cited in Brooks et al., p. 4).

Finally, 96% of all juvenile homicide arrests occur in urban and suburban communities. As a result, we would expect adults in these communities to be more concerned about school safety than those living in rural areas. Yet rural parents (56%) are more likely to report that they believe schools are unsafe than those living in urban (46%) or suburban (44%) communities (Brooks et al., 2000). Taken together, telephone polls and surveys reveal that the public's perception of school safety is inaccurate. Americans are greatly misinformed by the hyperbole that surrounds school shootings today (see Table 3.1).

TABLE 3.1   *Reality versus Public Perception of School Safety*

Reality	*Public Perception*
• 1 in 2 million chance that a child would die in a school in 1998–1999. • 40% decrease in school-associated violent deaths between 1997–1998 and 1998–1999 school years. • 56% decrease in juvenile homicide arrests between 1993 and 1998. • 4% of juvenile homicides occur in rural areas.	• 71% of the public believed that a school shooting was likely in their community. • 49% increase in the public's fear that a school shooting would occur in their community from 1998 to 1999. • 62% of the public believe that juvenile crime is on the increase. • People in rural areas fear more for their children's safety in schools than those living in urban and suburban communities.

What Are Some of the Consequences of Misconceptions about School Safety?

In this section, some of the consequences of misconceptions about school safety are examined. We highlight some of the primary problems associated with such misconceptions in two areas: the use of school safety technology and **profiling** students at risk for targeted violence, including its implications.

Use of School Safety Technology

As detailed above, recent school shootings and other reported acts of violence across the United States have caused some public policy makers and educators to consider ways to make schools safer (Agron, 1999). Safety technology, such as metal detectors, security cameras, access control systems, locked doors, and alarm systems, has been advocated as a way to ensure school safety (Agron, 1999; Townley, 1995).

The extant literature addressing the relationship between school violence and safety technology is limited, contradictory, and plagued by methodological problems. Most school violence research has been exploratory in nature, using surveys to address a large number of variables. It is not known if school safety technology actually deters violence or makes students feel safer (Hyman & Perone, 1998; Rosenblatt & Furlong, 1997). The literature has also been clouded by civil rights controversies. The Department of Justice (1997) School Crime Report indicated that students at schools that used security measures, such as monitors and patrols, had approximately the same number of violent incidents as schools without such measures. Furthermore, students at the schools with monitors and patrols were more afraid of being attacked. These findings suggest that school safety technology may not be addressing all aspects of the problem of school violence.

Mayer and Leone (1999) questioned the use of security technology and personnel to promote school order. Using a structural equation model, they found that schools using physical measures such as metal detectors, locked doors, and locker checks were more likely to have increased theft, gang presence, and student attacks. Mayer and Leone state that instead of "running schools in an overly restrictive manner" (p. 351), schools should better communicate rules to students and develop appropriate interventions, such as anger management, social skills training, peer mediation, and conflict resolution programs. Similarly, Hyman and Perone (1998) suggest that school officials may victimize their students by implementing overly stringent discipline procedures. They pointed to inflated school violence estimates as a factor in school administrator's implementation of overzealous disciplinary procedures. There is little question that schoolwide positive behavioral intervention and support programs are an effective alternative to school safety technology (e.g., Nelson, 1996b; Nelson, Martella, & Marchand-Martella, in press).

Finally, the use of safety technology to reduce school violence has raised civil rights concerns. Safety technology may violate students' Fourth Amendment right to be free from unreasonable search and seizure. Lower courts have issued rulings that student rights are not violated by metal detectors, but the U.S. Supreme Court has not ruled on this issue, and courts have been divided on when and where students can reasonably expect privacy (Hyman & Perone, 1998).

Profiling Students at Risk of Targeted Violence

A 1993 report on violence and youth by the American Psychological Association states: "Our schools and communities can intervene effectively in the lives of children and youth to reduce or prevent their involvement in violence. Violence involving youth is not random, uncontrollable or inevitable" (p. 3). Trust in such statements makes the use of profiles only more enticing and tempting.

The media often portray children who commit violent acts as troubled children who did exhibit unrecognized warning signs in their behavior and actions before they exploded in violence. Nancy Gibbs, in her 1999 article in *Time* magazine, refers to these troubled children in reference to the Columbine school shooting, for instance, as the "monsters next door." In her article and in countless accounts of school shootings, extensive descriptions of the student's activities prior to the shooting are provided, and we are left with the notion that educators, parents, and others should have seen the signs of future violent acts. In other words, profiling might be the solution to predicting violent behavior and apprehending criminals.

Profiling students involves identifying students at risk for targeted violence through the use of checklists and warning guides listing characteristics and behaviors that could potentially lead to violence. Next is an overview of the origins and uses of profiling, research on school shooters conducted by the U.S. Secret Service, the weaknesses of profiling, and implementation implications of profiling.

Origins and Uses of Profiling.   Since 1969, criminal investigators and criminologists in the United States have used profiling by the Federal Bureau of Investigation (FBI) (Fey, Nelson, & Roberts, 2000). A profile is a set of behavioral indicators forming a characteristic pattern of actions or emotions that tend to point to a particular condition. To arrive at the characteristics that compose a specific profile, a person's behavior is compared with case studies and evidence from other profiles (the results of this process conducted by the FBI with school shooters is detailed below).

Essentially, two different types of criminal profiling methods exist: inductive and deductive. In **inductive criminal profiling,** the profiler looks for patterns in the data present and induces possible outcomes (possible acts of targeted school violence committed by students who fit the pattern). The strategy is used to predict behavior and apprehend potential offenders before they commit a crime. Formal and informal studies of incarcerated criminals, practical experience of the profiler, and public data sources such as media reports are used to create profiles. General profiles are assembled relatively quickly and include general characteristics on a one- or two-page list.

There are two obvious problems with the use of inductive profiling. First, the generalizations that are made to construct the profile stem from limited and often very small population samples. Inductive profiles also only take into account the characteristics of apprehended offenders and neglect offenders who are at large. There is little question that the characteristics of nonapprehended offenders are likely to be missing from the profiles. Second, in inductive profiling, behavior and motivations are assumed to be constant over time. For targeted violence prediction for students, this assumption neglects the very nature of changes in children's behavior over time. For the use of inductive profiling, we need to ask, Could the targeted acts of violence committed by the youths in Santee, Littleton, Jonesboro, and

Springfield have been predicted with the use of inductive profiling? Did previous incidents in other schools point undoubtedly to the occurrence of these tragedies or allow the construction of a profile that would have identified the students involved in the incidents?

Deductive criminal profiling involves interpreting forensic evidence from a crime or crime scene to reconstruct behavior patterns and deduce offender characteristics, demographics, emotions, and motivations. Most FBI profiling is deductive in nature. Anyone who has read Sherlock Holmes stories has encountered deductive profiling. Holmes uses physical evidence, gut feelings, and his work experience to deduce a profile of the criminal. Deductive profiling requires a great deal of effort, skill, and specialized training in forensic science and crime scene reconstruction.

There is one obvious problem with deductive criminal profiling. Although an offender for a particular crime might be successfully identified through deductive profiling, it does not enable us to develop a reliable base of generalizations to use in the identifications of other offenders. For deductive profiling, the question arises whether the targeted acts of school violence that have occurred allow us to construct a general behavioral profile that could be used for the identification of students at risk for violent behavior.

Research on School Shooters. The U.S. Secret Service initiated a **Safe School Initiative** in an effort to determine if schools could prevent targeted violence (Vossekuil, Reddy, Fein, Borum, & Modzeleski, 2000). Targeted violence is a term developed by the Secret Service to refer to any incident of violence where a known (or knowable) attacker selects a particular target prior to his or her violent attack. The target may be an identified (or identifiable) person (e.g., teacher or classmate), or it could be a school building itself. Although, as discussed above, acts of targeted violence are random events that are declining, the Secret Service studied the most recent school shooters in an effort to help schools to consider steps they can take to prevent incidents of targeted violence. The remainder of this section summarizes the results of the Secret Services Safe School Initiative on targeted violence in schools (Vossekuil et al., 2000).

The Safe School Initiative is a collaborative partnership with the U.S. Department of Education's Safe and Drug Free Schools Program. The overall goal of the initiative was to provide information to educators, law enforcement professionals, and others interested in preventing incidents of targeted violence in schools. Personnel from the Secret Service National Threat Assessment Center studied documented school shooting incidents. School shootings were only included if the attackers were current or recent students at the school and they chose the school for a particular purpose. School shootings were not studied if they were clearly related to gang or drug activity or were due to an interpersonal dispute that just happened to occur at the school.

Researchers reviewed primary source materials (i.e., investigative, school, court, and mental health records) for each incident. Information gleaned from these sources included facts about the attacker's development of an idea and plan to harm the target, selection of the target, motivation for the incident, communications about ideas and intent, acquisition of weapons, and demographic and background information about each attacker. In addition, researchers conducted in-depth interviews with 10 of the attackers to get their perspective on their decision to engage in the attack. The primary attributes of the incidents are the following:

1. Thirty-seven incidents, involving 41 attackers, met the study criteria.
2. Targeted violence at school is not a new phenomenon. The earliest documented case occurred in 1974, when a student set off the fire alarm and shot the janitors and fire-fighters who responded.
3. The incidents took place in 26 states, with more than one incident occurring in Arkansas, California, Kentucky, Missouri, and Tennessee.
4. Males committed all the incidents.
5. The targets of the attacker included almost an equal number of students and school officials (i.e., school administrators, teachers, or other staff).
6. Students or school officials were killed in more than 66% of the incidents. Handguns, rifles, and shotguns were the primary weapons used.
7. More than 50% of the attacks occurred in the middle of the school day.

Consistent with our concerns regarding profiling students at risk for school violence, the results revealed that there is no accurate profile of the school shooter. A summary of the characteristics of the attackers include the following:

1. The ages of the attackers ranged from 11 to 21, and they came from a variety of racial and ethnic backgrounds.
2. They came from a variety of family situations (e.g., intact families, single-parent families).
3. Their academic performance ranged from poor to excellent.
4. Their friendship patterns ranged from socially isolated to popular.
5. Their behavioral histories ranged from no problems to multiple problems.
6. Attackers tended *not* to show any marked change in academic performance, friendship status, interest in school, or disciplinary problems at school.
7. Attackers were rarely diagnosed with any mental disorders prior to the attack.
8. Fewer than 33% of attackers had histories of drug or alcohol abuse.

Several findings suggest that incidents of targeted violence at school are rarely impulsive. First, in most cases, the attacker decided to harm the target before the attack, and more than 50% did so at least 2 weeks prior to the attack. Second, the attacker planned the attack in more than 75% of the incidents and more than 50% developed a plan at least 2 days prior to the incident. Third, 66% had multiple reasons for their attacks, and more than 50% had revenge as a motive. Finally, more than 75% of the attackers held a grievance at the time of the attack and communicated them to others prior to the attack.

The implications of the above findings are twofold. The *first implication of the findings* centers on the potential risks involved in using any given profile to identify students at risk for targeted violence. There are four potential risks associated with such profiling. First, the use of behavioral profiles is not effective for identifying students at risk for targeted violence. Knowing that a student exhibits characteristics consistent with the behavioral profiles detailed in the *Early Warning, Timely Response: A Guide to Safe Schools* (Dwyer et al., 1998) or the National School Safety Center's *List of Characteristics of Youth Who Have Caused School-Associated Violent Deaths* (National School Safety Center, 1999) will not help educators and others determine whether a student is at risk for targeted violence (Table 3.2 presents profiling lists by the U.S. Department of Education and by the

National School Safety Center). On one hand, there is little question that using any given profile to identify students at risk for targeted violence would lead to overidentification, because the majority of students who fit the profile will not actually pose a risk. On the other hand, the use of any given profile will fail to identify some students who in fact pose a risk of violence but share few if any of the characteristics.

Second, special services will be in demand as students are identified as being at risk for targeted violence through profiling. Will the students identified as at risk for targeted violence receive all their instruction away from the other children, or will that be limited to intervention programs as part of the regular school day? What will the interaction between these students and the other children in the school be like? What demands will be placed on school personnel, including increased responsibilities and necessary training?

Third, in lieu of or in addition to special programs for students at risk for targeted violence, suspensions, and expulsions are two alternative strategies to deal with the identified children. Educators will have to decide whether students who supposedly or actually exhibit the behavioral characteristics described in any given profile would benefit from the exclusion of the education process or would be more likely to commit violent acts if they are excluded from school.

Finally, aside from policy implications at the school system level, some issues arise regarding the treatment and rights of students when profiling is implemented. These issues include student privacy rights and related legal implications. Stereotyping, discriminating, and the wrongful identification of potential perpetrators are ethically unjustifiable, even if the intentions are to protect children from harm. Student privacy rights are likely to be violated with the use of profiling. Educators could face legal action in the form of civil rights suits and possibly class action suits, as well as negative media attention, especially if a student has been wrongfully identified as at risk for targeted violence.

The *second implication of the findings* focuses on the key issues educators should consider for preventing targeted violence. Rather than using behavioral profiles, educators should focus on students' behaviors and communications to determine if they appear to be planning an attack. In other words, educators should use a fact-based rather than a trait-based approach to identify whether students are preparing an attack. The findings highlighted above suggest that students often communicate their plans in advance and that they have access to weapons. Thus, educators should take seriously students' verbal communications (in many cases students were communicating their plans to others, and many knew the attackers' plans in advance) regarding a potential attack and assess whether students have access to weapons (most attackers had access to weapons). Some key questions for educators to include in their fact-based assessment are the following (a comprehensive description of key factors to consider in a fact-based approach is provided below):

1. Have the students developed a plan and communicated it to others? In a majority of cases, students have communicated their plans to commit a targeted act of violence in advance.
2. Have students been bullied? More than 66% of the attackers reported that they had been bullied, threatened, attacked, or injured by others prior to the incident.
3. Have students engaged in behaviors (e.g., efforts to get a gun, disturbing behaviors such as threats of homicide and suicide) that cause concern or indicate a need for

TABLE 3.2   *Profiling Lists by the U.S. Department of Education and the National School Safety Center*

U.S. Department of Education	*National School Safety Center*
1. Social withdrawal	1. Has a history of tantrums and uncontrollable angry outbursts
2. Excessive feelings of isolation and being alone	2. Characteristically resorts to name calling, cursing, or abusive language
3. Excessive feelings of rejection	3. Habitually makes violent threats when angry
4. Being a victim of violence	4. Has previously brought a weapon to school
5. Feelings of being picked on and persecuted	5. Has a background of serious disciplinary problems at school and in the community
6. Low school interest and poor academic performance	6. Has a background of drug, alcohol, or other substance abuse or dependency
7. Expression of violence in writings and drawings	7. Is on the fringe of his or her peer group, with few or no close friends
8. Uncontrolled anger	8. Is preoccupied with weapons, explosives, or other incendiary devices
9. History of discipline problems	9. Has previously been truant, suspended, or expelled from school
10. Past history of violent and aggressive behavior	10. Displays cruelty toward animals
11. Intolerance for differences and prejudicial attitudes	11. Has little or no supervision and support from parents and caring adults
12. Drug use and alcohol use	12. Has witnessed or been a victim of abuse or neglect in the home
13. Inappropriate access to, possession, and use of firearms	13. Has been bullied and or bullies or intimidates peers or younger children
14. Serious threats of violence	14. Tends to blame others for difficulties and problems he or she causes
	15. Consistently prefers television shows, movies, or music expressing violent themes and acts
	16. Prefers reading materials dealing with violent themes, rituals, and abuse
	17. Reflects anger, frustration, and the dark side of life in school essays or writing projects
	18. Is involved with a gang or an antisocial group on the fringe of acceptance
	19. Is often depressed or has significant mood swings
	20. Has threatened or attempted suicide

Source: U.S. Department of Education. (1998). *Early warning, timely response: A guide to safe schools.* Washington, DC: Author; and National School Safety Center. (1999). *Checklist of characteristics of youth who have caused school-associated violent deaths.* [online] Available: http://www.nssc1.org/reporter/checklist.htm.

help? Most attackers engaged in behavior that caused others to be concerned. Educators expressed concern for the attackers in more than 75% of the cases. The attackers had come to the concern of more than one individual in more than 50% of the cases.

4. Do the students have access to a weapon? The attackers got the gun(s) used in their attack from their own home or that of a relative in more than 66% of the cases.

Finally, although it may appear to be relatively straightforward to conduct a fact-based assessment of the extent to which students are at risk of targeted violence, it is difficult to identify students who are planning an attack. In cases in which there is a concern that students are planning an attack, the inquiry should focus on their difficulty coping with major losses, their perceived failures or injustices, and whether or not they had access to weapons. In addition, educators should develop a plan for how they will respond to students once they have been identified as being at risk for targeted violence. Although there are no definitive guidelines for how schools should respond to such students, we recommend that educators work with law enforcement and other social service agencies to develop an effective and supportive response to students and their family members.

How Do We Conduct a Fact-Based Threat Assessment?

All threats should be assessed in a timely manner, and decisions regarding how they are handled must be made quickly. That is not to say that all threats should all be treated the same. As discussed above, it is easy for educators to run the risk of over- and underestimating threats, unfairly punishing or stigmatizing students who are in fact not dangerous. The goal of the FBI's threat assessment approach is to make an informed judgment on two questions. How credible and serious is the threat itself? To what extent do the students appear to have the resources, intent, and motivation to carry out the threat? The FBI developed a risk assessment approach for schools to evaluate the students at risk for targeted violence to answer these two questions (O'Toole, 2000). In this section, we detail the key elements of the FBI's risk assessment approach, beginning with a discussion of some key concepts. This discussion is followed by a description of the FBI's four-pronged assessment approach.

Key Concepts

There are five key concepts in the FBI's risk assessment approach: threat, motivation, signposts, level of detail in the attackers' plan, and level of threat.

Threat. A **threat** is an expression of intent to do harm or act out violently against someone or something. A threat can be spoken, written, or symbolic (e.g., motioning with one's hands as though shooting at another person is a symbolic threat). There are four types of threats.

Direct Threat.   A **direct threat** identifies a specific act against a specific target and is delivered in a straightforward, clear, and explicit manner (e.g., "I am going to kill John"). The communication suggests that the targeted violence *will* occur.

Indirect Threat.   An **indirect threat** tends to be vague, unclear, and ambiguous. The plan, the intended victim, the motivation, and other aspects of the threat are phrased tentatively (e.g., "If I wanted to, I could kill everyone at this school!"). The communication suggests that the targeted violence *could* occur.

Veiled Threat.   A **veiled threat** is one that strongly implies but does not explicitly threaten violence (e.g., "We would be better off without you around anymore"). The communication *hints* at a possible violent act but leaves it to the potential victim to interpret the meaning of the message.

Conditional Threat.   A **conditional threat** warns that a violent act will happen unless a demand or set of demands is met (e.g., "If you don't pay me one million dollars, I will place a bomb in the school"). The communication suggests that the targeted violence is *contingent* upon a demand or set of demands.

Motivation.   Motivation is the reason behind the threat. Threats are made for a variety of reasons. A threat may be a warning signal, a reaction to fear of punishment or some other anxiety, or a demand for attention. It may be intended to taunt; intimidate; assert power or control; punish; manipulate or coerce; frighten; terrorize; compel someone to do something; strike back for an injury, injustice, or slight; disrupt someone's or some institution's life; test authority; or protect oneself.

Signposts.   **Signposts** are the behaviors that indicate that students are planning a targeted act of violence. The actual act of targeted violence is just the end observable behavior of an evolutionary path toward it; most students do not "just snap" or decide to commit an attack. Common signposts in the evolutionary path include (1) frustration and brooding about failures and disappointments, (2) fantasies about destruction of specific individuals, and (3) the development of a detailed plan. These behaviors are often evident in students' conversations, writings, drawings, and other actions.

Detail, Plausibility, and Emotional Content in the Attackers' Plans and Precipitating Stressors.   The higher degree of specificity and plausibility, the more problematic the threat of targeted violence. A high degree of specificity and plausibility indicate that students have thought a great deal about and planned for the targeted violence. Specific details can indicate that substantial thought, planning, and preparatory steps have been undertaken by the student, suggesting that there is a higher risk that students will carry out the targeted violence. Detailed plans include (1) the identity of the victim or victims; (2) the reason for making the threat; (3) the means (e.g., weapon and method); (4) the date, time, and place; (5) plans or preparations that have already been made, and (6) plausibility (i.e., how realistic is the plan). Likewise, a lack of specificity or plausibility indicates that students have not thought a great deal about the targeted violence. In such cases, students are just responding to a frustration or attempting to intimidate or frighten a particular student or disrupt a particular school event. Plans with limited specificity or plausibility tend to be general in nature (e.g., "I'm going to blow up the gym...") and/or implausible (e.g., "...with a nuclear bomb").

In addition to specificity and plausibility, it is important to consider the emotional content and any precipitating stressors that may increase the seriousness of the threat. The degree of emotionality embedded in the content of the threat should be examined to assess the temperament of students. Although emotions provide important information regarding their temperament, they provides little information with which to assess the degree of threat. Precipitating stressors can serve as catalysts for a targeted violence. The impact of a precipitating event may depend on personality traits, characteristics, and temperament that may be involved when students fantasize about violence or act violently.

Level of Threat.   In general, there are three levels of threat: low, medium, and high.

Low-Level Threat.   The overall content of the threat suggests that students are unlikely to carry it out. The information is (1) vague, (2) indirect, (3) inconsistent, (4) implausible, and (5) lacks detail or realism. The content of the threat suggests that students are unlikely to carry it out. An example is students who write in their journals that they are going to kill everyone in the gym with a nuclear bomb.

Medium-Level Threat.   The overall content of the threat suggests that students could carry it out, but it does not appear entirely realistic. The information (1) is more direct and more concrete than a low-level threat, (2) indicates that students have given some thought to how the act will be carried out, (3) provides an indication of a possible place and time (although not a detailed plan), (4) does not provide a strong indication that students have taken preparatory steps (although there may be some veiled reference or ambiguous or inconclusive evidence), and (5) contains a specific statement seeking to convey that the threat is not empty (e.g., "I'm serious!"). The content of the threat suggests that students might carry it out. An example is when students tell their friends that they know the specific times a particular group of students hangs out in the gym and that they are going to kill them someday.

High-Level Threat.   The overall content of the threat suggests that students are likely to carry it out. The information (1) is direct, specific to the victim, and plausible; (2) indicates that concrete steps have been taken toward carrying it out (e.g., students have acquired or practiced with a weapon or have had the victims under surveillance); and (3) provides detailed information on the place and time of the threat. The content of the threat suggests that the student is likely to carry it out. An example is students telling their friends that at 11:00 A.M. on Wednesday, they are going to kill a particular group of students with a shotgun.

In summary, the overall goal is to recognize and act on the most serious threats in a decisive manner and address those that are less serious in a standardized and timely fashion. In many cases the distinction between the levels of threat will not be obvious. Nevertheless, it is important for educators to understand that the higher the degree of specificity and planning, the more serious the threat.

Four-Pronged Threat Assessment Approach

The FBI uses a four-pronged threat assessment model to evaluate the likelihood that students will actually carry out a threat. The model is designed to provide educators with a framework for evaluating students to determine if they have the motivation, means, and intent to carry out a proclaimed threat. The assessment is based on the "totality of the circumstances" known about the students in four major areas or prongs: (1) personality of the students, (2) family dynamics, (3) school dynamics and the students' role in those dynamics, and (4) social dynamics.

The first step involves a preliminary or rapid assessment on the content of the information included in the threat itself. This assessment can be conducted by the school psychologist, counselor, or other individuals trained to conduct the threat assessment. The goal is to identify the level of the threat (i.e., low, medium, or high).

The rapid assessment can include the collection of information in all four areas or prongs (i.e., personality, family dynamics, school dynamics, and social dynamics) if the identities of the students are known. Information can come from a variety of sources, including teachers, staff, students, and other outside sources such as law enforcement agencies or mental health specialists. Threats assessed as medium or high and made by students who have serious problems in the majority of the four prongs should be taken more seriously. Appropriate intervention by school officials and law enforcement should be initiated immediately.

The following section outlines factors to be considered in each of the four prongs (i.e., personality, family dynamics, school dynamics, and social dynamics), including some of the types of behavior, personality traits, and contexts that should be considered seriously by school officials, law enforcement, and others. These variables should only be used in a **fact-based threat assessment** process and should not be used to profile students at risk for targeted violence. Furthermore, they are interconnected, and no trait or characteristic should be considered in isolation or given more weight than the others. All the characteristics can be identified in students not at risk for targeted violence.

Personality.   **Personality** is the pattern of traits or behaviors that characterize individual students. A trait is psychological characteristic of a person, including dispositions to discriminate between or among different situations similarly and to respond to them consistently despite changing stimulus conditions. These dispositions are thought to be a product of inherited temperament and environmental influences. Assessing the personality of students who have made a threat of violence requires knowledge of their behavior over time and in a variety of contexts. Thus, it is important to identify individuals who have had extensive contact with the students when assessing their personality or how they discriminate and respond to different situations. Key dispositions include (1) coping strategies (i.e., the skill to deal with conflicts, disappointments, failures, and insults); (2) expression of emotions (i.e., the skill to express internal behaviors such as anger, sadness, or frustration); (3) empathy (i.e., the skill to demonstrate compassion with the feelings and experiences of others), (4) resiliency (i.e., the skill to come back after a setback, a failure, perceived criticism, disappointment, or other negative experience); (5) responsiveness to authority figures (i.e., the skill at following rules and instructions); and (6) self-image (i.e., feelings about themselves and how they appear to others). Key personality characteristics include the following.

Leakage.   Students reveal clues (e.g., spoken, stories, diary entries, essays, poems, letters, songs, drawings, doodles, tattoos, or videos) to feelings, thoughts, fantasies, attitudes, or intentions that signal an incident of targeted violence. Another form of **leakage** occurs when students try to get unsuspecting friends or classmates to help with preparations for an incident of targeted violence.

Low Tolerance for Frustration.   Students are easily bruised, insulted, angered, and hurt by real or perceived injustices done to them by others.

Poor Coping Skills.   Students show exaggerated, immature, or disproportionate responses to frustration, criticism, disappointment, failure, rejections, or humiliation.

Lack of Resiliency.   Students have little capacity to bounce back (even when some time has elapsed) from a setback, putdown, or frustrating or disappointing experience.

Failed Love Relationship.   Students feel rejected or humiliated after the end of a love relationship and are unable to accept or come to terms with the rejection or humiliation.

Injustice Collector.   Students will not forget or forgive real or perceived injustices or the persons they feel are responsible (students might keep a hit list of these individuals).

Signs of Depression.   Students show signs of depression, such as lethargy, physical fatigue, a morose or dark outlook on life, a sense of malaise, and a loss of interest in activities that they once enjoyed. Other signs of depression can include unpredictable and uncontrolled outbursts of anger, a generalized and excessive hatred toward everyone, feelings of hopelessness, agitation, restlessness, inattention, and sleeping and eating disorders.

Narcissism.   Students lack insight into others' needs or feelings and blame others for failures and disappointments. This lack of insight manifests itself in several ways. Students might (1) embrace the role of a victim to evoke sympathy and to feel temporarily superior to others, (2) display signs of paranoia and assume an attitude of self-importance that masks feelings of unworthiness, or (3) be either very thin-skinned or very thick-skinned in response to criticism.

Alienation.   Students feel different or estranged from others. This isolation goes beyond being a loner and involves feelings of isolation, sadness, loneliness, not belonging, and not fitting in.

Dehumanize Others.   Students do not see others as fellow humans; they are nonpersons or objects to be thwarted.

Exaggerated Sense of Entitlement.   Students expect and react negatively if they do not get special treatment and consideration.

Attitude of Superiority.   Students believe that they are superior and present themselves as smarter, more creative, more talented, more experienced, and more worldly than others.

Exaggerated or Pathological Need for Attention.   Students show an exaggerated or pathological need for positive or negative attention regardless of the situation.

Externalize Blame.   Students do not take responsibility for their actions and fault others, events, or situations for their actions. They seem impervious to rational argument and common sense when placing blame.

Mask Low Self-Esteem.   Students mask a low self-esteem by displaying an arrogant, self-glorifying attitude and by avoiding high visibility or involvement in school activities.

Anger Management Problems.   Students tend to burst out in temper tantrums or melodramatic displays or to brood in sulky, seething silence. Students' anger is noticeably out of proportion to the cause or is redirected toward people who had nothing to do with the original incident. Students' anger may also be accompanied by expressions of unfounded prejudice, dislike, or hatred toward individuals or groups.

Intolerance.   Students often express (through words, slogans, symbols, or artwork) racial, religious, and other intolerant attitudes toward minorities.

Inappropriate Humor.   Students tend to display humor that is macabre, insulting, belittling, or mean.

Manipulate Others.   Students attempt to manipulate others in an effort to win their trust so that they can rationalize any aberrant or threatening behaviors.

Lack of Trust.   Students are untrusting and chronically suspicious of others' motives and intentions. This lack of trust can approach a clinically paranoid state. Students may express the belief that they must deal with matters on their own because there are no trustworthy mechanisms to achieve justice or resolve conflicts.

Closed Social Group.   Students appear introverted and have no close friendships, or they associate only with a single small **closed social group** that excludes everyone else. Students threaten or carry out targeted acts of violence and are not necessarily loners in the classic sense because they do associate with a small group of other students.

Change of Behavior.   Students' behavior changes (decline in academic performance, disregard for school rules, etc.).

Rigid and Opinionated.   Students are rigid, judgmental, and cynical. They voice strong opinions on subjects about which they have little or no knowledge, and they disregard facts, logic, and reasoning that might challenge their opinions.

Unusual Interest in Sensational Violence.   Students have an unusual interest in school shootings and other heavily publicized acts of violence. They will demonstrate their interest by declaring their admiration for those who committed the acts or criticizing them for their incompetence for failing to kill enough people. The students may express a desire to carry out a similar act in their own school.

Fascination with Violence-Filled Entertainment.   Students have an unusual fascination (i.e., spend an inordinate amount of time) with violent movies, television shows, computer games, music, or other forms of media that focus intensively on themes of violence, hatred, death, and destruction.

Negative Role Models.   Students are drawn to negative role models associated with violence and destruction, such as Adolf Hitler and Satan.

Behavior Appears Relevant to Carrying Out a Threat.   Students are occupied in activities that could be related to carrying out a threat (e.g., spending unusual amounts of time practicing with firearms or on other activities that will assist them in carrying out the threat). The time occupied in these activities results in the exclusion of normal everyday pursuits such as homework, attending classes, going to work, and spending time with friends.

Family Dynamics.   **Family dynamics** are patterns of behaviors, relationships, thinking, beliefs, traditions, and family crises that make up a family. The assessment of family dynamics includes determining each family member's opinion of the interrelationships among them. It is also important to identify key events that place a child at risk for psychiatric disorders. Key variables that have been found to be associated with child psychiatric disorders include (1) severe marital discord, (2) low socioeconomic status, (3) large family size, (4) a father with a criminal history, (5) maternal psychiatric problems, and (6) admission to care by authorities (Patterson, 1982b). Although exposure to any one of these variables does not necessarily place a student at risk for psychiatric disorders, there is an exponential increase in their likelihood (Patterson, 1982b). The key characteristics in family dynamics are as follows.

Turbulent Parent-Child Relationships.   Students have a difficult or turbulent relationship with their parents. They express contempt for their parents and dismiss or reject their parents' role in life. Factors such as multiple moves, the loss of a parent, or the addition of a stepparent can underlie students' turbulent relationships with their parents.

Acceptance of Pathological Behaviors.   Parents do not react or appear to be unconcerned about behavior that most parents would find disturbing or abnormal. The parents appear unable to recognize problems in their children and respond in a defensive manner to any criticism of their children. When contacted by school officials, the parents appear unconcerned, minimize the problem, or reject the reports of their children's troubling behaviors.

Access to Weapons.   Students have access to weapons or explosive materials in the home. The weapons and explosive materials are treated carelessly (e.g., guns are not locked away and are left loaded). Parents may handle the weapons or explosive materials casually or recklessly, conveying to their children that a weapon can be a useful and normal means of intimidating someone else or settling a dispute.

Lack of Intimacy.   The family appears to lack intimacy and closeness. The family has moved frequently or recently.

Student Rules the Roost.   The parents do not set limits on their children's conduct, regularly give in to their demands, and seem to be intimidated by their children. In other words, the traditional family roles are reversed, with the children being the authority figures. Students insist on an inordinate degree of privacy, and the parents have little information about their activities, school life, friends, or other relationships.

No Limits or Monitoring of Television and the Internet.   Parents do not limit or monitor their children's television watching or their use of the Internet. Students may have a television in their own rooms or are otherwise free to spend as much time as they like watching television or surfing the Internet rather than engaging in activities with the family or with friends.

School Dynamics.   Schools, like families, have patterns of behaviors, relationships, thinking, beliefs, and traditions that make up the school culture. There is no research on the relationship between school dynamics and threat assessment; nevertheless, these patterns have an effect on the students' behaviors, their feelings about themselves, their outlook on life, and so forth. The assessment of school dynamics involves evaluating the behaviors that are formally and informally reinforced in the school and the role that the students have within the school culture. The assessment should examine the perceptions of school staff and students because there may be significant discrepancies between their views. The key characteristics of social dynamics are as follows.

Attachment to School.   Students appear detached from school. Students appear not to have attachments with other students, teachers, and school activities.

School Tolerance for Disrespectful Behavior.   The school does little to prevent or punish disrespectful behavior between individual students or groups of students. Bullying is part of the school culture, and school officials appear oblivious to it. The school atmosphere promotes racial or class divisions or allows them to remain unchallenged.

Inequitable Discipline.   The use of discipline is inequitably applied, or staff and students perceive that it is so.

Inflexible Culture.   The school's culture (i.e., official and unofficial patterns of behaviors, values, and relationships among students and staff) is static, unyielding, and insensitive to the changing needs of newer students and staff.

Pecking Order among Students.   Certain groups of students are officially or unofficially given more prestige and respect than others. Staff and students treat those students in the high-prestige groups as though they are more important or more valuable than the other students.

Code of Silence.   A **code of silence** prevails among the students. Little trust exists between staff and students. As a result, few students think that they can tell staff if they are concerned about the behaviors or attitudes of another student.

Unsupervised Computer Access.   Students have unsupervised access to computers and the Internet. Students are able to play violent computer games or explore inappropriate web sites (e.g., those that promote violent hate groups or give instructions on making bombs).

Social Dynamics.   Communities, like families and schools, have patterns of behaviors, relationships, thinking, beliefs, and traditions that make up the larger community in which students live and go to school. Students' behaviors, beliefs, opinions, choice of friends, their feelings about themselves, their outlook on life, and their attitudes toward drugs, alcohol, and weapons will be shaped to some degree by the social dynamics of the community. Of particular interest are the students' peer groups, and their relationship with these groups will provide important information regarding the likelihood that they will carry out a threat. The key characteristics of social dynamics are as follows.

Media, Entertainment, and Technology.   Students have unmonitored and easy access to movies, television shows, computer games, and Internet sites with themes and images of extreme violence.

Peer Groups.   Students are intensely and exclusively involved with a group of peers who share a fascination with violence or extremist beliefs. The group excludes others who do not share its interests or beliefs. Thus, students spend little or no time with others who think differently and are shielded from a reality check that comes from hearing from others' views or perceptions.

Drugs and Alcohol.   Knowledge of the students' use of and attitude toward drugs and alcohol can be important.

Outside Interests.   Students' interests outside the school are important to consider. These interests can either mitigate or increase the level of concern, depending on the students' interests.

Copycat Effect.   Copycat behavior is very common. Thus, school shootings and other violent incidents that receive intense media attention can generate threats or copycat violence elsewhere. Staff, students, law enforcement, and parents should be more vigilant in the days, weeks, and even months following a heavily publicized incident elsewhere in the country.

Summary

Violence is a complex issue with complex causes and consequences. As such, school leaders face the difficult decision to implement strategies to prevent violence such as schoolwide positive behavioral intervention and to support programs in schools in response to pressures from parents, politicians, and the public. Schools are one of the safest places for students. Overall, the level of violence in U.S. schools is low and is declining. The following are some statistics on youth homicide in the United States that put school violence in perspective (Brooks et al., 2000):

1. Forty: the number of people (including some adults) who were shot and killed in school during the academic year 1997–1998.
2. Eleven: the number of children who died in 2 days from family violence (child abuse or neglect, at the hands of their parents or guardians).
3. Eight: the number of children who die from gunfire every day.
4. Three thousand and twenty-four: the number of children who die from gunfire every year.
5. Ninety percent: the percentage of children under age 12 who are homicide victims and are killed by adults.
6. Seventy-five percent: the percentage of youths between ages 12 and 17 who are homicide victims and who are killed by adults.

We hope we outlined profiling as a strategy and methodology to such an extent here that the decision to use or not use profiling will be facilitated for school leaders. The decision to use profiling reaches beyond pragmatic implementation issues and touches on the very core of what schools should and will look like with or without its use. The use of profiling in schools carries with it serious considerations. Its use can neither be justified by deferring to a climate of public pressure nor by using it as an emergency response to heightened concerns by the parents and general public about school safety.

We know that students will continue to make threats in schools (and, fortunately, most will never carry them out). Thus, we outlined the FBI's fact-based threat assessment approach to help schools assess the degree of risk that a threat poses. Although there is a clear need to field test, evaluate, and further develop the fact-based threat assessment approach, the four-pronged assessment approach detailed in this chapter provides clear guidelines. The threat assessment model can be used to identify and evaluate which students are at high risk for committing an act of targeted violence.

Finally, we hope we clarified key issues, concepts, and practices related to school safety so that teachers can better focus on how to create safe and disciplined learning environments that work for all students. As noted above, undue concerns regarding school safety can result in policies and practices that are harmful to students. How to develop, implement, maintain, and evaluate a schoolwide positive behavioral intervention and support program is covered in Chapter 4. The goals of such programs are to establish effective policies and procedures that create positive norms for behaviors, to improve the ecological arrangements of the school, and to identify and select evidence-based programs and strategies. A systematic process for planning, selecting, implementing, and evaluating evidence-based programs and strategies is covered in Chapter 5. Implementing evidence-based programs and strategies is important because not everything that is done in schoolwide discipline or violence prevention shows promise.

VIGNETTE • *Revisited*

Ms. Salinis was surprised to find that it is virtually impossible to determine how many school shootings actually occur in a given school year. She thought it would be relatively straightforward to determine the rate of school-related violent deaths occurring in any given year, but it proved difficult to obtain such figures. She found that not only are school-related deaths relatively rare, but they appear to be declining. She also found that the number of fights and gun possessions at school has been declining over recent years and that students and teachers feel safe at school. These findings were in direct contrast to the picture painted by the magnified national coverage of the school shootings.

Ms. Salinis was also surprised to find out that students who commit school shootings do not exhibit identifiable behavior patterns. In contrast to the picture presented by experts interviewed after each of the school shootings, school shooters do not exhibit any identifiable behavioral patterns or profiles. The ages, ethnicities, behavioral histories, friendship patterns, and academic performance of the attackers varied widely. Rather than looking for behavioral patterns, Ms. Salinis learned that she should conduct fact-based threat assessments.

Ms. Salinis decided that it was important for her to take threats of violence seriously. She learned, however, that she should focus more on the characteristics of the threat rather than on the characteristics of the student. Ms. Salinis would focus on the degree of specificity and plausibility of the threat. A high degree of specificity and plausibility in the threat would indicate that the student has thought a great deal about and planned a violent incident. On the other hand, a low degree of specificity or plausibility in the threat would indicate that the student has not thought a great deal about the targeted violence.

Discussion Questions

1. How safe are schools?

2. Why does the public have misconceptions of school safety?

3. What are the problems that arise with misconceptions of school safety?

4. What are the primary attributes of the recent incidents of school violence?

5. What are the characteristics of the students involved in recent incidents of school violence?

6. What is inductive profiling?

7. What is deductive profiling?

8. What is a threat? What are the different levels of threats?

9. What are the primary areas examined in the FBI's four-pronged threat assessment approach?

10. How should the factors included in the four-pronged threat assessment approach be viewed?

4

Managing the School Environment

Developing, Implementing, and Maintaining a Schoolwide Positive Behavioral Intervention and Support Program

Chapter Objectives _____

After studying this chapter, you should be able to:

- Depict the theoretical foundation and goals of schoolwide positive behavioral interventions and supports.
- Illustrate the key elements of schoolwide positive behavioral interventions and supports.
- Characterize the six organizational systems that make up a schoolwide positive behavioral intervention and support program.
- Describe the seven key attributes of the leadership organizational system.
- Illustrate the four key attributes of the schoolwide organizational system.
- Describe the four key attributes of the nonclassroom organizational system.
- Characterize the five key attributes of the classroom organizational system.
- Depict the four key attributes of the individual organizational system.
- Describe the three key attributes of the academic support system.
- Depict common barriers to the development, implementation, and maintenance of a schoolwide positive behavioral intervention program.
- Explain how the Safe School Evaluation Rubric is used to develop, implement, maintain, and evaluate a schoolwide positive behavioral intervention and support program.

VIGNETTE

MATHEMATICS TEACHER JEFF GAVIN appealed to his middle-school students in a big way. Turnout for sporting events had reached an all-time high in the 6 years since he had arrived at Lemuria, a middle school in a mostly Hispanic section of a large metropolis. Education carried a great deal of influence in the school community, and Lemuria provided students with unity and pride. Mr. Gavin's fellow faculty members had adopted a schoolwide program to identify problematic student behavior and implement discipline policies on which all teachers and support staff could agree. Thus, the stage was set to help students toward prosocial, cooperative behavior and to contain any possible deterrents to student learning.

Zach Garcia and his buddies signed up for Mr. Gavin's mathematics class. Zach struggled with mathematics, but his influence and leadership among his group of friends gave him some real social leverage. Most of the boys in Zach's group received free or reduced lunches, came from non-English-speaking homes, and had difficulty achieving high grades in school. To them, school was a place for social interaction within their group.

In Mr. Gavin's mathematics class, Zach and his friends felt that they were treated fairly. Grades depended on effort expended and personal progress. Attendance also figured into grading. For this reason as well as the contractual grading, each boy, even those who struggled with the mathematics concepts, could make an "A" based on personal efforts. Personal attention from Mr. Gavin felt good to them; his sense of humor, his warmth, and his equitable treatment of each member of the class according to the contract he developed assured them that they were on equal footing with others who were more successful in class. Attention paid to creating a safe learning environment had definitely paid off at Lemuria.

Overview

Concern about and a focus on the roles of schools in reducing problem behaviors is not new (McParland & McDill, 1977). Schools that promote prosocial, cooperative behaviors and academic success are central to preventing problem behaviors (Nelson, 1996b; Nelson, Martella, & Marchand-Martella, in press). For approximately 180 days per year and 6 hours each day, educators strive to provide learning environments that are conducive to learning. Unfortunately, schools face significant contemporary challenges that make it increasingly difficult to achieve such learning environments.

The challenges are many. First, schools are asked to do more each year with fewer resources. Initiatives to improve literacy, meet state-mandated standards, infuse information technologies, and facilitate school-to-work transitions are just a few of the challenges being added to the list of demands that schools are expected to meet. Second, schools must educate an increasingly heterogeneous population of students. Growing numbers of students in schools have limited English proficiency; significant learning and/or behavioral problems; and families in need of financial, social, and mental health support (Knitzer, Steinberg, & Fleish, 1990; Stevens & Price, 1992). Third, schools struggle to meet the needs of children who exhibit severe problem behaviors (Walker, Colvin, & Ramsey, 1995). Such students often account for more than 50% of the behavioral incidents handled by principals and support staff in schools even though they represent only 1% to 5% of the school population (Sugai, Sprague, Horner, & Walker, 1999). Further, many of these students need comprehensive and time-consuming wraparound planning and supports that involve families, schools, and communities (Eber & Nelson, 1997). Finally, schools often lack the capacity to identify, adopt, and maintain policies and practices that meet the needs of all students (Nelson et al., in press). Schools often provide staff professional development opportunities on behavioral interventions and supports in a piecemeal fashion with little concern regarding their "contextual fit" to the needs and attributes of the school. Such professional development models lead to a fragmentation in the knowledge and competencies of school staff working within a school and ultimately to less than optimal outcomes for all children (Nelson, 1996b).

The focus of this chapter is on creating safe and disciplined learning environments. The goal here is on maximizing student learning rather that simply reducing discipline problems. Few, if any, schools have achieved safe and disciplined learning environments that fully maximize student learning. Thus, all schools, regardless of whether or not they are experiencing high rates of discipline-related problems, should develop a **schoolwide positive behavioral intervention and support (SWPBIS) program** to ensure that the school environment maximizes student learning.

Although the school is the primary context of interest, our strategic planning process requires schools to examine the communities in which they are located; the nature of the surrounding social context has a significant influence on the intensity and structure of the SWPBIS program. In addition, the surrounding social context will affect the types of community-based behavioral interventions and supports that can be provided to children who exhibit severe problem behaviors and their families.

This chapter describes a strategic planning process for developing, implementing, maintaining, and evaluating a SWPBIS program (commonly referred to by educators as discipline policies and practices). The chapter should be of especial interest to present or future administrators; we believe, though, that all educational personnel should understand the process undertaken in strategic planning. Therefore, first discussed is the SWPBIS program, including its goals, elements, and organizational systems. This discussion is followed by a detailed description of the **School Evaluation Rubric (SER)** (Nelson & Ohlund, 1999), including information on its research base. The SER is a continuum of a progress evaluation rubric that is integrated within a strategic planning process. The SER is designed to help educators develop, implement, and maintain a SWPBIS program.

What Is Schoolwide Positive Behavioral Intervention and Support?

Schoolwide positive behavioral intervention and support (SWPBIS) is the application of positive behavioral interventions and supports to achieve socially important behavior change across all the school environments (described below). The goals and key elements of SIBIS follow.

Goals

The three primary goals of SWPBIS are to establish effective policies and procedures that create positive norms for behaviors, to improve the ecological arrangements of the school, and to identify and select evidence-based interventions and programs. A SWPBIS program applies a behaviorally based systems approach to enhance the capacity of schools, families, and communities to design school environments that improve the fit or link between research-validated practices and the environments in which teaching and learning occur. The SWPBIS approach examines the environments in which problem behaviors are observed; the development of interventions that consider the consequence variables that maintain occurrences of problem behaviors; the selection of interventions that give careful scrutiny to the range of possible lifestyle outcomes (e.g., personal, health, social, family, work, recreation); and the acceptability of procedures and outcomes by students, families, and the community.

Key Elements

The SWPBIS approach represents the integration of four key elements: a science of behavior, research-validated and practical interventions, attention to social values, and a systems approach (Sugai et al., 1999). A description of these elements follows.

1. The SWPBIS approach is founded on a science of human behavior that emphasizes that much of human behavior is learned, comes under the control of environmental factors, and can be changed. As our understanding of human behavior increases, so does our ability to teach and encourage more adaptive behaviors.

2. A SWPBIS program emphasizes the adoption and maintained use of evidence-based and practical interventions. Although procedures to prevent and reduce the likelihood of occurrences of problem behaviors are often associated with behavioral interventions, a SWPBIS program emphasizes strategies that use assessment information (such as functional behavioral assessment) to arrange learning and living environments so that factors that are likely to trigger or maintain problem behaviors are less likely to be present and so that adaptive behaviors are more likely to be taught, occasioned, and supported.

3. A SWPBIS program emphasizes the improvement of the living and learning options available to students, their peers, and their families. Thus, a central tenet of a SWPBIS program is that behavior change and the means by which behavior change is achieved need to be socially significant by being *comprehensive,* considering all parts of a student's day (before, during, and after school) and important social contexts (home, school, neighborhood, and community); *durable* so that change lasts for long periods of time; and *relevant* by enhancing prosocial behaviors that affect living and learning opportunities (academic, family, social, work).

4. A SWPBIS program emphasizes a systems approach, which considers the many contexts or organizational systems in which adaptive behavior is required. In schools, six organizational systems (described below) must be considered. A systems approach also focuses on prevention-based practices, team-based problem solving, active administrative support and participation, data-based decision making, and a full continuum of behavior support to accommodate the range of intensities of problem behaviors that occur in schools.

What Are the Organizational Systems within a SWPBIS Program?

Six organizational systems are included within a SWPBIS program. They include organizational systems focusing on (1) leadership, (2) schoolwide systems, (3) nonclassrooms,

(4) classrooms, (5) individual students, and (6) academic support system. Each is described below.

Leadership Organizational System

A leadership organizational system examines the school's role in effecting a leadership team that implements a continual strategic planning process to achieve a safe and disciplined school environment maximizing student learning. This system is central to the development, implementation, maintenance, and evaluation of a SWPBIS program. Although not necessarily distinct from other leadership activities used to direct and support the school efforts, this system focuses on establishing positive teaching and learning environments within all systems in the school: schoolwide (i.e., all students, all staff, and all settings), nonclassroom (i.e., particular times or places where supervision is emphasized), classroom (i.e., instructional settings), and individual student support (i.e., specific supports for students who are at risk of or engage in chronic problem behaviors). The goal of the leadership organizational system is to improve the school's vision and organization; stakeholder involvement and communication; allocation of resources (human, fiscal, and time); development, implementation, and maintenance of systems to support positive teaching and learning environments; and continual self-assessment.

There are seven key attributes of the leadership organizational system. They are (1) administrator support and representative representation, (2) parental involvement, (3) behavioral capacity, (4) building-level status, (5) support and commitment of staff, (6) sustained effort, and (7) central key part of the school improvement goals.

Administrator Support and Representative Representation.
The first key attribute of the leadership system is the support of the administrator. Support here is necessary because the administrative staff is central to discipline policies and procedures as well as provides a vision for all aspects of the school. In addition, the leadership team should be representative in terms of key areas addressed by the SWPBIS program. It is, however, important not to include too many members. Six to eight members usually help to ensure the representativeness of the leadership team and its efficiency.

Parental Involvement.
Parental involvement is important for two primary reasons. First, parental involvement plays an important role in establishing community support and commitment for the SWPBIS program. The community can provide many valuable resources and improve the SWPBIS program's outcomes. Second, parental involvement will facilitate communication of the goals, procedures, and practices of the SWPBIS program with families and others.

Behavioral Capacity.
The third key attribute of the leadership system is behavioral capacity. At least one member of the team should have training and experience in **applied behavior analysis.** Furthermore, the members of the leadership team should have broad and complimentary expertise, particularly when developing a SWPBIS program, because its successful development involves academic, social, family, and community factors. All members of the leadership team should be knowledgeable of evidence-based academic and

behavioral programs. It is difficult for the team to develop an effective SWPBIS program if the members are not familiar with basic applied behavior analysis and evidence-based interventions and programs.

Building-Level Status.   The leadership team must have building-level status, which simply means that the leadership team developing the SWPBIS program is a key part of the school's organizational structure. Because the SWPBIS program affects essentially all areas of the school (e.g., curriculum), the leadership system should be coordinated with the remaining functions of the school's overall organizational system. In addition, the team should not be seen as temporary or tangential to the organizational structure of the school.

Support and Commitment of Staff.   The support and commitment of the staff make up another attribute of the leadership system. The leadership system should not be based on a top-down process to build the SWPBIS program; rather, the teams should work to build consensus on all the SWPBIS program's policies, procedures, and practices. Although there is no set standard, schools generally try to achieve 80% consensus among staff prior to implementing any aspect of the SWPBIS program.

Sustained Effort.   Sustained effort on the part of the leadership team is also necessary to develop, implement, maintain, and evaluate a SWPBIS program. Building a SWPBIS program is an ongoing refinement and maintenance process that requires sustained effort. Effective SWPBIS programs are developed over time. Given the comprehensive nature of a SWPBIS program, it is beyond the capacity of staff to develop and implement a SWPBIS program in less than 2 to 3 years. This time frame, coupled with changes in staff and the need to update current staff, requires sustained effort.

Central Key Part of the School Improvement Goals.   The final attribute of the leadership system is that developing a SWPBIS program should be seen as central to achieving the school improvement goals. Achieving a school environment that maximizes the learning of all students should be a key part of the school improvement goals of all schools. The efforts of the leadership team must also be linked and coordinated to school reform efforts and activities and maintained over time. Achieving a safe and disciplined learning environment is a process of continual refinement.

Schoolwide Organizational System

The schoolwide organizational system is defined as involving all students and staff in all settings within a school. The goals of the schoolwide organizational system are to create a common language among staff, students, and families regarding the school's culture; to clarify staff roles in regard to discipline issues, problems, and crisis procedures; and to provide feedback to staff on a regular basis.

There are four key attributes of the schoolwide organizational system. They are (1) schoolwide guidelines for success (e.g., be safe, be responsible, and be respectful); (2) strategies for teaching staff, students, and families the guidelines for success; (3) clearly defined discipline roles and responsibilities; and (4) clearly defined crisis response plan.

Schoolwide Guidelines for Success.   The first key attribute of the schoolwide organizational system is the guidelines for success. These guidelines are a limited set of general expectations that represent the overall culture the school wants to achieve. Because of the general nature of the guidelines for success, they not only serve to encompass a great deal of behavior but also to provide the flexibility necessary for staff to connect more specific nonclassroom and classroom expectations to them. The guidelines for success provide a "common language" that staff can use to communicate with students and among themselves (e.g., was that safe, respectful, or responsible?) about behavioral issues. Using a common language improves the predictability of day-to-day interactions between students and staff as well as among staff. In addition, the guidelines for success provide a common foundation with which to connect nonclassroom and classroom rules or expectations.

Strategies for Teaching Staff, Students, and Families.   Strategies for teaching staff, students, and families the guidelines to success and associated nonclassroom and classroom expectations are the second key attribute of the schoolwide organizational system. Developing and implementing such teaching strategies is critical because educators often assume that students already know what appropriate school behavior is. Indeed, defining such expectations is one of the most unchallenged assumptions in schools today. Related to this issue is the notion that telling students the guidelines for success and associated nonclassroom and classroom expectations is the same as teaching students what is expected. Effective schools acquaint students with the key areas of the school (e.g., gym, cafeteria, and break areas) and actively teach the guidelines for success and associated nonclassroom and classroom expectations.

Clearly Defined Discipline Roles and Responsibilities.   The third key attribute of the schoolwide organizational system is defined discipline roles and responsibilities. It is important for all staff to understand the problem behaviors they are expected to handle and their role in doing so. For example, problem behaviors requiring an administrative response and the respective roles of the administrator and staff should be clearly defined. Clearly defined discipline roles and responsibilities reduce staff conflicts and improve communication among administrators, students, staff, and families.

Clearly Defined Crisis Response Plan.   A crisis response plan is the fourth key attribute of the schoolwide organizational system. When a school achieves an "exemplary" level of implementation in each of the six organizational systems (described later), the occurrence of crisis is reduced. Crisis, however, can happen at any time, anywhere. The crisis response plan should help schools prepare and resolve a range of crisis situations. Although the number of crisis events or situations that can be included in the response plan can vary, many schools focus on school-level events (e.g., anonymous threats to school safety and school shooting), nonclassroom and classroom level situations (e.g., defiance and verbal/physical aggression), and student level events (e.g., suicide threat). The crisis response plan should clearly define the roles and responsibilities for all school staff, establish an effective communication system, and establish an efficient process for securing support (internally and externally when needed).

Nonclassroom Organizational System

The **nonclassroom organizational system** is defined as particular times or places where supervision is emphasized (e.g., hallways, cafeteria, playground, and bus). The goals of the nonclassroom system are to improve the predictability of the day-to-day interactions between staff and students and among staff by ensuring that the behavioral expectations are linked to the schoolwide guidelines for success, to increase the participation of all staff in creating safe and disciplined nonclassroom areas, to maximize the ecological arrangements of the nonclassroom areas of the school to promote positive student behaviors, and to ensure active supervision of students and effective use of discipline procedures by supervisory staff.

The key attributes of the nonclassroom organizational system are (1) behavioral expectations that are linked to the schoolwide guidelines for success, (2) strategies for teaching behavioral expectations to students, (3) ecological arrangements that maximize positive student behaviors, and (4) staff training for active supervision and discipline procedures.

Behavioral Expectations That Are Linked to the Schoolwide Guidelines for Success. The first key attribute of a nonclassroom organizational system is the linkage of the behavioral expectations of the nonclassroom areas with the schoolwide guidelines to success. This linkage is more general and flexible in nature and improves the predictability of the day-to-day interactions between students and staff as well as among staff.

Strategies for Teaching Behavioral Expectations to Students. The second key attribute of the nonclassroom organizational system involves strategies for teaching staff and students expectations for each of the nonclassroom areas. Establishing strategies for teaching students, regardless of age, is critical to creating a safe and disciplined learning environment that maximizes student learning. Again, staff of older students often mistakenly assume that students already know the expectations required of them. Although the teaching strategies often differ (e.g., less rehearsing with older students), all staff should commit time at the beginning of the school year to teach students the expectations associated with each nonclassroom area of the schools. In addition, the behavioral expectations for each nonclassroom area should be linked to the guidelines to success when teaching and correcting students.

Ecological Arrangements That Maximize Positive Student Behaviors. The third key attribute of the nonclassroom organizational system is adjusting the ecological arrangements of the nonclassroom areas of the school to maximize positive student behavior. The basic assumption is that the proper design and effective use of the school environment reduces the incidence of problem behaviors in the nonclassroom areas of the school. Critical examination of the ecological arrangements is difficult because the human tendency is to overlook obvious solutions to problems. Clichés such as "If it had been a snake it would have bit me!" apply to the ecological arrangements of the school. Staff needs to view the ecological arrangements through a different lens and take advantage of the solutions that are inherent in the school environment itself.

Typical modifications to the ecological arrangements in the nonclassroom areas of the school include eliminating or adjusting unsafe physical arrangements and improving the scheduling and use of space. Eliminating or adjusting unsafe physical arrangements involves actual structural changes and adjustments in the use of the space. Although each site plan is unique, some problems could occur. First, campus and specific area borders are sometimes poorly defined. Even when fencing is used, it is sometimes obscured by foliage that shields the campus from natural surveillance. Second, undifferentiated campus areas (e.g., a hidden corner of the playground) present opportunities for informal gathering areas that are out of sight from adult supervision. These areas are not only used for prohibited activities, but they also have a tendency to increase the incidence of problem behaviors. Third, building layout and design often produce isolated spots (e.g., the end of a hallway) where students gravitate and may commit prohibited activities or be exposed to victimization. Finally, bus-loading areas are often in direct conflict with traffic flow or create conflict and congestion with automobile parking areas. These zones also tend to be in direct conflict with the flow of students leaving or entering the school grounds for extracurricular activities. Congestion created by traffic and student flow provides the occasion for problem behaviors and increases safety concerns.

One of the most effective ecological strategies for promoting positive social behaviors centers on improving the scheduling and use of space. For example, it not only takes longer to get groups through the lunch line because of congestion, but it also provides the occasion for more physical and undesirable social interactions between and among students. In elementary schools, reversing lunch and recess as well as mixing grades may eliminate many problems typically associated with the lunch or recess period. Although there are no set rules, general guidelines can be used to improve the scheduling and use of space. These guidelines include reducing the density of students by using all entrances and exits to a given area; increasing the space between groups, lines, and classes, and mixing age groups as the density of students increases; keeping wait time to a minimum; decreasing travel time and distance as much as possible; using physical signs such as clearly marked transition zones to indicate movement from less controlled to more controlled space or behavioral expectations for the common areas of the school; and sequencing events in common areas designed to facilitate the type of behavioral momentum desired (e.g., going to recess before lunch rather than going to lunch before recess results in students being better prepared for instruction).

Training Staff on Active Supervision and Discipline Procedures.

Training supervisory staff to supervise and use the discipline procedures is the final key attribute of the nonclassroom organizational system. Both certified and classified staff need training because the ratio of students to staff is the highest in the nonclassroom areas. The skill of staff to correct behavior in a positive fashion is greatly decreased. Teaching staff to move, observe, and engage students when they are exhibiting positive or problem behaviors is key to creating positive nonclassroom areas. In addition, supervisory staff needs to understand the disciplinary procedures in place for each of the common areas and how to challenge students exhibiting problem behaviors in a nonconfrontational and unemotional matter.

Classroom Organizational System

The classroom organizational system is defined as instructional settings in which teachers supervise and teach groups of students. The goals of this system are to ensure student learning outcomes, to improve the predictability of the day-to-day interactions between staff and students as well as among staff, and to build staff knowledge and competencies of effective teaching and behavioral interventions and supports.

There are five key attributes of the classroom organizational system. They are (1) curricula that focus on achieving academic success for all students, (2) behavioral expectations that are linked to the schoolwide guidelines for success, (3) consistent discipline procedures used by teachers, (4) teachers having access to effective assistance and recommendations for student behavioral and academic concerns, and (5) teachers having access to ongoing staff development activities.

Curricula That Focus on Achieving Academic Success for All Students. The first key attribute of the classroom organizational system is a curricula focus on achieving positive student outcomes. This attribute not only focuses on the overall curriculum but also on establishing a full continuum of academic supports (e.g., one-to-one tutoring programs) to ensure the success of all students.

Behavioral Expectations That Are Linked to the Schoolwide Guidelines for Success. Behavioral expectations should be linked to the schoolwide guidelines for success. The linkage of each teacher's specific expectations to these guidelines, which are more general and flexible in nature than the schoolwide guidelines, improves the predictability of day-to-day interactions between students and staff as well as among staff. That is not to say that every teacher has to have the same expectations. Rather, the linkage of each teacher's expectations to the schoolwide guidelines for success provides a common language with which to discuss student behaviors (both appropriate and inappropriate).

Consistent Discipline Procedures Used by Teachers. The third key attribute of the classroom organizational area of the school is the use of consistent disciplinary procedures for common classroom problem behaviors (e.g., off-task and noncompliance). The goal is to provide a common disciplinary response by teachers to improve predictability in the day-to-day interactions between teachers and students. Behavioral expectations linked to the schoolwide guidelines for success coupled with a common disciplinary response by the teachers provides predictability of the day-to-day interactions between staff and students. Although there are numerous common disciplinary responses, effective ones tend to reduce or eliminate warnings, provide the student a chance to regain control, and plan or problem solve alternative responses. It is important to maintain flexibility in administrative and classroom disciplinary responses for more severe problem behaviors (e.g., fighting and defiance). Such responses should be adjusted given the context associated with the problem behavior.

Teachers Having Access to Effective Assistance and Recommendations for Student Behavioral and Academic Concerns. Ensuring that teachers have access to effective assistance and recommendations for student behavioral and academic concerns is the fourth key attribute of the classroom organizational system. Schools must develop efficient and simple structures (e.g., common planning time once a week focused on academic and behavioral concerns) to support problem solving by teachers. Schools must also develop the knowledge and competencies of key members of their staff to ensure that teachers have access to evidence-based interventions and programs. That is, a number of staff should have in-depth knowledge of academic and behavioral interventions and supports as well as collaborative skills necessary to work with staff.

Teachers Having Access to Ongoing Staff Development Activities.   Finally, staff should have access to ongoing staff development opportunities. These opportunities should be designed to sustain current practices in the school as well as to explore potential additions. Staff development activities should be targeted and strategic in nature if they are to facilitate the implementation, refinement, and maintenance of the SWPBIS program.

Individual Organizational System

The **individual organizational system** is defined as specific supports for students who are at risk of or are experiencing school failure. The goals of this system are to establish prevention intervention procedures (academic and social) for students who are at risk of school failure and to provide individualized interventions and supports to students experiencing school failure.

Key attributes of the individual organizational system include (1) evidence-based interventions and programs for students who are at risk of or are experiencing school failure, (2) a common "solutions"-focused language or conceptual lens used by all staff to develop effective prevention and intervention practices, (3) an **established behavioral support team** that is easy to access and is not seen solely as a step in the special education referral process, and (4) the use of community resources as prevention and intervention practices for students and families.

Evidence-Based Interventions and Programs for Students Who Are at Risk of or Are Experiencing School Failure.   The first key attribute of the individual organizational system is the use of evidence-based interventions and programs. Evidence-based interventions and programs are punctuated by all the federal agencies (e.g., National Institutes of Mental Health) and professional organizations (e.g., National Association for School Psychologists) having established criteria to determine whether a particular intervention or program is evidence based or not. Establishing these criteria was done because schools tend to apply ineffective practices. Chapter 5 describes in detail how to develop or select evidence-based interventions and programs.

A Common "Solutions"-Focused Language or Conceptual Lens Used by All Staff to Develop Effective Prevention and Intervention Practices.   Second, a common language or conceptual model with which to view problem behaviors should be established. It is not only difficult to assess problem behaviors, but it is also difficult to develop behavioral intervention plans to treat the problem behaviors if staff members use different conceptual models. An effective conceptual model for viewing problem behaviors should have principles and concepts that are easily understood. If the concepts are too complex, they will be difficult to use with all staff in a school setting. The conceptual model should also naturally lead to school-based interventions. A conceptual model is of little use if it does not logically connect to variables that can be manipulated in a school setting. Finally, the conceptual model should be legally defensible. Courts will look closely to see if schools have applied evidenced-based processes and practices if a legal issue should arise in the treatment of a student. We believe that the only conceptual model that meets all three criteria is the one used as the foundation for this book: applied behavior analysis. Some of the more common conceptual models such as psychoanalytic (i.e., behaviors are the function of the constant interplay of unconscious processes within the individual), psychoeducational (i.e., similar to the psychoanalytic except that the focus of treatment is on the volitional aspect [ego] of the unconscious processes), and control theories (i.e., behaviors are internally controlled and not influenced by external events or individuals) do not meet the criteria for an effective conceptual model. Table 4.1 presents an analysis of these common conceptual models including applied behavior analysis, relative to the basic attributes of an effective model.

An Established Behavioral Support Team That Is Easy to Access and Is Not Seen Solely as a Step in the Special Education Referral Process. The third attribute of the individual organizational system is an established behavioral support team that is easy to access and is not seen solely as a step in the special education referral process. To ensure easy and efficient access, access to the team should be integrated into the organizational structure of the school. Behavioral support teams are composed of teachers, administrators, and support staff who possess the knowledge and competencies necessary to address complex student problems. The team works collaboratively with teachers to analyze the problem and to design interventions and supports to improve student outcomes (academic and social). The team should use the functional behavioral assessment processes and procedures described in Chapter 10 as a problem-solving framework to address student problem behaviors. In addition, the team should receive ongoing staff development to expand their capacity to address such behaviors.

TABLE 4.1 *Comparative Analysis of Common Conceptual Models*

Attribute	*Conceptual Model*			
	Psychoanalytic	*Psychoeducational*	*Control*	*Applied Behavior Analysis*
Easy to understand	No	No	Yes	Yes
Leads naturally to effective school-based interventions	No	No	No	Yes
Legally defensible	No	No	No	Yes

The Use of Community Resources as Prevention and Intervention Practices for Students and Families.   Fourth, community resources should be used in individual organization systems. The educational focus and training in today's schools often limit a school's ability to respond to the most serious needs of some students. Thus, schools must establish collaborative relationships and procedures to access those agencies in the community charged with meeting the more complex needs of students and families. Procedures should be developed to improve communication and networking among social service agencies, law enforcement, the juvenile justice system, and other relevant community resources. The use of community resources to address student problem behaviors is the final attribute of the individual organizational system. The problems presented by students experiencing school failure and their families are often complex and require resources beyond those provided the school. The educational focus and staff training of educators limit schools' ability to respond to the most serious needs of some students. Thus, schools should establish collaborative relationships and procedures to readily access community agencies charged with meeting the more complex needs associated with student and their families that are beyond the scope of the school. Community resources can be used to provide a wide range of services to students and families that are beyond the scope of the school, from mentoring programs to multisystemic approaches to therapy.

Academic Support System

The academic support system is defined as the integration of evidence-based academic skill support interventions and programs in three key skill areas (i.e., beginning reading, language, and mathematics) at the secondary (for students who are at risk of developing learning problems) and tertiary (for students who are experiencing learning problems) levels. The secondary and tertiary academic programs should build on the existing primary universal curriculum delivered to all students. In other words, the secondary- and tertiary-level programs should align and fit contextually within the primary universal curriculum program provided to all students. Furthermore, the interventions should address key skill areas in reading, language, and mathematics rather than the entire set of skills.

What are primary, secondary, and tertiary levels? In any school, three types of children can be identified: *typical children* not at risk for learning problems, *children at risk* for developing learning problems, and *children who show signs of life-course-persistent* learning problems and involvement in delinquent acts (Moffitt, 1994). Members of each group are candidates for differing levels or types of intervention that represent greater specificity, comprehensiveness, expense, and intensity (Reid, 1993). The interventions appropriate for each student group are primary, secondary, and tertiary forms or levels of curriculum and instruction. The primary-level curricular and instructional focus is on a schoolwide basis so that students do not become at risk for learning problems. Curriculum and instruction used for primary prevention are universal: all students are exposed to it. The secondary-level curriculum and instruction focus is on providing academic support and skill development to students at risk for learning problems. Students who do not respond to the primary curricular and instructional practices or demonstrate too many specific risk factors (e.g., poverty,

English language learners) are candidates for secondary-level practices. The tertiary-level curricular and instructional focus is on students who evince a life course of persistent learning problems. Successful curricular and instructional practices for these students are likely to be comprehensive, intensive, and collaborative across professionals.

Figure 4.1 presents an example of the primary, secondary, and tertiary emergent literacy program used by a Head Start program in the Midwest. The primary-level emergent literacy curriculum used by the program was broad based and focused on interactive and naturally occurring opportunities for learning. The secondary-level program focused on enhancing the phonological awareness skills of children who were at risk of developing reading disabilities. These skills were taught directly to children in a one-to-one format by direct service providers, volunteers, and parents. The tertiary-level program focused on enhancing the phonological awareness and language skills of students who were experiencing significant learning problems. The phonological awareness and language skills were taught directly to children by a team of specialists (i.e., special education teachers and speech therapists).

There are three key attributes of the academic support organizational system: (1) evidence-based secondary- and tertiary-level curricular and instructional interventions and programs; (2) primary-, secondary-, and tertiary-level curricular and instructional procedures are coordinated and integrated with one another; and (3) early identification procedures.

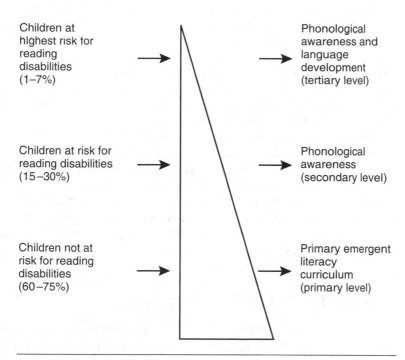

FIGURE 4.1 *Examples of a primary-, secondary-, and tertiary-level emergent literacy program for young children.*

Evidence-Based Secondary- and Tertiary-Level Curricular and Instructional Interventions and Programs.   The first attribute of the academic support organizational system is the use of evidence-based secondary- and tertiary-level curricular and instructional practices. Selecting such curricular and instructional practices is critical because these children with or at risk for learning problems need intensive sequenced instruction. Chapter 7 describes evidenced-based curricular and instructional practices.

Primary-, Secondary-, and Tertiary-Level Curricular and Instructional Procedures Are Coordinated and Integrated with One Another.   The second attribute of the academic support organizational system is the integration and coordination of the primary-, secondary-, and tertiary-level curricular and instructional practices. The overall goal of establishing these three levels is to provide an interconnected continuum of support for students with or at risk for learning problems rather than distinct approaches. In other words, the secondary- and tertiary-level curricular and instructional practices should target key skill areas necessary for students to access the primary-level curriculum.

Early Identification Procedures.   The final attribute of the academic support organizational system is the early identification of students with or at risk for learning problems. The goals of early identification are to prevent the emergence of learning problems in the case of at-risk students and to provide immediate support to those with learning problems. **Gated assessment processes** are commonly used to identify students with or at risk for learning and behavior problems. These processes consist of a series of assessments designed to screen out students with or at risk for learning problems systematically. Each assessment level (or "gate) consists of a finer-grained assessment. Initial gates are very broad and will include many students. Subsequent finer-grained gates pass only those students potentially at risk. The process is designed to be simple, efficient, and quick so as to impose as little as possible on teachers. A three-step gating procedure for identifying students with or at risk for learning problems is presented in Figure 4.2.

As illustrated, teachers systematically evaluate the students in the class via rank ordering according to how closely their observed skills correspond to the learning problem (e.g., beginning reading skills). These students are further assessed at gate 2 with a simple and efficient screening measure (e.g., oral reading rate). The two lowest scoring students move on to gate 3, whereas the remaining students receive the secondary-level program (e.g., one-to-one tutoring in beginning reading skills). Diagnostic assessment procedures are administered to the two students who proceeded on to gate 3, and they are provided an individualized tertiary-level program.

What Is the School Evaluation Rubric?

The School Evaluation Rubric (SER) (Nelson & Ohlund, 1999) is a continuum of progress evaluation rubric that describes three levels of implementation (beginning, developing, and exemplary) for each of the six organizational systems. The SER is shown in Appendix A on page 341. Evaluating progress in the six organizational systems using the three levels of implementation is necessary to achieve a school environment that maximizes student

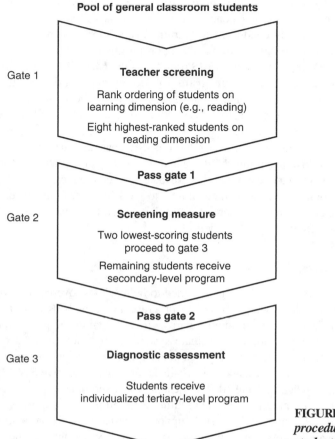

Pool of general classroom students

Gate 1

Teacher screening

Rank ordering of students on
learning dimension (e.g., reading)

Eight highest-ranked students on
reading dimension

Pass gate 1

Gate 2

Screening measure

Two lowest-scoring students
proceed to gate 3

Remaining students receive
secondary-level program

Pass gate 2

Gate 3

Diagnostic assessment

Students receive
individualized tertiary-level program

FIGURE 4.2 *Gating assessment procedure for the identification of students with learning problems.*

learning. The goal of the SER strategic planning process is to ensure that all six organizational systems are exemplary (i.e., include all the key attributes associated with each system). Only the key attributes identified by researchers to ensure the reliability and validity of the SER (Nelson et al., in press) are included here. A description of the key attributes of each organizational system is detailed below. Studying the three levels of implementation detailed in the SER helps one understand the attributes of each of the six organizational systems.

Research Base for the SER

The Effective Behavioral Support (EBS) model developed by Sugai and colleagues to increase the capacity of schools to prevent problem behaviors (e.g., Colvin, Kameenui, & Sugai, 1993) was used to develop the initial SER. As noted above and detailed below, a key component of the SER is a continual improvement process that leads to even more comprehensive integrated academic and behavioral interventions and supports for producing a school environment that is conducive to learning. This improvement process has led to even more comprehensive intervention and support programs.

A validated example of the SWPBIS program is the **Effective Academics Behavior Intervention in Support (EABIS) program.** EABIS program validation studies included (1) an experimental design, (2) evidence of a statistically significant and practically significant treatment effects, (3) replication at multiple sites with demonstrated effects, and (4) evidence that the treatment effects were sustained for more than 1 year (Nelson, 1996b; Nelson et al., in press). In general, research on the SER has demonstrated that it results in comprehensive SWPBIS programs that have had statistically and practically significant effects on formal disciplinary responses (i.e., suspensions, emergency removals, and expulsions); teachers' beliefs regarding their ability to work with difficult to teach children; overall academic achievement of schools; and the academic, social, and school survival skills of the most difficult to teach students.

Administering the SER

Overcoming Barriers.   The SER is designed to help schools overcome several barriers that often arise when developing a SWPBIS program. First, the SER is designed to overcome the tendency of schools to adopt a narrow focus when developing a SWPBIS program. The SER enables schools to evaluate systematically each of the six *interrelated* organizational systems that underlie a safe and disciplined school environment. Evaluating each of the six systems allows schools to create a more comprehensive SWPBIS program.

The second barrier that the SER is designed to overcome is the susceptibility of schools to either adopt practices that have little or no empirical support or fail to adapt them to their particular context. The SER supports data-based decision making regarding the current status and analysis of service gaps relative to key attributes of the six organizational systems identified in the research literature. The organizational systems are designed to support staff in the implementation of safe school practices, which are designed to maximize student learning. In addition, the consensus-based strategic planning process embedded within the SER ensures that the policies and practices adopted are "contextually fitted" to the school.

Third, the SER is designed to overcome the time constraints associated with developing a SWPBIS program. The SER relieves time constraints in several ways. First, the SER provides schools a clear and efficient structure for developing, implementing, maintaining, and evaluating a SWPBIS program. Schools do *not* have to spend extensive time thinking through the process they will use to develop, implement, maintain, and evaluate a SWPBIS program. Second, the SER is an effective staff development tool. Schools do *not* have to commit extensive time toward staff development activities or rely on outside expertise to develop, implement, maintain, and evaluate a SWPBIS program, because all staff become fluent in the key attributes of a SWPBIS program as they use the SER. Finally, the SER serves to improve and maintain the SWPBIS program over time. The readministration process embedded within the SER sets not only the context for the continual refinement of the SWPBIS program but also its renewal by providing a natural context for reeducating existing staff and educating new individuals each academic year.

Finally, the SER is designed to overcome the conflicts that often arise with the development of a SWPBIS program. Discipline-related issues in schools are often difficult because staff have different levels of expertise, perspectives, and commitment. In addition to ensuring that all staff understand the key attributes of an effective SWPBIS program, which in itself reduces conflict, the SER is a truly bottom-up process that helps build a common focus and commitment among staff.

Implementing the SER. The SER and associated action planning process have been field tested in numerous schools across the country. Before describing how to implement and administer the SER, it is important to note that there are numerous data-collection procedures that can be used to assess school environments. Thus, the SER and the other data-collection procedures presented here are not exhaustive, and at times additional procedures (e.g., observations, staff surveys, and inspection of formal disciplinary referrals) should be used along with the SER.

It is important to preface this description of the SER and how to administer it by noting that basic management responsibilities such as open communication, fair assignment of duties, and access to appropriate instructional materials must be attended to prior to the deeper discussion evoked by implementing the SER. Problems with inappropriate instructional materials, learning environments, or a school culture that is unwilling to accept the diversity and individuality of the students (especially those who exhibit problem behaviors) and families all take precedence over high-level discussions about creating a safe and disciplined school environment designed to maximize student learning.

This approach does not say that implementing the SER and developing an action plan to create a safe school environment require a perfectly functioning leadership and management system to move forward. Indeed, many of the problems mentioned above may be identified through the administration and implementation of the SER. Nevertheless, such problems must be addressed before individuals of the school community develop confidence that the school leadership has the ability to tackle the problems presented by students who exhibit problem behaviors.

The SER encompasses a four-stage strategic planning model to develop, implement, maintain, and evaluate a comprehensive safe school plan that encompasses the six organizational systems. Positive teaching and learning environments are maximized when a school is exemplary in all six systems. This model includes a set of concepts common to most strategic planning models. The stages in the strategic planning model are the following (see Figure 4.3):

Stage 1: Consensus-based administration of the SER (identification of problems and service gap analysis)

Stage 2: Formation of leadership team (guide the development, implementation, maintenance, and evaluation of the SWPBIS program)

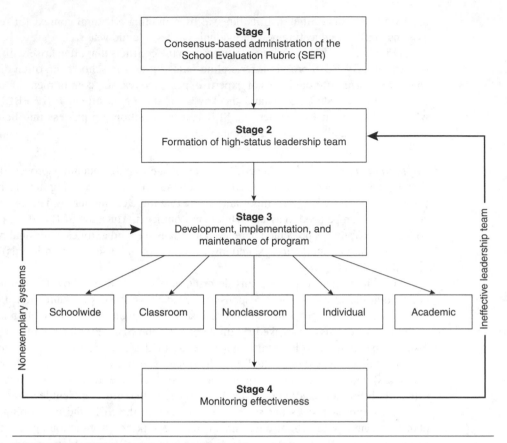

FIGURE 4.3   *SER four-stage strategic planning model.*

Stage 3: Development and implementation of a safe school action plan (practices to fill gaps in current services)

Stage 4: Monitoring effectiveness (ongoing evaluation of the effectiveness and refinement of the organizational systems)

Careful inspection of Figure 4.3 reveals that the administration of the SER is truly a bottom-up process in which all staff have input into the development of the SWPBIS program from the beginning. The first stage in the strategic planning model involves the consensus-based administration of the continuum of progress evaluation rubric within the SER. In the second stage, a leadership team is formed to guide the development, implementation, maintenance, and effectiveness of the safe school action plan. The remaining two stages focus on the development, implementation, and maintenance and on the evaluation of the SWPBIS program, respectively.

The SER presents each of the six organizational systems in sequence to facilitate its use (see page 341). The continuum of progress rubric for each organizational system and associated service gap analysis form are presented in sequence. The rubrics and associated service gap analysis forms are used in stage 1. The leadership team (formed in stage 2) uses the final page of the SER to develop and implement the SWPBIS program in stage 3. The SER is readministered on a regular basis in stage 4.

Stage 1: Consensus-Based Administration of the SER.   A consensus-based administration process is used to identify the current status (i.e., beginning, developing, and exemplary) of and service gaps for each of the six organizational systems. The goal of the consensus-based administration process is *not* only to ensure that everyone has input but also to increase staff's understanding of the key attributes associated with each of the six organizational systems.

A four-step process is used for each organizational system in stage 1. First, a staff member presents a brief overview of the key attributes of one organization system. Second, small groups study the continuum of progress rubric for each of the six organizational systems and achieve consensus on the current status (i.e., beginning, developing, and exemplary) of each one. Third, each group completes the associated service gap analysis form and preliminary action plan (i.e., potential solutions to fill the service gap needs) associated with each organizational system. Finally, the results from each group are reported and discussed by the larger group until they achieve consensus on the current status of and service gaps for each organizational system. The potential solutions are not typically discussed at this time. Rather, the leadership team will consider potential solutions suggested by staff when developing the SWPBIS program.

Stage 2: Formation of High-Status Leadership Team.   A leadership team should be formed to guide the development, implementation, maintenance, and evaluation of the SWPBIS program. The formation of this team and the designation of its responsibilities are important prerequisites to the success of the program. Although the committee will direct and guide the development, implementation, and evaluation process, the SWPBIS program is a joint venture, with staff at all levels working together. Achieving consensus on all aspects of the plan is essential to ensure its implementation and maintenance.

The overall *responsibility of the leadership team* is to direct the development, implementation, maintenance, and evaluation of the safe school action plan. The following are the responsibilities and general activities of the committee: to attend all planning meetings; to develop, implement, maintain, and revise the SWPBIS program; to evaluate new or revised components of the SWPBIS program; to communicate with staff members regarding the activities of the committee; and to conduct staff meetings to ensure the implementation and maintenance of the SWPBIS program. In addition, team members must be persistent in their efforts because effecting school change may be slow, can be intense, and may result in heated exchanges. Committee members must push through these exchanges in a positive manner.

Stage 3: Development, Implementation, and Maintenance of SWPBIS Program.   The leadership team uses the results obtained during stage 1 to develop a strategic SWPBIS program. The results obtained in stage 1 provide direction and momentum that the leadership team can use to develop the plan. Planning for a safe and disciplined school environment requires priority attention above and beyond the routine planning process that is common to schools. Schools must change current practices, which is not always easy to do. The leadership team may be faced with the following three challenges in relation to the planning process:

1. Adequate time is unavailable for planning due to the demand for immediate change.
2. The staff may pressure the leadership team to designate a significant amount of time toward immediate planning for a particularly troubling group of students.
3. The school may not have adequate resource support readily available to implement all the necessary practices.

Although the total planning, implementation, maintenance, and evaluation process may seem overwhelming, the leadership team can respond to the above demands in a prudent manner by prioritizing and working toward acquiring the resources necessary to implement the safe school plan. In addition, the leadership team should use an efficient team meeting format to reduce the time demands associated with the planning, implementation, maintenance, and evaluation process.

The leadership team uses a three-step process during stage 3. First, the overall consensus on the current status (i.e., beginning, developing, and exemplary) of each of the organizational systems is formally recorded. This baseline information provides the team a way to assess their progress toward achieving a SWPBIS program that is exemplary in each of the organizational systems. Second, the leadership team should record the results of the service gap analysis and prioritize those gaps that are of highest priority. Such prioritizing will enable the leadership team to develop a long-term strategic plan that will not overwhelm the staff. Third, the leadership team should develop a strategic plan to guide the development and implementation of the SWPBIS program. The "plan of action" form requires the team to identify the actions and associated strategies to achieve them. In addition, the team identifies a target date, the resources necessary, the person(s) responsible, and the evaluation procedure. The "plan of action" form included in the SER helps the team by providing a framework for making all decisions, facilitating teamwork through the development and implementation of the plan, providing effective communication for sharing progress in achieving goals, providing a mechanism for analyzing and enhancing the coordination of resources, focusing efforts on specific goals and objectives, and serving as a tool for measuring and demonstrating effectiveness.

Stage 4: Monitoring Effectiveness.   The leadership team readministers the SER to evaluate the effectiveness of and refine the SWPBIS program. In addition to serving an evaluative function, the readministration of the SER serves to re-educate existing staff and to educate new staff to the particular elements of the SWPBIS program. The dialogue associated with the readministration process provides a natural context for clarifying the elements of the SWPBIS program.

The leadership team uses the same steps detailed above in stage 1 to evaluate the SWPBIS program. Staff's views of the current status of each of the organizational systems are compared with those obtained with the previous administration of the SER. In addition, the readministration process will provide staff an opportunity to identify additional service gaps and potential solutions. The leadership team then uses the same process detailed above under stage 3 to refine the SWPBIS program. The overall goal is to achieve an exemplary status in each of the organization systems.

Summary

The development of SWPBIS programs represents one of the more important shifts in approaches to school discipline that have occurred in recent years. For the most part, traditional approaches to school discipline are based on punitive and exclusionary policies developed in the early 1900s, when schools were oriented toward academically inclined and socially acceptable students. Success in school was not necessary to obtain a job. Times have changed, though. Without a high-school education today, prospects for life success tend to be very poor. Although times have changed, schools have not. Administrators and teachers talk of lists of prohibitive rules and a series of increasingly severe punishments for the violators of these rules.

SWPBIS programs provide schools a systematic process with which to apply positive behavioral interventions and supports across all school organizational systems. The goal of a SWPBIS program is to apply a behaviorally based systems approach to enhance the capacity of schools, families, and communities to design school environments that improve the fit or link between research-validated practices and the environments in which teaching and learning occur. The practices and processes of the SWPBIS approach emphasize the systematic examination of the environments in which problem behaviors are observed; development of proactive evidence-based interventions and supports; and the importance of the acceptability of procedures and outcomes by the school staff, families, and community members.

The SER, which incorporates the key attributes of the six organizational systems of the school, provides staff an efficient process with which to develop, implement, maintain, and evaluate a SWPBIS program. The SER serves several important functions. First, the SER enables schools to evaluate each of the six *interrelated* organizational systems that underlie a safe and disciplined school environment systematically (i.e., leadership, school-wide, nonclassroom, classroom, individual, and academic support). Evaluating each system naturally leads schools to create a more comprehensive SWPBIS program.

Second, the SER supports data-based decision making regarding the current status, analysis of service gaps, and evaluation of the implementation and maintenance of practices in each of the six organizational areas. The organizational systems are designed to support staff in the implementation of safe school practices, which are designed to influence student behaviors positively. In addition, the strategic planning process embedded within the SER ensures that the policies and practices adopted are "contextually fitted" to the school.

Third, the SER provides schools a clear and efficient process with which to develop, implement, maintain, and evaluate a SWPBIS program. The SER also serves to improve and maintain the SWPBIS program over time. The readministration process embedded within the SER not only sets the context for the continual refinement of the SWPBIS program, but also its renewal by providing a natural context for reeducating existing staff and educating new individuals each academic year.

Finally, the SER reduces conflicts that often arise among staff when developing a SWPBIS program. The SER reduces such conflict because it ensures that all staff members understand the key attributes of an effective SWPBIS program. The SER is also a truly bottom-up process that helps build a common focus and commitment among staff.

VIGNETTE • *Revisited*

Several student behavioral incidents showed the staff how important it was to develop a school-wide positive behavioral intervention and support program that was supported by the community. In addition, the staff members were supported in their efforts to teach without having distracting discipline incidents. The consistent way in which behavioral incidents were handled enhanced teachers' feelings of being supported by disciplinary policies and being firmly linked to community values at the same time.

Mr. Gavin believed that one critical factor in the implementation of this program was the information given to students concerning schoolwide expectations for their behavior and the consequences of both meeting and violating these expectations. This information was dispersed at the beginning of each semester by every teacher on the staff. Students were made aware of acceptable levels of behavior, of the process that would be followed if those tenets were violated, and of consequences imposed. Therefore, when Mr. Gavin and his colleagues walked across the parking lot one Tuesday afternoon, he was surprised to see Zach and a couple of his friends gathered at the base of the bleachers. This territory was definitely off limits to students during the school day, and for months no violation of this nature had occurred. The ruling was usually easy to enforce because the distance from the school to the bleachers was too great for "between class" gatherings. When Zach saw Mr. Gavin, he gave recognition that he'd been caught and began a slow saunter back to the "slab" area with his friends in tow.

The slab was just that: a huge section of concrete flooring with vending machines, picnic tables, and benches for students to occupy as they took breaks, waited for buses, or visited before and after school. Mr. Gavin caught up with the boys and asked them their purpose in being so far from the building and in a restricted area. As they answered, he noticed their dilated pupils and caught what he thought was a faint smell of marijuana coming from their padded jackets. As they talked, Mr. Gavin discovered that the boys had skipped their third-period class but had full intention of attending his class, which happened during fourth period, following the lunch break.

According to the schoolwide positive behavioral intervention and support plan adopted by Lemuria Middle School, these students—Zach and his buddies—were children who showed signs of life-course-persistent delinquent acts. The policies used to enforce their break with behavioral expectations of the school were predetermined, equitable, and clear. Mr. Gavin and the students were clear about the next steps. Rather than using punitive, exclusionary policies, the students were treated according to the schoolwide plan that the school staff taught students thoroughly at the beginning of each semester.

Discussion Questions _____

1. What contemporary challenges are making it difficult for schools to achieve learning environments that maximize student learning? Are there others beyond those identified?

2. Why should all schools develop a SWPBIS program?

3. What are the key elements of a SWPBIS program?

4. What organizational systems within a school must be examined to achieve a learning environment that maximizes student learning?

5. What are the key attributes of each of the organizational systems?

6. What are the SER administration stages?

7. What are the goals associated with each of the SER administration stages?

8. What are the key processes used at each of the SER administration stages?

9. What are some of the common barriers to the development, implementation, maintenance, and evaluation of a SWPBIS program?

10. What are some of the barriers the leadership team will face when developing a SWPBIS program?

Managing the School Environment

Planning, Selecting, Implementing, and Evaluating Evidence-Based Interventions and Programs

Chapter Objectives _____

After studying this chapter, you should be able to:

- Illustrate a strategy, an intervention, and a program.
- Depict the relationship among a strategy, intervention, and program.
- Explain the process for identifying and describing a problem.
- Characterize the process for developing the capacity of the school to implement and sustain interventions and programs.
- Describe the process for selecting the target group and setting for interventions and programs.
- Illustrate the process for selecting interventions and programs.
- Depict the process for implementing and sustaining interventions and programs.
- Explain the process for evaluating interventions and programs.

VIGNETTE

FRED HELWIG GREW UP in a neighborhood in which the children had just about anything they wanted. His mother, a single parent, was seldom around, although she worked hard and made a respectable living. Rather than ask for the "extras" he wanted to gain status with his classmates, Fred's answer was to simply "take" what he needed from the lockers and backpacks of his fellow students. Fred's good looks and well-chosen wardrobe presented him as "respectable," although he was a loner at his upscale elementary school. In addition to his kleptomania, which was becoming more apparent to the teaching staff, however, his skill levels in reading and math were far behind the norm. Thus, he was unable to compete satisfactorily in the classroom hierarchy.

In the months following the opening of school in Fred's fifth-grade year, his mother began to date a man that Fred didn't like. In fact, it would have been hard for anyone to gain Fred's approval, because having his mother's attention—what there was of it, as she worked long hours—was what the boy most enjoyed. The addition of another relationship in his mother's busy life left Fred on his own many nights or at the home of a neighbor whose own fifth-grade son went to Fred's school. The two boys did not care for this arrangement, so Fred became almost an intruder when he was left with Seth Murray and his family.

Fred became increasingly unhappy in school. Once in a while, he even began playing "hooky," coming home early to watch television. Always a bit of a loner, he now became almost sullen in his approach to the teaching staff and to his fellow students. His former attempts to fit in were replaced by disinterest in his peer group. As a result, the other students sensed his hostility and began to leave him to himself, both on the playground and in the classroom.

On one occasion, when he was placed in a cooperative learning group for a science project, Fred refused to join the other children and instead worked alone at his desk until the teacher intervened. Mr. Allen, Fred's fifth-grade teacher, felt empathy for the boy even though he knew of Fred's kleptomania and saw his struggle to integrate into the class. Mr. Allen mentioned Fred to the school leadership team and was told that Fred had shown few signs of overt problematic behavior other than a general failure to thrive and an occasional bout of kleptomania. He probably qualified for a secondary intervention and thus was approached.

The inability to read on or near his grade level showed up on Fred's standardized tests that year. Not surprisingly, his scores showed him to be capable but to be a nonachiever. Fred also began to demonstrate behavior that verged on hostility. His stealing came to a head one day when a classmate, Jonathan, caught Fred taking a pocket speller from his backpack in his locker. Jonathan went to Mr. Allen and demanded that Fred be sent to the office or kicked out of the class.

Mr. Allen alleviated a fight by bringing the boys together and talking to Fred about the theft. He asked Fred why it was important to own the speller instead of just borrowing it and encouraged Fred to apologize. Jonathan's anger dissipated when he got beyond being righteously indignant and had a chance to confront Fred. After school, though, Mr. Allen called Fred's mother and scheduled a conference with both mother and son for the following afternoon.

Overview

The three primary goals of schoolwide positive behavioral intervention and support programs are (1) to establish effective policies and procedures that create positive norms for behaviors, (2) to improve the ecological arrangements of the school, and (3) to identify and select evidence-based interventions and programs. The focus of this chapter is how to plan, select, implement, and evaluate individual and academic support interventions and programs (i.e., the fifth and sixth organizational systems of the SER) that have been validated through experimental studies or rigorous evaluation designs. (Individual support interventions and programs in this chapter refer to targeting groups of students who are experiencing difficulties and designing interventions and programs for all the targeted individuals. Chapters 9 through 12 specifically describe interventions and programs for individual students experiencing behavior difficulties.) Research has demonstrated that educators and others should be cautious when selecting interventions or programs because not everything done in the name of schoolwide discipline or violence prevention shows promise. For example, the most common treatment for students who exhibit problem behaviors is insight-based counseling, even though research has demonstrated that it is ineffective (Sherman et al., 1998).

Students who experience behavior and academic problems are at risk for school failure. Although such students are consistently among the highest priority of schools and communities, they are the least well served segment of the school population. For example, it is conservatively estimated that approximately 8% of school-age students have significant emotional and behavioral disorders (Walker, 2000). Furthermore, the results of the National Assessment of Educational Progress (1998), a longitudinal study of educational progress, indicate that 25% to 40% of children in the United States are imperiled because they do not read well enough, quickly enough, or easily enough to ensure their success in school. The response of schools to these problems tends to be reactive rather than proactive. This reaction is unfortunate because we have the means with which to respond effectively to the academic and behavior problems that place students at risk for school failure.

In most cases, the failure of schools to plan, select, implement, and evaluate interventions and programs actively is, at least in part, a reaction; doing so appears to be an overwhelming task for members of a school leadership team to undertake. That is especially the case if the team has never been involved in such an effort. In this chapter, the steps a leadership team can use to plan, select, implement, and evaluate evidence-based interventions and programs are described. It is important for members of the leadership team to remember that as long as the school fails to address academic and behavior problems, they will continue to plague the daily operation of the schooling process. Moreover, failure to address these problems proactively will result in a massive waste of human potential, with all its accompanying problems.

This chapter describes a systematic process for identifying and describing the specific problems faced by schools; selecting strategies, interventions, and programs to prevent and remediate the problems; and implementing and evaluating those strategies, interventions, and programs in schools. As with Chapter 4, this chapter will be of special interest to present or future administrators; it is critical, however, that all educational personnel understand the process undertaken in strategic planning. First, key terms associated with the development and implementation of effective proactive interventions and programs to address the behavioral and academic problems of students are defined. These definitions are followed by a description of the process used to plan, select, implement, and evaluate such interventions and programs. The process is described in six sections: (1) identifying and describing the problem, (2) developing capacity to address the problem, (3) selecting the target group and setting, (4) selecting interventions and programs, (5) implementing and sustaining interventions and programs, and (6) evaluating interventions and programs.

What Are the Key Terms?

It is important to define three terms used in the prevention field and throughout this chapter: strategy, intervention, and program. These terms are often used differently in education.

Strategy

A **strategy** is a general conceptual approach or framework for preventing or remediating academic and/or behavior problems. The defining attribute of a strategy is that it is a general or conceptual approach rather than a specific set of activities and associated materials or procedures (i.e., interventions). Often, schools will initially identify a strategy that is then formalized as an intervention. For example, conflict resolution can offer basic training in social and problem-solving skills for students, or one-to-one tutoring in reading can offer basic training in key beginning reading skills for students.

A risk factors exposure model for explaining outcomes is often used in the prevention field (Hawkins, VonCleve, & Catalano, 1991; Lynam, 1996). This model is rooted in the notion that pervasive exposure to key risk factors is associated with negative, destructive long-term outcomes (Patterson, Reid, & Dishion, 1992). Empirical evidence suggests that this process likely operates in the following manner: (1) children and youth are exposed to a host of risk factors over time (e.g., dysfunctional families, drug and alcohol use by primary caregivers, child neglect or abuse, unemployment, lack of school readiness, ineffective school practices, reading failure); (2) these risk factors are associated with the development of maladaptive behaviors (e.g., defiance of adults, restlessness and overactivity, aggression, lack of self-regulation, disruptive classroom behavior, inability to focus and sustain attention, hostile attitudes toward school); (3) short-term outcomes include truancy, peer and teacher rejection, low academic achievement, school discipline contacts and referrals, and a larger than normal number of schools attended; and (4) these short-term outcomes are, in turn, predictive of much more serious, longer-term outcomes, including emotional disturbance, school failure and dropout, delinquency, drug and alcohol use, gang membership, adult criminality, and, in some cases, serious violent acts (Cicchetti & Nurcombe, 1993).

Intervention

An **intervention** is a specific set of activities and associated materials developed to prevent or remediate academic and/or behavior problems. The defining attribute of an intervention is that it is a specific set of activities and associated materials or procedures rather than a general or conceptual approach (i.e., strategy). For example, *Promoting Alternative Thinking Strategies* (PATHS) (Greenberg, Kusché, & Milhalic, 1998) promotes prevention of violence, aggression, and other behavior problems; improvement of critical thinking skills; and the development of emotional literacy, social problem-solving skills, and interpersonal competence for all children in all settings in grades K–6. The PATHS curriculum is organized into three units: self-control, feelings and relationships, and interpersonal cognitive problem solving.

In addition, as described in Chapter 4, in any school, three types of students can be identified: (1) *typical students* not at risk for academic and/or behavior problems, (2) *students at risk* for developing academic and/or behavior problems, and (3) *students who show signs of life-course-persistent* academic and/or behavior problems (Moffitt, 1994; Walker et al., 1996). Members of each group are candidates for differing levels or types of intervention that represent greater specificity, comprehensiveness, expense, and intensity (Reid, 1993). The interventions appropriate for each child group are *primary, secondary,* and *tertiary* forms of prevention (as noted in Chapter 4, but expanded to behavioral interventions).

1. *Primary.* Primary interventions focus on enhancing protective factors on a schoolwide basis so that students do not become at risk. Interventions used for primary prevention are universal; all students receive the services.
2. *Secondary.* Secondary interventions provide behavioral, social, or academic support, mentoring, skill development, and assistance to at-risk students. Students who do not respond to universal interventions or who demonstrate too many specific risk factors are candidates for secondary prevention services.
3. *Tertiary.* Tertiary interventions are appropriate for severely involved children who evince a life-course-persistent pattern of academic and/or behavior problems. Successful interventions for these students are likely to be comprehensive, intensive, and long term; to involve parents, siblings, peers, and natural supports; and to be collaborative across individuals and agencies. Strategies that encourage interventions at all three of these prevention levels are needed. To be maximally effective, primary, secondary, and tertiary interventions must be directly linked to and coordinated with each other within the context of the program (described below). In other words, primary, secondary, and tertiary prevention services and interventions should be available along a continuum within a program.

Program

A **program** is a grouping of interventions designed to prevent or remediate academic and/or behavior problems. The defining attribute of a program is that it includes a set of activities and associated materials or procedures rather than an individual intervention. For example, Nelson, Martella, and Marchand-Martella (in press) developed the EABIS program using the SER described in Chapter 4. EABIS is a multilevel schoolwide positive behavioral intervention and support program that provides a continuum of primary, secondary, and tertiary forms of interventions and supports for preventing problem behaviors.

The primary-level intervention was a schoolwide discipline program that had four components: (1) effective ecological arrangements of the common areas of the school (e.g., hallways, cafeteria, restrooms, playground), (2) clear and consistent behavioral expectations, (3) active supervision of the common area routines to prevent disruptive behavior and to respond effectively when it occurs, and (4) the **Think Time Strategy** (i.e., empirically validated disciplinary response used by classroom teachers and playground and lunchroom supervisors), which is designed to stabilize how staff members respond to problem behaviors in the classroom (see Chapter 8).

EABIS included three secondary-level interventions: one-to-one tutoring in reading, conflict resolution, and family management training. Sound Partners was used to provide one-to-one tutoring in early reading skills to first-grade students at highest risk of reading failure and remedial second and third graders (Vadasy, Jenkins, Antil, Wayne, & O'Connor, 1997). **Talk it Out** was used to teach the background knowledge necessary for children who are having conflicts to meet and resolve them (Porro, 1996). Finally, the family management program consisted of the videotape *SOS Help for Parents* (Clark, 1996) and two consumer-friendly handouts for parents. A family intervention specialist (i.e., school counselor, school psychologist, or school social worker) worked with the parents of children exhibiting problem behaviors to implement the program.

Functional behavioral assessment (FBA) and **behavioral intervention plan (BIP)** processes and strategies served as the tertiary intervention (see Chapter 10 for a detailed description of FBAs and BIPs). The FBA and BIP processes were based on those procedures developed by Nelson, Roberts, and Smith (1999). Teachers used FBA procedures to (1) identify the function of the problem behaviors (i.e., attention-seeking, escape/avoidant, autonomic, and multiple functions), (2) identify the conditions under which problem behaviors occur and do not occur, and (3) formulate a hypothesis regarding the function of the behaviors. Teachers then developed a BIP based on the identified function.

In summary, strategies, interventions, and programs are not only related to one another but also depict the evolution of the comprehensiveness of a schoolwide positive behavioral intervention and support program over time (see Figure 5.1). As depicted in Figure 5.1, initial discussions among members of the leadership team focus on the strategy or approach used to address a particular problem. Once a strategy is identified and adopted

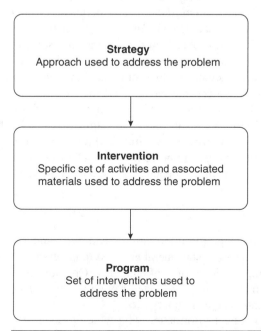

Strategy
Approach used to address the problem

Intervention
Specific set of activities and associated materials used to address the problem

Program
Set of interventions used to address the problem

FIGURE 5.1 *Relationship among strategy, intervention, and program.*

by the members of the leadership team, they plan, implement, and evaluate a particular intervention (i.e., specific set of activities and associated materials or procedures). Over time, the members of the leadership team often develop a program such as EABIS that includes several interventions to address the full array of factors underlying the academic and behavior problems faced by the school.

How Do We Identify and Describe the Problem?

The first step in planning, selecting, implementing, and evaluating an intervention or program is the identification and description of the behavioral and/or academic problem of concern. The goal of this first step is to identify who is affected most by the problem and what is the most frequently occurring problem or set of problems. (The singular term *problem* is used throughout the remainder of this chapter, even though schools typically must address multiple problems.) Identifying who is affected and what is the most frequently occurring problem will enable the members of the leadership team to target an intervention or program more directly. In addition, identifying and describing the problem will provide baseline information with which to set realistic goals (e.g., reduce disciplinary actions by 50%) and to evaluate the effectiveness of the intervention or program. Describing the problem and establishing baseline information will also help the members of the leadership team to achieve consensus among the staff that the intervention or program is necessary because it will address an issue with which they are struggling (e.g., reading failure).

Information or data needed to identify and describe the problem can be obtained from several sources. These information sources can be categorized into two primary categories: opinion and factual. **Opinion information** is often collected through interviews and surveys. Although members of the leadership team often rely solely on such information when identifying and describing the problems of the students they serve, doing so may not present an objective description of the problem. It is critical for schools to collect opinion information in combination with factual data to ensure that they have a clear and accurate description of the problem. Moreover, we recommend that opinion information be used to direct the collection of factual information (e.g., determine staff's views of the most critical needs). **Factual information** is quantitative in nature and should be collected in a systematic manner to ensure that it provides accurate and reliable data with which to make decisions. To this end, a multiple gating procedure that schools can use to identify and describe the most critical problems of the students they serve is described.

Opinion Information

The primary methods for collecting opinion information are surveys and interviews. Regardless of the method of data collection, staff members need to understand how their responses will be treated, including the level of confidentiality. One advantage of surveys over interviews is that the information can be collected from a relatively large number of people rather than from a small number, as in interviews.

Surveys and interviews to collect information with which to identify and describe can be targeted (i.e., focused on a specific academic or behavior problem) or exploratory in nature (i.e., used to identify potential academic and/or behavioral problems). Regardless of the focus, members of the leadership team should consider the following issues when designing a survey or interview.

1. *Who should be surveyed or interviewed?* One factor that the members of the leadership team should consider centers on who should be surveyed or interviewed. Should the entire staff be targeted, or should a specific group be designated? Respondents, even within a school, are less likely to complete a survey if it is general rather than specific in nature. In such cases, the members of the leadership team may want to consider asking the group to complete a survey at a designated time during a meeting to ensure high rates of participation on the part of staff (or others such as parents). In addition, achieving a high response rate is important to provide a more complete picture of staff views of a particular issue.

2. *Question format.* Another factor that members of the leadership team should consider focuses on the question format. Two categories of question formats are available to the members of the leadership team: open-ended and close-ended questions. With **open-ended questions,** respondents are asked to provide their own answers to questions. For example, respondents might be asked "What do you think is the most important student-related issue that the school should address?" and then be provided a space to write their answers or be told to report them verbally to interviewers. The primary shortcomings of open-ended questions are that information gained from such questions is usually incomplete, not comparable across respondents, and difficult to summarize.

In contrast, with **close-ended questions,** respondents are asked to select their answers from among those provided by the members of the leadership team. Using the preceding example, respondents might be asked to choose the most important student-related issue facing the school from a list of possible issues provided by the members of the leadership team (e.g., reading failure, disruptive behaviors, parent involvement). In addition, close-ended questions enable a variety of scales (e.g., Likert, forced choice) to be used. With Likert scales, respondents are presented with a question and are asked to indicate whether they "strongly agree," "agree," are "undecided," "disagree," or "strongly disagree." The primary shortcoming of close-ended questions lies in how members of the leadership team have chosen and structured the possible questions.

3. *Content of questions.* Prior to formatting and sequencing the questions and before conducting the survey or interview formally, the members of the leadership team should explore whether the draft questions are consistently understood and answered by respondents as expected. This step can be accomplished by testing the questions with a small number of representative staff. Members of the leadership team should interview these individuals about the content and the response format. The goal is to assess whether staff's comprehension and responses are consistent with the goals of the survey or interview.

4. *Formatting and sequencing questions.* When formatting and sequencing the questions, the primary goal is to minimize the work of respondents and any potential biasing effects associated with the sequencing of questions. The layout of the survey should be attractive, clear, and uncluttered; instructions should be self-explanatory; consistent question formats and responses should be used; and the length and time to complete the survey should be minimized.

In summary, opinion information can be used, at least in part, to identify and describe the problem or set of problems that staff members view as important. Opinion data by themselves are not that useful for providing objective information with which to identify and describe the problem. In the following section, a multiple gating procedure for providing factual information with which to describe and identify the problem is described.

Factual Information

Some form of a multiple gating procedure is the most effective strategy for collecting factual information. This information is used to identify and describe the most critical student-related problem to be addressed by the school (see Figure 5.2). Multiple gating procedures focus on teachers because they are the primary link between a student who is experiencing academic and behavior problems and intervention services. Classroom teachers have extensive knowledge of the academic and behavioral characteristics of the students in their classroom and are well positioned to provide invaluable information on academic and behavioral problems that need to be addressed in the school. Multiple gating procedures can use the considerable knowledge and expertise of teachers to develop proactive primary, secondary, and tertiary forms of interventions. Keep in mind, however, that teachers are not encouraged or trained to identify and refer students with academic and behavioral problems unless a child is extremely disruptive or is experiencing significant academic deficits. Thus, the members of the leadership team will have to develop a structured multiple gating procedure to tap into teachers' knowledge of the academic and behavioral characteristics of students.

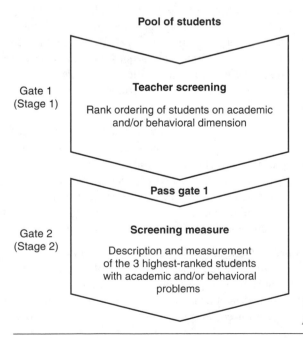

FIGURE 5.2   *Multiple gating procedures for identifying problems.*

Figure 5.2 graphically illustrates a two-stage multiple gating procedure, based on the work of Walker and Severson (1990), that can be used to identify and describe the most critical problem to be addressed by the school. At the *first stage,* a low-cost screening procedure is used to identify students who may be at risk for academic and/or behavioral problems. Stage 1 rank ordering of students is designed to give each child in the school an equal chance of being identified for the social and/or academic dimension of interest. Stage 1 relies totally on teacher judgment. Research has demonstrated that teachers' rankings are valid when teachers are provided a clear description of the academic or social dimension of interest (Walker et al., 1991). For example, in the case of social behaviors, the teachers' ranking can be made in relationship to the externalizing or internalizing behavioral profiles developed by Walker and Severson (1990). Similar specific definitions could be developed for academic dimensions of interest.

1. *Externalizing.* **Externalizing behavior** refers to all behavior problems that are directed outwardly, by the student, toward the external social environment. Externalizing behavior problems usually involve behavioral excesses (i.e., too much behavior) and are considered inappropriate by teachers and other school personnel. Examples of externalizing behavior problems include the following:

- Displaying aggression toward objects or persons
- Arguing
- Forcing the submission of others
- Defying the teacher
- Being out of the seat
- Not complying with teacher instructions or directives
- Having tantrums
- Being hyperactive
- Disturbing others
- Stealing
- Not following teacher- or school-imposed rules

2. *Internalizing.* **Internalizing behavior** refers to all behavior problems that are directed inwardly (i.e., away from external social environment) and that represent problems with self. Internalizing behavior problems are often self-imposed and frequently involve behavioral deficits and patterns of social avoidance. Examples of internalizing behavior problems include the following:

- Having low or restricted activity levels
- Not talking with other children
- Being shy
- Being timid and/or unassertive
- Avoiding or withdrawing from social situations
- Preferring to play or spend time alone
- Acting in a fearful manner
- Not participating in games and activities

- Being unresponsive to social initiations by others
- Not standing up for one's self

Providing clear definitions and criteria for teachers' judgment increases the objectivity of the screening process. Using the clear definition and criteria, teachers typically follow a two-step screening procedure. First, teachers are asked to identify groups of students in their classes whose characteristic academic and/or behavior patterns closely match

FIGURE 5.3   *Example of a stage 1 form for reading failure.*

Teacher: _____   Class: _____   Date: _____

Instructions.

1. Study the definition of reading failure.
2. In the first column, enter the names of eight students whose characteristic reading patterns most closely match the definition.
3. In the second column, rank order from most to least the students listed in the first column according to the degree to which each child's characteristic reading pattern matches the definition of reading failure.

Definition:

Reading failure refers to an inability to read aloud with accuracy and comprehension any grade-level text. The failure to read and comprehend grade-level text is primarily attributed to (1) limited letter-sound correspondence knowledge necessary to sound out words *fluently*, including the recognition of sight words, and (2) the limited self-monitoring of reading, including self-corrects, when an incorrectly identified word does not fit with cues provided by the letters in the word or the context surrounding the word.

Column 1 *General list*		*Column 2* *Rank order*
	Most like	1.
		2.
		3.
		4.
		5.
		6.
		7.
	Least like	8.

the dimension of interest. Second, teachers then rank order students according to the extent to which each one matches the academic and/or behavioral dimension of interest. This two-step procedure results in (1) the identification of the students who most exhibit the academic and/or behavioral dimension of interest and (2) the extent of the problem. An example of a stage 1 form used by an elementary school to identify students who are at risk for reading failure is presented in Figure 5.3. The specific directions for completing the two-step screening procedure at stage 1 are as follows:

1. Carefully study the definitions and examples of…(academic and/or behavioral dimension of interest) and select eight students whose academic and/or behavioral profile most closely matches it. Ordering or magnitude are not important at this point. The goal is simply to identify students whose academic and/or social behavioral profile is consistent with the definition.
2. Rank order the eight students on…(the academic and/or behavioral dimension of interest) according to the degree to which their academic and/or behavioral profile matches the definition of the dimension of interest. Keep in mind that the names of the students in columns 1 and 2 are the same. The students in column 1, however, are not rank ordered according to the extent to which their academic and/or behavioral profile aligns with the definition.

In stage 2, quick and efficient screening measures should be administered to describe and measure the academic and/or social dimension exhibited by the three highest ranked students identified in stage 1. Although the specific screening procedures would vary depending on the academic and/or social dimension of interest, they should be efficient (i.e., require little teacher time), reliable, and valid. Returning to the example of the elementary school interested in identifying children at risk for reading failure, oral reading rates (number of correct words read per minute) of the three highest ranking students in each grade were conducted (see Figure 5.4). The oral reading rates enabled the school to provide a clear description and measurement of the problem. As mentioned above, information collected in stage 2 can also be used to establish evaluation goals and objectives to assess the effectiveness of the interventions developed and implemented to address the problem.

This example could easily be adapted to deal with problem behaviors or any other issue of concern. For example, the definition of externalizing behavior problems detailed above could be substituted for the one on reading failure to identify students who exhibit disruptive behaviors. The key is to provide teachers a clear definition of the dimension of interest and then ask them to identify and rank order students systematically.

How Do We Develop Capacity to Address the Problem?

After the presenting problem has been identified, the members of the leadership team must develop the capacity of the school to address the problem. The leadership team must assess the school's organizational capacity to examine what resources (fiscal, human, and physical) are currently in place and to assess whether the required resources necessary to implement interventions and programs will be in place when needed.

FIGURE 5.4 *Example of an oral reading rate screening procedure.*

Perform the following steps to conduct reading rate checks.

1. Call one student to your desk to read to you aloud.
2. Instruct the student to read the selected narrative passage.
3. Record each error (i.e., substitutions, reversals, hesitations or assists, omissions) that the student makes on the below reading rate data form.
4. At exactly 1 minute, record the last word read aloud by the student.
5. Count the total number of words that the student read aloud.
6. Conduct the calculations of correct words per minute and incorrect words per minute using the following table.

Error Tally

1	2	3	4	5	6	7	8	9	10	11	12

1. Total number of words read   _____

2. Total errors   _____

3. Total correct   _____

Percentage correct   _____%   (line 3 divided by line 1)

Correct words per minute   _____   (line 3)

Incorrect words per minute   _____   (line 2)

The organizational capacity of schools is crucial to the scope of the interventions and programs that can be undertaken and ultimately sustained. What are the barriers to establishing a functional intervention or program? Will there be enough staff? Do staff members have the specialized technical knowledge necessary to address the problem? Are there resources for space and materials? Differing interventions and programs require differing levels of resources, and members of the leadership team need to determine what is available in advance of intervention and program implementation. These resources constitute the school's assets. Often, the members of the leadership team will be faced with deciding which interventions and programs can be dropped to accommodate others as needs and resources change. Members of the leadership team will constantly reassess these assets, or organizational capacity, as programs are added or subtracted. There are three areas of capacity to consider: human, technical, and funding capacity.

Human Capacity

Human capacity refers to the staff and volunteers who are currently available or could be available to address the problem. Which staff members are potentially available to implement the interventions and programs and which are needed to operate the organizational capacity necessary to implement them should be considered. In addition, staff members who could be available for the management, implementation, evaluation, and fund-raising (human and fiscal) activities associated with implementing interventions and programs should be identified.

The extent to which the members of the leadership team have the capacity to initiate, mobilize, and sustain interventions and programs should also be considered. Effective leadership teams promote communication, decision making, and conflict resolution to ensure that interventions and programs are implemented properly.

Finally, volunteers often are the fuel that will support interventions and programs and keep them operating. They provide a bridge between community and school and give much needed support to the work. Volunteers can supplement staff at any level of work, from intervention and program facilitation to clerical work. They should be involved and committed by providing proper training and feedback for the tasks they are asked to accomplish. All volunteers should have a well-defined task; if they are busy and think that they are an integral part of the school, they are more likely to stay involved. Volunteers have varying interests and time constraints that must be taken into consideration. A periodic review of the volunteer's task and time commitment gives both the volunteer and the staff an opportunity to evaluate and make changes in a positive way.

Technical Capacity

Technical capacity refers primarily to the administrative and specialized support necessary to address the problem. Administrative support provides the means for facility management, communications, operations, and logistics for implementing interventions and programs. Specialized support refers to the kinds of knowledge infrastructure that may be needed for specialized interventions and programs. Given the complexity of the factors underlying many problems addressed by contemporary schools, it is important for the members of the leadership team to assess the school's technical capacity to determine whether any staff have specialized knowledge related to the identified problem. It may be necessary for the school to bring in an individual from the community or identify a consultant to provide the technical knowledge necessary to address the problem in an effective and efficient manner.

Funding Capacity

Funding capacity refers to fiscal resources available to implement interventions and programs. Inadequate funding is often the reason new interventions and programs fail. Assessing funding capacity means determining how much funding is available to allocate toward the implementation of selected interventions and programs. It also means devising strategies for reorganizing current interventions and programs to match available funding resources. Most important, it means putting resources into the development of a long-term funding strategy for sustainable development of the selected interventions and programs. Finally, it is important to examine external resources that can be used to support the implementation of interventions and program. External resources not only include external funding but also include services, equipment, and funding support, often provided on an in-kind basis, that will enable the school to leverage its internal resources to greater benefit.

How Do We Select the Target Group and Setting?

After the problem has been identified and described and the capacity of the school developed, the members of the leadership team must select the target group to receive services and where they will be provided. This step can sometimes be the hardest because the problem often has a broad effect and requires resources (human, fiscal, and physical) beyond the capacity of the school. The opinion and factual data collected to identify and describe the problem as well as the capacity assessment provide a guide with which to select a target group. The identification of the target group and the type of primary, secondary, and tertiary interventions and programs needed in turn influence where the services are provided.

Selecting the Target Group

The members of the leadership group must consider two related issues when selecting the target group. The first issue centers on the level of the intervention (i.e., primary, secondary, and tertiary). In most cases, it is important for the school to develop a full continuum of primary, secondary, and tertiary interventions and programs to address the presenting problem. Primary-level interventions and programs directed at all the students needing services have both positive and negative aspects. On one hand, such interventions and programs reach large numbers of students. On the other hand, primary-level interventions and programs aimed at all the students needing services can be expensive and may not have the desired effect of more focused secondary and tertiary interventions and programs. Furthermore, because students in need of tertiary services (i.e., those who exhibit life-course-persistent academic and/or behavior problems) are often the most visible and challenge the resources of the school, members of the leadership team may tend to focus on tertiary-level interventions. In fact, contemporary schools often have primary-level interventions and programs (i.e., services that all students receive) and tertiary-level programs in the form of special education services. Such two-tiered interventions and programs are problematic because students must experience significant failure to receive the more intensive and focused interventions. In such cases, members of the leadership team should consider developing and implementing secondary-level interventions and programs that can be integrated into the existing primary- and tertiary-level ones.

The second issue the members of the leadership team must consider when selecting the target group focuses on who should receive the services. Selecting the target group for primary-level interventions and program is straightforward because the group is targeted at the general population of students. Selecting the target group for the secondary- and tertiary-level interventions and programs, however, is more difficult because they are targeted at students who are at risk for or already exhibiting life-course-persistent academic and behavior problems. The main considerations with selecting the target group for secondary- and tertiary-level interventions and programs are the early identification process used to detect these students and where the services are targeted.

The members of the leadership team can build on the multiple gating procedure they used to identify the primary problem. An example of a three-stage multiple gating procedure used by a Head Start agency to identify preschool-age children at risk for or with reading disabilities in need of secondary- and tertiary-level interventions is presented in Figure 5.5. As illustrated, teachers systematically evaluate the children in their class via rank ordering of them according to their observed emergent literacy skills. These children are further assessed at gate 2 with the Word Identification Phonological Awareness Screening (WIPS) and a Word Rhyme (WR) identification procedure (Nelson, Roberts, & Marshall, 1999). The WIPS procedure includes 10 items, ranging from compound words to sentences containing five single-syllable words. The items progress sequentially from simple (i.e., compound words) to difficult items (i.e., five-word phrases made up of single syllable words). The WR identification procedure includes five word pairs (three rhyming and two nonrhyming), totaling five items. Children respond verbally (yes or no) or physically (shaking of head) to the items. The two lowest scoring students move on to gate 3,

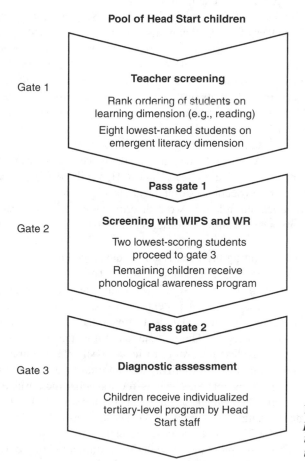

FIGURE 5.5 *Example of a gating procedure used to identify children in need of secondary- and tertiary-level interventions and supports.*

whereas the remaining students receive a secondary-level intensive instructional program in phonological awareness. Diagnostic assessment procedures are administered to the two students who passed on to gate 3; these students are provided an individualized tertiary-level program by preschool staff.

Again, similar multiple gating procedures can be used in behavioral areas as well. We illustrate with a four-stage gating procedure used by a school to identify first-grade children who were at risk for emotional and behavioral disorders and who had reading and language deficits.

The screening process focused on school behaviors (gates 1 and 2), reading readiness skills (gate 3), and language development skills (gate 4). The approach consisted of four stages that provided progressively more intensive levels of screening whereby only those students meeting or exceeding the predetermined cutoff criteria moved to the next step. The four stages are (1) teacher ratings of student behavior, (2) teacher ratings of critical event behaviors (i.e., high intensity–low frequency behaviors), (3) student's ability to recognize letters (i.e., phonological awareness), and (4) student's language development skills.

All first-grade children were screened. At stage 1, teachers completed the Teacher Report Form (TRF) (Achenbach, 1991) on all their students. Students who scored within the borderline and clinical ranges of the TRF continued to stage 2. At that stage 2, teachers completed a Critical Events Index (Walker & Severson, 1990), which asked respondents to check the occurrence or nonoccurrence of 33 items (e.g., steals, suddenly cries) that assess low frequency-high intensity behaviors, on the students from stage 1. Students who exceeded the normative criteria moved on for further assessment. At stage 3, a letter-recognition task was conducted. The children were shown 60 randomly sequenced uppercase and lowercase letters and were asked to name the letters in the order in which they were presented. Students who scored a standard deviation below the school norm on this task were referred for further screening. At stage 4, language competence was measured with the Test of Language Development-2 Primary (Newcomer & Hammill, 1997), which assesses seven language functions: picture vocabulary, oral vocabulary, grammatical understanding, sentence imitation, grammatical completion, word discrimination, and work articulation. Students who scored below one standardized deviation on this test were considered target students.

It is evident that multiple gating procedures can be developed to identify students in need of secondary and tertiary services in a number of areas. The Systematic Screening for Behavior Disorders (SSBD) (Walker & Severson, 1990) is an example of a multiple-gating procedure that can be used by schools for early identification of children who exhibit life-course-persistent behavior problems. The SSBD is a three-stage, multiple-gating system for identifying elementary-aged students. The first stage requires teachers to identify and then rank order students in their class according to how closely their characteristic observed behavior patterns correspond to externalizing and internalizing behavioral profiles, respectively (see profile descriptions above). The classroom teacher then uses two screening measures to assess the specific content of the behavior patterns of the three highest ranked students (both internalizing and externalizing). These measures include a 33-item Critical Events Checklist and a 23-item Combined Frequency Index. Teachers rate each student's status on behavioral descriptors of externalizing and internalizing behavioral dimensions built into the measures. Established normative criteria are then used to determine whether students qualify for further assessments in SSBD screening stage 3. A school professional other than the teacher (e.g., school psychologist, school counselor, special education teacher) observes the students exceeding the normative cutoff points. This professional uses structured observation and recording procedures to observe the students in classroom and playground settings. Students who exceed established normative criteria are then provided tertiary-level interventions and programs.

Finally, when selecting the target group, the members of the leadership group must also consider the multiple factors influencing the problem being addressed. For example, the risk factor exposure model underlying the development of behavioral disorders described above points to a number of factors that would have to be addressed by a comprehensive program (Hawkins et al., 1991; Lynam, 1996; Patterson et al., 1992). As illustrated in Figure 5.6, child (e.g., cognitive ability and resilience) and family (e.g., discipline style and family stressors) characteristics are associated with the development of maladaptive school-related behaviors that lead to academic failure (e.g., defiance of adults, restlessness and overactivity, aggression, lack of self-regulation, disruptive classroom behavior, inability to focus and sustain attention, hostile attitudes toward school) and peer rejection and alignment with deviant peer groups.

In other words, given the multiple factors that underlie any given problem, the members of the leadership team should consider other related groups that may also be targeted for interventions and programs. Secondary- and tertiary-level interventions and programs for students who have behavioral problems often focus on the multiple contexts (i.e., family, peers, and community) that the student encounters. For example, family experiences play a critical role in causing, promoting, or reinforcing problem behaviors. Therefore, it

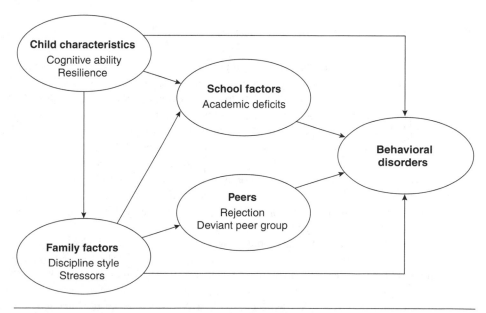

FIGURE 5.6   *The development of behavioral disorders.*

may be important to develop interventions and programs targeted toward parents, siblings, or the entire family unit. Considering related groups may enable the development of interventions and programs that compliment those aimed at the primary target group.

Selecting the Setting

Once the target group has been identified, the members of the leadership team must select the setting in which the interventions and programs will occur. Selecting the setting requires the leadership team to consider the characteristics of the target group and the interventions and programs to be provided. Although the context for providing primary-level interventions and programs is logical, it is not always obvious in the case of secondary- and tertiary programs. For example, at first blush, implementing a one-to-one tutoring intervention for children with or at risk for reading disabilities seems straightforward. Selecting a setting, however, is difficult. Will the tutoring sessions be conducted in the student's classroom, potentially disrupting the ongoing instructional activities provided to the remaining students? Or, will the tutoring sessions be conducted in the hallway or empty classroom, which would present a new set of concerns (e.g., seating for the student and tutor, transition time)?

It is clear that selecting the setting in which the interventions and supports will occur can be rather difficult. The members of the leadership team may have to collect additional data from the target group to determine where the secondary- and tertiary-level interventions and programs can be carried out most effectively and efficiently. These issues become even more problematic if the interventions and programs are targeted at associated groups such as parents.

How Do We Select Interventions and Programs?

After the problem has been identified and described, the capacity of the school developed, and target group selected, the members of the leadership team must select interventions or programs that will be provided. The team has extensive knowledge of how to prevent and remediate academic and behavior problems. Team members can help students acquire the social skills necessary to resolve conflicts and increase peer acceptance. They can help students acquire the academic skills necessary to be successful in school. With so many interventions and programs, one of the greatest challenges facing the members of the leadership team is identifying the ones that are evidence based. As noted above, selecting evidence-based programs is important because not everything done in the name of academic and behavior problems shows promise. Members of the leadership team and others should be cautious when selecting interventions and programs.

Although it might take some effort to identify evidence-based interventions and programs, taking the time to do so will enable the members of the leadership team to build on the experience of others, saving time in the long run and avoiding mistakes in the short run. Recall that strategies, interventions, and programs not only are related to one another but also depict the evolution of the comprehensiveness of schoolwide positive behavior and intervention programs over time (see Figure 5.1). Thus, the starting point for selecting interventions and programs is identifying a strategy or an approach that matches the characteristics of the problem and the target population, such as the risk factors exposure model described above. The members of the leadership team begin the process of identifying possible interventions once a strategy is adopted.

Because a single intervention implemented in isolation is unlikely to solve many of the academic and social problems facing schools, members of the leadership team should consider combining several interventions into a program. For example, a mentoring program to help children at risk for school failure may be complimented by a tutoring program in reading. Regardless of the problem addressed, it is important that the interventions included within a program be integrated and linked with one another. The overall goal of establishing a program that includes multiple interventions is to provide an interconnected continuum of support for students with or at risk for academic or learning problems rather than a set of distinct interventions.

Three criteria should be present for each intervention or program considered. The program must be (1) consistent with the school's strategy or approach, (2) within the school's capacity to implement (human, technical, funding), and (3) supported by experimental evidence.

The intervention or program under consideration may have produced positive outcomes, but not necessarily with the specific problem or target population that has been identified. The identified intervention or program should be identified to ensure that its goals support the school's approach. The school's level of readiness for specific interventions and programs, the agenda of key stakeholders, and the existence of other similar and/or conflicting interventions and programs should also be considered. These factors must be weighed in light of the intervention's or program's implementation requirements, its risks for negative effects, and its potential benefits.

The intervention or program under consideration must be within the capacity of the school to implement. Some interventions and programs are complex and can be difficult to implement. For each intervention or program selected, the resources needed to implement the intervention or program must be considered. The information gained from the capacity assessment process described above can be compared with the resources needed to implement the intervention or program to determine if the school has sufficient resources—human, technical and funding—to implement the program. If the costs of the proposed intervention or program and the resources required for its implementation are beyond the school's capacity, the members of the leadership team should select an alternative intervention or program.

Finally, the intervention or program must be evidence based. Fortunately, several agencies and organizations have joined forces to identify evidence-based practices within a variety of settings: home, school, mental health, and community. This information is easily accessible via the Internet and print sources. For example, the 1997 *Blue Print Programs* produced by the Center for the Study and Prevention of Violence established clear criteria for evaluating interventions and programs and provides a clear description of the programs in a Blueprint series. The objective of the Blueprint series was to identify violence prevention programs that met a very high scientific standard of program effectiveness. The overall goal of this series was to provide program descriptions that would allow states, communities, and individual agencies to (1) determine the appropriateness of the program for their context, (2) provide a realistic cost estimate for each program, (3) detail the organizational capacity required to ensure the program's implementation and maintenance, and (4) give detailed potential barriers and obstacles that might be encountered when attempting to implement each program. Complete copies of the Blueprint series can be obtained from the Center for the Study and Prevention of Violence in Boulder, Colorado (http://www.Colorado.edu/cspv/blueprints/Default.htm). Other efforts are currently under way. Thus, information on evidence-based programs will be increasingly easy to access as government agencies conduct systematic reviews of the literature to identify evidence-based programs.

Members of the leadership team should consider four standards for the selection of evidence-based programs. First, interventions and programs should only be considered if they have been validated with a true (i.e., random assignment of participants to experimental and comparison groups) or quasi-experimental (i.e., use of experimental and comparison groups without random assignment) design. Second, interventions and programs should only be considered if they produced a statistically and practically significant effect. Third, interventions and programs should be viewed more positively if they have been replicated at multiple sites with demonstrated effects. Finally, interventions and programs should be viewed more positively if they have demonstrated durable effects (e.g., sustained for at least 1 year posttreatment).

How Do We Implement and Sustain Interventions and Programs?

After the problem has been identified and described, the capacity of the school developed, and the target group and intervention or program selected, the members of the leadership team must set some implementation goals and objectives. The **goal** is a broad statement of what the members of the leadership team would like to accomplish. **Objectives** are the sequence of activities and tasks that must be accomplished to implement interventions and programs and in turn achieve the goal. Laying out a set of sequential objectives provides the members of the leadership team a means with which to track the implementation of interventions and programs. Implementation objectives should identify (1) who is responsible, (2) what activities and tasks must be carried out, (3) where they are carried out, and (4) the anticipated completion date. An example of a goal and its associated implementation objectives for a schoolwide discipline program are presented in Table 5.1.

It is important to limit the number of implementation objectives to make it easier for the school staff and other key stakeholders to identify the accomplishments. Furthermore, implementation objectives are not static. Objectives should be modified as resources change, activities proceed faster or slower than planned, or new information becomes available. Some guidelines for the members of the leadership team to keep in mind include the following:

- Ensure that the objectives are realistic and match the available resources and the capacity of the staff to implement interventions and programs.
- Ensure that input is obtained from outside agencies that will assist with the implementation of interventions and programs and will make certain that the implementation objectives are consistent with those of agencies.

TABLE 5.1 *Example of an Implementation Goal and Associated Objectives*

Goal

Reduce the number of formal disciplinary office referrals.

Objectives

1. Establish effective ecological arrangements to achieve a safe school environment.

   Who: Members of the leadership team.
   What: Conduct site analysis, eliminate or adjust unsafe physical arrangements, and
           improve the scheduling and use of space.
   Where: Entire school campus.
   Date: Fall, 2003

2. Establish consistent behavioral expectations and provide active supervision.

   Who: Entire school staff.
   What: Develop consensus among staff on behavioral expectations and levels of
           supervision.
   Where: Entire school campus.
   Date: Fall, 2003

3. Implement the Think Time Strategy for responding to problem behaviors.

   Who: Entire school staff.
   What: One 2-hour training session with two 1-hour problem-solving sessions.
   Where: School library.
   Date: January, 2003

4. Establish behavioral support team.

   Who: Members of the behavioral support team.
   What: Three 2-hour training sessions on functional behavioral assessment and behavioral
           intervention plans.
   Where: School Library.
   Date: January, 2003

Establishing realistic implementation goals and associated objectives will ensure that interventions and programs are implemented in a systematic fashion. The implementation objectives will not only clarify the tasks to be done but will also provide the leadership team members a means with which to track the implementation of interventions and programs. It is important for the members of the leadership team to make midcourse changes in the implementation objectives, if necessary.

Finally, the members of the leadership team should ensure the sustainability of interventions and programs. Sustainability means that an intervention or program is flexible, durable, likely to continue over a period of time, and has the resources to support it. Of course, members of the leadership teams should first ascertain if interventions or programs should be sustained. Changes in circumstances, staff, and school needs might suggest that the intervention or program is not a good "fit" for the school. Perhaps the desired outcomes were not achieved. The careful planning that was undertaken to select interventions and programs in the first place, however, suggests the likelihood that sustaining them will be a priority. Moreover, ending interventions and programs that achieve positive results is counterproductive if the problem for which it was chosen still exists. Creating interventions and programs requires significant start-up costs that can be amortized over future years if continued. If interventions and programs are successful but not sustainable, future ones may meet staff resistance. Some things for the members of the leadership team to consider with regard to the sustainability of interventions and programs include the following:

- Making sure the assessed needs of the school are continually driving the intervention or program
- Ensuring through a high-quality evaluation process that the intervention or program is producing desired outcomes
- Assessing capacity to identify natural supports for the intervention or program
- Preparing clear plans for sustaining the intervention or program
- Creating a strong organizational base for the intervention or program
- Considering integration of specific interventions into a comprehensive program
- Considering a scaled-down version of the intervention or program that will still be effective

How Do We Evaluate Interventions and Programs?

After the problem has been identified and described, the capacity of the school developed, and the target group and intervention or program selected and implemented, the members of the leadership team must evaluate the interventions and programs. The two goals of the evaluation are to provide feedback to staff regarding the implementation of interventions and programs (process evaluation) and to determine the extent to which interventions and programs have accomplished their established goals (outcome evaluation). Process evaluations focus on how interventions and programs can be modified to make them more effective. Outcome evaluations center on whether interventions and programs are effective and meet the established goals. Conducting process and outcome evaluations is complex. Thus, this section is not meant to be a comprehensive discussion of evaluation methodologies but rather a brief overview of the focus of process and outcome evaluations.

Process evaluations should focus on the extent to which the interventions and programs have been implemented as intended, serve the identified target population, and operate as expected. Although the information collected through a process evaluation varies depending on the particular intervention or program, three types of information are usually considered. First, because the intervention or program is directed at a specific target population, the characteristics of the individuals who actually receive the intervention or program activities should be examined. Second, it is important to establish the extent to which interventions and programs are being carried out as prescribed because they are designed to be delivered in a specific manner if they are to produce positive effects. Finally, because key stakeholders must value interventions and programs if they are to be sustained, it is important to study their perspectives.

Outcome evaluations focus on the effectiveness of interventions and programs or the extent to which they are meeting the established goals. In other words, outcome evaluations are summative in nature and provide information with which to judge the value of interventions and programs. Furthermore, outcome evaluations can take on several levels of complexity. At the first level, an outcome evaluation might be designed only to determine whether the target population has improved. At the second level, an outcome evaluation may be designed to determine whether the target population has improved relative to a similar group not receiving services. At the third level, an outcome evaluation might be designed to compare the relative effectiveness of two different types of interventions or programs.

Some guidelines for conducting evaluations of interventions and programs are as follows:

1. *Decide what to assess.* Focus on what the intervention or program can realistically accomplish. For example, examining the school's overall standardized reading scores to assess the effects of a one-to-one tutoring program on 2nd-grade students at risk for reading failure would not be realistic.
2. *Use several outcomes.* It is usually better to use several measurable outcomes when assessing interventions and programs. Once the outcomes are selected, deciding on an evaluation design and creating data-collection methods will be much easier.
3. *Select an evaluation design to fit the intervention or program.* It is important to select an evaluation design that will provide a clear picture of the extent to which any changes can be attributable to the intervention or program. Naturally, the strength of the evaluation design will enhance confidence in the findings.
4. *Determine when to assess.* The timing of measurements is important and will result from the evaluation design. For example, if the design uses a pre- and post-test, the measurements must be conducted before the implementation of the intervention or program as well as after it.
5. *Gather the data.* Decide who and how the data will be collected. The person selected to collect the data may affect the results. Will the members of the target population feel comfortable with the person? Can the person gathering data be as objective as the task requires? Some important issues that might arise include consent, confidentiality, and anonymity. These issues must be considered carefully prior to collecting any data.
6. *Analyze the data.* Just as there are quantitative and qualitative data-collection methods, there are quantitative and qualitative data-analysis methods. The data-analysis procedures used should be consistent with the evaluation design and measures used.
7. *Interpret the data.* The process and outcome data obtained through the evaluation must be interpreted to guide improvements in interventions and programs as well as improve them over time. The data should be interpreted against the established goals or benchmarks and the results weighed against the intervention's or program's cost.

Summary

One of the three primary goals of schoolwide positive behavioral intervention and support programs is to identify and select evidence-based interventions and programs. This chapter focused on how to plan, select, implement, and evaluate interventions and programs (i.e., the fifth and sixth organizational systems of the SER) that have been validated through experimental studies or rigorous evaluation designs. Planning, selecting, implementing, and evaluating evidence-based interventions and programs is key to achieving an effective schoolwide positive behavioral intervention and support program.

The key terms underlying the entire process used to plan, select, implement, and evaluate evidence-based interventions and programs are strategy, intervention, and program. Strategies, interventions, and programs are not only related to one another; they also depict the evolution of the comprehensiveness of a schoolwide positive behavioral intervention and support program over time. Identifying a strategy or conceptual approach to address the problem is important in guiding the selection of interventions and programs. Furthermore, selecting a set of primary, secondary, and tertiary interventions to address a problem leads to the development of an effective and comprehensive program.

Members of the leadership team use six steps to plan, select, implement, and evaluate evidence-based interventions and programs. First, the leadership team collects information from several sources in an effort to identify and describe the problem clearly. Although opinion data can be collected during this step, it is important that factual information is primarily used to do so. Second, after the problem has been identified and described, the leadership team must develop the capacity of the school to address the problem. Building the capacity of the school involves an assessment of the human, technical, and fiscal capacity of the school to support the implementation of the intervention or program. Third, the leadership team must select the target group and settings. Selecting the target group may be one of the most difficult tasks because the problem typically cuts across several groups (e.g., ages). Fourth, the leadership team must select the intervention or program that will be used to address the problem. The intervention or program selected should be validated through experimental research (i.e., true experimental) or rigorous (i.e., quasi-experimental) designs. Fifth, the leadership team must develop a strategic plan to implement and sustain the intervention or program. The plan should consider the capacity of the school to ensure that the implementation goals and objectives are realistic. Finally, the leadership team must conduct a process and outcome evaluation of the intervention or program. Conducting and evaluation of the intervention and program is important to ensure that the program meets established goals.

VIGNETTE • *Revisited*

Having handled the incident well, Mr. Allen now thought it was time to submit Fred to the leadership team as a genuine and immediate problem. The team had spent the last several years identifying and implementing behavioral and learning programs to address the needs of students such as Fred more directly.

The leadership team focused on identifying programs that had been developed and validated with studies that included quasi- or true experimental designs, evidence of statistically significant and practically significant treatment effects, and replication at multiple sites with demonstrated effects. The team focused on these programs because they typically meet the twin goals of validated practice and consumer friendliness.

The team, having built a capacity within the school to address a problem like Fred's, began a tertiary-level intervention with Fred, a student they considered "severely involved."

Rather than focusing on punitive behavior, the team arranged for Fred to have one-on-one tutoring in reading and math. In addition, Fred's mother was given family management training, through which she learned how to give herself a social life and to include Fred so that his needs were met, too.

Gradually, through the monitoring of the school leadership team, Fred began to emerge as a capable student. His acceptance was not complete until the end of his sixth-grade year, and yet the improvement was noticed almost immediately. Knowing how to read and being competent in math seemed to help Fred's confidence level. His kleptomania was another problem that led to Fred's untrustworthiness in the eyes of other students. When his social acceptance began to increase, however, his need to "take" things seemed to decrease.

Discussion Questions

1. What are strategies, interventions, and programs?

2. How are strategies, interventions, and programs related to one another?

3. What are primary-, secondary-, and tertiary-level interventions? What types of students is each intervention designed to address?

4. How does the leadership team identify and describe a problem?

5. How does the leadership team develop the capacity of the school to implement and sustain interventions and programs?

6. How does the leadership team select the target group and setting for interventions and programs?

7. How does the leadership team select interventions and programs?

8. What standards should the leadership team apply when selecting interventions and programs?

9. How does the leadership team implement and sustain interventions and programs?

10. How does the leadership team evaluate interventions and programs?

6

Managing Behavior within the Classroom
Preliminary Considerations

Chapter Objectives _____

After studying this chapter, you should be able to:

- Explain why it is important to have good classroom management skills.
- Illustrate effective classroom and seating arrangements.
- Characterize the nonverbal communication methods.
- Depict how to set effective classroom rules.
- Describe how rule-governed behavior is learned.
- Illustrate how to establish routines.
- Describe the purpose of precorrection procedures.
- Explain why we should teach social skills.
- Depict the different group-oriented contingencies.
- Characterize the advantages and disadvantages of each of the group-oriented contingencies and explain how each is implemented.

VIGNETTE

OVER THE PAST 5 YEARS, MS. HERNANDEZ, a seventh-grade teacher, has had difficulty getting students to follow rules and routines in her classroom. Many students tend to move about the room and talk with one another without her permission. She has noticed that the students who are most likely to disobey rules are those students who were disruptive from the first day of class. She has also noticed that other students follow the lead of these few students as the school year progresses. Therefore, over the year, Ms. Hernandez finds that more and more of her time is spent on disruptive behavior and less and less time is spent on instruction.

Ms. Hernandez is unsure what to do. She tries to respond the best she can to problem behavior. She uses warnings to try to get students on task and has sent students out of the room on occasion, but she wonders if she can do more. She seems to be simply reacting to the students' misbehavior. She wonders if she can take specific steps to prevent these problems from occurring in the first place.

To find answers to her questions, Ms. Hernandez decides to take behavior management workshops over the summer. She is hopeful that she can find preventative strategies to use in the classroom that will allow her to spend less time on getting disruptive students on task and more time on instruction. She believes that if she can spend more time on her instruction, her students will have higher academic achievement than they are currently displaying.

Overview

Behavior management is often thought of as a "child problem," but behavior management problems are often an indication of weaknesses in the management procedures used in the classroom. Management problems should be seen as an opportunity to teach students how to behave appropriately (Colvin, Sugai, & Patching, 1993) rather than blaming students for their behaviors or lack of achievement, which is typically the first response to a student who acts out (Walker, 1995). As stated by Bloom (1980), students come to school with two categories of variables that affect their achievement, **nonalterable variables** and alterable variables (see Table 6.1). Nonalterable variables are ethnicity, socioeconomic status, gender, and home background. An example of how these variables can affect school success was found in an investigation by Hart and Risley (1995), who reported that 3-year-old children from poor backgrounds have fewer than 600 words in their vocabulary. Middle-class children have slightly fewer than 800 words by age 3. Finally, children from affluent backgrounds have more than 1,000 words in their vocabulary. Thus, compared with affluent children, poor children have slightly more than half the number of words in their vocabulary. Clearly, teachers have a difficult responsibility in teaching students from such varied backgrounds. Making it even more problematic is that as children from poorer homes go through school, they tend to fall farther and farther behind their peers. Therefore, by the time these students are in sixth grade, they are far different than their peers in terms of academic success. According to one report, "By the end of sixth grade, a child of poverty would need to go to school an additional 2 years to have the same amount of academic experience in school as a more advantaged child" (Carnine, 1994, p. 343). Also, many of these students are prone to exhibit behavior problems in the classrooms (Engelmann, 1997; Kerr & Nelson, 1998; Meese, 2001; Walker, 1995).

TABLE 6.1   *Nonalterable and Alterable Variables*

Nonalterable Variables	*Alterable Variables*
Ethnicity	Use of time
Socioeconomic status	Teaching skills
Gender	Quantity of teacher-to-student
Home background	interactions

Obviously, educators must be concerned about the environments from which students come. Educators may also attempt to provide these children with extra stimulation before they enter into school so that they can catch up to their peers. Head Start is such an attempt. Teachers, however, are not in control of these environmental variables once the students enter school. Therefore, because teachers cannot alter these variables, it does no good to blame student deficiencies on the home environment or the parents.

The second category of variables includes those that are alterable. These variables include teaching skills, the quantity of teacher-to-student interactions, and the use of time. Therefore, teachers can go far in overcoming the deficiencies at home by providing better instruction and management in the classroom. Teachers must determine if there is a problem in their classrooms and how these problems can be altered.

Teachers can go a long way by thinking of management problems in the classroom as a *classroom* issue rather than a *student* issue. Approaching behavior management in this manner allows teachers to plan how to prevent or respond to management issues as part of the overall classroom planning process. This chapter is concerned with three areas of **alterable variables.** First, teachers must consider preventative strategies that can be used in behavior management, including seating arrangements and the establishment of rules and routines. Second, teachers must consider the types of group contingencies to be used in the classroom. Third, teachers must consider methods of teaching appropriate behaviors to decrease the likelihood of unwanted behavior.

Why Is Classroom Management Critical?

Although we are frequently tempted to explain away behavior difficulties by assuming they are developmental in nature and that the student will eventually "grow out of them," or we frequently shrug our shoulders and say, "Boys will be boys," we must take each behavior problem seriously. The single best predictor of delinquency in adolescence is behavior difficulties exhibited in elementary school (Walker, 1995). Research also suggests that for those students who have the more severe problem behaviors, the problem behaviors do not simply disappear over time. In fact, Walker indicates that the stability of aggressive behavior over a 10-year period is about the same as the stability of intelligence over the same time period. The stability of IQ scores is approximately .70, whereas the stability of aggressive behavior is .60 to .80. Therefore, problem behavior must be changed as early as possible in elementary school. If problem behavior persists after then, the likelihood of making successful changes later in a student's academic career diminishes radically (Walker, 1995). Thus, the teachers who should have the very best behavior management skills are in the primary grades.

The reason the early grades are so critical is because that is where adults have the most influence over a student's behavior. Thereafter, peers take on a more important role in a student's behavior. Patterson (1982a) has provided a model to show how behavior problems develop. As shown in Figure 6.1, problem behaviors frequently begin in the home. The process begins with family stressors that in turn put severe pressure on family members. These stressors then begin to escalate into negative-aggressive interactions, which then result in coercive techniques to force submission on the part of the child. **Aversive**

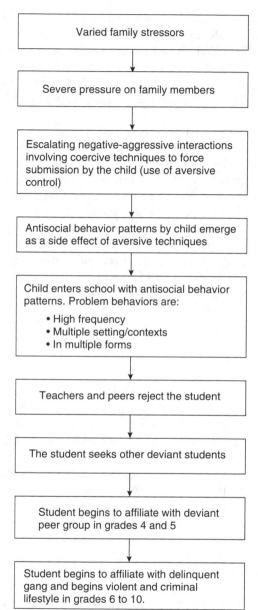

FIGURE 6.1 *The development of antisocial behavior patterns.*
Source: Adapted from *Coercive Family Process: A Social Learning Approach* by G. R. Patterson, 1982.

control is used in these families to control unwanted behaviors. Next, antisocial behavior patterns begin to emerge as the student enters school. Note that antisocial behaviors begin to become problematic around age 3 or 4. At this age, children who will exhibit antisocial behaviors later when they enter school can be fairly reliably identified. Once these students enter school, the antisocial behaviors should be fairly salient. The problem behaviors become frequent in nature and occur under many different settings and in multiple forms. Teachers and peers begin to reject the students, so they begin to seek out other deviant students with whom to interact. By the time they enter the fourth and fifth grades, they begin to affiliate with a deviant peer group. Finally, by the time they enter into sixth to tenth grades, the students are affiliated with a delinquent gang and begin a violent and criminal lifestyle.

Although the progression is fairly obvious, school personnel may not respond in time to prevent this negative spiral. The positive side is that the negative progression can be stopped, but teachers must be ready and willing to set up their classrooms to stop the cycle. Teachers cannot wait. They must begin to consider how they are going to prevent management problems from the first day of classes. Make no mistake: with the inclusion movement, more students with severe behavior problems are entering the general education classroom. Therefore, teachers need to be better at classroom management today than perhaps at any other time in educational history.

The first step at better classroom management is to prevent problem behavior from occurring in the first place. These preliminary steps to prevent management problems are discussed throughout the rest of this chapter.

What Are Effective Classroom and Seating Arrangements?

Clearly, many different seating arrangements are effective for different grades. Certain general statements, however, can be made about effective physical environmental and seating arrangements. Evertson (1987) described three aspects to consider when designing the physical arrangement of the classroom. First, teachers must consider the visibility of important aspects of a classroom. For example, the chalkboard or dry erase board, overhead projector screen, and other displays must be seen by all students. The projector screen, for example, must be high enough so that the projector does not interfere with the vision of the students located directly behind it. Also, any visuals presented at the front of the room should be able to be read clearly by the students at the back of the room. Second, teachers should consider the accessibility of highly visited areas. For example, pencil sharpeners should be located in an area that is free of student desks or other obstacles. Also, teachers must be able to move from one area of the room to another without having to step over objects or go around them. Traffic paths should be kept clear to avoid students getting in each other's way. Finally, teachers must arrange their classrooms in a manner that decreases the potential for distractibility.

The arrangement of the classroom to decrease distractions involves four general areas. First, teachers must consider where to place student desks (Paine, Radicchi, Rosellini, Deutchman, & Darch, 1983). Students should never have their backs to the speaker. During a teacher-directed lesson, the teacher should be the center of attention. Therefore, all desks should face the front of the room and be arranged to limit the amount of distractions. For example, desks should be separated in rows and should face away from the windows. Row seating decreases the level of interaction between students. Also, teachers should be able to view each student. Rows allow teachers to view all students. Students should not be hidden by an obstruction such as a permanent partition or a support beam in the room. Such obstructions make it more difficult for teachers to view each student and increase the likelihood of student misbehavior.

In addition, teachers must consider where to place each student. According to Jones and Jones (1995), teachers tend to place the highest performing students near the front of the classroom. The lowest performing students tend to be seated near the back of the room. Effective seating arrangements suggest that the opposite should occur. The highest performing students should sit near the back of the class, and the lowest performing students and those with behavior difficulties should sit near the front of the class. Seating the lower performers near the teacher takes advantage of proximity control and allows the teacher to gain and maintain the attention of those students.

If the purpose of instruction is for students to work together, student groups should face one another. Using a circle, square, or U-shaped arrangement works well with such tasks. The focus of attention should be on the other members of the group.

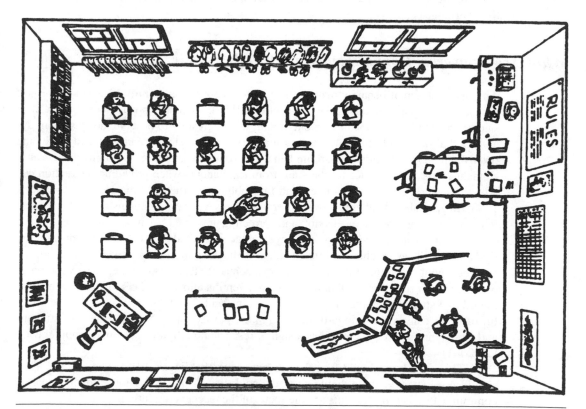

FIGURE 6.2 *Physical arrangement of the classroom.*

Source: From *Structuring Your Classroom for Academic Success* (p. 21) by S. C. Paine, J. Radicchi, L. C. Rosellini, L. Deutchman, and C. B. Darch, 1983, Champaign, IL: Research Press. Copyright 1983 by the authors. Reprinted by permission.

Second, placement of the teacher's desk must be considered. According to Paine et al. (1983), the teacher's desk should be placed in one of the front corners of the room, facing the students. Paine et al. also suggest that if an instructional aide's desk is in the room, it should be placed at the back of the room on the opposite side of the teacher's desk. This arrangement allows for student monitoring when the teacher and aide are at their desks.

Third, classroom partitions can be used in an advantageous manner. Paine et al. (1983) recommend having partitions on wheels for easy maneuverability. If small group instruction is occurring, a partition can be easily moved to shield the small group from the larger group's activity. This movement of partitions allows for a decrease in the distractions that tend to hamper small group instruction.

Finally, materials should be located where they are readily available. According to Paine et al. (1983), materials should be placed at the front of the room on a table. This placement allows for easy access to the materials by teachers and students.

Figure 6.2 shows an example of an effectively arranged classroom. Obviously, the classroom arrangement shown here may not be perfectly appropriate for all classrooms. The classroom in the figure, however, contains all of the essential elements of an effectively arranged one.

What Are Nonverbal Communication Methods?

An important area of behavior management involves **nonverbal communication** on the part of teachers (Eggen & Kauchak, 1997; Woolfolk, 1998). Students respond not only to what is said but also to what is done in the classroom. It is interesting to observe the classroom dynamics that occur between students and teachers. Nonverbal cues can go far in producing positive and not-so-positive classroom behavior. Nonverbal communication involves several elements. First, the distance teachers are from the students when providing instruction can affect whether the students will respond favorably to instruction (Van Houten & Doleys, 1983). In general, it is better to move closer to students when providing instruction, providing reinforcement for a positive behavior, and correcting unwanted behavior.

Second, teachers should provide eye contact with students (Good & Brophy, 1990). Eye contact allows teachers to inform students that they are being spoken to. In addition, teachers should have the students provide eye contact to teachers (saying, "All eyes on me" or "I need your attention"). Obtaining student attention allows teachers to increase the likelihood that students are attending to what is being said. Teachers, however, must be mindful of other cultures with regard to eye contact. For example, Native American students and adults may avoid eye contact as a sign of respect and religious custom (Zirpoli & Melloy, 2001).

Third, teachers should face the students squarely (Eggan & Kauchak, 1997). They should not look over their shoulders at the students. Again, facing the students squarely communicates that the students are the focus of the teachers' attention.

Fourth, teachers should be aware of their facial expressions toward students. There must be congruence between what is said and the facial expression (Eggan & Kauchak, 1997). For example, if a student engages in an unwanted behavior, reprimanding the student with a smile will likely decrease the reprimand's effectiveness. Likewise, frowning at a student while praising positive behavior can make the praise less effective. On the other hand, smiling while providing praise is an instance of congruence. Teachers should try to refrain from having an angry look on their faces when a student engages in an unwanted behavior. Many students will find such angry expressions as an indication that the behavior bothered the teacher, which may prove reinforcing for the student. Therefore, if students engage in unwanted behaviors, the facial response to the students should be as neutral as possible.

Fifth, teachers should use gestures in a manner that is congruent with the instruction (Eggan & Kauchak, 1997). For example, pointing to the door while telling the student to close it is an instance of congruence; pointing to the window while telling the student to close the door is not. Gestures can be used to increase the likelihood of students complying to a directive. In fact, if a student does not respond favorably to a directive to hang up her coat, the teacher can attempt to provide the directive again while pointing to the coat. Gestures simply provide additional information to the student.

Finally, teachers should vary the tone, loudness, or pitch of their voices when providing instructions (Eggan & Kauchak, 1997). This vocal variation (called **"pause and punch"**) also provides additional information to students. For example, providing emphasis on one part of the instruction—such as using a pause and punch on the word *door*, as in "Close the…*door* please"—can increase the likelihood that the student will respond. As with facial expressions, teachers should have a positive voice tone when students behave well; teachers should, however, attempt to refrain from a negative tone of voice when correcting unwanted behavior. Doing so could make students react against teachers in a negative manner. In such circumstances, the tone should be neutral or matter of fact.

How Do We Set Effective Classroom Rules?

Rules are an important aspect of classroom management. They provide students with the expectations of the teacher and other school personnel. Rules, then, are essentially attempts to prevent behavior problems from occurring. Effective teachers have rules to attempt to prevent management problems from occurring (Woolfolk, 1998). Unfortunately, all rules are not created equal. Many classrooms have rules that are ineffective for one of several reasons.

To determine what makes a good rule, what rules are and how they work must be clarified. One of the more important things that can occur in a student's life is the development of **rule-governed behavior.** When we are born, our behaviors are determined by two major sources: genetics and direct consequences. Genetically, we are born with certain behaviors that allow our species to survive. For example, the sucking response allows us to eat and obtain sustenance. From direct acting we also learn the consequences of our early behaviors. When babies engage in the sucking response, the milk reinforces the response. Babies also quickly learn that crying will bring them food and other necessary comforts such as warmth. Very young infants, however, do not learn through rules. Telling a newborn that crying will not be tolerated will have little effect on the crying behavior. Likewise, telling a very young infant to not touch a hot stove will usually result in the child touching it, unless the child has learned to follow your rules. Thus, most, if not all, of our very early behaviors are not affected by rules at all. This situation changes as we get older. The older we get, the more important role rules play in our lives. Most of us usually do not have to experience the direct consequences of all our behaviors. For example, if we only learned by experiencing the consequences, we would not learn to cross the street without looking both ways unless we got hit by a car or at least came close to getting hit.

Fortunately, we can tell children to look both ways before crossing the street and they will do so. In this case, following rules allows for the avoidance of the serious **consequences** of not following rules. Think of what goes on in the classroom. The most well behaved students are those students who follow the rules. Thus, we go through this very important transition as we grow older. This transition involves learning by experiencing the direct consequences of behaving and following rules. Much of our learning in society is dependent on rules. Rules are how the culture or society takes control of most of our behaviors.

Unfortunately, some individuals do not follow rules. These individuals break rules (laws) and may have to experience the direct consequences of not obeying the rules (laws). Some students do not follow the rules of the classroom and may have to experience the direct consequences of not following these classroom rules. What can be done with these students? How can the likelihood of rule-following behavior be increased? To answer this question, we must look at what rules are.

Rules are defined as contingency-specifying stimuli (Sulzer-Azaroff & Mayer, 1991). Contingency-specifying stimuli are statements that contain one or more of the three terms in the three-term contingency (i.e., **antecedent,** behavior, consequence). For example, the rule "Walk in the hallway" contains the behavior. The rule "When in the school, walk in the hallway" contains the antecedent (when in the school) and the behavior. Finally, the rule "When in the school, walk in the hallway to avoid getting hurt" contains the antecedent, the behavior, and the consequence (avoid getting hurt). Thus, rule-governed behavior is behavior that is controlled by these stimuli. Rule-governed behavior has also been called verbally governed behavior (Vargas, 1988) in that rules are stated in some verbal form such as in writing or in speech. Thus, when rules have obtained control over a behavior, that behavior is called rule governed or verbally governed. When rules fail to have an effect on a student's behavior, the contingency-specifying stimuli have not enacted control over the behavior. This lack of control may be because potential consequences are too improbable (say when someone shoplifts, the probability of actually being caught may be remote), the engagement of the behavior opposed to the rule may be reinforcing (such as skipping class to go "on the town;" recall the movie *Ferris Bueller's Day Off*), or the consequences of the rules may be too delayed (such as cheating now may result in a lack of skills later in life). Whatever the reason for not following rules, teachers can still attempt to teach rule-following behavior to students.

Rules are developed by experiencing the consequences of following rules (gaining reinforcement by receiving a positive reinforcer or by escaping or avoiding an aversive stimulus) (Sulzer-Azaroff & Mayer, 1991). For example, the child who goes to touch the hot stove is told not to touch it because it is hot and she will get burned. The statement, telling the child not to touch the stove, is the behavior; the antecedent would be because it is hot; and the consequence is getting burned. Most young children, however, will touch the hot stove and receive a minor burn. When something like that occurs, the parents may say, "I told you not to touch it." The parents are essentially teaching rule following. Most children will learn to avoid touching something hot when told it is hot because of their earlier experiences. They will also begin to follow other rules because they learn that following rules leads to reinforcement or prevents something negative from happening. Therefore, when teachers provide rules to students, those students who have learned to follow rules in the past will likely follow directions. Students who have not learned to follow rules will not follow directions. Teachers should make sure that when students follow rules there is a high likelihood that the rule-following behavior will be reinforced; likewise, when students do not follow rules, there is a high likelihood that they will not be reinforced or will face the negative consequences of not following the rules. In addition, teachers can increase the likelihood of rule following for students who are less likely to follow rules by being more specific. In other words, develop rules for these students that include all three of the terms in the three-term contingency (i.e., antecedent, behavior, and consequence).

That said, what should teachers do to develop effective rules in the classroom? Consider the following statement by Purkey and Smith (1983): "Evidence exists indicating that clear, reasonable rules, fairly and consistently enforced, not only can reduce behavior problems that interfere with learning but also can promote a feeling of pride and responsibility in the school community" (cited in Eggen & Kauchak, 1997, p. 445). It seems that the critical aspects of rules are that they are fair and that they are implemented the same for all students. Thus, once rules are created, they should be seen by the students as being reasonable and equally enforced. Teachers can meet these goals by carefully creating rules.

Creating Effective Classroom Rules

To create effective classroom rules, teachers must take the time to develop them. Rules are not something that is developed overnight and put up on the board the first day of class. The development of effective rules contains several steps (see Table 6.2). First, a discussion with the students on the value of rules should be provided (Eggan & Kauchak, 1997). This discussion should focus on telling students the importance of rules. For example, a statement such as "Rules allow us all to know what is expected of us" could be used. In addition, a discussion on why it is important to follow rules and why it is important to have consequences for violating the rules should be held. A comparison of society in general

TABLE 6.2 *Development of Effective Rules*

---

1. Discuss the value of rules with students.
2. Gather student input to develop rules while keeping in mind the following:
   - Develop only three to five rules.
   - Use simple language.
   - State rules positively.
   - Use different sets of rules for different situations, if needed.
   - Keep class and school rules consistent.
3. Gain student commitment to follow the rules.
4. Teach rules explicitly.
5. Post rules in a prominent location.
6. Monitor and review rule following.

---

could be used. Laws are essentially rules of society. Teachers could discuss what would happen in society if there were no laws. For example, speed limit signs are statements of rules. A discussion on why it is important to have speed limits could be conducted.

Second, effective rules should be developed with student input. According to Lickona (1991), gaining student input allows students to have ownership over the classroom rules. Students are also more likely to follow rules if they have a say in the development of the rules. Students are more apt to think that teachers respect what they have to say in the development of the rules. That is not to say that students have the final say in the development of the rules; ultimately, teachers have the final say. If, however, there is a disagreement with a particular rule, it is much better to identify what the disagreement is early in the development of the rules rather than later, when the rules are already solidified. In addition, gaining student input allows teachers to provide rationales for each rule as it is being developed. Effective rules must be developed with the following in mind.

1. *Rules must be kept to a minimum.* The general rule of thumb is to keep the number of rules to three or four (Paine et al., 1983) or four or five (Eggen & Kauchak, 1997). A short list is important because students must be able to repeat the rules without referencing the written rules. In other words, students should be able to memorize the rules. The importance of knowing what the rules are without referring to written rules is that if students break a rule, they are not surprised. It is not acceptable for students to indicate that they did not know what the rule was that was broken. Many students break rules because they do not know what the rules are. Therefore, keeping the list short will help avoid this problem.

Many teachers will have difficulty limiting the list to only three to five rules. If this difficulty arises, it is likely that the rules are too specific. Many rules can be combined into a more general rule. For example, if there are several rules such as "keep your hands to yourself," "say nice things to others," "keep negative comments to yourself," and "aid others who are in need of help," one general rule, such as "treat others with respect," could include them all.

2. *Rules should contain simple language.* Teachers have a variety of students with different strengths and weaknesses. Clearly, rules should not contain language that any student in class cannot understand. For example, rather than stating "treat others with deference," say "treat others with respect." Rules are not meant to be used as a vocabulary lesson. Keeping the wording simple also allow students to better remember those rules.

3. *Rules should be stated positively.* This characteristic is perhaps one that is violated more than the others. Many teachers tell students what they do not want them doing versus what they do want them to do. For example, rather than having the rule, "Do not treat others with disrespect," state the behavior wanted, such as, "Treat others with respect." Instead of stating "No cheating," say, "Keep your eyes on your own work." Likewise, instead of saying, "No running in the hall," say, "Walk in the hall." This characteristic of effective rules should also spill over to those instances when instructions to students are provided. For example, rather than stating that students should "not show up for class late," we should tell them to "get to class on time." The importance of this characteristic cannot be overstated; telling a student what not to do does not necessarily tell the student what to do. Telling a student not to use foul language does not tell a student to use appropriate language. Instead, the result could be a student who simply stops talking in class, which reduces foul language but does not improve the student's use of appropriate language. In addition, stating rules positively helps teachers scan for positive behaviors rather than negative ones.

4. *There may be different sets of rules for different situations, if needed.* For example, having a rule of walking in the classroom is not appropriate in physical education. Also, having a rule for students to keep their eyes on their own work is not relevant during cooperative learning situations, when the sharing of work may be wanted. Therefore, depending on the situation, some rules may be appropriate in one context but inappropriate in others.

5. *Class rules and school rules must be consistent.* Obviously, if classroom rules were not in agreement with school rules, students would not know how to react. Therefore, teachers should review the school rules and ensure that these rules are consistent with the classroom rules. For example, a school may require a hall pass. Therefore, teachers should make that a classroom rule if students need to access the hallway.

Third, there should be an effort to gain student commitment to follow the rules. The teacher should state each rule, and a discussion should ensue to determine if all students are in agreement of the rules.

Fourth, once a commitment has been obtained from all the students, the rules should be taught. Following an "I do, we do, you do" procedure, the teacher can model following the rules ("I do"); practice rule following, providing feedback to students ("we do"); and give students opportunities to practice rule following on their own ("you do"). Role-playing is an excellent method to teach rules. Examples and nonexamples of rules can be provided. For instance, for the rule "be respectful of others," examples of respect (e.g., asking politely for a piece of paper from another student) and of disrespect (e.g., taking another student's paper without asking) could be discussed. Teachers could also request examples and nonexamples of rules from the students. In addition, when nonexamples of rule following are provided, the teacher should model what the consequence would be, such as sending the student to time out. Once it is apparent that students are discriminating between examples and nonexamples of rule following, the rules can be written for display.

Fifth, rules should be posted in a prominent location. This posting is a reminder to the students of what the rules actually are. The positioning also allows visitors to the classroom to learn what is expected of the students. In addition, posting allows other staff such as substitute teachers to learn classroom expectations and informs the students that visitors to the classroom also know what is expected.

Finally, rule following must be monitored and reviewed. Teachers should observe how the rules affect student behavior. If students begin to break rules consistently, the reason for the infraction should be determined. Many times, students, especially younger students, simply do not remember what the rules are. To avoid or prevent this potential problem, rules should be reviewed on a consistent basis (e.g., once a week). Once students master the rules (i.e., can recite the rules without referencing the posted rules), the review can be faded out. Students may also break rules because the rules are not clear. If so, rules should be modified until all students can explain what is meant by each one. Using unison or choral responding provides all students an opportunity to say the rules back to the teacher. In addition, rules may not be followed because they are not enforced. In other words, rule following is not reinforced and rule breaking is not punished or ignored. Teachers must make sure that rule following is reinforced as immediately and consistently as possible. Once the students demonstrate rule following behavior, reinforcement can be faded to an intermittent basis. Teachers must also make sure that they do not reinforce rule breaking at any time, because doing so only makes breaking rules in the future more likely.

How Do We Establish Routines?

The development of rules is a critical aspect of preventing behavior management problems in the classroom. An equally important and sometimes overlooked area, however, is the teaching of routines. If we were to observe an orderly classroom, we would see one in which the teacher has taken the time to teach students how to follow certain prescribed routines. For example, there should be a procedure for using the restroom or for sharpening pencils. There may be a routine for indicating whether a hot lunch is needed for a student at the elementary level. There may be start-up routines to get students ready for the day, such as having a short activity for students to begin while the teacher completes tasks such as taking role are completed. Procedures should be taught in any area that will help with the smooth flow of activities in a classroom. Evertson and Emmer (1982) defined five such general areas in which teachers should teach routines to their students:

1. Students' use of classroom space and facilities
2. Students' behavior in areas outside the classroom (e.g., bathroom, lunchroom, drinking fountain, playground)
3. Whole-class activity routines (e.g., raising hand to speak, where and when to turn in completed work, how to get help during independent seatwork)
4. Small group routines (e.g., how to gain the teacher's attention, choral responding, taking turns in shared reading)
5. Additional routines (e.g., how to behave at the beginning or end of class or the school day, how to respond to another student with disabilities, how to behave when a visitor is present, what to do during announcements)

The teaching process for routines is the same as for teaching any other task. First, the teacher should model ("I do") what the procedure is for the students. For example, the teacher may model taking the bathroom card from the wall and going from the classroom to the bathroom. The teacher may model how to flush the toilet and how to wash her hands. Second, the teacher should take students and guide them through the routine while providing feedback along the way ("we do"). Third, the teacher should have each student practice the bathroom routine independently while again providing feedback ("you do"). Once the students have demonstrated the skill of the bathroom routine, another procedure can be taught. Finally, the teacher should continuously monitor the students in how they perform the procedure, providing positive and corrective feedback over time.

Although teaching routines is not often thought of as an important behavior management tool, procedures that are adequately taught can have a dramatic impact on preventing student misbehavior (Witt, LaFleur, Naquin, & Gilbertson, 1999). Many so-called misbehaviors are simply behaviors that students display because they have not been taught the appropriate or expected procedures. Therefore, the time commitment involved in teaching procedures will be well worth it.

What Are Precorrection Strategies?

One fundamental assumption that can be made about classroom behavior problems is that they are learned. In addition, appropriate classroom behavior can be taught. Thus, problem behavior can be seen not only as a management issue but also as an instructional one. As stated by Colvin et al. (1993), a preventative management approach (i.e., a precorrection strategy) is to use the instructional skills known by staff to manage problem behaviors. The instructional approach is based on three assumptions. First, problem behaviors are learned through our interactions with our environments. Second, students need to learn appropriate behavior; thus, they need to be taught. Third, emphasis should be placed on teaching social skills. Therefore, if management problems can be corrected by instructional techniques, these problems can also be prevented by the same techniques. Essentially, teachers could prevent management problems by attempting to anticipate where problems are likely to be encountered (e.g., during transitions) and then by designing a lesson plan to teach the relevant skills to students to prevent the anticipated problem behaviors.

Colvin et al. (1993) described the similarities of academic correction and behavior problem correction. For example, suppose a student writes a story and uses "it's" to refer to possession (it's cage is clean) instead of "its." The teacher could correct the error by explaining to the student that "it's" does not refer to possession but rather means "it is" (e.g., it is cage is clean). Then the teacher could have the student repeat what "it's" means, have the student correct the mistake in the story, and then praise the student for the correction. Similarly, if a student swears at another student, the teacher could remind the student of the rule to treat others with respect, have the student repeat the rule, ask the student to apologize to the other student, and then praise the apology. Thus, the teacher treats the problem behavior as an opportunity to teach appropriate behavior.

Suppose now that the student is still having difficulty with discriminating when to use or not use "it's." Good teachers would take a step back and reteach the rule of when to use "it's" and "its." This reteaching would continue until the student could demonstrate **mastery** of the concept. This teaching is called precorrection by Colvin et al. (1993). In another example, the student above again directed swear words toward another student, most teachers would attempt to punish the misbehavior in some fashion. If, however, an instructional method to solve problem behaviors is to be used, the teacher, rather than simply attempting to punish the swearing behavior, would take a step back with the student and reteach classroom rules until the student could demonstrate an understanding of the rules. Colvin et al. call the difference between the two methods of responding to misbehavior "correction" and "precorrection." As shown in Table 6.3, Colvin et al. demonstrate the differences between correction and precorrection procedures. Precorrection procedures are more instructional in nature.

Colvin et al. (1993) provide a seven-step plan that leads through the precorrection planning process. First, the context of the predictable behavior should be identified. In others words, teachers should determine when and where problem behaviors are likely to occur. For example, based on experience, most teachers can predict when problem behaviors are most likely to occur, such as during lunch, transitions, and assemblies or with substitutes. Teachers can also document when and where behavior problems usually occur by using any of the assessment methods described in Chapter 10. Teachers should consider when these problem behaviors will occur. This planning is no different than when teachers plan for academic problems that are likely to occur during certain academic tasks. Teachers should consider ahead of time what they will do when a student has an academic problem and should set out to prevent the problem from occurring. Again, this planning is not different from what should occur when considering behavior problems.

Second, the predictable and expected behaviors should be specified. For example, during transitions, teachers may expect that pushing is likely to occur. Then, they need to determine what behaviors are appropriate under the circumstances such as "Keep your hands to yourself."

Third, teachers should consider how to modify the context of the situation. For example, proximity control can be used to prevent students from pushing during a transition. Teachers or other adults can be near the students during a transition to make the behavior less likely.

Fourth, teachers should rehearse the appropriate behaviors with the students. For example, before the students transition to lunch, the teacher could stand near the students and have them repeat the rule about keeping their hands to themselves. Reminders of appropriate behaviors before students have an opportunity to engage in unwanted behaviors can prevent the unwanted behaviors from occurring. Again, this step is similar to reminding students about a rule in the use of a word such as "it's" before they begin to write.

Fifth, teachers should determine how they will reinforce appropriate student behavior. For example, when students transition to lunch appropriately, the teacher could reinforce the students by providing them with 5 extra minutes of free time when they reenter the room. Note that reinforcement does not always have to be receiving something tangible or as activities; praise from teachers may also function as a strong form of reinforcement.

Sixth, expected behaviors should be prompted by teachers. That is, when students begin to break a rule, teachers should first attempt to bring about the appropriate behavior

TABLE 6.3   *Comparison of Correction and Precorrection Procedures*

Correction	*Precorrection*
1. Is reactive	Is proactive
2. Involves a manipulation of consequences	Involves a manipulation of antecedents
3. May lead to negative teacher-student interactions	May lead to positive teacher-student interactions
4. Focuses on inappropriate behavior	Focuses on appropriate behavior
5. May lead to escalating behavior	May lead to appropriate behavior
6. Focuses on immediate events	Focuses on future events

Precorrection Checklist and Plan	Teacher:_____ Student:_____ Date:_____/_____/_____
☐ 1. Context	
Predictable behavior	
☐ 2. Expected behavior	
☐ 3. Context modification	
☐ 4. Behavior rehearsal	
☐ 5. Strong reinforcement	
☐ 6. Prompts	
☐ 7. Monitoring plan	

FIGURE 6.3 *Precorrection checklist and plan.*

Source: From "Precorrection: An instructional approach for managing predictable problem behaviors" by G. Colvin, G. Sugia, and B. Patching, 1993, *Intervention in School and Clinic,* 28, pp. 143–150. Copyright 1993 by PRO-ED, Inc. Reprinted by permission.

by prompting it to occur. For example, if a student begins to push another student during a transition, the teacher could say, "Remember the rule about keeping your hands to yourself." If the prompt does not work and the student continues the unwanted behavior, the teacher should then have a predetermined response to this noncompliance. For example, if the student continues to push, the teacher may need to remove the student from the group during the transition and provide a brief time-out.

Finally, the plan must be monitored. Teaches should continue to determine if appropriate behaviors are being exhibited. If a problem persists, an individualized intervention may be needed (described in Part IV).

Figure 6.3 shows a precorrection plan outlined by Colvin et al. (1993). As shown in the figure, the plan requires planning in a similar manner as would occur during an academic task. Notice that the example plan shown in the figure is for an individual student. The precorrection plan, however, can also be used for the entire class. Precorrection is placed in the classroom change section because effective classroom change takes planning. The precorrection plan provides an excellent model for achieving the goal of designing a classroom environment that prevents or reduces the probability that management problems will occur.

What Are Social Skills?

To have meaningful relationships with their peers, teachers, and parents, students must acquire social skills. According to Elliott and Gresham (1991), students who lack social skills experience negative student-adult or student-student relationships. They state, "Because socialization is an important outcome of schooling, training programs which teach children how to improve interactions with their teachers, peers, and parents can be a useful instructional tool for educators and mental health professionals" (Elliott & Gresham, 1991, p. 2).

Social behaviors can be viewed in five domains: cooperation, assertion, responsibility, empathy, and self-control (Elliott & Gresham, 1991). Others view social and personal competence in areas such as social skills and social problem solving (Polloway, Patton, & Serna, 2001). Social skills include reciprocal interactions of individuals involved in a social exchange. Social problem solving involves a sequence of behaviors including (1) problem orientation, (2) problem definition and formulation, (3) generalization of solutions, (4) decision making, and (5) implementation of plan and evaluation and verification of the outcome (D'Zurilla & Goldfried, 1971; Polloway et al., 2001).

Social skills and social problem solving may need to be directly taught to students and treated just like academic skills. Olson and Platt (2000) discuss the use of modeling, role-playing, peer tutoring, cooperative learning, and videos to teach social skills. Whatever the intervention chosen, students should first observe effective modeling of the skill to be learned, practice displaying the skill while receiving teacher feedback, and then have opportunities to display the skill independently in contrived or in real-life contexts.

How Do We Provide Group-Oriented Contingencies?

When setting out to prevent behavior problems in the classroom, teachers must determine how to respond to wanted and unwanted behavior. The response to student behavior should be well planned. Therefore, a decision must be made regarding what type of contingency to arrange for the students. Although reinforcing student behavior is typically thought of as an individual student procedure, reinforcement systems can be thought of as based on a group. There are three types of **group-oriented contingencies:** independent, dependent, and interdependent (Sulzer-Azaroff & Mayer, 1991). Each type has its advantages and disadvantages.

Independent Group Contingencies

Independent group contingencies are the contingencies typically considered when working with students. They are perhaps the most common forms of contingencies in the classroom. Independent group contingencies involve the same response contingencies for each student while providing these contingencies based on each individual student's behavior (Sulzer-Azaroff & Mayer, 1991). The behavior requirement can be the same for each student (e.g., all students must follow the rules in the classroom) or different (e.g., some students may not be required to maintain the same on-task level as other students). To use independent group contingencies, teachers must set what the response requirement is for all students or must individualize these response requirements for each student but provide reinforcement based on each individual's response. An example with this form of group contingency is receiving a grade based on a test. Criteria are set for varying levels of test scores (e.g., 90% = A, 80% = B). Students have the same response requirements. In addition, students can study together for a test. Individual performance, however, is consequated. All students do not receive the same grade if all students do not score the same. Likewise, if a cooperative learning group were set up and students worked together on a problem, but students were required to turn in individual products such as a report resulting from the cooperative learning group, each individual in the cooperative learning group would receive an individual score. The group as a whole would not suffer if one individual in the group scored poorly, nor would the group as a whole benefit if a member in the group scored particularly well.

Dependent Group Contingencies

Dependent group contingencies make access to reinforcers by the group based on the behavior of a selected group member. Reinforcement does not depend on every member's performance; reinforcement is dependent on only one member of the group (Sulzer-Azaroff & Mayer, 1991). Dependent group contingencies can be readily viewed in classrooms under some circumstances. For example, if the teacher tells the students that they can go out to recess as soon as everyone in the class finishes the assignment, the contingency is dependent on when the last student finishes. Therefore, the selected student in this case would be the last to finish. Another example is where an item is missing and the whole group is punished if the person who has taken the item does not come forward. Although the selected student is not known, the whole group faces the consequences of a particular individual. Yet another example is when the class is consequated if a particular student does not behave well. A teacher stating that no one can go out to play because Mary was not in her seat illustrates a dependent group contingency.

    Dependent group contingencies are not only used to improve the classroom behavior of a student who behaves poorly. If a teacher places an academically struggling student in a cooperative learning group with higher achievers and indicates that the group's grade is dependent on the lowest performer, dependent group contingencies are used to encourage the higher-achieving students to aid the lower-achieving student. The critical aspect, then, of dependent group contingencies is that reinforcement is dependent on one group member who is either self-selected (such as the stealing example) or is selected by the teacher.

Interdependent Group Contingencies

Interdependent group contingencies involve treating a group of students as a single individual. In other words, the same response contingencies are set for all group members (Sulzer-Azaroff & Mayer, 1991). The students in a group are then interdependent on each other for reinforcement. Interdependent group contingencies are typically built into cooperative learning groups (Slavin, 1995). In such a group, the progress of the group as a whole accounts for the group's grade. Thus, each and every member of the group has incentives to help the others with the task.

Teachers can use interdependent group contingencies to aid with classroom behavior management. In such an approach, teachers can reinforce a class as a whole on their behavior during a specified time. For example, if a substitute reports to the teacher that the students were well behaved during his time in the class, the teacher could reinforce the class with extra free time. Therefore, every student in the class is dependent on one another for access to the reinforcer. Interdependent group contingencies use the advantages of peer pressure to encourage good behavior on everyone's part.

The Good Behavior Game.

An example of interdependent group contingencies that has an extensive research base is the good behavior game. Barrish, Saunders, and Wolf (1969) researched the game in the 1960s. The good behavior game involves separating the students in a class into separate groups. Unwanted behaviors are targeted and defined. Next, a criterion level of maximum allowed behaviors is set. When any member of a team displays a target behavior, the team as a whole receives a mark. The team(s) with fewer marks than the criterion allowed or the team with the fewest marks wins the game. Consequences for winning could involve special privileges, such as extra recess or computer time. The losing team(s) would not be punished but would not receive the reinforcer. The good behavior game typically occurs on a daily basis. Unless the class is especially unruly, however, playing the game over a week would be appropriate.

Several modifications of the game have been made. For example, if a team has a member who frequently misbehaves, rather than continually providing marks to the team, a combined interdependent and independent group contingency can be used. For instance, Butterworth and Vogler (1975) placed any fifth-grade student who committed two target behaviors in a time-out (see Chapter 12 for a discussion of time-out). The first infraction would count against the team, but the second would not. If the team won, the student would not receive the reinforcer with the team (cited in Sulzer-Azaroff & Mayer, 1991).

Harris and Sherman (1973) made another modification. In this investigation, fifth- and sixth-grade students who decided not to play the game were placed on their own team. The game continued as described above with the addition of a consequence for the team of having to stay 5 minutes after school for more marks than the criterion allowed. This extra consequence was added to decrease the probability that the team of students who refused to participate would have high levels of misbehavior.

Sulzer-Azaroff and Mayer (1991) warn that the good behavior game may be set up to reduce disruptive behavior rather than to increase desirable behavior. Therefore, they describe one further modification: a process in which five to seven positive behaviors are targeted that can earn points and five to seven behaviors are targeted that can lose points. This modification is essentially a combination of the good behavior game, a token system (see Chapter 11), and a response cost system (see Chapter 12). Before the last half-hour of the day, the team with the most points wins the game. Also, any team that has no negative points is awarded bonus points.

Advantages and Disadvantages of Each Group-Oriented Contingency

The group contingencies described can be effective in managing a classroom. Each group contingency requires planning similar to planning for instruction. Each contingency however, has advantages and disadvantages that must be taken into account during the planning process.

Independent Group Contingencies

Advantages. Independent group contingencies have several advantages. First, they allow teachers to individualize their consequences for wanted and unwanted behaviors. Some teachers may think that it is unfair to consequate students for the behavior of others. Second, independent group contingencies are already in practice in classrooms. Grades are based on individual performance. It is rare to see classroom teachers provide a subject grade based on classroom performance as a whole. Third, individual responsibility is usually expected of people in society. Thus, individual group contingencies resemble society in general. Finally, individual group contingencies are effective in changing unwanted behaviors and increasing desirable ones.

Disadvantages. The disadvantages of independent group contingencies are that they do not foster group cooperation and that they do not take advantage of peer pressure in solving behavior difficulties. In addition, some students are singled out for reasons other than simply their behavior. Some students may be treated differently due to things beyond their control, such as gender, ethnicity, or physical attributes. Of course, teachers should be aware of such biases and work to prevent them from occurring.

Dependent Group Contingencies

Advantages. Dependent group contingencies have the advantage of using group pressure to aid the target student academically or to modify the behavior of a particular student. Dependent group contingencies attempt to get the group as a whole to aid the target student. Improved behavior has been shown in research involving dependent group contingencies (Pigott & Heggie, 1986; Sulzer-Azaroff & Mayer, 1991). Research has shown that social reinforcement delivered by peers can be more powerful than when the same reinforcer is delivered by a teacher (Wolery, Bailey, & Sugai, 1988). Therefore, dependent group contingencies take advantage of the powerful influence peers can have over their fellow student's behavior.

Disadvantages. The one major disadvantage of dependent group contingencies is the possibility that the target student will become the brunt of threats by his or her peers (Axelrod, 1973). The other students could chastise the target student in that they all suffer if the target student misbehaves. This disadvantage may be serious enough to prevent its use altogether.

Interdependent Group Contingencies

Advantages.   Interdependent group contingencies have a long and successful history in education. Clearly, cooperative learning groups are popular in education, and these groups are frequently exposed to interdependent group contingencies (Slavin, 1995). As with dependent group contingencies, there is evidence that when interdependent group contingencies are in effect, students tend to work more closely, which promotes higher academic performance and cooperation compared with individual contingencies (Pigott & Heggie, 1986; Slavin, 1983). Similarly, interdependent group contingencies take advantage of peer pressure to improve the behavior of students in the classroom (Wolery et al., 1988).

Disadvantages.   The disadvantages of interdependent group contingencies are similar to those of dependent group contingencies except that rather than one particular student being the target of ridicule, any student in the group could be subjected to threats. The possibility of threats and ridicule, however, may be less overall for each student than for the targeted student in dependent group contingencies.

How to Implement Group Contingencies

Although there are differences with each type of group contingency, what ties them together is that they all require the provision of consequences. Therefore, it is important to understand how to apply consequences appropriately. There are four important points to remember. First, make consequences for both wanted and unwanted behaviors known to students before they are applied. There is no point in making consequences a surprise to the students.

Second, keep the reinforcers as simple and natural as possible. For example, natural reinforcers (such as smiles, praise, and privileges) should be used before more artificial reinforcers (such as tokens, point systems, and edibles) are implemented. Although artificial reinforcement systems are effective, they are not always needed. In other words, the use of artificial reinforcers may be overkill. If natural reinforcers work, use them. If they do not work, see if they can be provided differently, such as using more **specific praise** instead of general praise. If they still do not work, artificial reinforcers may then be attempted.

Third, consequences, especially those that are unenforceable or unreasonable, should never be threatened. For example, threatening to keep the student(s) after school for the next 4 weeks is not a good idea because most students know that a teacher will not be able to follow through with this threat. Making unreasonable or unenforceable threats only makes teachers look incompetent.

A fourth important point is that teachers should attempt to use reinforcers to improve teacher-to-pupil interactions. Positive teacher-to-student interactions contain three aspects, as follows (Latham, 1992).

1. *Teachers must avoid negative traps.* **Negative traps** involve the provision of punishment techniques in such a manner that the negative interactions escalate. For example, if we are working with our classroom and the students are not listening to our instruction, we may have a tendency to reprimand the class. Unfortunately, reprimanding the class may result in the class becoming more unruly. As the class becomes more unruly, we may begin to threaten the students with having to stay after school. Some of the students may continue to escalate further by beginning to argue with us. We in turn may begin to argue with the students. This escalation continues until the interaction begin to get out of hand. Figure 6.4 shows this trap, with teacher and students becoming entangled in an almost endless tug-of-war. A much better response to the class would have been to provide a start-up request, such as, "Everyone's attention on me, please. Now, let's begin the unit on the Civil War." If a few of the students continue to misbehave, we would then take them aside and handle the problem behaviors on an individual basis away from the class. Traps shown to escalate behaviors include the following: (1) criticism (e.g., "You never listen to me"), (2) sarcasm (e.g., "You all are listening so well today"), (3) threats (e.g., "If you don't stop talking, I will keep everyone after school"), (4) logic (e.g., "You know, if you don't listen to me, you will not learn the material and will fail the class. Therefore, I need you all to listen so that you can learn what caused the Civil War"), (5) arguing (e.g., "I don't care if you find the Civil War boring"), (6) questioning (e.g., "How many times do I need to tell everyone to listen?"), (7) physical force (e.g., taking a student who is talking and physi-

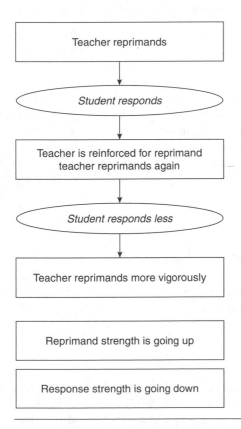

FIGURE 6.4 *Reprimands: A Trap for the Unwary.*

Source: From *Research Into Practice: Implementing Effective Teaching Strategies,* by A. Hofmeister and M. Lubke, 1991, Boston: Allyn and Bacon. Reprinted by permission.

cally turning her head toward you), and (8) despair or pleading and hopelessness ("I can't continue teaching this way. Could you all please just try for me?").

2. *We should actively practice positive interaction skills.*We must attempt to improve the positive atmosphere of the classroom. The way teachers can do so is by decreasing the level of negative interactions with students and increasing the positive interactions. According to Latham (1992), teachers allow 90% of all appropriate behaviors to go unrecognized. Unfortunately, we too often become prone to **negative scanning,** or trying to find students misbehaving. Latham also indicates that teachers are five times more likely to respond to unwanted behavior as they are to respond to wanted behavior. Walker, Hops, and Fiegenbaum (1976) presented data that showed that teacher praise was provided for appropriate student behavior 0.6 time per hour (or 2.4 times per school day) and provided active disapproval of unwanted student behavior 9.1 times per hour (or 36 times per day). Therefore, Walker et al. provided data showing teachers making 17 negative statements to each positive one. Making this fact more troubling is that the attention teachers provide to unwanted behavior can actually make the unwanted behavior stronger by feeding it with the desired attention. If teachers are to create a more positive learning environment and improve the interaction with students, they should aim for eight to nine positives to every one negative statement. Therefore, teachers should consider how often they are praising students compared with how often they are reacting negatively to student behavior.

3. *We should use a teaching interaction strategy when we attempt to correct an unwanted behavior.* This interaction strategy may decrease the probability of a negative interaction with the student. First, we should say something positive (if possible) to the students, such as, "You all did a good job on your homework." Second, we should briefly describe the problem behavior, such as, "Everyone is not attending to me when I am speaking." Third, we should describe the desired alternative behavior, such as, "I would like everyone's attention when I am teaching." Fourth, we need to give a reason the new behavior is more desirable, such as, "If everyone listens, tonight's homework will not be too difficult." Fifth, we should have the students exhibit the desired behavior. Finally, we should provide positive feedback for the desired behavior, such as, "I appreciate you providing me with your attention."

Conclusion

Teachers should consider the type of group contingency they will use in their classrooms. Group contingencies can be used to improve classroom behaviors, but each has advantages and disadvantages. Teachers must determine which contingency is most appropriate under different circumstances for different students.

Summary

Teachers are in a unique and important position to improve the behaviors of students who exhibit unwanted behavior. They are in control of the physical arrangements of the classroom, what the rules and routines will be, and how to respond to both positive and negative classroom behaviors. We know that the best way to improve the classroom behavior of students is to prevent any unwanted behavior from occurring in the first place. We also know that for some of the students, it is critical to stop the progress of antisocial behavior as soon as possible. Therefore, teachers must plan how the classroom will be arranged, including how the students will be seated, what routines will be required, and how to teach wanted behavior before unwanted behavior occurs through precorrection, social skills, and social problem-solving strategies. Everything that happens in the classroom, including the teacher's nonverbal behaviors, can and will affect the likelihood that students will display unwanted behaviors. Teachers must look at each of the aforementioned factors as part of their management plan for the classroom. Doing so will not eliminate all unwanted behaviors but will improve the probability of a positive classroom climate that will be conducive to learning.

As indicated by Hofmeister and Lubke (1990), classroom management is not the creation of an orderly environment but the creation of a learning environment; classroom management does not involve the reduction of misbehavior but involves increasing appropriate behavior. Teachers can achieve these goals by carefully planning before problem behaviors occur.

VIGNETTE • *Revisited*

After studying classroom management procedures, Ms. Hernandez realized that she should be spending more time teaching students how to behave properly in the classroom. Therefore, on the first and second days of class, she sat down with the students and developed a set of classroom rules. She also went over classroom routines. Once the rules were developed and the routines were described, Ms. Hernandez actually modeled rule-following behavior, coming into the classroom and sitting at a desk ready to begin work. She also modeled routines such as what to do when one needs to sharpen a pencil or get a drink. Once Ms. Hernandez modeled the rules and routines for the students, she asked several students to show her proper rule- and routine-following behavior while she discussed why the behavior shown by the students was correct. Ms. Hernandez also discussed examples of not following rules and routines and asked the students why it was important to follow the proper ones instead. Once she was confident that all students knew what the rules and routines were, she began to focus on academics while continually reinforcing rule and routine following.

Although Ms. Hernandez lost 2 days of instruction at the beginning of the year, she knew that she would gain back those days and then some by having a well-managed classroom.

Unfortunately, Ms. Hernandez also knew that there will always be a few students who do not follow the rules and routines. Therefore, she decided on the consequences for such behavior. Ms. Hernandez also decided to approach such misbehavior as an instructional problem. She knew that simply punishing infractions does not teach students what to do instead. Therefore, Ms. Hernandez established a seven-step precorrection routine that she uses when students fail to follow rules or routines: identify the context of the predictable behavior, specify the predictable and expected behaviors, consider how to modify the context of the situation, rehearse the appropriate behaviors with the students, determine how to reinforce appropriate student behavior, prompt expected behaviors, and monitor the plan.

Discussion Questions

1. According to Bloom, what alterable variables is the teacher in control of? Explain.

2. Why is it important to correct misbehavior as early in a student's career as possible?

3. Draw a plan of a classroom that is effectively arranged. Why is your classroom arranged this way? How can your arrangement help prevent management problems from occurring?

4. How can nonverbal procedures aid in behavior management? Describe these procedures.

5. Develop four effective rules. How do your rules have the characteristics of effective rules? How would your students learn to follow these rules?

6. Provide an example of routines you would have in your classroom. How would you teach these routines?

7. How would a teacher use precorrection strategies? Provide an example.

8. Why would social skills be important to teach students who display behavior problems?

9. What type of group contingencies would you use in your classroom. Why?

10. What are the three types of group contingencies? What are the advantages and disadvantages of each?

7

Managing Behavior within the Classroom

Instructional Variables

Chapter Objectives _____

After studying this chapter, you should be able to:

- Illustrate the levels of time.
- Explain how teachers can improve their use of allocated time and improve students' engaged and academic learning times.
- Depict how to plan for transitions.
- Characterize what effective instruction involves.
- Describe teaching functions.
- Depict the stages of learning.
- Illustrate different response prompting strategies.
- Depict what an effective lesson plan format involves.
- Describe three critical components for providing effective instruction.
- Explain what is meant by the term *mastery*.
- Illustrate three teaching behaviors that can help reduce behavior problems.
- Describe how to complete an academic functional assessment.
- Characterize the different evidence-based practices.
- Depict the key features of effective instructional methods.

VIGNETTE

MR. THOMPSON, A FOURTH-GRADE TEACHER, is experiencing difficulty with student behavior in his classroom. He has trouble getting and keeping his students on task and has noticed that they are not learning at the rate he would like. He thinks that the problem with the students' academic progress has to do with his lack of instructional time. Mr. Thompson has also informally observed that the majority of the behavior problems he sees occur when there is downtime in the classroom. In other words, when there are managerial tasks to be done, during transitions from one academic topic to another, or during independent work time, there is a high likelihood of behavior problems.

A further difficulty is that students seem to take a long time to transition from an activity such as physical education or recess. He has observed students wandering around aimlessly as well as engaging in play behavior. Unfortunately, transitions are beginning to interfere with instructional activities because the class is constantly 10 to 15 minutes behind schedule.

Mr. Thompson fears that if something is not done soon, he will lose control of the classroom. More important, he fears that his fourth graders will not learn what they need to know when they move to fifth grade. Therefore, Mr. Thompson has begun to look for solutions to his dilemma.

Overview

Classroom management has been considered separately from classroom instruction over the years, yet teachers should think of everything that goes on in the classroom as instruction. As stated in Chapter 6, behavior management involves the creation of a learning environment. Therefore, teachers should focus their attention on how they provide instruction. Specifically, teachers should instruct in a manner that is consistent with what has been found to be effective through empirical investigation. Teacher performance creates an environment for student learning experiences, which then contribute to positive or negative student performance. The reason it is important to consider student outcomes is that research has demonstrated that low student performance can be related to increased behavior management problems (Kerr & Nelson, 1998). In other words, a classroom in which there is a great deal of academic achievement for all students will be a classroom that will likely have low levels of behavior difficulties. This point is critical. Students do not come to school hating to be there. Students learn to hate school because they experience failure and do not experience much success (Kerr & Nelson, 1998). As Scott, Nelson, and Liaupsin (2001) note, "academics become aversive" (p. 313). These failures are in large part determined by how well teachers provide instruction to their students. Also, be assured that the more students find the classroom aversive, the more likely they will be to exhibit unwanted behaviors (Kerr & Nelson, 1998; Scott et al., 2001).

The effective teaching research has shown what excellent teacher performance is. Excellent teacher performance comes from having appropriate curriculum **pacing,** lesson pacing, and transition management (Hofmeister & Lubke, 1990). As shown in Figure 7.1, these teacher behaviors contribute to instructional momentum. **Instructional momentum** means that the students are moving through the curriculum at their own speed; these students, however, are also successful when they progress through the curriculum. Instructional momentum in turn reduces student misbehavior. This reduction in unwanted student behavior comes about for at least two reasons (Hofmeister & Lubke, 1990). First, when students are successful, they are less likely to misbehave. Second, when there is momen-

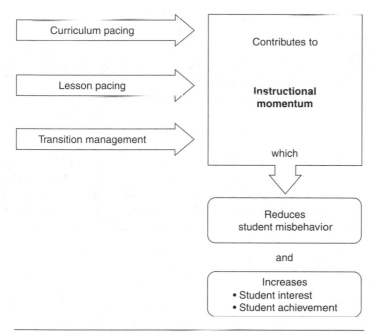

FIGURE 7.1 *Instructional momentum.*

Source: From *Research Into Practice: Implementing Effective Teaching Strategies,* by A. Hofmeister and M. Lubke, 1990, Boston: Allyn and Bacon. Reprinted by permission.

tum, students have less time to misbehave. Stated another way, the more downtime (i.e., unstructured activities) students have, the more likely they will exhibit misbehavior; the less downtime students have, however, the less likely they will go off task (Hofmeister & Lubke, 1990; Witt et al., 1999). Instructional momentum also increases student interest and student achievement (Hofmeister & Lubke, 1990). Again, students who are interested in what is going on in the classroom and who are achieving at high levels are less likely to misbehave than other students.

Therefore, the goal for educators is to help students become successful in the classroom. The methods of doing so are the focus of this chapter. Here, the levels of time teachers have available and how that time can be maximized are discussed.

What Are the Levels of Time?

One of the most important aspects of teaching is the use of time that teachers are afforded each academic day. The more teachers are able to use their time effectively and efficiently, the more students will learn and the more progress they will make. Paine et al. (1983) liken time to money: (1) time is *like* money (it can be managed; it can slip through your hands; it is cumulative) and (2) time *is* money (it is the basic currency in education and is the only resource directly converted into student learning). Paine et al. note that "you are wealthy or poor in this resource depending on how skilled or unskilled you are in managing your time" (1983, p. 67).

If teachers manage their time well, students will make academic progress and will be less likely to have behavior problems in the classroom. As shown in Figure 7.2, there are four basic levels of time: available, allocated, engaged, and academic learning.

Available Time

Available time involves the amount of time available for all instruction. In other words, if a school day is 6 hours, the total available time is 6 hours. Schools, however, never have 6 hours available for instruction. Students have recess or other types of breaks such as lunch; assemblies also take away from available time. Therefore, the amount of time actually available for instruction is less than 6 hours. The amount of time left for teaching academic subjects is allocated time.

Allocated Time

Allocated time is the amount of time a teacher or school delegates for a content/subject area. As shown in Figure 7.2, teachers use approximately 79% of the total available time (Hofmeister & Lubke, 1990). In other words, out of a 6-hour day, the amount of time actually allocated for instruction is 4 hours and 44 minutes. Thus, approximately 1 hour and 16 minutes is unused allocated time. Unfortunately, the amount of time allocated for a content/subject area is not the actual amount of time spent instructing students. Time for tran-

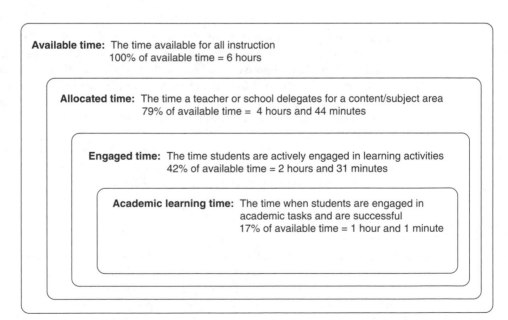

FIGURE 7.2   *Levels of time.*

sitions (discussed in detail later), completion of classroom tasks (e.g., handing out papers, taking roll), and handling disruptions take away from the teacher's instructional time (i.e., the amount of time the teacher spends providing instruction in an academic content/subject area). Possibly due to these disruptions in allocated time, it is not strongly related to student achievement (Wolery et al., 1988).

The problem with not using as much allocated time as possible is that the more downtime there is in the classroom, the higher the likelihood that students will misbehave (Hofmeister & Lubke, 1990; Witt et al., 1999). Management issues also take away from a teacher's instructional time. As behavior problems persist and become worse, the less time teachers have to teach and the more unused allocated time there is. The more noninstructional time there is, the more behavior problems there are likely to be.

Fortunately, teachers can have a significant effect on the amount of time they have to instruct. Allocated time can be used fully or poorly, depending on factors such as teacher planning and behavior management skills. According to Hofmeister and Lubke (1990), there are four general areas in which teachers can better plan to use their allocated time. First, teachers should keep sufficient materials and supplies such as workbooks, pencils, paper, handouts, or other lesson materials available. When these materials are not available, teachers waste time locating ample materials for students. All materials needing preparation should be done beforehand.

Second, teachers should have necessary equipment available before teaching a lesson. For example, audiovisual equipment should be in the classroom or be easily accessible. Also, the equipment should be tested before class to make sure it is working properly. Nothing is more frustrating than turning on an overhead projector and having a burned-out bulb. Such delays only waste instructional time and allow students to go off task.

Third, materials should be stored in easily accessible areas in the classroom. Organization of materials is critical to prevent delays in finding these materials. Classroom materials should be filed in an orderly fashion and allow easy access for teachers and students. Paine et al. (1983) recommend designating an area in the classroom for collected work and materials and teaching rules for passing and collecting materials. These rules include the following: pass or collect materials quietly, have paper monitors (assigned helpers in the classroom), pick up materials quickly, have paper monitors pass or collect in their zone only, pass or collect materials keeping your hands to yourself, and have monitors return materials to correct storage area. By teaching these rules explicitly, students learn what is expected of them, which helps prevent difficulties when managing materials in the classroom.

Fourth, the collection and correction of homework should be planned. Hofmeister and Lubke (1990) state that homework checking procedures should take less than 5 minutes. Paine et al. (1983) recommend a student self-correction station for homework or other seatwork done in the classroom. Again, rules should be developed and taught directly to students so that they can be more successful at the self-correction station. Rules include the following: only one person at each answer key, leave your pens or pencils at your desk (only correcting pens are allowed at the station), check your work quietly, and put all corrected work in the box.

Additional concerns related to allocated time include coming to class prepared and organized. Organized teachers are able to begin class on time and have a minimal number of delays before and during their instruction. Paine et al. (1983) also suggest finding effective ways to deal with student requests for assistance. Without teaching students how to seek help, teachers may find that students raise their hands and wait for the teacher, losing precious time to work on other problems or complete parts of their assignment that they can do at their desk and thus increasing the opportunities for misbehavior. Paine et al. developed an assistance card that could be taped to the end of each student's desk. On one side were the words "please keep working" and on the other were the words "please help me." The sign can be raised so that students would see their prompt (please keep working), and the teacher would see his or her prompt (please help me). While waiting, students accessed a "surefire" work folder containing materials that could be done without teacher assistance. Students were taught to work on these materials until the teacher was able to provide assistance.

Engaged Time

Engaged time involves the amount of time students are actively engaged in learning activities. Engaged time is also called *on-task time.* According to Hofmeister and Lubke (1990), students are actively engaged in learning activities an average of 42%, with a range of 25% to 58% (see Figure 7.2). In other words, students spend approximately 2 hours and 31 minutes on task in a school day. Given that students are more likely to misbehave during down time, teachers must be concerned with the amount of time students are *actually engaged.* Teachers should consider methods of getting and keeping students on task to maximize learning and prevent misbehavior.

Getting and Keeping Students on Task.   Latham (1992) sets general guidelines in getting and keeping students on task. According to Latham, the sooner teachers can get students on task, the easier it is to keep them on task. It is also easier to get students back on task if and when they go off task. Therefore, a key to increasing the likelihood of on-task behavior is to get students on task as soon as possible. To achieve this goal, teachers should begin instruction immediately. Unwarranted delays at the beginning of a class period only makes off-task behavior more likely. Second, to better manage on-task behavior, teachers should walk around during the instructional time. Paine et al. (1983) also recommend these four steps. First, teachers should "move" or circulate about the classroom in an unpredictable pattern. Second, teachers should scan the classroom, searching for students who are doing well. Third, teachers should use their attention to manage student behavior by praising students' efforts. Circulating and scanning can help in this end. Finally, teachers can use the **"praise around technique"** by praising students around the student who is off task and then, according to Paine et al., following up with the student by providing immediate praise when he or she comes back on task.

Latham (1992) outlines steps to increase the likelihood that students will get on task early in the period and maintain their on-task behavior. First, teachers should state and role-play their expectations. For example, a teacher could tell students that they are expected to work hard throughout the period. If they do so, they will be able to do something different sooner. Role-playing these expectations can be an important step, especially for younger students who can see what on-task behavior looks like. Second, teachers should state and apply consequences for on-task and off-task behavior. When students are on task, every attempt should be made to reinforce that behavior. Praising students for being on task is critical to keeping them on task over time. When students are not on task, a simple redirect to get on task can be tried. In most instances, the redirect will work. The redirect (or start-up request) should state exactly the behavior the teacher wishes the student to perform, such as, "You need to be working on your math sheet." If students still do not get on task, the teacher should have some appropriate response planned such as that described in Chapter 8. Finally, teachers should deal proactively with distracters. For example, moving students away from windows or from the back of the room to the front and telling students of the expectations before instruction begins can increase the likelihood of on task behavior. Paine et al. (1983) recommend teaching rules (or expectations) for various activities in the classroom, modeling them for students, practicing them and providing ample feedback to ensure that students have learned what to do, and then fading these procedures out, being sure to praise students intermittently when they do what they need to do in the classroom.

Academic Learning Time

Similar to engaged time, **academic learning time** is when students are actively involved in learning activities. Academic learning time, however, involves the time when students are also *successful.* Olson and Platt (2000) note that "for academic progress to occur, students must not only be on-task, but must also achieve at high accuracy levels" (p. 172). Academic learning time is the time when true learning takes place. Simply being engaged does not mean that students are actually learning. Students can be engaged while making mistakes. When students are making mistakes, they are not learning. Therefore, the old adage that we learn through our mistakes is incorrect. When we make mistakes, we only learn how to make mistakes. On the other hand, when we respond correctly, we are learning how to make the correct response. Unfortunately, the amount of time that students are actually learning is small. As shown in Figure 7.2, the academic learning time is approximately 17%, with a range of 10% to 25% (Hofmeister & Lubke, 1990), to 18% (Latham, 1992). Therefore, in a school day, only slightly over 1 hour of a 6-hour school day is spent actually learning.

A misconception that many have is that as long as students are paying attention, they are learning. Another is that practice makes perfect. In truth, because we can practice the incorrect responses to a problem, practice does not make perfect. For example, if a student follows an incorrect process for answering a math problem, the student could be making the same mistakes consistently. Unless some form of corrective feedback is provided, the student is unlikely to learn the correct process for solving the problem. Once the student has learned the incorrect process to solving math problems, it is much more difficult to teach the student the correct process. Students then become frustrated, and this frustration could lead to unwanted classroom behavior. Instead of assuming that practice makes perfect, teachers would be better served with the saying that "perfect practice makes perfect." With this perspective, teachers should continuously attempt to aid students in making correct or successful responses while decreasing the likelihood of mistakes. Thus, teachers must closely supervise their students and make sure that they are responding appropriately to assigned material. This supervision requires constant checking for student understanding.

Hofmeister and Lubke (1990) make several suggestions to aid in increasing the academic learning time of students. First, students' involvement must be enhanced. Teachers can enhance student involvement by connecting their instruction with the students' personal lives. For example, students could practice language arts by writing a story about what they did over the summer break. Second, teachers must make sure that students attend to initial presentations. For example, requiring eye contact during instruction and checking for understanding initially through questioning during a lesson will increase students' attention.

Third, students should be involved in the instructional activity. For example, students can be asked questions throughout instruction or teachers can use unison responding (described later in this chapter) to engage an entire group of students in the learning process. Fourth, teachers should provide relevant lessons and assignments. Busy work should be avoided because students learn that the work is not very relevant to them. Unfortunately, this attitude could extend to more meaningful tasks. Teachers should attempt to build their instruction around student interests. For example, many students are interested in dinosaurs. Teachers could build a lesson on western geography around the locations different dinosaur species lived. Also, teachers should focus their instruction on the skills that students most need in their daily lives. Telling time, counting money, and measuring objects are examples of critical skills for students. Finally, teacher instruction should be organized. Lessons can be scripted or outlined. They should be sequenced so that there is a logical order to the tasks to be learned, keeping errors to a minimum. Also, instruction should be planned at the students' levels of skill development and rate of learning. Grouping for instruction (described later in this chapter) could be used.

Academic learning time is perhaps the most important area of time usage for teachers. It is when learning actually takes place. Teachers can have all the allocated time available to them, but if students are not successfully engaged, this time is wasted. To increase the time available to teach further, teachers must also be aware of the curriculum, lesson pacing, and the time taken for transitions. As stated by Carnine, Silbert, and Kameenui (1997), "We now know for certain what we have suspected for a long time, that is, that adequate academic-engaged time is essential if students are to succeed in school" (p. 8).

What Is the Importance of Curriculum and Lesson Pacing?

Curriculum pacing and lesson pacing are important aspects of instruction. Curriculum pacing is concerned with the rate at which students progress through the curricula (e.g., basal reading series) or program used in the classroom. Lesson pacing deals with the pace at which teachers conduct individual or daily lessons. According to Hofmeister and Lubke (1990), "There is a direct relationship between the amount of material covered and the amount students learn" (p. 42). That is, the more the teacher covers, the more the students learn (Berliner, 1984). The principal objective of curriculum and lesson pacing is to accelerate the performance of students. If students are accelerated in a particular skill, they become relatively "smart" compared with students who have not been accelerated (Adams & Engelmann, 1996). According to Adams and Engelmann, acceleration is possible if well-designed instruction—teaching more skills in less time with more substantial generalizations—is used. Just because students may be working below grade level does not mean that information should be presented at a slower pace (provided the students are appropriately placed in the curricula or program used).

How Do We Plan for Transitions?

One area that takes up much of the allocated time is transitions, which occur for a variety of reasons throughout the school day. Witt et al. (1999) report that transitions occur an average of 15 times per day. As stated by Witt et al., if these transitions take an average of 10 minutes each, students spend 2.5 hours in transition. Therefore, transitions would take over 2 hours away from students' academics. For example, transitioning from recess to the classroom takes time. The time it takes for the students to come in from recess until they are seated and ready to work cuts into the teacher's allocated time. Likewise, lunchtime transitions also tend to decrease the amount of time available to instruct students. Transitions from one topic to another, such as from reading to math, can also adversely affect allocated time. Essentially, any time students break from one activity to go to another is considered noninstructional in nature. Interestingly, the time at which many behavior management problems occur is during these transitions (Witt et al., 1999). Therefore, teachers should attempt to decrease their transition times as much as possible. Doing so achieves two things. First, decreasing transition times increases the time teachers have to instruct. Although simply increasing instructional time does not necessarily result in improved academic achievement, it does increase the possible time when students can be engaged and successful (which is correlated with academic achievement [Wolery et al., 1988]). Second, decreasing transition times can decrease behavior management problems (Witt et al., 1999) because students simply have less time to misbehave.

To help with these transitions, Paine et al. (1983) recommend teaching students how to transition and posting these expectations on a chart. Teaching students to move quietly, put books away and get what they need for the next activity, move chairs quietly, and keep hands and feet to oneself can actually decrease transition times because students learn what to do in an effective and efficient manner.

In addition, several other steps can be taken to decrease transition times (see Table 7.1). First, teachers should set a goal for the desired length of each transition (Witt et al., 1999). For example, a teacher may wish to decrease the time it takes for transitions by half, with the goal of having transitions completed within 5 minutes. Second, students should be prepared in advance for the transition (Hofmeister & Lubke, 1990). For example, students can be told that they will be transitioning in a few minutes. Third, the teacher should signal for student attention (Witt et al., 1999). For example, the teacher would ask for all students to look at her. Once all students are looking at the teacher, she can then move to the next step. Fourth, the activity should be brought to a closure (Hofmeister & Lubke, 1990). For example, summarize the lesson or have students put materials away before the transition begins. Fifth, tell the students exactly what needs to be done (Witt et al., 1999). For example, state the following: "I need you to put your reading materials away and take out your math books" or "I need you to form a single line at the door and walk down the hall to the library when the bell rings." According to Hofmeister and Lubke (1990), the same signal

TABLE 7.1   *Steps to Decrease Transition Times*

1. Set a goal for the desired length of each transition.
2. Prepare students in advance for the transition.
3. Signal for student attention.
4. Bring the activity to a close.
5. Tell the students exactly what needs to be done.
6. Monitor the time it takes for the transition to occur.
7. Monitor which students are following the instruction and prompt those who are off task.
8. Provide feedback to students who meet the time goal, and instruct students who were too slow to try to transition within the goal time.
9. Begin the lesson when all students are ready to learn.

should be used for each transition. Sixth, the teacher should monitor the time it takes for the transition to occur (Witt et al., 1999). Seventh, the teacher must monitor which students are following the instruction and prompt those who are off task (Witt et al., 1999). Eighth, the teacher should provide feedback to the students who meet the time goal and instruct the students who were too slow to try to transition within the goal time (Witt et al., 1999). For example, the teacher could say, "Great job to those of you who have your books on your desk and are ready to get started. Those of you who are not ready yet, let's try to beat the clock tomorrow." Finally, the teacher should begin the lesson when all students are ready to learn (Witt et al., 1999).

In this example, if the teacher is able to decrease her transitions from 10 minutes to 5 minutes, the teacher gains 1 hour and 15 minutes of instructional time. Over a year, the teacher would gain approximately 237 hours of instructional time. Essentially, this gain in hours is equivalent to almost 40 extra days of instruction. Therefore, although moving from 10-minute to 5-minute transitions may seem like a small gain, in the end a great deal of time is gained.

Figure 7.3 shows a transition planning sheet developed by Hofmeister and Lubke (1990). As shown in the figure, two types of activities are to be listed (i.e., between and within activities). Between activities could include moving from math to reading, recess to music, or lunch to science. Within activities could include passing out independent reading assignments, passing out math worksheets, or returning graded homework assignments. In the planning form, the teacher documents the time of day the transition occurs, what the transition involves, and the length of time it takes for the transition. At the end of the day, the teacher calculates the total time it takes for transitions. If the teacher wishes to decrease transition times, those transitions that take too much time can be readily determined. At this point, the teacher would go through the planning process as outlined in Figure 7.3.

What Is Effective Instruction?

There continues to be an intense concern about the need to improve education. The focus of this concern often centers on economic, cultural, and social issues. People tend to blame

School _____   Date _____

Teacher _____   Observer _____

| Time of day | Description of transition | | Length of transition |
| | Between activities | Within activities | |
	From To	(Describe)	
	⟶		
	⟶		
	⟶		
	⟶		
	⟶		
	⟶		
	⟶		
	⟶		
	⟶		
	⟶		
	⟶		
	⟶		
	⟶		
	⟶		
	⟶		
	⟶		

FIGURE 7.3 *Transitions.*

Source: From *Research Into Practice: Implementing Effective Teaching Strategies,* by A. Hofmeister and M. Lubke, 1990, Boston: Allyn & Bacon. Reprinted by permission.

failures on the cultural and socioeconomic factors of our communities, a lack of support from parents/families, and other factors out of our direct control. Failures in the schools are often seen as student and family failures. Effective teachers, however, assume full responsibility for their students and classrooms and focus on variables over which they have control (Meese, 2001).

The cry for educational reform in both general and special education classrooms is heard across the United States (Vaughn, Moody, & Schumm, 1998); reform efforts tend to focus on evaluation methods, extended school days or years, reduced class size, increased teacher pay, technology in every classroom, and the like. Crandall, Jacobson, and Sloane

(1997) note that "surprisingly little attention has been paid to the problem of improving how students are taught" (p. 3). Much of the failure seen in schools can be attributed to instructional system deficits (Carnine et al., 1997). Thus, attention must be paid to effective instructional practices and the teaching functions of which they are composed.

What Are Teaching Functions?

Teaching functions are classroom experiences that move students from a lack of skill mastery (no or little knowledge) to mastery (demonstration of skills or knowledge at high levels) (Hofmeister & Lubke, 1990). Hofmeister and Lubke (based on the work of Rosenshine and Stevens, 1986, in a synthesis of the research on effective teaching) consolidate teaching functions into five groups: (1) daily reviews and prerequisite checks, (2) presentation of new content, (3) **guided practice,** (4) **independent practice,** and (5) weekly and monthly reviews (see Figure 7.4). Each of these is described below.

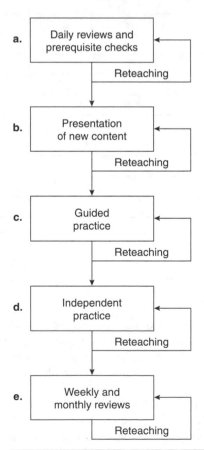

FIGURE 7.4 *Major teaching functions.*

Source: From *Research Into Practice: Implementing Effective Teaching Strategies,* by A. Hofmeister and M. Lubke, 1990, Boston: Allyn and Bacon. Reprinted by permission.

Daily Reviews

Effective teachers review material covered in previous lessons, check on homework completed the night before, check on prerequisite skills needed for the upcoming lesson, and reteach, if needed (Hofmeister & Lubke, 1990). To review, teachers may provide several problems on the board or overhead that require written responses from students. This activity helps establish a work-oriented tone and gives students an opportunity to be successful (error rates should be low). Homework completed the night before should be checked promptly; going over homework serves as an additional review for students. Effective teachers try to prevent errors from occurring in upcoming lessons by making sure that necessary prerequisite skills are mastered. For example, to solve more advanced word problems in math, students should have mastered basic math skills and more simplistic word problems. If students do not show mastery during the daily review, reteaching is necessary. It is better to delay the introduction of new material than to place students in a remedial situation, having them experience errors rather than successful learning.

Presentation of New Content

After the daily review, effective teachers present new content. They provide clear goals and objectives for the lesson, step-by-step instructions and directions, careful modeling of the skill (when appropriate), plenty of examples, and a check for student understanding (Hofmeister & Lubke, 1990). The presentation of new content is often referred to as teacher demonstration (Meese, 2001), or "I do." Effective teachers are clear about their objectives for the lesson. They organize material so that one step builds on the mastery of the previous step, giving clear and explicit instructions along the way. During modeling of new information, effective teachers model or demonstrate the skill (when appropriate). This step is called the "I do" step because the teacher is explicitly showing the students what to do ("Now watch me"). Numerous examples should be demonstrated to ensure that students are learning this new information. Checking for student understanding may involve having the students answer questions in unison (compared with saying, "Do you understand?"), having students summarize the main points, and reteaching if necessary (again based on what students are able to perform).

Guided Practice

Following the presentation of new content, effective teachers provide opportunities for guided practice. This step is also called prompted practice (Meese, 2001) or the "we do" of instruction because the teacher is actively participating in the learning with the students ("let's do some together"). Guided practice is referred to as the "bridge" between the presentation of new information and independent practice (Hofmeister & Lubke, 1990). Students must traverse this bridge to ensure that they can perform the skill when they get to the other side (independent practice, or doing it on their own). Guided practice involves asking questions and giving feedback (Meese, 2001). This acquisition stage of learning (during which students are first acquiring the skill) should have focused questions that have only one correct answer. Unison responding or the use of response cards (preprinted cards with answers or the use of chalkboards or laminate boards on which students write their answers) can be used to provide practice opportunities for students. These procedures focus on group responding, thereby giving everyone an opportunity to respond and receive feedback. Teacher feedback (praise or error corrections) is critical in guided practice and should be immediate (as close to the response as possible) and specific (telling the students what they have done the right way or what they need to do to remediate) to ensure successful student learning.

Independent Practice

According to Hofmeister and Lubke, "The transition from guided practice to independent practice should not occur until students are at least 80% successful in their guided practice" (1990, p. 61). That is, students should not move into the "you do" phase of learning until they can demonstrate success with the teacher (during the "we do"). During independent practice, students may do seatwork tasks or other practice activities (working on the computer, reading to a peer tutor) (Meese, 2001). Teachers must still actively monitor student performance.

Effective teachers provide homework only when students are successful, that is, during independent practice. Students should not receive homework that they do not know how to do. They should be able to do the work on their own with a high degree of success. New material should not be encountered; high error rates should not be shown (Hofmeister & Lubke, 1990). Likewise, cooperative learning activities (with students working together on a common assignment) should only be introduced when students have the skills to perform the task. Cooperative learning should be used during independent practice to ensure that all group members can work together and be successful when performing the activity.

Weekly and Monthly Reviews

Weekly and monthly reviews help ensure that students have opportunities to perform the skills over time so that skills are not forgotten. For example, weekly comprehensive mastery tests help students maintain skills. If skill atrophy is shown, reteaching is warranted. Reteaching involves "I do, we do, you do," giving the students more opportunities to learn and practice the skills. It is critical to provide this distributed practice so that students have opportunities to perform the skill and receive feedback over time.

What Are the Stages of Learning?

In addition to the teaching functions, teachers should also keep in mind four learning stages when planning lessons for students. These learning stages are acquisition, proficiency, maintenance, and generalization (Meese, 2001).

Acquisition Stage

The **acquisition stage** is the first stage of learning; it is the entry point when learning a skill. Students typically have little or no knowledge about the task at hand and require some level of teacher assistance (Meese, 2001). The most effective way of getting students to learn a skill is by following the teaching functions noted above, with particular emphasis on presentation of new content, guided practice, and independent practice. This stage of learning is highly teacher directed; unison responding and frequent teacher questioning are requirements to ensure increased opportunities for students to respond and receive feedback. When effective instruction is delivered at the acquisition stage of learning, errors are diminished and the chances of future generalization and maintenance of the skill are enhanced. At the end of the acquisition stage, students should perform the skill at a high rate of accuracy (usually 80–90%) (Wolery et al., 1988). These students, however, may not be fluent in skill performance or able to perform the skill under different situations (generalization). For example, given a worksheet of 10 double-digit addition problems, the student completes the problems with two errors and takes 5 minutes to complete the activity. Therefore, once acquisition is achieved, students must move to the proficiency stage of learning.

Proficiency Stage

The **proficiency stage** of learning follows acquisition. That is, once students have acquired a skill, they must be able to perform the skill at a fluent or automatic level (Meese, 2001). Drill and practice activities are used, fluency building is conducted (e.g., time trials using precision teaching), and less teacher-directed instruction is provided. Peer tutoring or computer-assisted instruction may be used to provide additional feedback and practice to students. Students may engage in repeated reading of a story to improve their reading speed. All these procedures help produce fluent student responding. Wolery et al. (1988) discuss such objectives as duration and latency of response during this stage of learning. Thus, the focus is on *rate* of learning or the time it takes to perform a particular skill. In the previous example, given a worksheet of 10 double-digit addition problems, the student completes the problems in 1 minute with no errors.

Maintenance Stage

According to Meese (2001), "As students become proficient with a new skill or concept, teachers must help them retain the material over time" (p. 178). The **maintenance stage** of learning involves periodic practice and review of the skill to ensure that students maintain skill mastery over time. Instruction is no longer needed, but practice is important (Wolery et al., 1988). Homework and seatwork activities are provided to keep students practicing and familiar with the task at hand. Students must have opportunities to continue to perform the skill; if not, the skill may atrophy over time. In the previous example, given a worksheet of 10 double-digit addition problems, the student completes the problems as homework.

Generalization Stage

Many consider the **generalization stage** to be the most important stage of learning because students use their newly learned skills in novel situations. In the previous example, the student can calculate the answers to double-digit addition problems in story problems or during a math fact game. Wolery et al. (1988) note that for a skill to be considered mastered, the student can perform it in different settings (a student exhibits appropriate social skills in other classrooms and in the community), across different persons (a student is able to ask for help from another teacher and a job supervisor), across behaviors (new or similar behaviors, such as a student who exhibits a reduction in swearing after learning to self-manage his talking outbursts), or differing materials (a student is able to read the newspaper after being taught to read in a basal reader). Teachers may ask for the help of teachers, parents, or other students to prompt or praise others when skills are demonstrated in the natural environment (Meese, 2001).

What Are Response Prompting Strategies?

Response prompting strategies are similar to what Vygotsky called "scaffolding." These strategies allow teachers to teach while decreasing the chances of students making errors and increasing their chances of success. There are several prompting and fading strategies: antecedent prompt and test, most to least, antecedent prompt and fade, least to most, graduated guidance, and time delay (Cooper et al., 1987; Martin & Pear, 1999; Wolery et al., 1988).

Antecedent Prompt and Test Procedure

The **antecedent prompt and test** procedure involves prompting students during instruction and then providing them with practice or test trials after removing all prompts. This procedure should sound familiar; it was discussed earlier with teaching functions as "I do" (model), "we do" (guided practice), and "you do" (independent practice). This procedure has also been called the model-test, model-lead-test, and prompt-practice strategy (Wolery et al., 1988). It involves having the teacher present a prompt such as a model (e.g., "That word is *blue*"). Next, the teacher performs the skill or task with the student or presents a test or practice trial. This test or practice trial can occur immediately after the initial prompt or sometime later (e.g., "That word is *blue*. What word?"). Correct independent responses are reinforced (e.g., "Yes, that word is *blue*"). Incorrect responses are corrected and feedback is provided (e.g., "That word is *blue*"; "Say it with me. Blue"; "What word?").

Most-to-Least Prompting

Most-to-least prompting involves decreasing assistance to a student in a progressive fashion (Wolery et al., 1988) and creating a prompt hierarchy. This hierarchy involves a number of prompts listed in order of intrusiveness (i.e., the amount of control exerted over the student's response). For example, a physical prompt (e.g., hand-over-hand prompting) is much more intrusive than a verbal prompt (e.g., telling a student what to do). With this approach, the teacher begins with the most intrusive prompt (e.g., guiding the student's hand when writing the letter "A"). Once the student is able to meet a predetermined criterion for this prompt (freely moves hand with teacher with no resistance for three consecutive trials), the next intrusive prompt of the hierarchy is provided (e.g., placing teacher's hand on student's elbow to guide the writing of the letter). This continues until the student can perform the skill independently, with the least intrusive level of prompting (e.g., telling the student to write the letter on his or her own).

Antecedent Prompt and Fade Procedure

The **antecedent prompt and fade** procedure involves providing a more intrusive prompt on initial instructional trials and then fading out the prompt in a systematic manner (Wolery et al., 1988). Fading of prompts can involve presenting the controlling prompt less frequently (e.g., teacher pointing to every "b" when student is asked to color each "b" red in a discrimination task between "b" and "d" to pointing to just some of the "b"s) or fading the intensity of the prompt (e.g., loud voice to a soft voice). For example, the teacher may wish to teach a student how to write her name. Therefore, the teacher physically guides the student's hand initially when writing her name. Once the student seems to be moving her hand appropriately to write her name, the teacher provides less pressure on the student's hand. Again, once the student is able to continue to write her name, the teacher provides even less pressure until the teacher's hand is moving just above the student's hand. If a student makes a mistake, the teacher provides an error correction (e.g., "You put the 'm' before the 'o' in your name. Let's go back and try again"). The decision of when to move from one level of prompt to another is not typically defined (Wolery et al., 1998). Therefore, this decision is based on teacher judgement. A critical aspect of this strategy is to assess whether student errors increase as prompts are faded. If so, the more intrusive prompt may need to be re-implemented.

Least-to-Most Prompting

Least-to-most prompting involves increasing assistance when a student does not perform a behavior (Wolery et al., 1988); thus, a prompt is necessary to get the behavior to occur. Similar to the most-to-least procedure, here a list of prompts is developed in order of their level of intrusiveness. The difference between this procedure and the most-to-least procedure is that the beginning prompt in the least-to-most procedure is the least intrusive prompt. In addition, all levels of the prompts may be used in a single trial. For example, a teacher could define a list of prompts from verbal (least) to full physical (most) prompts. The teacher may provide an instruction to copy the material from the board. The teacher waits for a predetermined time (response interval) to see if the student begins to copy the material. If the student makes a mistake or does not copy from the board, the teacher moves to the next level of prompt, such as a verbal and gestural prompt (e.g., verbalizing to the student to copy from the board while pointing to the board and then to the student's paper). If the student continues to make mistakes or does not begin copying within the response interval, the teacher moves to the next level of prompt, such as a verbal-gestural-light physical prompt (e.g., touching the student on the shoulder). If the student makes the correct response (e.g., copies the material from the board) when the initial instruction to copy the board is provided, the student is reinforced. In essence, the student determines the level of prompt that will be provided by his or her behavior.

Graduated Guidance

Graduated guidance is similar to the most-to-least prompting procedure except that it involves more of a fluid movement from the highest level of prompt to the lowest level. In other words, prompts are removed immediately as needed by students (Wolery et al., 1988). A good way to picture graduated guidance is when teaching a child to ride a bike without training wheels. First, we grasp the bike firmly while the child is riding and gradually lessen the amount of assistance we provide until the child is riding independently. The difference between this method and most-to-least prompting is that the latter involves a series of steps the child would need to ride successfully with us holding on, then moving to the child riding successfully with us lightly touching the bike, and so on. With graduated guidance the teacher's prompts are adjusted moment to moment and gradually faded out. For example, if a student is instructed to write her name, the teacher provides a hand-over-hand physical prompt at first while the student is attempting to write. As the student is writing more independently, the teacher immediately removes the level of prompt. In other words, the level of prompt provided is dependent on the student's level of need.

Time Delay

Time delay involves presenting the final desired stimulus and the starting stimulus at the same time. This process occurs for several trials (Wolery et al., 1988). Then, a time delay is provided between the two stimuli (constant time delay), or the time delay between the two stimuli is gradually increased (progressive time delay) on subsequent learning trials (Wolery et al., 1998). With constant time delay, a delay interval is decided upon based on the normal time it takes students to respond to an instruction (e.g., 5 seconds). If the student responds within the time delay, the student is reinforced. When that occurs, there is a transfer in stimulus control from the desired prompt (e.g., instruction) to the delayed prompt. The point when this begins to occur is called the moment of transfer (Sulzer-Azaroff & Mayer, 1991). If there is no response, there is a prompt.

For example, suppose that a teacher has a student who will not provide the answer to math problems unless the teacher specifically requests the answer. Therefore, the teacher presents math division problems initially on cards and asks for each card, "What is the answer to this problem?" After these beginning trials, the teacher holds up each card and waits for a response. If the student provides the correct response before the verbal prompt, the student is reinforced. If the student provides an incorrect response before or after the prompt, the teacher goes through an error correction procedure (i.e., model ["The answer is 12"], lead ["Say the answer with me. 12"], and test ["What is the answer to this problem?"]) and then puts the card in the pile of problems to be retested. If the student does not respond within the delay period, the teacher provides the prompt (e.g., "What is the answer to this problem?"). If the student answers correctly after this prompt, the student is reinforced, but the response does not count toward the criterion for completion of the task (in other words, the cards can be put back into the pile of problems that have not been answered correctly before the prompt was provided). If the student still does not respond to the delayed prompt, the stimulus used to consequate the correct responses should be reviewed.

With the progressive time delay procedure, the same procedure is used except that the time delay is gradually and systematically expanded. For example, the teacher provides the prompt (e.g., instruction to provide an answer) at 0 seconds initially over five trials, then at 1 second for 3 trials, then 2 seconds for the next three trials, and so on.

What Is an Effective Lesson Plan Format?

Lesson plans are used by teachers to deliver instruction on a daily basis. One strategy to help the effective implementation of lesson plans is direct instruction, which emphasizes fast-paced and well-sequenced instruction typically delivered to small groups of students who are given many opportunities to respond and receive feedback (Adams & Engelmann, 1996; Meese, 2001). Teachers use repetition and emphasize engaged time, pacing, and effective error corrections. An effective lesson plan format is shown in Table 7.2 (as noted by Meese, 2001). Its elements should be familiar, given the teaching functions previously described and the **effective instructional cycle.**

TABLE 7.2   *Example of an Effective Lesson Plan Format*

Lesson Plan Element	*Contents*
Opening the lesson	• Gain student attention. • Review or summarize previous learning. • Remind students of important rules. • State the purpose of the lesson. • State why the skill should be learned.
Demonstrating the new skill or concept	• Break the skill into a careful sequence of steps. • Model steps to students.
Giving guided practice	• Provide numerous opportunities to practice. • Ask questions. • Use choral responding. • Give feedback.
Providing independent practice	• Provide seatwork or other practice opportunities directly related to the lesson. • Actively monitor performance.
Closing the lesson	• Review or summarize the main points learned. • Remind students of the usefulness of information. • Provide specific directions on what will happen next.
Evaluating the lesson	• Provide formative evaluation (have students accomplished the objectives of the lesson?). • Provide summative evaluation (have students accomplished the objectives of multiple lessons following a period of instruction?).

What Are Three Critical Components for Providing Effective Instruction in the Classroom?

Carnine et al. (1997) describe three critical components for providing effective instruction in the classroom. They are: (1) organization of instruction, (2) program design, and (3) teacher presentation techniques. Each of these components is described below.

Organization of Instruction

Before focusing on the curricula and how teachers actually deliver instruction in the classroom, it is necessary to ensure that the organization of the classroom is efficient and appropriate for students. Three key elements should be considered: (1) time in the classroom, (2) scheduling, and (3) arranging materials. First, as previously noted, the time in the classroom (engaged time and academic learning time) needs to be examined and maximized to ensure better student outcomes. The more students are *actively* and *successfully* engaged, the more they will learn. Second, an emphasis must be made on academics and curriculum-related activities; thus, this time must be scheduled in the classroom. Finally, how the physical setting is arranged and how instructional materials are provided can also affect how instruction is delivered in the classroom. The organization of instruction can be compared to having effective roadways when driving a car. Without a safe place to travel, driving might prove difficult, if not impossible.

Program Design

After examining the organization of instruction (the "roadways for driving a car"), attention is turned to the programs or curricula used in the classroom ("the car"). The "car" should be reliable and run smoothly. It should be able to go down the road without fail and do so efficiently. The same is true of program design. The curricula teachers use in the classroom should have many key elements for more effective use in the classroom: (1) specifying objectives, (2) devising strategies, (3) developing teaching procedures, (4) selecting examples, (5) sequencing skills, and (6) providing practice and review. First, the program should state what will be taught using observable behaviors that are amenable to direct measurement (saying that students will learn to appreciate literature is not enough; it is better to specify reading rate per minute and accuracy levels, for example). Second, according to Carnine et al. (1997), "whenever possible, programs should teach students to rely on strategies rather than require them to memorize information" (p. 10). These strategies (e.g., learning sounds and blending) can be used to tackle new words (increases generalized performance). Thus, teachers get more than they expected. They get much more learning from their students than if they taught one skill and got one skill; now, their students can do many more things than were actually taught.

Third, after specifying the objectives and devising the strategies, a good program specifies the formats for how teachers will actually present the information to students. This element relates to the teaching procedures used. These formats should be specific so that teachers do not have to guess how to present the information to students. Formats should be easy for students to understand and contain only one skill at a time so as to decrease the chance of student errors. Some programs provide scripting for teachers to follow. Fourth, skills should be sequenced as to avoid unnecessary errors and promote efficient learning. Carnine et al. (1997, p. 12) recommend the following:

1. Preskills of a strategy are taught before the strategy itself is presented.
2. Instances that are consistent with strategy are introduced before exceptions.
3. High utility skills are introduced before less useful ones.
4. Easy skills are taught before more difficult ones.
5. Strategies and information likely to be confused are not introduced at the same time.

For example, teachers should not teach the letters and sounds "b" and "d" at the same time because they look and sound similar and could promote confusion (and reversals!). Carnine et al. note that the most critical principle is teaching components of a strategy before the entire strategy is introduced.

Finally, the program should provide ample opportunities for practice and review. Repetitions are necessary because students are naïve and need to practice correctly (as previously discussed, it is perfect practice that makes perfect, not simply practice that makes perfect).

Teacher Presentation Techniques

After examining the organization of instruction (the "roadways for driving a car") and program design ("the car"), attention now turns to how to "drive the car." We can have the best car in the world and the smoothest and safest roadways around, but if we do not know how to drive the car, we cannot take the car down the road. Likewise, we could be the best driver in the world, but without a good car to drive, we cannot access the roadways. Teachers need all three components: good organization in the classroom, a good curriculum, and good instructional delivery. They can take a great curriculum and ruin it by not knowing how to present instruction to students. How teachers present instruction in the classroom includes many key elements: (1) small group instruction, (2) unison oral responding, (3) wait time, (4) pacing, (5) monitoring, (6) **diagnosis and correction,** and (7) motivation.

First, small group instruction should be used. These groups should be formed using homogeneous and flexible skill grouping. That is, students are grouped according to skill but can move into other groups depending on their skill performance. Grouping this way is very efficient for teachers; they have more engaged and academic learning time because students are being successful. Second, when small groups are used, **unison oral responding,** another opportunity for students to respond and receive feedback from the teacher, should be conducted. Third, wait time is critical to include when delivering instruction. **Wait time** (also called "think time") gives students an opportunity to think about the answer before they actually say it. To provide wait time opportunities, teachers use signals (cues that prompt student responses). Without these cues, higher-performing students would monopolize the instructional sessions, jumping to the answer before other students could respond.

Fourth, pacing should be varied and fast (providing more opportunities for students to respond and receive feedback). So-called perky pacing contributes to better student achievement and decreased behavior problems. Students do not have time to go off task. Fifth, monitoring student performance is critical. Teachers can monitor student performance while students respond in unison (are they correct and responding together?). Individual turns should be provided after groups respond and responses should be firm (i.e., say it like they know it) to check individual student performance (another monitoring approach). Names should always be used at the end of the instruction provided to individual students (e.g., "Read the next sentence, Joseph" rather than "Joseph, read the next sentence") to ensure that all students will pay attention to the task at hand. Sixth, diagnosis and correction should be maximized. Error correction procedures should focus on providing an effective model (e.g., "That word is *brother*"), a lead ("Say it with me. Brother"), a test (e.g., "What word?"), and a delayed test (e.g., "Starting over") to ensure firm responding. Other error correction procedures can be used for more advanced items but are beyond the scope of this book. Finally, motivation should be key to instructional delivery. Students respond well to praise. Saying "yes" to the correct answers provided by students provides them yet another repetition of hearing the correct answer and tells them that what they said was correct ("yes, the word is *brother*" or "yes, *brother*"). Artificial reinforcers (as noted in Chapter 2) can be used initially and then faded out to more naturally occurring reinforcers to maximize student performance.

What Is Mastery?

Mastery involves performing skills at high levels. Engelmann (1999) likens mastery to a stairway, saying "Mastery is the guarantee that students are able to reach each stair without falling" (p. 4). Effective teachers carefully design their instruction (or use curricula specifically designed for this purpose) toward that goal. To ensure that mastery will be achieved, Engelmann recommends an examination of first-time corrects. Each time a task is presented, students either respond correctly (in unison) or incorrectly (one or more students provide the wrong response or do not answer). Four criteria allow precise interpretation of how students respond during the lesson.

1. Students should be at least 70% correct on information that is being introduced for the first time. (If they are only at 50%, they are at chance level and are guessing.)
2. Students should be at least 90% correct on skills taught earlier in the program sequence (this assumes previous skill mastery).
3. At the end of the lesson, all students should be "virtually 100% firm on all tasks and activities" (p. 6).
4. Student error rates should be low enough to ensure that teachers have sufficient time to complete lessons.

To calculate first-time corrects, teachers count the number of tasks in which students provide responses and the number of times students respond correctly and then divide the correct responses by the total responses, multiplying by 100 for a percentage of first-time corrects. So, if a teacher provides 10 tasks and the students respond correctly to 8 of these tasks, the percentage of first-time corrects is 80%. Ensuring skill mastery leads to higher academic performance that in turn leads to better behavior in the classroom. Students who are successful in school are less likely to be disruptive in class.

What Are Three Teaching Behaviors That Can Help Reduce Behavior Problems in the Classroom?

Martella and colleagues pinpointed three behaviors—appropriate instructions, specific praise, and appropriate error corrections—that should be taught to those interacting with students in the classroom. In order to teach classroom staff these behaviors, Martella, Marchand-Martella, Macfarlane, and Young (1993) and Martella, Marchand-Martella, Miller, Young, and Macfarlane (1995) recommend modeling appropriate use of these behaviors. Following that step, opportunities for guided practice (including role-playing) should be conducted. Feedback on correct use of the behaviors and corrective feedback should be provided. Finally, observations should be made.

Appropriate Instructions

Appropriate instructions (called instructional commands by Martella, Marchand-Martella, Miller, et al., 1995) include statements that

> state the command succinctly without phrasing it as a question (e.g., "Susan, tell me the word on this card," rather than "Can you tell me the word on this card?"); specify a desired motoric or verbal response (e.g., "Tom, erase the number 6 on your paper," rather than "Tom, erase it"); use a neutral or positive/pleasant tone of voice; and have a time delay of 5 seconds between commands, as opposed to rapidly repeating the command several times. (p. 54)

The performance criterion for appropriate instructions is 100%. The number of appropriate instructions is tracked, as are the number of inappropriate instructions. The total number of appropriate instructions is divided by the total number of instructions and multiplied by 100 for a percentage of appropriate instructions. For example, if 8 appropriate instructions were observed and 2 inappropriate instructions were observed, the percentage of appropriate instructions is $8/10 \times 100 = 80\%$.

Specific Praise

Specific praise statements are "precise statements in a neutral or positive/pleasant tone of voice that reflect a positive response to a desired behavior (e.g., 'Good job putting your coat in the closet, Joe,' rather than 'Good job, Joe')" (Martella, Marchand-Martella, Miller, et al., 1995, p. 54). The performance criterion for specific praise is 50%. That is, half of all praise statements should be specific rather than nonspecific (general to the task or behavior, such as "good" or "super"). The number of specific praise statements is tracked, as are the number of nonspecific praise statements. The total number of specific praise statements is divided by the total number of praise statements and multiplied by 100 for a percentage of specific praise statements. For example, if 5 specific praise statements were observed and 5 nonspecific praise statements were observed, the percentage of appropriate specific praise statements is $5/10 \times 100 = 50\%$.

Appropriate Error Corrections

Appropriate error corrections include the following:

> If the student makes an incorrect response (e.g., says "stop" when the word is *go*) or does not respond within 5 seconds of the instruction, tell the student the correct response and have him or her repeat it (e.g., "This word is *go*"). Error correction procedures should be stated in a neutral tone of voice. Avoid using an inflected tone of voice that indicates negativity and saying phrases such as "That's not right," "You're guessing," and "You can do better than that." (Martella, Marchand-Martella, Miller, et al., 1995, pp. 54–55)

The performance criterion for appropriate error corrections is 100%. The number of appropriate error corrections is tracked, as are the number of inappropriate error corrections. The total number of appropriate error corrections is divided by the total number of error corrections and multiplied by 100 for a percentage of appropriate error corrections. For example, if 7 appropriate error corrections were observed and 3 inappropriate error corrections were observed, the percentage of appropriate error corrections is $7/10 \times 100 = 70\%$.

What Is an Academic Functional Assessment?

An **academic functional assessment** helps determine the function or purpose of a student's behavior. (Chapter 10 presents a detailed description of functional behavioral assessments.) Of course, if these reasons are not effectively remediated, behavior problems in the classroom often result. Instructional performance is closely tied to how students behave in the classroom. Witt and Beck (1999) analyze what happens before and after students' academic performance that can help or hinder how they do in the classroom. They recommend maximizing effective instructional activities before students' academic performance occurs as well as maximizing effective feedback (or consequences) after they perform. In addition, detractions, distractions, and disruptions should be minimized before academic performance occurs; consequences that may decrease how students do following academic performance (e.g., attention from peers for nonacademic behavior such as playing or whispering) should also be minimized.

According to Witt and Beck (1999): "There are two, and only two, reasons a student does not perform academic work: he can't do it or he won't do it. That means he either lacks the skills to do the work or he simply prefers not to do the work" (p. 46). One-minute functional assessments are recommended to determine four basic reasons why students fail to progress academically (Witt & Beck, 1999). These reasons are (1) the student won't do the work (motivation problem), (2) the material is too hard (the student can't do the work), (3) the student needs more practice (the student can't do the work), and (4) the student needs more help (the student can't do the work).

One-minute functional assessments should be conducted to determine if students exhibit won't do or can't do deficits. These assessments include the following four key parts (Witt & Beck, 1999).

1. *Monitor student performance to get a baseline.* Data are taken on precision teaching charts [three-cycle academic charts] on rate of performance in academic areas such as oral reading; examples of student performance include flat lining, high variability, progress is too slow, and satisfactory.
2. *Evaluate student performance.* Students are expected to progress 25% per week; if more than 25%, progress is deemed satisfactory; if less than 25%, it is time to analyze the learner.
3. *Analyze the learner.* This step pertains to finding things under the teacher's control that can make a difference in academic performance, such as providing motivation if a student exhibits a "won't do" deficit and determining the effects or, for "can't do" deficits, testing the use of easier materials if the material is too hard, adding practice if more practice may be needed, and providing assistance if a student may need more help and determining the corresponding effects.
4. *Teach with precision.* Link the assessment previously conducted with intervention ideas such as goal setting for motivation problems, peer tutoring for students who need more practice, interspersing easy work with more difficult work when material is too hard, and using response cards when students need more help; these interventions—along with many other good ideas—are provided by Witt and Beck (1999).

What Are Evidence-Based Practices?

When viewing educational effectiveness, teachers should take more of a pragmatic approach and

> identify what students need to know to succeed in our society, then use the most effective instructional practices to teach these skills and concepts. Implicit in this view is the assumption that the same scientific method that solved many complex problems in medicine and industry is up to the challenge of determining which teaching methods are the most effective. (Crandall et al., 1997, p. 3)

Educational effectiveness must rest on the principles of the scientific method. The scientific method helps us gain an understanding of the world. It includes the following steps: (1) identification of a problem, (2) definition of the problem, (3) formulation of a hypothesis or research question, (4) determination of the observable consequences of the hypothesis or research question, and (5) a testing of the hypothesis or an attempt to answer the research question (Martella et al., 1999). The scientific method helps describe, explain, predict, and improve the world around us (Martella et al., 1999). It is important to use the scientific method to guide the selection of effective programs and instructional methods in schools.

Key Features of Effective Programs

As noted by Adams and Engelmann (1996), an effective program has seven key features. These features can serve as criteria with which to assess the effectiveness and possible adoption of programs used by schools. They include:

1. Would teachers, even those with below average teaching skills, be able to teach the program successfully after receiving relatively small amounts of training?
2. Does the program permit reliable predictions about how much student progress may be anticipated for a given period?
3. Is the sum of the "promised" skills relatively substantial compared with the sum of skills currently mastered by students during the same period?
4. Is there an analytical basis to suggest that these gains are at least plausible?
5. Are there sufficient tests of student performance to serve as a guide for adjusting the rate of presentation to students?
6. Do priority skills receive relatively more instructional attention than trivial skills?
7. Is there consumer protection information to suggest that the outcomes are possible? (p. 7)

Direct Instruction

One program meeting all seven criteria is **Direct Instruction** (published by Science Research Associates and authored by Siegfried Engelmann and colleagues). Direct Instruction provides a model of instruction that increases student achievement through carefully focused instruction; its aim is to provide intense and efficient lessons that allow all students, even the lowest performing, to achieve mastery of academic skills. This program can be used with minimal training (of course, the more training, the better). It permits reliable predictions about student progress because of homogeneous and flexible skill grouping as well as a scripted presentation format, allowing predictions about what can be accomplished in an academic year. In addition, it has a wealth of published (empirically based) research and field testing documenting its use. It provides scope and sequences of skills to be taught so that the sum of promised skills are substantial over time. Direct Instruction offers theoretical support and, more importantly, empirical evidence (it is noted as one of only three school reform models offering evidence of positive effects on student achievement by the American Institutes for Research [see the *Education Week* article by Olson, February 17, 1999]). For further information on the empirical support offered by Direct Instruction, readers are referred to the work of Adams and Engelmann (1996) involving a meta-analysis of the Direct Instruction research and an analysis of Project Follow Through results by Watkins (1997).

In addition, Direct Instruction offers multiple opportunities for students to respond (unison responding) and curriculum-based assessments to ensure program mastery. An emphasis on priority skills is a key feature of Direct Instruction. These skills are carefully sequenced so that higher-order thinking skills can be easily accomplished (based on prior mastery of prerequisite skills). Finally, the main form of consumer protection available for Direct Instruction comes through empirical investigations comparing the program with other approaches. Again, the field testing of Direct Instruction makes it one of the most widely researched programs in the country.

Success for All

Another school reform model shown to have strong and positive effects on student achievement (as noted by the American Institutes for Research [see the *Education Week* article by Olson, February 17, 1999]) is **Success for All** by Robert Slavin and Nancy Madden, a comprehensive approach to restructuring schools that serve (in particular) those students at risk for school failure. The approach ensures that every child learns how to read. It includes nine components: (1) a reading curriculum with at least 90 minutes of daily instruction, (2) continual assessment, (3) one-on-one tutoring, (4) emphasis on language development and reading in prekindergarten and kindergarten classrooms, (5) cooperative learning, (6) a family support team, (7) a local facilitator to provide mentoring to schools, (8) staff support teams, and (9) training and technical assistance provided by Success for All staff.

High Schools That Work

The third school reform model that demonstrated strong and positive effects on student achievement was **High Schools That Work** (see the *Education Week* article by Olson, February 17, 1999). This model is designed to raise the academic achievement of career-bound high schoolers by combining college preparatory studies with vocational studies. The following key practices are noteworthy to the program: (1) high expectations for student learning, (2) rigorous vocational courses, (3) more required academic courses, (4) learning in work environments, (5) collaboration among academic and vocational teachers, (6) an individualized advising system, (7) active student engagement, (8) extra help outside of school and in the summer, and (9) use of assessment and evaluation data to improve student learning.

Results Noted by the American Institutes for Research

Only 3 of the 24 (12.5%) school reform models reviewed by the American Institute for Research offered strong (positive) effects on student achievement. Sixteen of the school reform models (67%) offered marginal, mixed/weak, or no research evidence yet were still being used in schools. Thus, the report from the American Institutes for Research (see Appendix B for web site) should help guide the selection of effective school practices.

National Reading Panel Results

The National Reading Panel (a congressionally mandated independent panel) conducted the largest, most comprehensive research-based review ever on how children learn to read. Rigorous scientific standards to evaluate the research were used, and the work was conducted in a public forum. Results indicated the following:

> The panel determined that effective reading instruction includes teaching children to break apart and manipulate the sounds in words (**phonemic awareness**), teaching them that these sounds are represented by letters of the alphabet which can then be blended together to form words (**phonics**), having them practice what they've learned by reading aloud with guidance and feedback (**guided oral reading**), and applying reading comprehension strategies to guide and improve reading (emphasis added) (http://www.nichd.nih.gov/new/releases/ nrp/htm, p. 1).

The web site for the National Reading Panel can be found in Appendix B.

Key Features of Effective Instructional Methods

Effective instructional methods include the design features big ideas, mediated scaffolding, conspicuous strategies, strategic integration, primed background knowledge, and judicious review (Kameenui & Carnine, 1998). Each of these features is described below.

1. *Big ideas.* **Big ideas** are the underlying concepts or skills that allow students to apply or generalize what they learn. An example related to reading acquisition is phonemic awareness; directly teaching this skill has positive effects on early reading success (National Research Council, 1998).

2. *Mediated scaffolding.* **Mediated scaffolding** enables students to bridge the gap between their current skill levels and the goal of instruction. Content, task, materials, and instructional approach support initial skills instruction and facilitate student mastery of skills. One-to-one instructional formats are an example of mediated scaffolding. That format enables teachers to adjust the level of scaffolding provided to students as they acquire skills and move through content.

3. *Conspicuous strategies.* Related to mediated scaffolding, **conspicuous strategies** are explicit teaching strategies to ensure student mastery of skills. To make teaching strategies conspicuous, a program should stress teacher modeling and effective error corrections.

4. *Strategic integration.* **Strategic integration** involves integration of concepts, content, and skills that are mutually facilitative of each other or are arranged so that instruction communicates generalizations to new areas removed from the original area of instruction. For example, integrating phonemic awareness, alphabetic understanding (student's understanding that words are made up of individual letters called graphemes), and automaticity (student shows automatic decoding or fluency) is more effective for teaching beginning reading than instruction in alphabetic understanding alone (Kameenui & Carnine, 1998).

5. *Primed background knowledge.* **Primed background knowledge** involves connecting previously acquired knowledge of the skills about to be taught. For example, teachers can prompt students to use their segmenting (breaking down words into component sounds; *m/a/n* would be the sounds said in *man*) and blending skills (running sounds together to form a word; *mmmaaannn* would be how the sounds in *man* are said via blending, without stopping between them) when decoding a word. Primed knowledge also involves ensuring the teaching of prerequisite skills. A hierarchical structure of the scope and sequence ensures that students acquire prerequisite skills to enhance later learning of more complex skills.

6. *Judicious review.* **Judicious review** refers to the sequence and schedule of opportunities for students to apply and develop fluency with newly acquired skills. Programs should be structured to include immediate practice, varied review activities, and intermittent review to ensure that students fully acquire the skills being taught.

Other Resources

Other resources emphasizing effective programs, strategies, and instructional practices include but are not limited to *Direct Instruction Reading* (Carnine et al., 1997), *What Works in Education* (Crandall et al., 1997), *Teaching Learners with Mild Disabilities: Integrating Research and Practice* (Meese, 2001), *Preventing Reading Difficulties in Young Children* (National Research Council, 1998), *Designing Effective Mathematics Instruction: A Direct Instruction Approach* (Stein, Silbert, & Carnine, 1997), *The Surefire Way to Better Spelling* (Dixon, 1993), and *Effective Teaching Strategies That Accommodate Diverse Learners* (Kameenui & Carnine, 1998) as well as ERIC/OSEP library books on adapting curricular materials in language arts, social studies, and science (Schumaker & Lenz, 1999) and reading and mathematics (Shumm, 1999) and on promoting successful inclusion through the architecture of instruction (Kameenui & Simmons, 1999).

Summary

Behavior management is frequently thought of separately from academic instruction. Unwanted behavior (e.g., acting out in class), however, is no different in form or function from academic behavior (e.g., reading). In other words, behaviors (both positive and negative) are affected by the same thing: what goes on in the classroom. Therefore, rather than thinking about unwanted behavior as separate and distinct from academic behaviors, they both should be considered classroom behaviors. Once this consideration is made, then how instruction in the classroom positively or negatively affects the behavior of students can be considered. In general, the students who display behavior problems are frequently poor performers in the classroom (Engelmann, 1997; Kerr & Nelson, 1998; Meese, 2001). The connection can be explained in one of three ways. First, misbehavior adversely affects student academic performance. Second, poor academic performance adversely affects student behavior. Third, something else such as dysfunctional family relationships adversely affects both. All three of these explanations have validity. Teachers, however, have little or no control over the third explanation; they do have control over the first two. Unfortunately, improving classroom behavior does not necessarily result in improved academic performance. Students still need to be instructed appropriately. On the other hand, improved academic instruction has been shown to improve classroom behavior (Hofmeister & Lubke, 1990). Therefore, one of the best methods of improving classroom management is to improve the way students are instructed.

In this chapter, several considerations teachers should make when planning their instruction and when considering their behavior management procedures were covered. Teachers owe it to their students to use the time available for instruction wisely. Also, as educators, teachers owe students the opportunity to be instructed in a manner that has been shown to be effective through the scientific research literature. This instruction involves several important areas of teaching, including the use of scientifically validated curricular materials. If teachers work on improving their instruction, improved classroom behavior will result. There will still be unwanted behavior from time to time, and teachers must have an appropriate response to these behaviors. Chapter 8 addresses what teachers can do when students still misbehave in the face of excellent classroom instructional methods.

VIGNETTE • *Revisited*

Mr. Thompson decides to research methods of improving the classroom behavior of his students and their academic progress. The first thing he decides to do is calculate how much of his instructional time is lost due to transitions. Once he realizes that a full 25% of his allocated time is spent trying to get students through their transitions, he considers methods of decreasing that time. He teaches his students how to transition (e.g., how to line up at the door, where to go upon entering the room).

Mr. Thompson also thinks that he needs to increase the rate at which he provides instruction. He believes that there is too much downtime during the day. These downtimes involve prompting other students to get on task and conducting managerial tasks such as handing out papers. Therefore, Mr. Thompson modifies how he delivers instruction throughout the day by increasing the pace of his instruction, attempting to praise appropriate student behavior more specifically and frequently, and having student assistants assist in managerial tasks so these tasks can be completed in half the time.

With these minor changes, Mr. Thompson sees improved student behavior through higher percentages of on-task behavior and lower disruptions and higher student achievement after only 2 weeks.

Discussion Questions

1. Why should instruction be considered an important component of behavior management?

2. How can teachers improve academic achievement via the use of classroom time? How can teachers improve the use of their time?

3. What is the importance of curriculum and lesson pacing in preventing management problems?

4. Why should teachers improve their transitions? How can teachers do so?

5. What are the considerations teachers should make with regard to teaching functions? How do these functions relate to the stages of learning?

6. How can teachers use different prompting strategies to increase student correct responding?

7. What are the three components for providing effective instruction? Provide an example of each.

8. What are three teaching behaviors that can help to reduce behavior problems in the classroom? Provide an example of each.

9. What is an academic functional assessment? Provide an example of how to conduct such an assessment.

10. What are the key features of effective instructional methods? Why are they important?

8

Managing Behavior within the Classroom

The Think Time Strategy

Chapter Objectives

After studying this chapter, you should be able to:

- Characterize the distinctive properties of classrooms.
- Depict the underlying developmental psychology research base for the Think Time Strategy.
- Describe the underlying research base for the Think Time Strategy involving families of children who exhibit antisocial behaviors.
- Illustrate the underlying research base for the Think Time Strategy involving individuals with developmental delays.
- Describe the underlying research base for the Think Time Strategy involving student-teacher interactions in the classroom.
- Depict the underlying research base for the Think Time Strategy involving language deficits in students with social adjustment problems.
- Characterize the results of research conducted on the Think Time Strategy.
- Explain what teachers need to do to implement the Think Time Strategy.
- Illustrate the five parts to teaching students how the Think Time Strategy works in the classroom.
- Explain how Think Time is used.
- Describe common questions that arise when implementing the Think Time Strategy and be able to answer those questions.

VIGNETTE

SIXTH-GRADE TEACHER MS. KAMP has just finished a lesson in mathematics. She now expects the students to complete a number of assigned problems. Al begins disrupting his peers. Ms. Kamp tries to get Al to begin his assignment and stop bothering his peers. The interaction goes something like this:

Ms. Kamp:	Moving close to Al. "Al, it is time to get started with your math."
Al:	"What math?"
Ms. Kamp:	"The problems on page 12."
Al:	Starts on his math problems.
Ms. Kamp:	"Good work!" Moves away and begins to work with another student.
Al:	Calls out to a peer sitting across the room. "This math is stupid."
Ms. Kamp:	"Al, I need you to start working on your math and to be quiet. If you choose not to be quiet, you will get a yellow card."
Al:	"I don't care."
Ms. Kamp:	Places a yellow card on his desk (the first of two warnings she uses in her classroom management system before taking away a student's recess privilege).
Al:	Muttering under his breath. "She thinks I care about a yellow card."
Ms. Kamp:	In an agitated voice. "I really need you to be quiet and to get to work on your math."
Al:	Begins to work on his math but starts to talk to a classmate sitting close by.
Ms. Kamp:	"Al! I said stop. If you choose not to stop, that will be a blue card." (The blue card is his second warning.)
Al:	"Blue card, smue card."
Ms. Kamp:	Places a blue card on his desk (signifying that Al will lose his recess privilege).
Al:	"I don't care about your stupid recess." He throws his books on the floor.
Ms. Kamp:	"That behavior is unacceptable. I'm going to write an office referral."
Al:	"Go ahead, you'll pay."
Ms. Kamp:	Writes the office referral and sends Al to the office.

Ms. Kamp is finding that teacher-student interactions like this one are becoming far too common in her classroom. Growing numbers of students are coming to her classroom exhibiting chronic and severe forms of disruptive behaviors, and she wonders if there is anything she should be doing differently. The multiple warnings she gives students do not work very well for those with whom she has the most difficulty.

Overview

Unfortunately, many classroom management systems or strategies used by teachers do not work well. Teachers often respond to a student's problem behavior by ignoring it until they can no longer stand it or by using elaborate warning systems such as checks after a name or pulling different-colored cards. These responses to problem behaviors often result in more persistent chronic behavior patterns or escalate minor behaviors into more severe forms. The varying staff responses to problem behaviors are especially troublesome for difficult-to-teach students who are experiencing or are at risk for school failure. These students often work with several professionals throughout the day, each with different responses to problem behaviors. Although many students can handle the wide range of responses from staff, many of the difficult-to-teach students with whom teachers struggle are unable to manage these varying teacher responses.

This chapter describes the Think Time Strategy (Nelson & Carr, 2000), a validated classroom management strategy that can be used throughout the school, in individual classrooms, or with specific students. (A video-based training program is available from Sopris West: www.sopriswest.com.) The Think Time Strategy has been designated as an exemplary program by the U.S. Department of Education's Expert Panel on Safe, Disciplined, and Drug-Free Schools. The distinctive properties of the classroom environment that the Think Time Strategy is designed to address are discussed first, followed by an overview of the research base for the Think Time Strategy. Then comes a description of the process used to prepare for and implement the Think Time Strategy. The process is described in three sections: (1) preparing to implement the Think Time Strategy, (2) using the Think Time Strategy, and (3) answering common implementation questions.

What Are the Distinctive Properties of Classrooms That the Think Time Strategy Is Designed to Address?

Classrooms have distinctive properties that greatly affect teachers, regardless of how they organize students for learning or what management system they use (Doyle, 1986). In other words, a set of universal properties is in place in every classroom. These properties create constant pressures that shape teaching and classroom management. Although the intensity of their effects with regard to student behavior will vary with the particular conditions of every school, these pressures operate in all classrooms, regardless of how classrooms are organized and managed.

This discussion of the distinctive properties of classrooms comes first for a very important reason. Discussions of classroom management or the handling of misbehavior tend to emphasize the individual student as the target of the teacher's thinking and action, failing to capture the group or social dimension. Although the description of the Think Time Strategy is directed at how teachers respond to the problem behaviors of individual students, its effects must be viewed within the group dimension. The Think Time Strategy is designed to have a positive and powerful influence not only on individual students, but also on the group dynamics of classrooms and schools.

The group dynamics of classrooms and schools have several universal properties, including (1) multidimensionality, (2) simultaneity, (3) immediacy, (4) unpredictability, (5) publicness, and (6) history. Each of these is described below.

Multidimensionality

Multidimensionality refers to the large quantity of events and activities that occur on a continuous basis in classrooms. Classrooms are crowded places in which students with differing preferences and skills must use a restricted supply of resources to accomplish a broad range of social, academic, and personnel objectives. Instructional activities must be developed, carried off, and evaluated. A multitude of organizational functions, ranging from ordering and organizing supplies to taking roll and collecting student work, must be completed each day. Single events can have multiple collateral effects. For example, pausing to wait for a student to answer a question can not only influence that student's behavior and motivation but also throw off the pace of the lesson and the attention of the other students. In short, there are numerous choices that the teacher must make, none of them simple.

Simultaneity

Simultaneity refers to numerous events occurring at the same time in classrooms. While teaching a lesson, the teacher must monitor students' attention, acknowledge questions, keep track of time, and respond to problem behaviors. The number of simultaneous events can increase dramatically under common teaching arrangements. For example, the number of these events increases dramatically when the teacher moves from whole group instruction to cooperative groups or individual learning activities.

Immediacy

Immediacy refers to the rapid pace of classroom events. It is estimated that an elementary teacher has over 500 exchanges with individual students in a single day (Jackson, 1968). Of these exchanges, 20% to 50% can involve publicly evaluating student classroom conduct with either praise or reprimands. In such a fast-paced environment, teachers do not have the luxury of reflecting before acting.

Unpredictability

Unpredictability refers to classroom events taking unexpected turns. Distractions, interruptions, and unexpected events are common occurrences in classrooms. In short, it is often difficult for teachers to anticipate fully how a given activity or day will go.

Publicness

Publicness refers to the public places in which all events are witnessed by a large proportion of the students. Discipline-related issues are especially public events. Students notice if a teacher fails to recognize that a student is violating a rule or reprimands an innocent bystander. The publicness of discipline issues may actively encourage a student to continue or may cause others to join in once a disruption starts. Thus, the publicness of discipline matters can be magnified very quickly.

History

History refers to the class's accumulation of a common set of experiences, routines, and norms that provide the foundation for the classroom environment. Early exchanges, at a group or an individual level, often shape events for the rest of the year. Classes are also influenced by seasonal variations and the broad cycle of the school year. In short, planning for or responding to a single event must be done in the broader context of the class's history.

Taken together, the universal properties of classrooms described above play a large role in classroom management. The Think Time Strategy is designed to reduce the negative effects often associated with responses to problem behaviors that rely on multiple warnings and steps embedded within all classroom management approaches used in schools. A comparison of the relative effects of typical classroom management approaches that rely on multiple warnings and steps and the Think Time Strategy for each of the distinctive properties of classrooms is presented in Table 8.1.

What Is the Research Base for the Think Time Strategy?

In contrast to common classroom management strategies, the Think Time Strategy treats the problem behaviors of difficult-to-teach students as a chain rather than an event. In other words, the Think Time Strategy is built on the premise that there is an interpersonal relationship between the problem behaviors of difficult-to-teach students and the responses of their teachers (i.e., reciprocal effect between student-teacher behaviors) as well as an intrapersonal relationship across student and teacher behaviors (i.e., each individual's behav-

TABLE 8.1   *Potential Problems and Solutions to Each of the Distinctive Properties of Classrooms*

Property	Typical	Think Time
Multidimensionality	Increases the number of events that must be managed by the teacher and the number of collateral effects from discipline-related events	Does not add to the number of events that must be managed by the teacher and reduces the number of collateral effects from discipline-related events
Simultaneity	Increases the number of simultaneous events that occur in classroom	Does not add to the number of simultaneous events that occur in the classroom
Immediacy	Increases number of reprimands used by the teacher Requires extensive reflection on the part of the teacher prior to reacting	Decreases the number of reprimands used by the teacher Does not require extensive reflection on the part of the teacher prior to reacting
Unpredictability	Decreases the predictability of discipline-related events	Increases the predictability of discipline-related events
Publicness	Encourages the student to continue and/or others to join in	Discourages the student from continuing and others from joining in
History	Creates a negative historical connection across misbehaviors	Eliminates or reduces historical connection across misbehaviors

ior serves as an antecedent for subsequent behaviors). The net result of these inter- and intrapersonal effects is that problem behaviors develop into chronic behavior patterns or escalate minor problem behaviors into more severe forms.

Also in contrast to traditional classroom management strategies, the Think Time Strategy minimizes verbal interactions with students. Students who exhibit problem behaviors tend to have language deficits that make it difficult for them to manage the excessive dialogue of teachers' attempts to adjust student behavior. In the remainder of this section, six areas of research underlying the Think Time Strategy are discussed: (1) developmental psychology, (2) families of children who exhibit **antisocial behaviors,** (3) individuals with developmental delays, (4) student-teacher interactions in the classroom, (5) language deficits of students with social adjustment problems, and (6) research conducted on the Think Time Strategy. The first five areas of research focus on evidence supporting the premise that the problem behaviors of difficult-to-teach students should be viewed as chains rather than events. The last section focuses on studies conducted on the Think Time Strategy.

Developmental Psychology

A plethora of research on the reciprocal or interpersonal effects of child-adult behaviors has been conducted in developmental psychology. Reciprocal adult-child interactions occur when an individual's behavior serves as antecedents to subsequent behaviors. In the case of developmental psychology, evidence suggests that even global traits such as temperament systematically influence child-adult behaviors (Thomas, Chess, & Birch, 1968). Similarly, more subtle discrete child behaviors such as vocalization (Gewirtz & Boyd, 1977), crying (Murray, 1979), smiling (Bates, 1976), activity level (Stevens-Long, 1973), aggression (Faggot, 1984), and speech (Bohannon & Marquis, 1977) have an effect on adult behaviors and vice versa. Regardless of the area, developmental psychologists have demonstrated that much of what children learn occurs through a reciprocal process in which the adult models for and responds to the particular behaviors of children. For example, in the case of social interactions, most of the intricacies of what children must learn about complex social behaviors and language are acquired in this manner through reciprocal interactions with their parents or caregivers by the age of 5 (Patterson, 1982b).

Families of Children Who Exhibit Antisocial Behaviors

Patterson (1982a) developed a theoretical framework (i.e., coercion theory) and provided supporting evidence for the interpersonal nature of child-parent interactions within families of children who exhibit antisocial behaviors. Patterson reported that the immediate effects of parents' attempts to stop (i.e., threats and scolding) the problem behaviors of their children not only made the situation worse (in terms of persistence and escalation) but also played a key role in establishing ongoing coercive family interactions.

The coercive family interaction patterns work as follows. Instead of withdrawing their command, the parent appeals for compliance; the child in turn increases the intensity of his or her behavior, which evokes physical guidance from the parent. This behavior in turn evokes a resistant push from the child, which evokes physical guidance from the parent, which is then followed by a slap on the buttocks from the parent, resulting in a tantrum by the child, to which the parent responds finally by withdrawing the command. Within this context is a shaping process that leads to more coercive interactions, resulting in powerful training of children in antisocial behaviors.

In general, parents of children with antisocial behavior seldom follow through on their threats. Children are aware of that and respond to most of the parents' threats, insults, humiliations, and scolding with counterattacks. From the children's standpoint, these attempts do not signal that punishment will follow. That is, children do not consider aversive consequences delivered by their parents as signals for them to stop but rather as irritants and elicitors of counterattack. This process has been called *nattering*. An example of the nattering process that occurs in families is depicted in Figure 8.1.

Individuals with Developmental Delays

Individuals with developmental delays who exhibit problem behaviors typically exhibit a sequence of such behaviors (e.g., off task, arguing, defiance, physical aggression) that occur together in some manner. Behaviors that occur together (covary) have been described or categorized as a functional response class (Evans & Meyer, 1985; Evans, Meyer, Kurkjian, & Kishi, 1988; Foxx, 1982; Millenson & Leslie, 1979; Voeltz & Evans, 1982; Wahler, 1975). A functional response class is defined as a group of topographically different behaviors that produce the same functional effect (Carr, 1988; Johnston & Pennypacker, 1980; Millenson & Leslie, 1979). For example, a student may use many different responses, some valued and others considered problematic, to obtain attention from a teacher (e.g., raise hand, look at the teacher and smile, throw materials and scream). To the

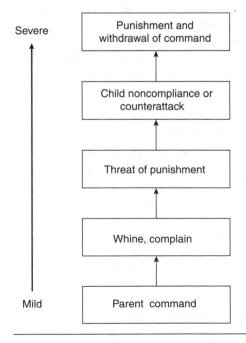

FIGURE 8.1   *Example of the nattering process.*

extent that each response (regardless of whether it is valued or not) is maintained (i.e., re-inforced) by access to teacher attention, these responses may all be viewed as members of the same functional response class.

Finally, as in developmental psychology, the problem behaviors individuals with developmental disabilities exhibit are a dyadic (i.e., a chain of responses) phenomenon rather than a monadic (i.e., a single event) phenomenon (e.g., Johnston & Pennypacker, 1980). That is, individuals with developmental delays who exhibit problem behaviors typically engage in behaviors that are offensive to those with whom they interact. The reciprocal nature of this interaction often results in the maintenance or escalation of the intensity of the problematic behaviors over time. Indeed, recent advances in the use of functional behavioral assessments (described in Chapter 10) were derived from an increased understanding of the reciprocal nature of problem behaviors.

Student-Teacher Interactions in the Classroom

Research on student-teacher interactions in the classroom supports the notion that problem behaviors should be viewed as chains rather than events. Shores and his colleagues (e.g., Shores, Gunter, Denny, & Jack, 1993; Shores, Jack, et al., 1993) demonstrated that the aggressive behaviors of students have a negative interpersonal effect on the extent to which teachers interact with children. Similarly, teachers' use of positive statements has a positive interpersonal effect on the rates of problem behaviors exhibited by children with emotional or behavioral disorders.

Nelson and Roberts (2000) extended the work of Shores and his colleagues by studying the *ongoing* interpersonal (i.e., reciprocal effect between student-teacher behaviors) and intrapersonal (i.e., individual's behaviors serve as an antecedent for subsequent ones) sequence of child-teacher interactions around classroom problems in general education classrooms. They reported that the ongoing interaction behaviors of children and teachers around such problems remained relatively constant over time and appeared to be uninfluenced by contextual factors (e.g., content area, time of day, and teacher proximity). These findings suggest strong intra- and interpersonal effects associated with child-teacher interactions around classroom problems.

In summary, the findings parallel those from research conducted with families of children who exhibit antisocial behaviors. As a general case, the findings indicate that teachers seldom follow through on their threats or warnings to difficult-to-teach students to stop problem behaviors, replicating the nattering process that occurs in families of children who exhibit antisocial behaviors (see Figure 8.2). Teachers experience some behaviors of students as unpleasant and wish them to stop. They usually indicate their initial displeasure with these behaviors by using subtle nonverbal cues such as eye contact or physical proximity. To the difficult-to-teach students, these cues signal no intention to follow through. Teachers then resort to using threats or warnings (usually a part of their classroom management system) to signal their displeasure with the students' behavior. The net goal of teachers is to avoid a conflict with the students that would accompany their efforts to confront them and make them stop what they are doing. In other words, teachers do not actually try to stop the problem behavior of students; rather, they only ineptly meddle in it. The effect of teacher nattering is to produce extensions of the problem behaviors that only evoke more intense displeasure on their part.

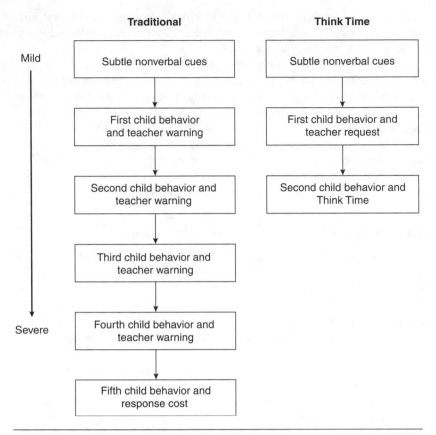

FIGURE 8.2   *Traditional classroom management systems versus the Think Time Strategy.*

Language Deficits of Students with Social Adjustment Problems

Successful language acquisition is critical for achieving positive social adjustment and responding to teacher requests to adjust students' problem behaviors. Many school-age children with social adjustment problems also exhibit deficits in the area of language (Kaiser, Hancock, Cai, Foster, & Hester, 2000). Both language problems and social adjustment problems emerge from the same etiological and environmental factors (e.g., parent-child interactions). Conversely, delays in language may worsen social adjustment problems.

The co-occurrence of language deficit and social adjustment problems is well documented (Redmond & Rice, 1998). Moreover, there is evidence of increased risk for school failure and for long-term social adjustment problems associated with the co-occurrence of language and behavior problems (Hinshaw, 1992). For example, young children from low-income families are more likely to evidence both language and behavioral problems than are middle-class children (Delaney & Kaiser, 1997). In general, this research has found that students with emotional or behavioral disorders differed from typical peers in that they (1) scored significantly below average in language ability, (2) made more errors in language, (3) showed poor topic maintenance, (4) produced more inappropriate responses, (5) demonstrated a greater use of situationally inappropriate language, and (6) had greater difficulties with nonverbal communication (Camarata, Hughes, & Ruhl, 1988; McConough, 1989; Walker & Leister, 1994).

Research Conducted on the Think Time Strategy

Taken together, research in developmental psychology—with families, with individuals with developmental delays, and in classrooms—on the reciprocal effects of child-adult behaviors suggests that the problem behaviors exhibited by difficult-to-teach students are dyadic events (chain of responses) rather than monadic ones (single events). Because such behaviors may be dyadic events, the intra- and interpersonal reciprocal influences that occur around minor problems may lead to more severe forms of challenging behaviors in the classroom. In addition, research on the language deficits of students with behavioral disorders suggests that many difficult-to-teach students are incapable of dealing with the excessive dialogue of teachers around incidents of problem behavior, resulting in frustration on the part of the students and an increased probability of severe challenging behaviors.

Based on this research, Nelson and his colleagues (Nelson, 1996a; Nelson, Martella, & Galand, 1998) hypothesized that teachers' responses (e.g., turning of cards, checks after names, repeated warnings and reprimands) to the minor problems of students who exhibit behavior problems may actually result in intra- and interpersonal reciprocal behavioral sequences in which individuals' responses (both students and teachers) become more intense and problematic. If that is the case, the minor classroom problems of students who exhibit behavior problems may not only serve as antecedents for teachers' responses (e.g., reprimands) but also serve as antecedents for subsequent severe challenging behaviors (see Figure 8.2).

Nelson (1996b) examined the effects of setting clear limits in combination with the Think Time Strategy for problem behaviors on school survival skills, social adjustment, and academic performance of a group of difficult-to-teach students. Comparisons between target (i.e., those with or at risk of emotional and behavioral disorders) and criterion (i.e., those without and not at risk of emotional and behavioral disorders) students indicated positive effects on the social adjustment (effect size = 0.81), academic performance (effect size = 0.92), and school survival skills (effect size = 0.84) of the target students.

Building on this work, Nelson et al. (1998) conducted a component analysis to provide more conclusive information on the effects of the Think Time Strategy on severe challenging behaviors that require an administrative intervention (e.g., suspension). The results indicated that the strategy alone resulted in a 70% decrease in such behaviors. Finally, Nelson, Gutierrez-Ohrman, Roberts, and Smith (2000) examined the effects of the Think Time Strategy on the severe challenging behaviors (behavioral earthquakes) of 24 students with behavior difficulties. The results indicated that the group of students who exhibited behavior problems had fewer severe challenging behaviors following the implementation of the Think Time Strategy. If the average treatment effects were extrapolated over the course of the school year, the group of children with emotional and behavioral disorders would have exhibited more than 1,200 fewer severe challenging behaviors. Further, individual children would have exhibited approximately 20 severe challenging behaviors over the course of the school year, compared with more than 90 prior to the implementation of the Think Time Strategy.

What Do Teachers Need to Do to Implement the Think Time Strategy?

The four steps in preparing to implement the Think Time Strategy are relatively simple and straightforward: (1) identify cooperating teachers, (2) physically prepare the classroom, (3) inform parents, and (4) teach students how the Think Time Strategy works in the classroom.

Identify Cooperating Teachers

The first step in preparing to implement the Think Time Strategy is to identify a cooperating set of teachers. The Think Time Strategy requires teamwork between two or more teachers. The cooperating teachers' classroom (Think Time classroom) should be located in close proximity to a second classroom, thereby reducing the amount of travel time and the potential for problems when these students are moving to the Think Time classroom.

Physically Prepare the Classroom

The second step in preparing to implement the Think Time Strategy is to physically prepare the classroom. Typically, teachers will place two to three desks in a designated Think Time area, an area free of visual distractions such as posters or traffic. Furthermore, this area should be located in a low-use area of the classroom that is *not* in close proximity to where the students in the classroom are working.

Inform Parents

The third step in preparing to implement the Think Time Strategy is to inform parents how the Think Time Strategy will be used in the classroom. Teachers should develop and send home a parent information letter. A sample parent information letter is presented in Table 8.2. The Think Time Strategy should also be discussed with parents during conference time or other informational meetings.

Teach Students How the Think Time Strategy Works in the Classroom

The final step in preparing to implement the Think Time Strategy is to teach students how the procedure works in the classroom. Like all procedures, rehearsing and making the Think Time Strategy a routine will make it less susceptible to breakdowns, because students will have learned the normal sequence of steps. It is important that students learn classroom rules and expectations before they are taught the Think Time Strategy. In addi-

TABLE 8.2 *Example of a Parent Letter*

Dear Parent/Guardian:

I am writing in regard to my classroom discipline plan. I am committed to quality education for all students. All students deserve the most positive educational climate possible for academic and social growth. I have a set of well-defined classroom rules that were developed to promote a safe, nurturing classroom environment that is conducive to learning. To create such an environment, I teach, encourage, coach, and reinforce appropriate behavior to help students follow the classroom rules.

I also use a discipline technique called THINK TIME to create a positive educational climate whenever any student exhibits a behavior that is disruptive to the class. The technique emphasizes the seriousness of education, respectfulness of the classroom environment, and the importance of students taking responsibility for their own behavior. THINK TIME has two parts. The first part is designed to allow students to focus and gain self-control by asking them to either sit off to the side or move to another classroom. The second part involves providing the student with feedback about his or her behavior and an opportunity for him or her to plan for future success in the classroom.

I will notify you when your child has been directed to THINK TIME three or more times within a school week. In addition, I will ask for your assistance if problems persist or if a problem is unusually challenging.

I encourage you to join me in a cooperative and supportive effort to provide a safe school and classroom environment that is conducive to learning. Feel free to call me at _____ if you should have any questions. Please sign the section below to indicate that you have read this letter, and return it to me as soon as possible.

I look forward to working with you to make this a productive school year for your child.

Sincerely,

_____   _____

Parent/Guardian Signature   Date

tion, the instruction should be carried out in the natural context of the classroom and the receiving classroom to help acclimate the students to the procedure. This step is especially important for younger students and those students who exhibit challenging behavior. These students should be provided with additional practice to ensure mastery of the steps involved in the Think Time Strategy.

There are five distinct parts to a teaching plan on how the Think Time Strategy will be used in the classroom: (1) providing a rationale, (2) teaching that certain behaviors will result in the use of the Think Time Strategy, (3) teaching how to move to and enter the designated Think Time classroom, (4) showing what is involved during the Think Time period and behavioral debriefing process, and (5) instructing students about how to rejoin the classroom. Teaching how the Think Time Strategy will be used is much the same as teaching any other classroom routine. The teacher should actively discuss the procedure, give examples and nonexamples of problem behaviors, check for understanding, and provide practice in how the procedure is accomplished. Actively teaching students how the Think Time Strategy will work in the classroom will ensure that students fully understand why the teacher is using this strategy and how it will work in the classroom. Such knowledge will lead to more time to teach content because students will have already learned how to go through the process. In addition, the entire instructional sequence should be positive and matter of fact.

The specific teaching plan for teaching students how the Think Time Strategy will work in the classroom follows.

Rationale.   The rationale for the Think Time Strategy should focus on three areas. First, the teacher should communicate that the overall goal is for the students to succeed and enjoy the class. Teachers will not allow students to do anything that interferes with their or someone else's success. Second, teachers should communicate the importance of creating a safe and orderly learning environment to ensure everyone's success. They should indicate that a safe and orderly learning environment will set a positive tone for learning in the classroom. Finally, teachers must communicate that it is important for everyone to control their own behavior and that the Think Time Strategy will help them learn how to develop self-control.

Understanding Those Behaviors That Will Result in the Use of the Think Time Strategy.   Following the rationale for the use of the Think Time Strategy, teachers should discuss and model for students those behaviors that interfere with the learning and teaching processes. This discussion does not center solely on classroom rules. Rather, teachers should discuss with students the full range of behaviors that interfere with these processes. Teachers can brainstorm with students to identify these behaviors. Older students (second grade and up) are fully aware of those behaviors that interfere with the teaching and learning processes.

Next, teachers must tell students that teachers will *not* necessarily respond immediately with the Think Time Strategy because they believe that students can control their own behavior. Sometimes they will give students some subtle reminders such as eye contact, physical proximity, and or purposely ignore their behaviors in an attempt to help them gain self-control. If these subtle reminders do *not* work, teachers will use the Think Time Strategy. At other times, the Think Time Strategy is used immediately if it is necessary (e.g., chronic or serious behavior). The overall goal is to give students an opportunity to self-correct their behavior.

Regardless of the situation, the Think Time Strategy is used after students fail to comply with a teacher's request to change their behavior (e.g., "I need your attention"). It is important to highlight for students that teachers will respond more quickly (for lower-level behaviors) than they are accustomed. In addition, teachers should let students know that in Think Time, they need to be completely silent and only respond to the classroom teacher. Students in the Think Time classroom who are not in Think Time should ignore the student in their classroom who is in the designated Think Time area. Teachers should discuss with students the importance of not becoming involved in the problems of other students and inform students that it will be considered a serious infraction if they do (e.g., warranting an immediate Think Time or some other established response cost).

Moving to and Entering the Designated Think Time Classroom. Teaching students to leave the room for Think Time involves teaching them (1) the signal used to cue students to leave the classroom, (2) how they are to leave the classroom, and (3) how they are to enter the designated Think Time classroom. Teachers should discuss and model for the students the signal used to cue them to leave the room for Think Time. Although there are numerous ways to signal students to leave the room, the least intrusive signal to classroom activities that involves little or no verbal communication with the students should be used. Teachers may use a hand signal, hand students a pass, or give students a short verbal directive. Students should be given time to comply; if not, the signal might be perceived as an ultimatum. Teachers should ensure that their verbal directives are not delivered as threats, ultimatums, or warnings, such as, "If you don't…, you will have to go to the Think Time classroom."

Next, teachers should discuss and model for students how they would like them to leave the classroom and what teachers want students to do. The following are some examples and nonexamples that can be used to demonstrate this step in the classroom.

Examples
- Leave the classroom quickly without argument.
- Leave the classroom in a controlled fashion.
- Proceed quickly to the designated Think Time classroom when directed to do so by the teacher.

Nonexamples
- Ignore signal, leave slowly, or argue with the teacher.
- Leave noisily (e.g., stomping, slamming books or door, rolling eyes, pouting).
- Walk slowly, talk to other teachers and students, or stop in the restroom.

Finally, teachers should discuss and model what the students are to do when they get to the designated Think Time classroom. There are two distinct things to teach students: (1) the signal that the receiving teacher will use to direct students to the designated desk in the classroom for Think Time and (2) how to enter the designated room properly. Step 1 is best accomplished by having the teacher actually teach students the signal ahead of time. Again, although there are numerous ways to signal students to proceed to the designated desk, the teacher should select one that is the least intrusive to classroom activities and involves little or no verbal communication with the students. The teacher can use a hand signal or short verbal directive similar to the one used by the former classroom teacher.

For the second step, teachers should discuss and model for students how they would like students to enter the Think Time classroom (in a controlled fashion) and what teachers do not want them to do (act in an uncontrolled fashion). The following are some examples and nonexamples that can be used to demonstrate this step to the class.

Examples
- Enter the classroom and stand quietly in the doorway until directed to a designated desk by the teacher.
- Stand in the doorway in a controlled fashion.
- Proceed quickly to the designated desk when directed to do so by the teacher.

Nonexamples
- Enter the classroom and proceed immediately to the designated desk without teacher direction.
- Stand noisily (e.g., stomping, moving around, slamming the door, rolling eyes, pouting).
- Ignore the signal, walk slowly, talk to students, stop and look at something.

Think Time Period and Debriefing Process.   Teachers should discuss and model for students how they are to sit at the designated desk in the Think Time classroom including: (1) sit quietly and (2) wait for instructions from the teacher. The goal is to give students an opportunity to calm down and regain self-control. Keep in mind that although students should sit quietly and wait for the teacher to give them instructions, teachers should limit the number of tasks students have to accomplish at the same time (e.g., having their feet flat on the floor, back straight). The following are some examples and nonexamples that can be used to demonstrate this step in the classroom.

Examples
- Sit quietly at the desk in a controlled fashion and wait for the teacher.
- Wait for instructions from the teacher.

Nonexamples
- Sit noisily at the desk (e.g., tapping fingers, slamming fists).
- Slump in the desk, roll eyes, and pout.
- Raise hand or call out to the teacher in an inappropriate fashion.

Next, teachers should discuss and model for the students how the debriefing process is conducted: (1) the **debriefing** process is initiated by the teacher when students are calm, (2) the debriefing process begins when the cooperating teacher asks students to describe the behavior that initiated Think Time objectively, (3) the debriefing form is completed, and (4) the debriefing responses are checked by the cooperating teacher. The debriefing form asks students three questions (see Table 8.3). The goals of debriefing are to check whether students have gained self-control and to provide them an opportunity to plan or think about how they can avoid going to Think Time in the future. Keep in mind that the student's behavior is more important than the amount of time spent in Think Time. The

TABLE 8.3   *Behavior Debriefing Form*

Name: _____   Date: _____

Teacher: _____   Grade: _____

Arrival Time: _____   Departure Time: _____

1. What was your behavior? _____

_____

_____

2. What behavior do you need to display when you go back to your classroom?

_____

_____

3. Will you be able to do it? ___ Yes ___ No ___ I need to see the teacher

_____

_____

following are some examples and nonexamples that can be used to demonstrate this step in the classroom.

Examples
- When asked by the teacher, identify inappropriate behavior that initiated the Think Time.
- Complete the debriefing form by accurately identifying inappropriate behavior, what the students need to do (replacement behavior) when they go back to the classroom (e.g., follow directions if they did not follow directions before), and whether the students think they can or cannot do the new action(s).
- Wait for the teacher to check the debriefing responses.

Nonexamples
- Ignore teacher instructions.
- When asked by the teacher, fail to respond (e.g., "I don't know") to the teacher's question regarding the inappropriate behavior that initiated the Think Time.
- Fail to complete the debriefing form or do not accurately identify the inappropriate behavior or what they need to do (replacement behavior) when the students go back to the classroom (e.g., follow directions if the student did not follow directions before).
- Do not wait for the teacher to check the debriefing responses.

Rejoining the Class

Teaching the students to rejoin the class involves teaching them (1) to wait at the door in a controlled fashion until the teachers can check the accuracy of the debriefing form, (2) how the debriefing form will be handled, and (3) the reentry procedures the teachers will use to ensure that students are able to make up the work they missed. The teacher should discuss and model for students that they are to wait at the door in a controlled fashion (e.g., quietly and no physical movement and gestures) until the teacher can check the accuracy of the debriefing form. Furthermore, the teacher should note that the students will simply be directed to sit at their desk when the teacher is engaged in teaching a lesson. In those situations, the teacher will check their debriefing form after finishing the lesson.

Next, teachers should discuss and model for students how the debriefing form is handled and checked for accuracy. If the form is inaccurate, teachers will simply direct students back to the Think Time classroom. Teachers will not discuss what information is inaccurate on the debriefing form, and students cannot ask teachers. Students are to proceed back to the Think Time classroom in a controlled fashion, decide what information is inaccurate, and correct it on a new debriefing form. If the form is accurate, teachers will direct students in a positive manner (positive voice inflection, praise, etc.) to join the class. Students should learn the types of reentry procedures that will be used to ensure that they make up the work they missed (e.g., peer assistance, assignment sheet, or teacher works with students directly). The following are some examples and nonexamples that can be used to demonstrate this step in the classroom.

Examples
- Enter the classroom and stand in the doorway in a controlled fashion (e.g., quietly and no physical movement and gestures).
- Wait for the teacher to check the debriefing form.
- Join the class when prompted by the teacher.
- Complete work missed while in Think Time.

Nonexamples
- Enter the classroom and proceed immediately to the designated desk without teacher prompting.
- Stand at the door in an uncontrolled fashion (e.g., stomping, shuffling, slamming the door, rolling eyes, laughing).
- Do not complete work missed while in Think Time.

How Is the Think Time Strategy Used?

Before describing the key steps in the Think Time Strategy, it is important to discuss the importance of "withitness" to the implementation of the Think Time Strategy. **"Withitness"** is defined as a teacher's ability to communicate an overall awareness of the classroom to the students. Students' tendency to exhibit problem behaviors is directly linked to the teacher's level of awareness of what is occurring in the classroom. A "witht" teacher demonstrates an awareness of times of high probability for problem behaviors, increases monitoring, and takes preventative steps. A "witit" teacher also demonstrates an awareness of whether or not students comply with teacher attempts to redirect behavior. For example, the teacher who tells a student to stop disturbing her classmate and then ignores that the student failed to comply is inviting challenges and is reducing credibility. Although the elimination of threats or warnings in the Think Time Strategy increases the "withitness" of teachers, it is critical that teachers demonstrate "withitness."

The Think Time Strategy includes three interventions common to schools: (1) effective request (i.e., elimination of threats, ultimatums, warnings, or repeated requests), (2) **antiseptic bounding** (quiet reflective period in which everyone disengages from the student), and (3) behavioral debriefing. Again, the Think Time Strategy requires teamwork between two or more teachers (i.e., the homeroom teacher and a cooperating teacher who provided the designated Think Time area). There are five interrelated steps in the Think Time Strategy: (1) catching problem behavior early, (2) moving to and entering the designated Think Time classroom, (3) experiencing the Think Time period and debriefing process, (4) checking students' debriefing responses, (5) and rejoining the class. Many of the steps presented here are restatements of the Think Time Strategy presented earlier, but it is critical to understand and implement the strategy for it to be effective.

Catching Problem Behavior Early

It is critical that teachers catch the problem behavior of students early and eliminate the use of threats, ultimatums, warnings, or repeated requests. In the case of minor behavior (e.g., off task), teachers should reinforce (e.g., praise) students if they comply with a request or prompt to adjust their behavior. If students do not comply, they are directed to a designated classroom for Think Time. For more serious problem behaviors (e.g., profanity), teachers should simply direct students to a designated classroom for Think Time. Communication with students in both cases should be limited, unemotional, and matter of fact. The goal is to reduce verbal communication with students due to the potential reinforcing effects of teacher behavior on the problem behavior.

Moving to and Entering the Designated Think Time Classroom

Students will move independently to the designated Think Time classroom. For problematic students, teachers should use a strategy to ensure that students move quickly and efficiently to the designated classroom. Some of the strategies that might be considered are tracking the amount of time students take to arrive at the designated classroom, using a student escort, or using a designated classroom in close proximity that will enable easy monitoring of students (e.g., classroom directly across the hallway or next door). Once students arrive at the designated classroom, they stand by the classroom door and wait until the cooperating teacher directs them to a designated Think Time desk. Again, the desk should be located in an area that is free from distractions and that limits the ability of students to engage teachers or other students.

Experiencing the Think Time Period and Debriefing Process

After the cooperating teacher has observed students sitting calmly during the Think Time period or antiseptic bounding condition, the teacher approaches them and initiates the debriefing process. The debriefing is always conducted at the first opportunity after students have been calm and ideally after allowing the misbehaving students a minimum of 3 to 5 minutes to "think about" their behavior and gain self-control. The antiseptic bounding condition is behavior dependent (not time dependent). The debriefing process begins when the cooperating teacher asks the students to describe the behavior that initiated Think Time objectively. This brief question helps the teacher determine if the students have gained self-control and are ready to return to the classroom. After an acceptable (e.g., calm, objective) description of the behavior has been provided by the students, the cooperating teacher gives them a behavior debriefing form to complete (see Table 8.3). The form is completed independently unless students are unable to do so. In such cases, the cooperating teacher conducts a verbal debriefing and writes the students' responses on the form. If the students are not responsive to the question about the behavior that led to Think Time, the teacher responds by saying, "I'll get back to you," and then returns to regular duties until another appropriate break arrives and the students are sitting calmly. Throughout this process, the cooperating teacher does not cajole the students and is not drawn into a discussion with them. The students must figure out the inappropriate behavior on their own and gain self-control. Again, all interactions with students should be limited, unemotional, and matter of fact.

Checking Students' Debriefing Responses

After the students complete the behavior debriefing form, they wait for the cooperating teacher to check the form to see if it was completed correctly (inappropriate and replacement behaviors were stated in objective terms, and the students indicated that they were ready to go back to their classroom). At this point, the cooperating teacher does not know which problem behavior the students had actually exhibited that initiated the Think Time. If the form is filled out correctly, the cooperating teacher directs the students back to their classroom with the completed form. If the form is filled out incorrectly, the students remain in Think Time. The cooperating teacher responds by saying "I'll get back to you" and returns to regular duties until another appropriate break arrives (and the students are sitting calmly). The entire debriefing process is repeated until the students complete the form correctly.

Rejoining the Class

When the students reenter the classroom, they stand by the door and wait until the teacher acknowledges them. The teachers then assess the accuracy of the completed form. If the debriefing form is inaccurate, the students are directed back to the designated classroom to repeat Think Time.

Summary

In summary, the Think Time Strategy is used in combination with other interventions and approaches. Throughout Think Time, teachers are not drawn into a discussion with students. All interactions are limited, unemotional, and matter of fact. There is no set time limit on when the cooperating teacher approaches students to complete the debriefing process. The time required for the Think Time Strategy is dependent on the student (how long it takes him or her to calm down and be responsive to positive adult-student interactions) and on when the cooperating teacher has a moment to conduct the debriefing (waiting for an appropriate moment when interacting with students will be least disruptive to the class).

What Common Questions Arise When Implementing the Think Time Strategy?

A number of common questions arise when the Think Time Strategy is implemented in the classroom. The questions and associated answers follow.

Should We Use Other Consequences or Responses to Problem Behaviors?

The use of the Think Time Strategy should not be viewed as the only response to problem behaviors. It should be used flexibly with other school and classroom strategies and consequences (e.g., proximity, eye contact, planned ignoring). The Think Time Strategy in itself is a powerful enough response to most minor problem behaviors, but additional contingencies such as parent contacts, response cost, and administrative referrals in the case of chronic or severe problem behaviors may also be appropriate. Teachers should establish some other consequences for a certain number (e.g., 3 or 4 per week) of Think Times to ensure parent contact and the development of a comprehensive behavioral intervention and support plan.

What Should We Expect from Students during Think Time?

The Think Time Strategy is designed to provide the students an opportunity to gain self-control, reflect on their behavior, and plan for future success. Students are expected to meet two behavioral guidelines: keeping completely silent and controlled, and only responding to the teacher. Students are not expected to meet overly rigid behavioral guidelines such as keeping their feet flat on the floor or their eyes straight ahead.

What Do We Expect from Other Students throughout the Think Time Strategy?

Other students are expected to ignore students going to or already in Think Time. Failure to do so is considered a serious infraction, and offending students immediately go to Think Time or receive an additional response cost.

Does Every Teacher in the School Need to Use the Think Time Strategy?

Although, as described in Chapter 3, it is important for schools to use a consistent response to problem behaviors, it is not necessary for all teachers to use the Think Time Strategy. Only two or more teachers are needed to implement the Think Time Strategy.

What Happens When a Student Will Not Leave the Classroom?

Before directly addressing this question, teachers should look carefully at whether the problem behavior was caught early. Teachers sometimes inadvertently engage students several times before using the Think Time Strategy. This engagement sometimes agitates students and causes them to be highly defiant.

Instead, a strategy called "meeting force with patience" should be implemented. This strategy involves cueing (e.g., telephoning) a colleague (e.g., counselor, administrator, or crisis response team) to come to the classroom and sit next to the student. Teachers continue to work with the other students. A colleague comes into the room, sits next to the student and waits a few minutes or until he or she believes that the student is calm, and then cues the student to leave the classroom. If the student complies, the student is directed to the principal's office and receives the established administrative-level disciplinary response for defiance. If the student does not comply, this colleague should stop attending to the student and wait until the next appropriate moment (i.e., believes the student is calm) to cue the student to leave the classroom. The student is directed to complete Think Time when he or she returns from the principal's office. The student completes Think Time regardless of the administrative response. Although it is not necessarily problematic for students to be noncompliant periodically, teachers should look closely at developing a comprehensive behavioral program for those students who are continually resistant and noncompliant.

What Should We Do with a Student Who Is in Think Time during Lunch, Recess, Planning Times, or at the End of the School Day?

Although it would be ideal for students to complete Think Time prior to re-engaging in any activity, that is often difficult to accomplish in schools. In such cases, the students complete the activity and then must complete Think Time prior to returning to the classroom. For example, say it is the end of the day and a student is still in Think Time. The cooperating teacher would simply let the student leave at the end of the day (student would stop at the classroom to pick up needed items). The next day the teacher would direct the student back to the Think Time classroom at the start of the day.

What Should We Do about Substitute Teachers?

Substitute teachers typically send students to Think Time but do not receive students unless they have been trained to use the Think Time Strategy. Many schools have substitute teachers watch the training tape *The Think Time™ Strategy for Schools...Bringing Order to the Classroom* available from Sopris West (www.sopriswest.com) and have them implement the strategy as typically used in the classroom. When substitute teachers have not been trained, they should be provided with a guide to help them understand how they can use the Think Time Strategy. An example of a substitute teacher's guide is presented in Table 8.4.

Can We Start the Think Time Strategy Anytime?

Although, as with all classroom routines, it is easier to implement the Think Time Strategy at the start of the school year, teachers can easily implement it anytime. Of course, if it is implemented later in the year, the first few days will be a little busy.

How Long Is Too Long for Think Time?

If a student spends a long time in Think Time, the problem behavior may not have been caught early enough. Teachers should implement an administrative intervention if students are still noncompliant and defiant after 30 to 40 minutes. Again, students would complete Think Time when they return from the principal's office or, in those cases in which the principal suspended students, the next time they enter the classroom. Again, teachers should consider developing a comprehensive behavioral program for students who are continually resistant and noncompliant.

TABLE 8.4   *Example of a Substitute Teacher's Guide*

The Think Time Strategy is the technique I use in response to disruptive behavior. Think Time is designed to be educational, not punitive. Therefore, it is important not to threaten a student with Think Time. Just do it! The remainder of this letter describes how you should use the Think Time Strategy.

Redirect, remind, or encourage the student to adjust his or her behavior only *once* when you believe that a student is misbehaving. If the student's behavior does not change, simply say, "Go to room _____." Say this in a matter-of-fact, unemotional way. Then go on teaching as if nothing happened. Expect the student to do as he or she was told. All the students in my class are familiar with the steps in the Think Time Strategy. If the student does not go to room _____, simply send him or her to the office. If the student will not go call the office, ask for the assistance of the principal. It is the student's responsibility to behave, not yours. You are responsible for teaching.

When the student returns from "Think Time," check the Behavior Debriefing Form to be sure that it accurately reflects the reason he or she was sent from the classroom. If the Behavior Debriefing Form is blatantly false or if there is subsequent misbehavior, simply repeat the process. Be helpful and positive to the student if he or she has completed the Behavior Debriefing Form accurately. Help the student get back on track. Leave a note for me if the student does not complete Think Time before school is dismissed. It may also be helpful to alert the principal.

You are not expected to receive students sent in for "Think Time." Simply direct a student to room _____ if one should come in.

Please feel free to ask one of the students to explain Think Time to you if you have any questions. Have a great day!

How Often Should We Use the Think Time Strategy?

Teachers should establish a specific level of Think Time usage per week (e.g., 3 or 4 per student), with an additional response cost such as parent contact or detention when a student reaches or exceeds that level. This strategy typically keeps Think Time usage to a minimum. Teachers should also monitor students who receive that additional response cost and develop a comprehensive behavioral program for students who are in Think Time too frequently.

What about the Loss of Instructional Time?

Research (e.g., Nelson, 1996b) has shown that the Think Time Strategy does not adversely affect academic achievement. Indeed, the Think Time Strategy typically has a positive effect on academic achievement because it enables teachers to maintain a focus on teaching by suppressing problem behaviors quickly and efficiently. Consequently, the level of problem behaviors exhibited by students decreases because they are actively engaged in the learning activity.

How Should We Use the Think Time Strategy with Students Who Exhibit Highly Explosive and Challenging Behaviors?

The Think Time Strategy can be effectively used with students who exhibit highly explosive and challenging behaviors. Before going on, note that a comprehensive behavioral program needs to be developed for these students. It is clear that the Think Time Strategy alone will not address all the factors underlying explosive and challenging behaviors.

Teachers should use the Think Time Strategy when they see the subtle signs or triggers that precede explosive and challenging behaviors. The Think Time Strategy should be used when teachers encounter the subtle signs such as being nonconversational, sighing loudly, or slamming books and chairs that precede such behaviors. In these cases, it is important to discuss with students how the Think Time Strategy will be used. For example, a teacher might say, "John, I've noticed that when you…., things do not go well. When I see you…, I'm going to ask you to go to Think Time. I'm not sending you to Think Time because…is a problem behavior. Rather, I'm sending you to Think Time so that you don't exhibit a problem behavior."

How Can We Tell If We Are Using the Think Time Strategy Appropriately?

As detailed above, the Think Time Strategy fits contextually with classroom routines and interventions. Thus, the appropriate use of the Think Time Strategy must be viewed within all the other contextual factors related to classroom management. An evaluation form to evaluate whether the Think Time Strategy is being used appropriately is presented in Table 8.5.

TABLE 8.5 *Think Time Strategy Evaluation Checklist*

The Think Time Strategy evaluation checklist is designed to assess a teacher's strengths when implementing Think Time. The checklist can be used by an independent observer or can be completed by the teacher. The evaluation questions are provided as a guide to the primary behaviors that exemplify the effective use of the Think Time Strategy. Feel free to add evaluation questions if you think such additions will increase the practicality and sensitivity of the evaluation process. In addition, please make supporting notes that will help describe any problems in more detail.

Rating scale: 1, No change; 2, Minor problems; 3, Major problems

Skill 1. Setting and implementing rules and routines

Evaluation Questions	Rating and Notes
a. Does the teacher provide a set of rules?	
b. Do the rules specify behaviors needed for productive instructional and classroom interactions?	
c. Does the teacher have well-established classroom routines?	

Skill 2. Appropriate behavior recognized and validated

Evaluation Questions	Rating and Notes
a. Is teacher praise specific and contingent?	
b. Is teacher praise delivered in a credible manner?	
c. Does the teacher recognize appropriate academic and classroom interaction?	

Skill 3. Prevention of Problem Behavior

Evaluation Questions	Rating and Notes
a. Does the teacher demonstrate increased vigilance at appropriate times?	
b. Does the teacher effectively use nonintrusive measures such as eye contact and physical placement to monitor students?	
c. Does the teacher coach and remind students to follow the classroom rules and routines?	

(continued)

TABLE 8.5 *Continued*

Skill 4. Responding to behavior efficiently

Evaluation Questions	Rating and Notes	
a. Does the teacher use limited warnings, requests, and so forth?		
b. Are the teacher's reactions to misbehavior limited, unemotional, and matter of fact?		
c. Does the teacher use contingent and specific requests to encourage students to stop the misbehavior?		
d. Does the tone and content of the requests threaten or demean students?		

Skill 5. Managing the Think Time period and debriefing process

Evaluation Questions	Rating and Notes	
a. Does the placement of Think Time area limit social interactions with the teacher, other students, and materials?		
b. Are the rules for the Think Time period unnecessarily restrictive?		
c. Does the teacher direct the student to the Think Time area quickly and efficiently?		
d. Are the social interactions of the teacher during the debriefing process unemotional and matter of fact?		
e. Does the teacher keep Think Time to a minimum?		

Skill 6. Managing the reentry

Evaluation Questions	Rating and Notes	
a. Does the teacher respond quickly and efficiently to the student?		
b. Does the teacher demonstrate a willingness to engage the students positively?		
c. Does the teacher provide direction or strategies to the student regarding any missed work?		

Summary

Classrooms have six distinctive properties that greatly affect the classroom management systems used by teachers: (1) multidimensionality, (2) simultaneity, (3) immediacy, (4) unpredictability, (5) publicness, and (6) history. These distinctive properties create constant pressures that shape the task of teaching and classroom management. Although the intensity of their effects varies with the particular conditions of every school, these pressures operate in all classrooms, regardless of how classrooms are organized and managed.

The Think Time Strategy is designed to alleviate some of the problems that arise with traditional classroom management systems that involve multiple warnings and steps embedded within all approaches used in schools (see Table 8.1). The chapter began with a discussion of the distinctive properties of classrooms for a very important reason. Discussions of classroom management or handling misbehavior tend to emphasize the individual student as the target of the teacher's thinking and action, failing to capture the group or social dimension. In other words, the Think Time Strategy is not only designed to have a positive and powerful influence on individual students but also on the group dynamics of classrooms and schools.

In addition, the problem behaviors of students exhibited in schools can be divided into two types: events (monadic) and chains (dyadic). Fortunately, the problem behaviors of most students in schools are events (monadic); the students comply with teachers' first attempt to change their behaviors. Because almost any classroom management system will work with students who exhibit problem behaviors that are events, the multiple warnings embedded within most systems will work quite well.

The problem behaviors of students who are difficult to teach, however, tend to be chains (dyadic); these students rarely comply with teachers' multiple attempts to change their behaviors. They exhibit a coercive interaction style that works as follows. Instead of complying with a teacher's request to stop a problem behavior, the students in turn continue to exhibit the problem behavior (or a topographically different one), which evokes a warning (e.g., stop…or…), which in turn evokes a noncompliant response from the students, which evokes another warning from the teacher (albeit more intense), which is then followed by a defiant (more intense noncompliant) response from the students, which results in the teacher withdrawing the request for compliance or a response cost (e.g., loss of recess, administrative intervention). Within this context is a shaping process that leads to more coercive interactions, resulting in powerful training of students in problem classroom behaviors.

Finally, the Think Time Strategy is designed to address directly the problem behaviors of students that are chains. Because students who exhibit event problem behaviors generally comply with teacher's requests, the Think Time Strategy can be used with all students in the classroom even though it is specifically designed to address problem behaviors that are chains. Of course, the Think Time Strategy should not be viewed as the only response to problem behaviors. It should be used flexibly with other school and classroom strategies (e.g., proximity, eye contact, planned ignoring) and consequences. The Think Time Strategy in itself is a powerful enough response to most minor problem behaviors. Nonetheless, additional contingencies such as parent contacts, response cost, and administrative referrals in the case of chronic or severe problem behaviors might also be used, and a comprehensive behavioral intervention and support plan might also be developed.

VIGNETTE • *Revisited*

Ms. Kamp and the other teachers at her school decided to implement the Think Time Strategy. A number of their colleagues who taught at other schools had indicated that the Think Time Strategy had worked very well in their schools. In addition, school staff had found that what they were doing was not working well. It was increasingly difficult to teach because they were continually warning students about their behavior. Although the staff used different systems, they all involved multiple warnings. For some students, the repeated warnings only seemed to escalate the student's behavior. Teachers also found that they tended to become irritated, frustrated, and angry at times when students did not attend to the warnings.

Ms. Kamp found the implementation of the Think Time Strategy to be relatively easy. It was easy to teach students, and they really bought into the notion that it was important for them to gain self-control. With the exception of multiple warnings, the Think Time Strategy did not require the staff to abandon many of their classroom management strategies such as proximity, problem solving, and parent contact. Overall, Ms. Kamp found that the Think Time Strategy helped her maintain a positive teacher-student relationship, even with difficult-to-teach children.

Discussion Questions

1. What are the distinctive properties of classrooms that affect teaching and classroom management? Are there others beyond those identified?

2. How do common classroom management systems exacerbate the distinctive properties of classrooms?

3. How does the Think Time strategy alleviate the distinctive properties of classrooms?

4. What does a coercive student-teacher interaction look like?

5. What areas of research underlie the Think Time Strategy?

6. How does a teacher prepare to implement the Think Time Strategy?

7. How does a teacher implement the Think Time Strategy?

8. How does the Think Time Strategy fit contextually with subtle classroom management strategies (e.g., eye contact)?

9. How does the Think Time Strategy fit contextually with more intensive classroom management strategies?

10. When would a teacher consider developing a comprehensive behavioral intervention and support plan?

9

Managing Individualized Behavior

Pinpointing and Tracking a Behavior Problem

Chapter Objectives _____

After studying this chapter, you should be able to:

- Characterize the considerations to be made before deciding to develop an individualized behavior management system.
- Explain why writing goals and objectives for behavior problems is important and describe the four components that should be present in objectives.
- Illustrate how to write behavioral definitions.
- Depict different recording methods.
- Illustrate how to develop recording instruments to track behavior.
- Explain the purpose of conducting interobserver agreement checks and describe the calculation methods.
- Describe the factors that influence interobserver agreement.
- Depict different single-case experimental designs.

VIGNETTE

MRS. LOPEZ WAS INFORMED that she was going to have a new student, Karl, in her 10th-grade class. The student was from an alternative school that educated students who had behavior problems. Mrs. Lopez was concerned that Karl was going to be disruptive to her classroom. The teachers at the alternative school, however, assured her that Karl was much better behaved now.

The time came for Karl to enter Mrs. Lopez's room. He was pleasant in the beginning. He followed rules and was polite. He seemed to try hard on his assigned work. Then, Mrs. Lopez noticed that Karl was beginning to swear more and said negative things about her and his classmates when frustrated. He also began to finish fewer and fewer assignments. Mrs. Lopez phoned Karl's former teacher at the alternative school and asked what she should do. The teacher told Mrs. Lopez that she should first consider if there was indeed a problem. The teacher's concern was that Karl's reputation was affecting how Mrs. Lopez viewed his behavior. In other words, the teacher asked Mrs. Lopez if she thought that Karl's behavior could have been consistent with her other students but was considered more disruptive due to her knowledge of his past behavior problems. Mrs. Lopez indicated that she did not think that her knowledge of Karl's past problems was affecting her view of him and his behaviors but would consider this possibility.

Mrs. Lopez asked other teachers if they had noticed a change in Karl's behavior and if they found his school behavior to be problematic. Mrs. Lopez also compared Karl's performance with the rest of the class and found that he was functioning much differently that the other students. She also had evidence that his problem behaviors were getting worse.

Overview

Until now, the focus of this book had been on schoolwide and classroomwide procedures that school district personnel can use to decrease the likelihood of behavior management problems. For some students, however, the aforementioned strategies do not work. Teachers may have to move to the third level of behavior management—the individualized level—for students who do not respond positively to widescale attempts to prevent behavior problems. At this level, teachers must become more systematic in their interactions when developing plans for these individuals.

A concern for many teachers is for the other students. An individualized management system, by its very nature, means treating some students differently from others. As shown up to this point in this book, however, every effort should be made to prevent having to design individualized management systems. Some students simply need a more prescribed system. It is no different than with instruction. If a student is having difficulty with reading, teachers should not refocus instruction for that student, because that would mean treating the student differently. Some students just do not respond to instruction and management systems as all the other students do. Therefore, designing an individualized management system should not be an obstacle. The one major consideration teachers should make is what to tell the other students. In most cases, it will not be necessary to tell them anything. In some cases, it may be worthwhile to tell the students that it is sometimes necessary to have special management procedures for students who need extra help in their good **behavior.** This explanation can and should be made without specifically naming the student or students involved.

We all know who these students are. These students are those who stand out from the others. Nelson (1996b) calls them "target" students, ones who always test the system. They seem to defy attempts to correct their behavior difficulties. Unfortunately, larger-scale management methods such as those designed at the building or classroom level do little to nothing to solve the problem.

When students continue to misbehave despite attempts to improve their behaviors, several decisions need to be made. First, the need for individualized intervention is discussed. Second, a method of measuring the behavior must be determined. Measuring the behavior tells how severe the behavior is and then helps determine if the individualized behavior management procedure was effective. Finally, the data collected must be represented in some fashion. Graphing is one of the most helpful methods of representing the data. In addition, the attempt to solve the behavior difficulty can be subjected to an experimental design that will help determine if the management program was successful and responsible for the observed changes in the student.

What Are the Considerations We Must Make?

Before any intervention takes place, teachers must ask whether or not an intervention *should* take place. To answer this question, several factors should be considered (see Table 9.1) (Sulzer-Azaroff & Mayer, 1991). We must ask these questions to ensure that our interventions are both realistic and ethical.

What Are Goals and Behavioral Objectives?

One of the more important skills a teacher can have is the skill to write behavioral objectives. As stated by Alberto and Troutman (1999), objectives should be written

to clarify the goals of a behavior-change program and thus to facilitate communication among people involved in the program. Because it is a written statement targeting a specific behavior,

TABLE 9.1 *Considerations before a Behavior Management System is Developed*

- Do we have a realistic identification of the problems and goals?
- Are there several independent requests for assistance with the same student?
- Is the student functioning differently from members of a comparison group?
- Are there dramatic changes in the student's behavior as seen by multiple sources?
- Is the behavior related to a physical or medical problem?
- Is this system for our benefit or for the student's?
- Are there logistical problems, such as the physical surroundings, staff responsibilities, and types of demands?
- Is the student willing to change?
- Are the procedures in use demonstrated to be effective?
- Is this an emergency or a critical event?
- Do we have public or supervisory support?
- Do we have control of the goals, including the antecedents and consequences?

the objective serves as an agreement among school personnel, parents, and students about the academic or social learning for which school personnel are taking responsibility.

A second reason for writing behavioral objectives is that a clearly stated target for instruction facilitates effective programming by the teacher and ancillary personnel. A clearly stated instructional target provides a basis for selecting appropriate materials and instructional strategies. (pp. 60–61)

Before writing a behavioral objective, a teacher must first write a goal.

Goals

A goal is a statement about outcomes that teachers expect to occur by the end of an academic year (Lignugaris/Kraft, Marchand-Martella, & Martella, 2001). If we had difficulty keeping a child on task for an instructional period, our goal might state the following: Given reading materials and a 30-minute reading period, Bobby will remain on task for the entire period for 5 consecutive days. Other examples of goals are the following: During a 20-minute free play period, Latoya will interact with other children in an appropriate manner for the entire period for 3 consecutive days. During transition time from lunch, Jorge will enter the social studies class before the class bell rings every day for 2 consecutive days.

Once the goal is identified, objectives are determined. (Goals are not restricted only to individual students. They should be written for the entire class.) At the beginning of the school year, teachers determine how they would like the class behaving by the end of the year and work toward that goal. For example, having all students turn in homework when assigned is a worthy goal.

Behavioral Objectives

A good format for writing behavioral objectives is based on the model proposed by Mager (1962) and Lignugaris/Kraft et al. (2001). This format proposes the following parts to an adequate objective: condition, student's name, behavior, and criterion. Objectives are short-term statements that are designed to lead to the goal. These short-term statements usually are based on what can be accomplished in 12 to 16 weeks.

Identify the Condition.   The condition is a description of the context under which the target behavior is measured. For example, "when provided a worksheet and told to complete it" is the context to "Bobby working on the sheet quietly." The condition should be stated in such a manner that another person reading the objective could replicate the context for the behavior. Examples of conditions include "Given a written list of…," "When verbally requested to…," "When provided with a verbal directive by the teacher…," and "Given a second-grade level basal reader and told to read a passage…."

Identify the Student.   Writing behavioral objectives individualizes the behavior management system. Thus, statements such as Bobby will…, Susan will…, and Jacob will… are part of the objective. (As with goals, behavioral objectives are not restricted only to an individual student. They can be developed for the entire class as well. Therefore, statements such as, "The class will…" could be used.).

Identify the Behavior.   Once it has been determined that there is a problem and that an intervention is warranted, the behavior of concern should be determined. This behavior should be defined in such a manner that it can be observed and measured. Vague terms should be eliminated from the definition. Behavioral definitions are discussed later in this chapter.

Identify the Criterion.   Behavioral objectives should include the minimum level required for acceptable performance. This level is set by the teacher with feedback from others, such as parents, administrators, school counselors, and school psychologists. The criterion tells teachers when the student has acquired the appropriate behavior. The criterion level should be specific so someone naïve to the program could determine how well the student is expected to perform the skill. This criterion level should be ambitious yet attainable. It is not unreasonable to expect all students to be well behaved in class. Examples of criterion levels include: "80% correct for 3 consecutive days," "100% of the time for five consecutive sessions," and "at least 70% of the intervals for 8 out of 10 consecutive days." The criterion that is set is essentially arbitrary, but teachers can use some standard by which to set these criteria: the behavior of well-behaved students. If other students are on task 70% of the time, a realistic level of on-task behavior is 70%. If successful students turn in their homework 80% of the time, a criterion of 100% of the time for the target student would not be realistic. Thus, look at what "model" students do and use this as the criterion level.

Methods of recording behaviors to determine if the student has met the criterion level are described later in the chapter.

Common Problems in Writing Objectives.   As shown in Table 9.2, several possible problems can result in writing behavioral objectives (Lignugaris/Kraft et al., 2001). These problems often involve missing or ambiguous parts to objectives.

Expanding the Scope of Behavioral Objectives

One consideration that must be made in the planning process of behavior change is to determine how the behavior will be maintained. Maintenance and generalization of behavioral gains must be considered. These concepts are covered in Chapters 11 and 12.

How Are Behaviors Assessed?

The first step to be completed before an intervention is implemented to decrease unwanted behavior and/or to increase wanted behavior is to determine the current level of the unwanted and/or wanted behavior. To achieve this step, the behavior(s) must be operationally defined and then which recording methods to use must be determined (Martella et al., 1999).

TABLE 9.2   *Common Problems in Objectives*

Poor Objective	Problem	Improved Objective
Upon entering the classroom, Ben will sit in his seat, ready to work.	Criterion is missing. Behavior is not well specified.	Ben will sit in his seat with materials on his desk within 15 seconds upon entering the classroom for 3 consecutive days.
When given independent seat work, Sarah will improve her on-task performance to 70% of the time.	Behavior is not appropriate. Criteria is incomplete.	When given independent seat work, Sarah will remain on task 70% of the instructional time for 5 consecutive days.
Jerry will engage in no negative verbalizations.	Condition is not specified. Criterion is incomplete. Objective is negatively worded.	When provided an academic task, Jerry will have no negative verbalizations for 4 consecutive days.
When engaged in free play activities with other students, Jackie will respect the rights of others 100% of the time for 3 consecutive days.	Behavior is not observable.	When engaged in free play with other students, Jackie will engage in appropriate play behavior 100% of the time for 3 consecutive days.
When given instructions, Barry will follow them 80% of the time for 3 consecutive days.	Criterion is not complete.	When given at least 10 instructions, Barry will follow 80% of them within 5 seconds across 3 consecutive days.
Terry will turn in her homework completed 100% of the time for 5 consecutive days.	Condition is not specified. Criterion is not complete.	Within 30 seconds of entering the classroom at the beginning of each school day, Terry will turn in her completed homework for 5 consecutive days.

Behavioral Definitions

Before a behavior can be recorded, it must be defined in such a manner that it can be measured (Martella et al., 1999). This requirement means that a behavior must be defined so that minimal inferences are used. For example, recall the magic carpet in the Disney movie *Aladdin*. When the carpet slumped over and walked slowly, most people said that the carpet was "sad" or "depressed." Sadness or depression in this case is clearly an example of an inference. Sadness or depression, however, are not observable. The behaviors we see that allow us to make the inference are the behaviors on which we should focus. Therefore, if teachers are concerned with a student being sad or depressed, they must work with the behaviors they see that allow them to make that inference. Another example is the term *angry*. Angry is not a behavior. Behaviors such as getting red in the face, clenching one's teeth, or swearing are examples of behaviors that can be labeled as angry. Table 9.3 lists a series of words that are not behaviors and a list of words that are indicative of observable behaviors. As shown on the left side of the list, many terms used to refer to behaviors are really inferences of behaviors. Therefore, to write a good behavioral definition, what exactly the behavior of concern is must be considered. The label of the behavior is not critical; the definition of the behavior to which the label refers is.

According to Hawkins and Dobes (1977), definitions must contain three characteristics:

1. The definition should be objective, referring only to observable characteristics of the behavior (and environment, if needed) or translating any inferential terms (such as "expressing hostile feelings, "intended to help," or "showing interest in") into more objective terms.
2. The definition should be clear in that it should be readable and unambiguous so that experienced observers could read it and readily paraphrase it accurately.
3. The definition should be complete, delineating the "boundaries" of what is to be included as an instance of the response and what is to be excluded, thereby directing the observers in all situations that are likely to occur and leaving little to their judgment. (p. 169)

Table 9.4 lists examples of definitions. As seen in the table, the definitions meet the three criteria described above. Writing behavioral definitions takes practice. The best way to think of behavioral definitions is what experts say to teachers when they are experiencing difficult behavior: "What exactly do you see the student doing? Describe the behavior to us so that if we went into your classroom we would see it and immediately recognize it from your description." Therefore, when writing definitions, pretend to be explaining the behavior to a friend. Another positive practice is to provide examples of the behavior within the definition. These examples should cover as many of the possible behaviors the student will display. Finally, think of what the student might do that would be an example of the behavior but does not meet the definition. For example, suppose noncompliance was defined as not following directions once an instruction is provided. What if the student followed through with the instruction, but did so 1 hour after it was delivered? Most people

TABLE 9.3 *Examples of Observable and Unobservable Behaviors*

Observable Behaviors		*Unobservable Behaviors*	
Speaks	Kicks	Appreciates	Discovers
Verbalizes	Hands in	Comprehends	Initiates
Hits	Arrives	Perceives	Respects
Sits	Swears	Believes	Intends
Asks	Gives	Knows	Commits
Waits	Touches	Recognizes	Realizes

TABLE 9.4 *Examples of Behavioral Definitions*

Positive Statements

Positive words or statements separated by a break in speech directed toward self/others/objects/tasks (e.g., "I can do this," "You look nice today," "That is a nice shirt," "I like to read")

Negative Statements

Derogatory single words or statements separated by a break in speech directed toward self/others/objects/tasks (e.g., "I'm so stupid," "I'm going to kill you," "I hate this f_____ calculator," "math sucks")

On Task

In seat (buttocks on the seat of the chair unless otherwise permitted [feet do not have to be on the floor]), remaining quiet during the task (no verbalizations unless permitted), working on the assigned task, and engaging in bodily movements related to the assigned task, such as using a pencil

Off Task

Not in seat (buttocks not on the seat of chair unless permitted [feet do not have to be on the floor]), talking with others (talking, whispering, or mouthing to others without permission), interrupting others (passing a note, touching another student's body or possessions), not working on the assigned task (such as scribbling or doodling instead of writing or reading a magazine instead of the text), and engaging in bodily movements unrelated or interfering with assigned task (such as playing with a pencil or ripping paper)

Compliance

Responding either motorically or verbally to an instruction (including instructional stimuli or cues such as, "Tell me this word") within 5 seconds

Aggression

Any pushing, shoving, hitting, or pinching that could result in damage (does not include behaviors that occur when playing, such as when wrestling)

Destruction

Any throwing, kicking, punching, tearing, or biting objects that could result in damage

---

would still consider this behavior to be noncompliance; the latency was too long. The behavior of the student meets the definition, however, because the student followed the instruction, albeit late. Therefore, some time element, such as "responding to the instruction within 5 seconds," should be added. Once the behavioral definitions have been written, the methods of recording the behavior can be considered.

Recording Methods

Measuring behavior can take various forms, from standardized tests to direct observations. For the purposes of this book, observation methods, because they are most often used by teachers, are covered. Information on other measurement methods such as standardized tests, rating scales, and checklists can be found in most assessment textbooks (e.g., Cohen & Spenciner, 1998; McLoughlin & Lewis, 2001; Salvia & Ysseldyke, 1995).

Several direct observation methods, including permanent product, event or frequency, duration, latency, and time sampling recordings, are available (Martella et al., 1999; Sulzer-Azaroff & Mayer, 1991). Table 9.5 provides a brief description of each recording method as well as information on when each is appropriate to use.

Measures of Permanent Products. Perhaps the most frequently used method of recording by teachers is **permanent product recording** (e.g., completed worksheets or puzzles, written examinations, written spelling words) to assess the effects of instruction (Martella et al., 1999). With this observation procedure, the teacher observes the product of a student's behavior. The actual behavior itself is not observed. For example, a teacher

TABLE 9.5 *Direct Observation Recording Methods*

Measure	*Definition*	*Example*	*Use When:*
Permanent products	Observation of the student's behavior	Number of windows or chairs broken	Behavior leaves an enduring product
Event recording	Record each behavior as a frequency	Number of times tardy, number of times student uses profanity	Behavior is discrete, equal in duration, and transitory
Duration recording	Record the length of time a behavior occurs	Length of a tantrum, length of time engaged in an academic task	Behavior is discrete and transitory
Latency recording	Record length of time between onset of antecedent and behavior	Length of time it takes from instruction to compliance	Behavior is discrete and transitory
Interval recording	Record the presence or absence of a behavior within a specified time frame	See below	Behavior does not have a clear beginning and end, is continuous, and/or occurs at a high rate
Whole interval	Record behavior if it occurred for the entire interval	On-task behavior, in-seat behavior	Behavior is to be increased
Partial interval	Record behavior if it occurred at least once during the interval	Off-task behavior, out-of-seat behavior	Behavior is to be decreased
Momentary time sample	Record if behavior is occurring at the end of the interval	Same as above	There is not enough available time to observe the entire interval

might use the number of windows or chairs broken during an aggressive episode. Permanent product recording is used whenever a behavior leaves an endurable product. In other words, whenever there is something left over from a behavior that can be observed or counted at a later time, permanent product recording is being conducted.

Event Recording.   Teachers may simply tally the number of times a response (e.g., talk outs) occurs within a defined period of time to assess the effects of an intervention (Martella et al., 1999). **Event recording** establishes the numerical dimension of behavior. This observation procedure is used in cases in which there is a discrete behavior with a clear beginning and end and the behavior is roughly equivalent in duration. Examples of behaviors that are amenable to event recording include a tally of the number of times a student is tardy or absent, the number of times a student uses profanity, and the number of aggressive episodes a student exhibits such as hitting someone. Examples of behaviors without a clear beginning and end include off-task behavior, being out of one's seat, and poor social engagement. Event recording is also limited when high-frequency behaviors occur (e.g., motor movement of a child with attention deficit disorder) because the observer becomes overwhelmed and may lose count when trying to tally the behaviors.

Duration and Latency Recording.   Duration and latency recording procedures, like event recording, are used in cases in which there is a discrete behavior with a clear beginning and end (Sulzer-Azaroff & Mayer, 1991); in contrast with event recording, however, the behaviors exhibited are not roughly equivalent in time. For example, say that tantrums occur often for a young child but vary in length (e.g., one lasts 10 minutes, the next lasts 15 minutes). Simply counting these behaviors loses large amounts of information. What is worse, one tantrum or two? The answer is not really known; one tantrum may have lasted 45 minutes, but two other tantrums lasted a total of 10 minutes. **Duration recording** could also be used to measure the amount of time a student appropriately interacts with others on the playground.

   Latency recording involves recording the time from a specified event to the start of the targeted behavior or completion of the response. For example, latency recording could be used to measure the time between a request from a teacher to begin work on an assignment to the actual completion of the assignment by the student. Latency recording is especially appropriate when conducting compliance training (i.e., teaching a student to follow directions in the classroom). As noted above, event recording establishes the numerical dimension of behavior; duration and latency recording provides the temporal dimension.

   The difference between duration and latency recording methods is that duration recording simply involves measuring the length of time a response lasts, whereas latency recording involves the length of time between a stimulus (e.g., instruction) and the behavior.

Interval Recording.   Teachers often use interval recording to provide an estimate of the number of occurrences and the duration of behaviors (Martella et al., 1999). **Interval recording** is useful for nondiscrete behaviors that do not have a clear beginning and end, that occur over time, and that occur relatively frequently. Interval recording procedures involve dividing observational periods into units of time. There are three basic types of interval recording procedures: whole-interval recording, partial-interval recording, and momentary time sampling.

Whole-Interval Recording. **Whole-interval recording** requires the observer to record that the target behavior occurred only if it did so throughout the entire specified time interval. This procedure provides a conservative estimate (i.e., underestimates the occurrence) of an observed behavior because it does not count a behavior unless it occurs for the entire interval. For example, Figure 9.1 shows that a particular behavior occurred in the middle of interval 2 and progressed to the middle of interval 4. The tally of when the behavior occurred, however, is only in interval 3 because that is the only interval during which the behavior occurred the entire time. We would conclude that the behavior occurred 20% of the time. Notice that the behavior actually occurred 40% of time. Therefore, we have a conservative estimate of the level of the behavior, which is an underestimation of the behavior's occurrence. Whole-interval recording should be used only when there is a behavior we want to increase because interval recordings will not always accurately represent the level of behavior. We attempt to improve the accuracy of the recordings but will usually be off by some amount. If we are going to make mistakes, we want to make a mistake that will make the behavior look worse than it actually is rather than making it look better than it actually is. Therefore, for behaviors such as being in one's seat or being on task, we would rather say than the child is in seat or on task less than she actually is so that a management program will not be withdrawn prematurely.

An example helps illustrate why a whole interval is used for behaviors we want to increase. Say we wish to decrease Marybeth's pencil-tapping behavior in the classroom during independent seatwork. We set up 15-second whole intervals for 10 minutes. If Marybeth taps her pencil for 13 of the 15 seconds for each interval, she receives a "negative" in each interval. She could do that for all the intervals. In essence, she could be tapping her pencil quite extensively yet receive 0% of intervals of pencil tapping using whole-interval recording.

Partial-Interval Recording. **Partial-interval recording** requires that the teacher record that the target behavior occurred if it did so at any point during the specified time interval.

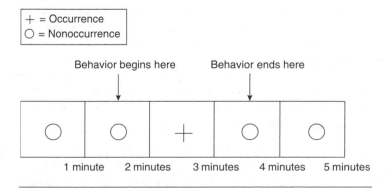

FIGURE 9.1 *Example of whole-interval recording.*

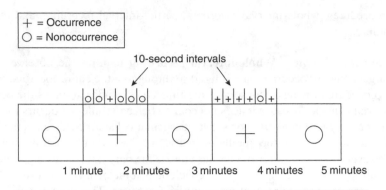

FIGURE 9.2   *Example of partial-interval recording.*

This procedure provides a more liberal estimate (i.e., overestimates the occurrence) of the observed behavior than the whole-interval procedure. Figure 9.2 shows that the behavior occurred one time in interval 2 and five times in interval 5, but the occurrence of the behaviors is counted the same in both intervals. Also, each instance of the behavior lasted only an average of 10 seconds. Thus, there were 10 seconds of behavior in interval 2 and 50 seconds of behavior in interval 5. The actual percentage of occurrence of the behavior would be 60 total seconds (or 1 minute) divided by 300 total seconds (or 5 minutes) of the observation period, or 20%. The recorded percentage is 40% (two intervals divided by five intervals). Therefore, we have an overestimate of the behavior. Partial-interval recording should be used only when we have a behavior we want to decrease. As stated previously, if we are going to make mistakes, we want to make a mistake that will make the behavior look worse than it actually is rather than making it look better than it actually is. Therefore, for behaviors such as being out of one's seat or being off task, we would rather say that the child is out of seat or off task more than he or she actually is, again so that a management program will not be withdrawn prematurely.

An example helps illustrate why a partial-interval recording system should be used with behaviors we want to decrease. Say we wish to take partial interval data on in-seat behavior. We would like this behavior to increase. We define this behavior as "buttocks flat on chair seat, child facing forward in seat, feet flat on floor." We set up 10-second intervals for 5 minutes. If Jerry, a student whose in-seat behavior needs to be improved, stays seated for 2 seconds for each 10-second interval, he receives a "plus" for the interval because he was in-seat at least part of the time. He could do that for all 30 intervals (six 10-second intervals per minute for 5 minutes) and achieve a percentage of 100% for staying in his seat. This method obviously inflates (overestimates) Jerry's behavior. On the other hand, if we were using whole-interval recording, Jerry would receive 0% of intervals of being in his seat because no interval included a full 10 seconds of sitting in his seat.

Momentary Time Sampling.   **Momentary time sampling** requires the teacher to record that the target behavior occurred if it did so immediately after the end of the specified time interval. This procedure provides the most liberal estimate of the observed behavior because the behavior has to occur only at the end of the interval but is counted as an occurrence interval.

How Do We Develop Recording Instruments?

Once the method used to record the data has been determined, a data sheet must be developed. The most frequently used data sheet is paper and pencil (Miltenberger, 2001). All teachers use a recording instrument of some form; a grade book is one example. Obviously, the main reason to use a data-recording instrument is to aid in being efficient and organized. To be efficient and organized, however, the data sheet must be developed before data are taken.

To create a data sheet, what information is to be recorded must be determined. For example, the student's name or identification number, location, teacher's name, date,

Student _____   Observer _____

Teacher _____   Classroom/School _____

_____

Behavioral definition(s):

_____
Date: _____ | Note: Place mark for each behavior seen.
Start time: _____:_____
End time: _____:_____

÷ _____ (Total number of behaviors)
   _____ (Total number of minutes)
   _____ = Rate

_____
Date: _____ | Note: Place mark for each behavior seen.
Start time: _____:_____
End time: _____:_____

÷ _____ (Total number of behaviors)
   _____ (Total number of minutes)
   _____ = Rate

_____
Date: _____ | Note: Place mark for each behavior seen.
Start time: _____:_____
End time: _____:_____

÷ _____ (Total number of behaviors)
   _____ (Total number of minutes)
   _____ = Rate

FIGURE 9.3 *Event recording data sheet.*

Student _____   Observer _____

Teacher _____   Classroom/School _____

Behavioral definition(s):

Date: _____

Start time: _____:_____

End time: _____:_____

÷ _____ (Total duration)
_____ (Total number of behaviors)
_____ = Average duration per behavior

| Note: Record duration of each behavior seen. |

÷ _____ (Total duration)
_____ (Total session length)
_____ = Percentage of total session time

Date: _____

Start time: _____:_____

End time: _____:_____

÷ _____ (Total duration)
_____ (Total number of behaviors)
_____ = Average duration per behavior

| Note: Record duration of each behavior seen. |

÷ _____ (Total duration)
_____ (Total session length)
_____ = Percentage of total session time

FIGURE 9.4   *Duration recording data sheet.*

length of observation, and definition of the target behavior should be placed on the data sheet. Another consideration is how much data should go on each data sheet. Should there be one page of data per day or several days of data on one sheet? Also, the data sheet should be clear and easy to use. Many data sheets are simply too involved and take a great deal of training to implement. Therefore, the simpler the data sheet, the better. The best way to create a data sheet is to develop a rough one and then modify it after it has been tried several times. Gradually refine the data sheet until it meets your needs. Figures 9.3 through 9.6 show different data sheets. Figure 9.3 shows a sample data sheet for event recording, Figure 9.4 shows a sample data sheet for duration recording, Figure 9.5 shows a sample data sheet for latency recording, and Figure 9.6 shows a sample data sheet for interval recording.

Student _____   Observer _____

Teacher _____   Classroom/School _____

Behavioral definition(s):

Date: _____

Start time: _____:_____

End time: _____:_____

$\div$ _____ (Total number of latency minutes)
_____ (Total number of antecedent events)
_____ = Average latency per event

> Note: Record each latency here.

Date: _____

Start time: _____:_____

End time: _____:_____

$\div$ _____ (Total number of latency minutes)
_____ (Total number of antecedent events)
_____ = Average latency per event

> Note: Record each latency here.

FIGURE 9.5 *Latency recording data sheet.*

A couple of suggestions can be made with regard to the use of a data recording system (Wolery et al., 1988). First, the recording sheet must be practical. It must not cause much disruption to ongoing class activities, such as requiring the teacher to stop instruction to make a recording. The data sheet should not draw attention to the teacher. The instrument should not cause reactivity on the part of the student who is being observed. Second, the data should be recorded immediately or as soon as possible. The longer the wait to record data, the more likely there are inaccuracies in the data. Thus, the longer the wait, the higher the likelihood that the particular behavior(s) that occurred and to what extent will be forgotten (Miltenberger, 2001).

What Is Interobserver Agreement?

A critical aspect of observation is determining if the manner in which the data are gathered is consistent. For example, we could change the way we define a behavior. A negative verbalization one day may not be viewed as inappropriate at another time. It is critical, however,

Student _____ Observer _____

Teacher _____ Classroom/School _____

Behavioral definition(s):

Date: _____   _____ (Total number of "+" intervals)
Start time: _____:_____   ÷_____ (Total number of intervals)
End time: _____:_____   _____ = Percentage of occurrence
Interval length: _____

Note: "+" = occurrence; "–" = nonoccurrence

1	2	3	4	5	6
7	8	9	10	11	12

Date: _____   _____ (Total number of "+" intervals)
Start time: _____:_____   ÷_____ (Total number of intervals)
End time: _____:_____   _____ = Percentage of occurrence
Interval length: _____

Note: "+" = occurrence; "–" = nonoccurrence

1	2	3	4	5	6
7	8	9	10	11	12

FIGURE 9.6   *Interval recording data sheet.*

that we remain consistent in the collection of the data so that each observation day can be compared with a previous or future one. To make the determination of how consistently we are observing and recording the instances of behavior, we can conduct interobserver agreement assessments. Through these assessments, we will be able to determine if we are consistent in our collection of the data. We should aim for approximately 25% of our data-collection sessions or days to have **interobserver agreement** assessments. These assessments require a second observer to collect the data at the same time the teacher does, and then a comparison of the data collected is made. The two observers should record the data independently so that the data one observer collects do not affect the data the other observer collects. The level of agreement to obtain for each interobserver agreement assessment is at least 80%. Following is a description of each of the types of interobserver agreement methods used in the classroom environment.

Permanent Products

The following formula is used to establish the percentage of agreement between independent observers measuring permanent products. The percentage of agreement equals the number of agreements divided by the total number of agreements and disagreements multiplied by 100:

$$\text{percentage of agreement} = \frac{\text{agreements}}{\text{agreements} + \text{disagreements}} \times 100$$

Inspection of the above formula reveals that as the number of disagreements goes up, the lower the percentage of agreement. For example, say that interobserver agreement was achieved on three of four damaged desks. In this scenario, disagreement between observers occurred on one desk. Substituting these numbers into the above formula, the percentage of interobserver agreement is 75% (i.e., 3 agreements/[3 agreements + 1 disagreement], with a result of .75 multiplied by 100).

Event or Frequency Recording

The following formula is used to establish the percentage of agreement between independent observers measuring events. The percentage of agreement equals the smaller total divided by the larger total multiplied by 100. As the discrepancy between the smaller total and larger total becomes greater, the level of interobserver agreement decreases.

$$\text{percentage of agreement} = \frac{\text{smaller total}}{\text{larger total}} \times 100$$

The percentage of agreement with event recording should be interpreted cautiously because it does not provide any assurance that the two observers were recording the same behavior. For example, one observer recorded that a child had said 20 swear words during a 60-minute observation period, and a second observer recorded 25 swear words during the sample period. The first observer, however, recorded 15 occurrences during the first 30 minutes of the observation period and 5 occurrences during the last 30 minutes, whereas the second observer recorded only 5 occurrences during the first 30 minutes of the observation period and 20 occurrences during the last 30 minutes. The calculation for this observation is the smaller total of 20 divided by the larger total of 25, resulting in .80, which is then multiplied by 100 for a percentage agreement of 80%. Thus, the percentage of agreement would have been inflated and would not accurately reflect the observer's actual level of agreement. A solution to this problem is to shorten the time interval within which inter-observer agreement is computed. The 60-minute observation period used in the above example could be broken down into six 10-minute intervals. The percentage of agreement could then be calculated for each interval. Thus, it is important to look at the length of interval used to compute the percentage of agreement in the case of event recording.

Duration Recording

The following formula is used to establish the percentage of agreement between independent observers measuring the latency or duration of behavior.

$$\text{percentage of agreement} \ = \ \frac{\text{shorter latency or duration}}{\text{longer latency or duration}} \times 100$$

An example of using this formula to calculate interobserver agreement is as follows. Say one observer recorded 10 minutes of a student's off-task behavior, and the other observer recorded 12 minutes of off-task behavior. The interobserver agreement percentage is 10 (short duration), divided by 12 (longer duration), which equals .83. This value is then multiplied by 100 for a percentage of agreement of 83%.

Two problems are experienced by observers when interpreting interobserver agreement using latency and duration recording. First, the procedures for ensuring that both of the observers begin the observation period at the same time must be established. Small variations between observers can distort the percentage of agreement. Second, as with event recording, high agreements do not necessarily ensure that the observers reported the same latencies or durations for the same occurrences of behavior. These issues should be examined whenever the results of a management program are assessed.

Interval Recording

The following formula is used to establish the percentage of agreement between independent observers for each of the interval recording procedures. The percentage of agreement equals the number of agreement intervals divided by the total number of agreement and disagreement intervals multiplied by 100.

$$\text{percentage of agreement} \ = \ \frac{\text{agreement intervals}}{\text{agreement intervals} + \text{disagreement intevals}} \times 100$$

The basic method for establishing interobserver agreement with interval recording involves computing the level of agreement for all the intervals (total agreement). To provide a more conservative estimate of interobserver agreement, both the scored interval (i.e., occurrence agreement) and unscored interval (i.e., nonoccurrence agreement) methods for establishing interobserver agreement should be used (Cooper et al., 1987; Hawkins & Dotson, 1975). Both methods use the above formula (agreement intervals [scored or unscored] divided by the total agreement and disagreement intervals [scored or unscored] multiplied by 100). An example of total scored and unscored interval interobserver agreement follows.

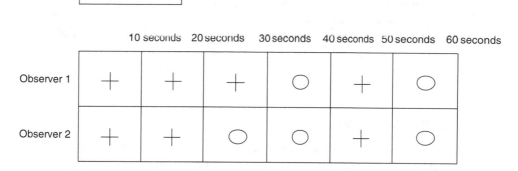

FIGURE 9.7 *Example of interobserver agreement with interval recording.*

Look at the example of the scored intervals provided in Figure 9.7. One minute's worth of 10-second intervals will be compared. Now, total interobserver agreement can be computed. Total interobserver agreement relates to how well both observers agreed on what they saw and what they did not see. Agreement was noted for intervals 1, 2, 4, 5, and 6. Therefore, the number of agreements (5) is divided by the number of agreements (5) plus disagreements (1) and then multiplied by 100 for a total agreement percentage of 83%. Now look at scored interval interobserver agreement. There is agreement on intervals that were scored (i.e., behavior occurred recorded as a check) for intervals 1, 2, and 5. There was disagreement on when the behavior occurred in interval 3. Therefore, the number of agreements of when the behavior was scored as occurring (3) is divided by the number of agreements (3) plus disagreements (1) and then multiplied by 100 for an agreement percentage of 75% for scored intervals. Finally, look at unscored interval interobserver agreement. There is agreement on intervals that were unscored (i.e., agreement that the behavior did not occur recorded as a zero) for intervals 4 and 6, but disagreement on when the behavior occurred in interval 3. Therefore, the number of agreements of when the behavior was scored as not occurring (2) is divided by the number of agreements (2) plus disagreements (1) and then multiplied by 100 for an agreement percentage of 67% for unscored intervals. Analyzing the data in this way gives the important information that the observers agreed on what they saw and what they did not see. This information helps inform us of the agreement we have with another person about whether or not the behavior occurred.

What Factors Influence Interobserver Agreement?

A number of environmental conditions can affect observers and can influence the quality of data collected (Martella et al., 1999). These environmental conditions include reactivity, observer drift, complexity of the measurement system, and observer expectations (Kazdin, 1977; Martella et al., 1999).

Reactivity

Reactivity refers to differences in interobserver agreement that result from observers being aware that their observations will be checked. Reactivity typically results in higher levels of interobserver agreement and accuracy of observations (Reid, 1970). It can be overcome by providing random interobserver checks, audio- or videotaping the observations and randomly selecting those that will be scored, or conducting interobserver agreement checks 100% of time.

Observer Drift

Observer drift occurs when observers change the way they employ the definition of behavior over the course of a study. In contrast to what we may think, observer drift does not necessarily result in lower levels of interobserver agreement. Observers can develop a similar drift if they work closely together and communicate about how they record the observed behavior. This drift will affect the accuracy of the data. Conversely, observer agreement will decrease over the course of the study if observers do not work closely together and do not communicate about how they record the observed behavior. Observer drift can be prevented or at least diminished through booster training on the definitions of the behavior(s) and by having data collected by individuals experienced in conducting observation sessions.

Complexity of the Measurement System

The complexity of the measurement system is influenced by the number of individuals observed, the number of behaviors recorded, the duration of the observations, the duration of the time intervals in interval recording, and the complexity of the data-recording instrument. Generally, the greater the complexity, the lower the levels of interobserver agreement. Thus, researchers or practitioners must balance the complexity of the measurement system with the need to obtain reasonable levels of interobserver agreement. Achieving this balance can involve observing fewer individuals, recording fewer behaviors, changing the duration of the interval, or simplifying the recording instrument.

Observer Expectations

Observer expectations can influence their observations. If observers expect the intervention to have a specific effect, they are more likely to record some change in a behavior that is not present. In other words, the observers' observation and recordings do not accurately reflect what is actually going on with the behavior. Observers' expectations appear to be most problematic when someone provides them feedback about how the management program is progressing, what the intervention is, in what condition the program is, and how the individuals are responding (Kazdin, 1977). The effect of observer expectations can be decreased by keeping the observers "blind" as to the specifics of the program (e.g., the program condition, purpose of the program) and by using individuals experienced in conducting observations.

What Are Single-Case Experimental Designs?

One of the more important questions a teacher or any practitioner has is, "Did my instruction, behavior management plan, or counseling make a change in the student's behavior?" To answer this question, data must be collected and analyzed. When teachers perform this function, they become scientist practitioners and conduct action research (Martella et al., 1999). Below are descriptions of **single-case experimental designs** that teachers can use to make data-based decisions with regard to the effectiveness of their behavior management efforts. (See Barlow & Hersen, 1984, Kazdin, 1982, Martella et al., 1999, and Tawney & Gast, 1984, for additional information on these designs.)

A-B Design

To understand single-case designs, the meaning of symbols must be known. In single-case designs, "A" refers to baseline. A **baseline** is the repeated measurement of a behavior under natural conditions. The baseline indicates the level at which the student performs a behavior without the intervention. It is of critical importance when considering single-case designs because it is the best estimate of what would have occurred had the intervention not been applied. The baseline, then, provides a comparison to the intervention condition, or "B." The intervention condition is the time that the independent variable or behavior management program is in effect. Typically, the "B" condition is used in isolation (Tawney & Gast, 1984). In other words, a skill is usually taught and measured over a period of time. A "B" design, however, is especially problematic because it is not possible to indicate where the student was before the intervention. Unfortunately, the "B" design is how many teachers attempt to determine the effects of the management program. To solve for this difficulty, several assessments can be provided before the intervention to determine where the students are at present. Also, it is important to make sure that students are not improving on their own; if so, the intervention may not be warranted. Therefore, the **A-B design** combines the baseline or preintervention measurements with a "B" condition to determine the effectiveness of an intervention. The A-B design should be the minimal level of data analysis a teacher uses before and during the implementation of a behavior management program.

Figure 9.8 shows an A-B design. As can be seen, several assessments occur before the intervention and several more occur during the intervention. In Figure 9.8, the intervention seems to be effective, but there is a major problem with A-B designs: they fail to demonstrate convincingly that a management program caused a change in a student's behavior. To solve this problem, the A-B design can be extended into an A-B-A or **withdrawal design.**

Withdrawal Design

The elaboration of the A-B design that Risley and Wolf (1972) called for was the withdrawal, or A-B-A, design. The A-B-A design has been called a withdrawal design and a reversal design (Barlow & Hersen, 1984). Technically, however, it is probably more appropriate to label the design a withdrawal rather than a reversal (i.e., the reversal design may signify an

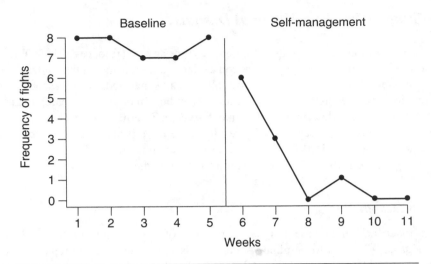

FIGURE 9.8   *The frequency of fights across baseline and self-management conditions.*

Source: From R. C. Martella, J. R. Nelson, and N. E. Marchand-Martella, *Research Methods: Learning to Become a Critical Research Consumer.* Copyright © 1999 by Allyn & Bacon. Reprinted by permission.

active attempt on the part of the teacher to change the level of student behavior during the "B" condition, such as reinforcing the behavior opposite of the desired one rather than simply removing the intervention [Barlow & Hersen, 1984]; see the later description of the changing criterion design for an elaboration of this concept).

The withdrawal design is a methodologically powerful tool used to determine if a behavior management program caused changes in the student's behavior (Kazdin, 1982). In the withdrawal design, the baseline is the first condition, followed by the intervention and ending on a return to baseline. The logic behind the withdrawal design is that if a behavior changed during the "B" condition and then returned to the first baseline level during the second baseline condition, the management program would have been shown to be effective. In this way, a functional (or causal) relationship between the intervention and the behavior can be shown. Figure 9.9 provides data indicating a functional relationship using a withdrawal design.

Multiple-Baseline Designs

One alternative to the withdrawal design is the **multiple-baseline design.** Multiple-baseline designs can be thought of as a series of A-B designs (Barlow & Hersen, 1984). In this way, multiple-baseline designs have several advantages over withdrawal designs. For example, in a multiple-baseline design, there is no requirement to remove or withdraw the intervention. There is not a need to return to baseline levels in the future. Thus, multiple-baseline designs are appropriate for investigations of skill acquisitions as well as motivational problems and

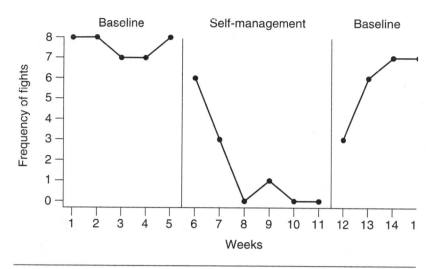

FIGURE 9.9   *The frequency of fights across baseline and self-management conditions.*

Source: From R. C. Martella, J. R. Nelson, and N. E. Marchand-Martella, *Research Methods: Learning to Become a Critical Research Consumer.* Copyright © 1999 by Allyn & Bacon. Reprinted by permission.

the reduction of unwanted behaviors. In many ways, multiple-baseline designs are more versatile than withdrawal designs. In addition, multiple-baseline designs allow for the replication of intervention effects across behaviors, students, and settings.

Multiple-Baseline Design across Behaviors.   The multiple-baseline design across behaviors requires at least two separate behaviors, which are independent of one another. In other words, if a teacher applies an intervention to one behavior, there should not be a corresponding change in the other behavior. Once these behaviors are targeted and a measurement system is put into place, baseline data should be collected for each behavior. Figure 9.10 shows the results of a behavior management program across two different behaviors.

Multiple-Baseline Design across Students.   The multiple-baseline design across students is similar to the multiple-baseline design across behaviors in that two or more baselines are required. There is, however, a need for two or more students. The teacher then takes frequent measures of the targeted behavior for each student during and after baseline. Figure 9.11 shows a multiple-baseline design across students. As can be seen, the graphs indicate who the students are. Also notice how the teacher kept the second student in baseline while the first student received the program.

Multiple-Baseline Design across Settings.   The multiple-baseline design across settings is similar to the previous two designs except that the teacher selects two or more settings. This design is especially useful in determining the generalizability of a behavior

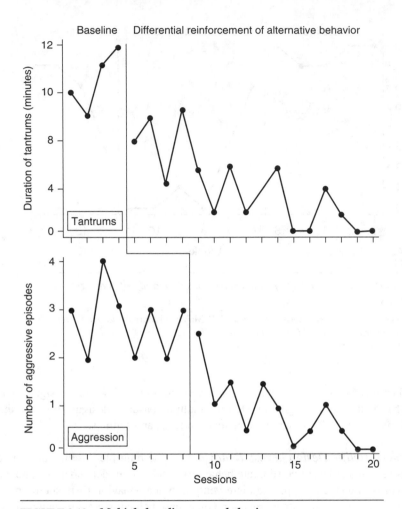

FIGURE 9.10   *Multiple baseline across behaviors.*

management program to other classrooms or other settings such as the lunchroom, playground, or physical education class. The teacher measures the student's behavior in each of these settings. The teacher takes baseline measures in each setting and then introduces the management program in only the first setting. The student's behavior in the second setting is not exposed to the program until later. Figure 9.12 displays data for a multiple-baseline design across settings. The figure indicates that there are two settings included in the assessment.

Multiple-Probe Design.   One potential problem with multiple baseline designs is the need for repeated measurements. At times, repeated measurements may result in reactivity during baseline (Horner & Baer, 1978). At other times, frequent assessments may not be

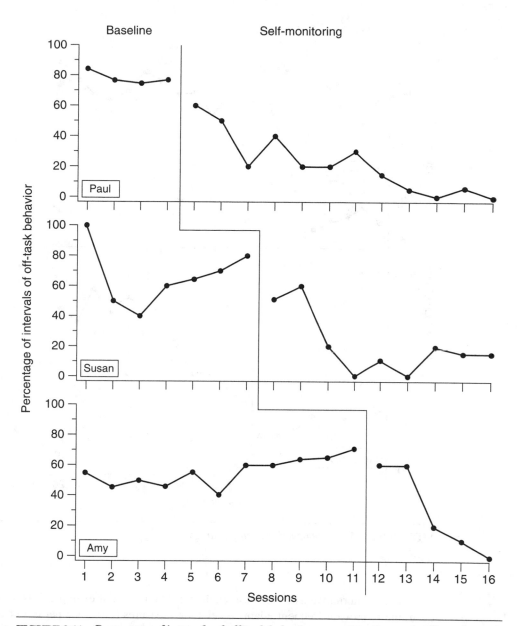

FIGURE 9.11 *Percentage of intervals of off-task behavior across baseline and self-monitoring conditions for Paul, Susan, and Amy.*

Source: From R. C. Martella, J. R. Nelson, and N. E. Marchand-Martella, *Research Methods: Learning to Become a Critical Research Consumer.* Copyright © 1999 by Allyn & Bacon. Reprinted by permission.

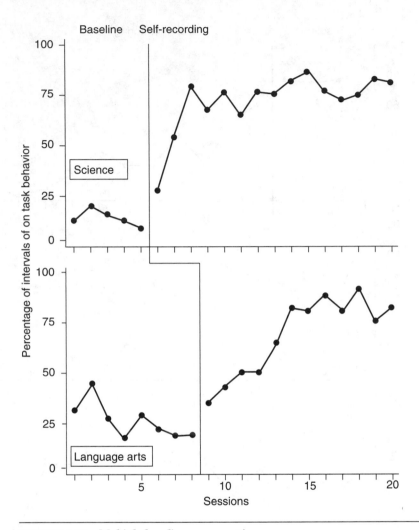

FIGURE 9.12   *Multiple baseline across settings.*

feasible and alternative assessment methods must be used. For example, it is probably not desirable to provide frequent adaptive behavior measures (i.e., once per day) over a long period of time for several reasons. First, providing standardized tests will most likely lead to reactivity. Second, frequent adaptive behavior testing may be too costly and time consuming. An alternative to frequent or repeated measurements is to "probe" the behavior every so often (e.g., once per week) during the baseline condition.

A third concern surrounding repeated measures involves the frequency with which teachers measure the behavior during the behavior management condition. According to

Barlow and Hersen (1984), if reactivity of measurement is the reason the multiple-probe technique is used, probes should also continue in the behavior management condition.

Finally, Kazdin (1982) indicated that probes may be used in situations in which behaviors were not the target for intervention, as in the case of assessing generalization/transfer or maintenance of behavior management program effects. For example, if a teacher were to determine the extent to which the improved classroom performance translated into improved

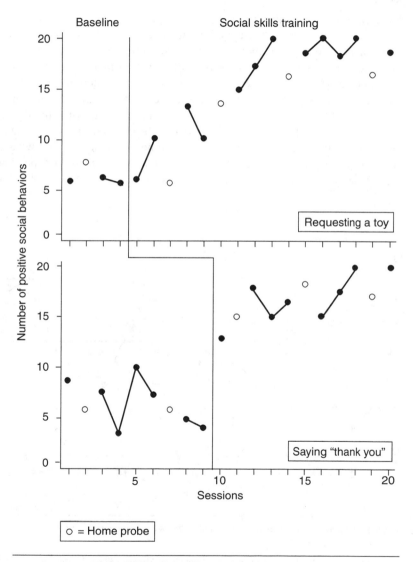

FIGURE 9.13 *Multiple baseline across behaviors with home probes.*

behavior at home, he or she could have the parents take less frequent measures at home (see Figure 9.13 for home probes). In this case, a combination of multiple-baseline and **multiple-probe designs** may be used in situations in which frequent measurements are applied to behaviors that are targeted for change and probes are conducted to assess generalization or transfer.

Changing-Criterion Design

The **changing-criterion design** has not been a popular design in classroom environments (Martella et al., 1999). It is, however, an important design teachers can use under appropriate circumstances. Figure 9.14 shows a changing-criterion design. As seen in the figure, a baseline condition is conducted, followed by the behavior management condition. Essentially, without the "phase" lines (i.e., changes within the intervention condition), the design looks the same as an A-B design. The difference between a changing-criterion design and an A-B design is the use of a criterion within each phase. As shown in the figure, the horizontal lines between each set of phase lines depict the criteria. Think of a changing-criterion design as an attempt to reduce or increase some behavior in a step-wise manner. In fact, that is what the design is intended to do: increase or decrease a dependent variable gradually. Thus, the changing-criterion design is useful for dealing with behaviors that

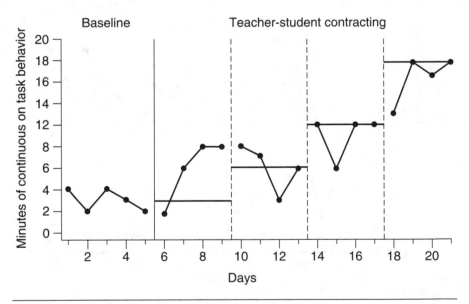

FIGURE 9.14 *Minutes of continuous on-task behavior across baseline and teacher-student contracting conditions.*

Source: From R. C. Martella, J. R. Nelson, and N. E. Marchand-Martella, *Research Methods: Learning to Become a Critical Research Consumer.* Copyright © 1999 by Allyn & Bacon. Reprinted by permission.

occur at a high rate and have a long history of reinforcement. The changing-criterion design is specially suited for such an attempt.

The method of implementing a changing-criterion design is a combination of planning and good (educated) guessing. In other words, teachers should plan the implementation of a behavior management program as they would any other program. The program and target behavior(s) must be well defined, the method of data collection must be determined, and the student(s) must be prepared to become involved in the program. Teachers need to rely on good guessing because they must determine the level of criterion changes throughout the program and hope that the steps are not too large or too small. To implement a changing-criterion design, teachers must do the following. First, they must collect baseline data. Second, the first criterion level should be set around the average of the baseline (Hall & Fox, 1977). Third, once the student meets some predetermined criterion level such as three data points at or below (in cases where the behavior is to decrease) the criterion, the criterion should be changed to a new level.

The difficulty with this final step is determining how large the change should be. For example, if the change is too large, the student may not be able to meet the new level. Suppose that a student engaged in an average of 50 inappropriate verbalizations per day. The first criterion is then set at 50 inappropriate verbalizations. Once the student engages in 50 or fewer inappropriate verbalizations per day for five consecutive days, we move to 10 inappropriate verbalizations per day. The step may be too much. That is a frequent mistake made in a classroom behavior management program. Although we want the behavior to stop quickly, for whatever reason, some behaviors take longer to reduce. Thus, the teacher is doomed to fail by requiring the behavior to be decreased too rapidly. What will happen in this case is that the student will not be able to reach the criterion level and the behavior will likely go back to a higher level. On the other hand, if the teacher decided to go from 50 to 49 inappropriate verbalizations after five consecutive days, the move may be too small; it would take too long to get down to zero inappropriate verbalizations per day. Thus, teachers must determine how quickly to reduce the unwanted behavior.

Alternating Treatments Design

Suppose that we wished to implement a behavior management program with a student who exhibited unwanted behaviors. We had a choice of one of two behavior management procedures. For example, we could use a time-out or a response cost system (described in detail in Chapter 12). How would we decide which method would be the most effective in reducing the unwanted behavior, other than a "best guess"? One way to determine which method would work best for a particular student is to use an **alternating treatments design** (ATD) (Barlow & Hersen, 1984). The main purpose of an ATD is to make comparisons between or among two or more conditions or behavior management methods, such as baseline and a management procedure or multiple behavior management procedures. The other single-case designs discussed thus far are planned only to determine if a management method works. On the other hand, an ATD attempts to demonstrate the superiority of one management procedure over the other.

Essentially, an ATD splits the student into equal parts and provides different methods to each part. For example, suppose that we wished to compare two methods of classroom management, such as in-class time-out and reprimands. We alternate the management procedures to see the relative effects of each on the classroom behavior of the student. The manner in which we alternate the management procedures can vary. For example, we could split the day in half and run one management procedure in the morning and the other in the afternoon. We could also run one on Monday, Wednesday, and Friday during the first week and Tuesday and Thursday during the second week and then repeat the sequence. We would then run the other management procedure on the other days. We must randomly determine when each management procedure is in effect.

Suppose that we elect to alternate days rather than time of day. We randomly determine when each management procedure is in effect. Teachers may set a rule on the number of consecutive times the same intervention can occur. Due to the chance factor, it would be possible to have an entire week with the same management procedure. Thus, a rule such as a maximum of two consecutive days with the same management procedure may be made. Once it is determined when each management procedure will be implemented, data can be collected on the effects of each method. Figure 9.15 shows an example of an ATD. In the figure, no more than two consecutive days of the same behavior management procedure are allowed. The interventions are alternated daily. Conclusions can be drawn based on the

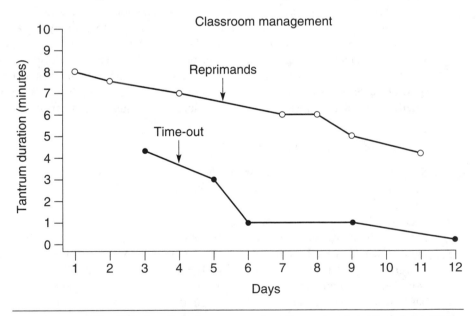

FIGURE 9.15 *The daily duration of tantrums across time-out and reprimand conditions.*

Source: From R. C. Martella, J. R. Nelson, and N. E. Marchand-Martella, *Research Methods: Learning to Become a Critical Research Consumer.* Copyright © 1999 by Allyn & Bacon. Reprinted by permission.

data in the figure. It seems as though the time-out was more effective than the reprimands, which can be determined by looking at the spread in the data. The wider the spread, the greater the differential effects of the management procedures. Notice that there is no baseline condition shown. The teacher only sought to determine which management method was most effective. A baseline condition was not needed.

A difficulty with an ATD is that it is not appropriate for comparing skill acquisition programs. Therefore, Sindelar, Rosenberg, and Wilson (1985) proposed the adapted alternating treatments design (AATD) for instructional research, and Gast and Wolery (1988) proposed the parallel treatments design (PTD) as an alternative.

Essentially, the AATD and PTD are modifications of the ATD. These designs help solve the problem of investigating the relative effectiveness of different instructional methods on skill acquisition dependent variables (Martella et al., 1999). The AATD and PTD require that two or more "sets" of dependent variables or behaviors be developed. These dependent variables or behaviors should be similar in difficulty and effort to perform. For example, suppose that a teacher is teaching math skills. The teacher would take two aspects of mathematics that are equal in difficulty and randomly assign these aspects to the different instructional methods; the sets, however, must be independent. If one method of instruction is effective in teaching some aspect of math, there should be no carryover to the other behaviors or aspects involved in math.

Summary

An interesting aspect of teacher preparation is that preservice teachers are trained how to undergo detailed planning for instruction. Instructional goals are laid out, and methods of instruction are decided upon. A frequently missed area of planning is behavior management (Colvin et al., 1993). Behavior management should be looked at no differently than any other instructional planning process. As such, goals and objectives should be developed for classroom behavior. It is critical that goals and objectives be developed in a manner that allows for the assessment and measurement of the target behavior.

Assessment and measurement of classroom behavior first involve defining the behavior in such a way that the behavior can be observed and measured. Once behaviors have been defined, they must be recorded in some manner. Teachers should develop data-recording instruments to track the levels of behaviors. Developing these instruments is no different from setting up a recording system for academic skills. Some form of accuracy check should be used when the data are recorded. In addition, if teachers wish to determine if the behavior management system was responsible for a change in student behavior, a single-case design can easily be integrated into the behavior management system used in the classroom.

Frequent arguments made against developing a comprehensive behavior management program for students is that such systems are too difficult, too time consuming, or a waste of effort (Wolery et al., 1988). Behavior management systems are difficult in some cases and they are time consuming, but they are never a waste of time. As with planning for instruction, the more planning and effort that go into behavior management, the more likely there will be success. Teachers who are good at managing student behavior take the time to do it correctly.

VIGNETTE • *Revisited*

After careful deliberation, Mrs. Lopez found that Karl's behaviors were indeed problematic. Therefore, she conducted a functional behavioral assessment (described in Chapter 10). She also defined as best she could what she believed to be Karl's problem behaviors. She knew that her definitions must be observable for her to track Karl's behavior. For example, her definition of "negative statements" was "any derogatory statements and/or words that contained commonly considered four-letter swear words directed at self or others without a break in speech." Mrs. Lopez also considered the goals for Karl's behavior. In other words, she thought about what she could reasonably expect from him by the end of the year. For instance, for appropriate classroom behavior statements, Mrs. Lopez's goal was as follows: "When in the classroom during instruction, Karl will work quietly for five consecutive school days." She then worked backward from where she would like Karl to be by then and where he is now. She planned three steps toward her goal. In other words, Mrs. Lopez wrote three short-term objectives that she thought Karl could reach on his way to improved behavior. For example, the first objective for working quietly was as follows: "When in the classroom during instruction, Karl will work quietly for two consecutive school days." (Another goal that Mrs. Lopez developed to go along with working quietly was to improve Karl's social skills.)

Next, Mrs. Lopez designed a method of tracking Karl's behaviors. She marked down every instance of swearing she heard. She also documented the percentage of time Karl was on task. She kept detailed information on Karl's seatwork completion and performance levels.

Finally, Mrs. Lopez set up a graph to provide a visual description of Karl's behavior. She plans to use this graph to track where Karl is now and how he progresses once she develops an individualized behavior plan for him. Using this graph, Mrs. Lopez will be able to determine if her efforts were successful or not.

Discussion Questions

1. Why is it important to consider carefully whether to develop an individualized intervention, and what are the considerations that must be made?

2. What are behavioral goals and objectives? Why should they be stated in a specific observable manner?

3. Why should behaviors be defined in a manner that allows for their observation?

4. Under what conditions would you use each of the recording methods?

5. How would you develop a recording instrument for off-task behavior for a student in the first grade?

6. What interobserver agreement calculation method(s) would be appropriate for partial-interval recording? What about for a duration count?

7. You are concerned with the integrity of your observations. What factors should you be concerned about and why? How could you prevent these factors?

8. Say that you wanted to demonstrate that a behavior management program worked across three classrooms. What type of design could you use to demonstrate that? Give fictitious data showing that your intervention worked.

9. Say that you did not know what behavior management intervention to use in your classroom. What design could you use to determine which intervention would be most effective? Give fictitious data making such a comparison.

10. How would you respond to someone who says that writing behavioral goals and objectives for unwanted behaviors and recording these behaviors are not worth the time and effort?

10

Managing
Individualized Behavior
Functional Behavioral Assessments

Chapter Objectives _____

After studying this chapter, you should be able to:

- Explain what it means to say that behavior is contextual.
- Illustrate different functions of behaviors.
- Depict other assumptions of behavior.
- Explain why functional behavioral assessments are important.
- Describe the types of indirect assessments.
- Characterize the types of descriptive analyses.
- Illustrate the types of functional behavioral analyses.
- Describe the advantages and disadvantages of each type of functional behavioral assessment.
- Depict when each type of assessment should be conducted.
- Characterize how to develop an individualized intervention based on assessment data.

VIGNETTE

MR. MALONE WAS A SIXTH-GRADE TEACHER. He seemed to have good management methods in his classroom, and the students were generally well behaved. Mr. Malone set good rules and routines, and the students followed them for the most part. Mr. Malone also provided effective instruction. The students' academic performance was good on the whole.

Unfortunately, Mr. Malone had a female student named Katrina who seemed to have difficulties following rules. She was frequently out of her seat and rarely raised her hand to ask a question, tending to blurt out questions and disturbing the other students. Mr. Malone tried warnings and time-outs for Katrina when she broke a rule or caused disruptions. These techniques worked at first but quickly lost their effectiveness. Mr. Malone was at the end of his rope. He had tried every management technique he could think of, even going as far as asking Katrina's parents for suggestions. Katrina seemed to know what she was doing. When asked to explain what she had done, Katrina would correctly describe her behavior. She could also describe why her behavior was inappropriate. Katrina indicated, however, that she could not help her behavior. She could not tell Mr. Malone why she was misbehaving, but would only say that she was sorry and not do it again. Then, at a later time, she would repeat the unwanted behavior.

Mr. Malone was not sure what to do. He generally liked Katrina. She could be pleasant to be around when she was behaving appropriately. He knew something had to be done, though, because her unwanted behavior was becoming more frequent. Mr. Malone was also concerned about improving Katrina's behavior soon because he was becoming convinced that Katrina might have an emotional disturbance, causing her to act this way.

Overview

Typically, there are three explanations for a student's behavior. First, it can be said that a student is behaving in a certain manner due to some physiological reason. She was born with a particular temperament, which is why she acts as she does. Second, a student may act a certain way because she comes from a dysfunctional home. Finally, a student may behave a certain way because she simply has chosen to act this way. As shown in Figure 10.1, there are three main reasons we behave as we do. The first reason is due to physiological reasons, the second is due to cultural reasons, and the third is due to the past or the immediate environment. Thus, physiology, cultures, and the learning environment account for why we do what we do.

Going back to the explanations teachers usually give for student misbehavior, temperament refers to physiological reasons and dysfunctional home life could refer to cultural reasons. The third reason teachers give for misbehavior, however, does not fit within the three possibilities. When we talk of choices, such as "you chose to act that way," we are talking about choices made independent of physiological, cultural, or environmental reasons. Thus, a student's choice will not be considered a reason a behavior occurs unless we talk of a choice as influenced by one of the three possibilities described above.

Suppose that we take each of the three possibilities to describe why a behavior occurs. First, physiology is a critical aspect of a behavior. We are all physiological beings, and our physiologies interact with the environment. Without our physiologies, we would

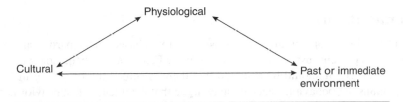

FIGURE 10.1 *Causes of behavior.*

not be around to discuss why students do what they do. Are physiologies, however, sufficient in explaining why we do something? The answer is no. As stated before, physiologies interact with the environment and are to a large extent dependent on the environment. What we know of natural selection shows us that the environment has a rather large influence on our physiological makeup. Cultures are also important in allowing us to understand our behavior. Cultures, however, have to enact controls over the people in those cultures. Thus, cultures by themselves tell us little about why people respond as they do. The environment is critical in explaining behavior, but again, by itself, it does not tell us the influence physiology and culture have over the behavior. Thus, to understand why we do what we do, we must consider these three aspects of human behavior.

Unfortunately, teachers have no control over two of the sources of behavior, physiology and cultures. Teachers cannot change a student's genetic makeup, and they cannot change student's culture. They can, however, have a tremendous influence over a student's immediate environment. Teachers can change the way they teach, the way they interact, and the way they respond to a student. Therefore, when discussing why students do what they do, teachers must look for clues in the immediate classroom environment, because that is all that is available. That is not to argue that the classroom environment explains everything; instead, the classroom environment and its corresponding effect on behavior are what teachers should focus on when it comes to changing student behavior.

This chapter describes environmental reasons why students behave as they do. The purposes of this chapter are to provide explanations for student behavior, describe how assessments aimed at finding these explanations are conducted, and explain how the results of these assessments can be used to develop effective individualized behavior management programs.

What Are the Assumptions of Behavior Management?

Whenever developing a behavior management program, certain assumptions must be made for it to be successful. These assumptions come from a particular conceptual system or how we have been taught to interpret human behavior. There are several such conceptual systems, including psychoanalytic, constructivist, cognitive, humanistic, and behavioral systems. The conceptual system used throughout this book comes from a social learning one. As such, assumptions made will be assumptions from this particular perspective. There are two major assumptions made with regard to human behavior (Iwata, Vollmer, & Zarcone, 1990). First, human behavior is contextual; second, human behavior serves a function.

Contextual Behavior

Human behavior is contextual; it should be interpreted based on the particular environmental conditions present just before and just after the behavior. If a behavior is occurring in a particular context, it should be assumed that there is something occurring in that context that maintains the behavior. Teachers may argue that a student's misbehavior is due to his or her home environment. A statement such as "He is like that because he comes from a dysfunctional home" is an example. Although a dysfunctional home environment certainly is something to be concerned about, it does not tell the whole story. The type of home environment a student comes from may affect a student's classroom behavior when the student first enters the room, but if that behavior continues after that point in time, the assumption is that there is something occurring in that classroom context that is maintaining the unwanted behavior. Therefore, the context of where a behavior is occurring has a critical effect on a student's behavior. So, what is a teacher to do? A teacher must determine what is going on in that particular context that may be reinforcing the behavior. In other words, a teacher must find the function of the behavior.

Functions of Behavior

There are several functions of a behavior. What is meant by function is that when a behavior occurs, something is likely to happen. That something may be a reinforcer. If so, the behavior will be more likely to be repeated in the future under similar circumstances. This something is a function. In other words, the behavior served a particular function (nontechnically speaking, it serves a purpose for the individual). Therefore, what we are trying to identify is a functional relationship between a behavior and particular contextual events. These contextual events will reliably occur either just before the behavior or just after the behavior. Determining a functional relationship is similar to when others talk of a cause-and-effect relationship (e.g., my behavior management system caused an improvement in student behavior). Although it may not always be possible to determine the true cause of a behavior, we can determine a functional relationship.

Now consider the information required to know the function of a behavior. Say we know that when a teacher provides an instruction to begin work (antecedent), there is a high likelihood that a tantrum (behavior) will result, or when the student has a tantrum (behavior), the teacher will send the student away from the group (consequence). Therefore, the probability of a particular behavior occurring is higher when a particular instruction is provided or when the teacher responds to the behavior in a certain way. What would this information provide to the teacher? Once the function of a behavior is known, it may become possible to change the instruction to avoid the unwanted behavior or to react to the unwanted behavior in another way. Thus, determining the function of a behavior can be critical in developing an adequate behavior program for the student.

To determine the function of a behavior, the possible functions must be known. Essentially, functions can be divided into two categories. As shown in Figure 10.2, the categories involve positive reinforcement and negative reinforcement. Under positive reinforcement are several subcategories: sensory (internal stimuli), social (attention), and tangible (objects/activities). Under negative reinforcement, the subcategories are sensory, social, and tangible. Notice the examples under each of the subcategories. (Some experts in the field of behavior management will place sensory feedback into its own category, signifying that it is not an environmental event, but an internal stimulation.). Two questions come to mind. First, why do the social subcategories have the same examples? Second, how can things we consider positive, such as hugs, be negative reinforcers and things we usually consider aversive, such as spankings, be positive reinforcers? The answer to both of questions is that the examples are the same to show that positive and negative reinforcers are not

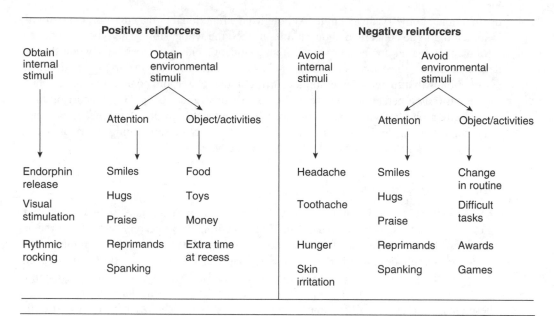

FIGURE 10.2   *Potential functions of behavior.*

subjectively determined. What determines if a stimulus such as a hug is a positive or negative reinforcer is determined by the student's behavior. Recall that an aversive stimulus is anything that occasions an escape or avoidance response. Therefore, if the student attempts to avoid a hug and continues to do so in the future, the hug is a negative reinforcer for the avoidance response. On the other hand, if a student behaved in such a manner to obtain a hug, the hug may be a positive reinforcer if the probability of the behavior increases in the future. (As stated in Chapter 2, technically we do not respond *for* reinforcers; we respond because we have received a reinforcer in the past for a particular behavior under similar conditions.)

Also, notice the sensory feedback category. Many times, we respond due to the automatic (Skinner, 1953) reinforcement of a behavior. In the positive reinforcement category, we see that students could behave to obtain some type of feedback from one or more of the senses, such as visual stimulation, rhythmic rocking, or an endorphin release. Likewise, at times we attempt to escape or avoid sensory stimulation by emitting a behavior to do so. For example, we take pain medication to escape pain, we may put pressure on our heads when we have a headache, or we may attempt to escape a toothache by pushing on our jaw where the pain resonates.

Several other possible variables influence challenging behavior (Foster-Johnson & Dunlap, 1993). Many can be considered setting events (see Chapter 2 for a description of these events). It is important, however, to realize that a number of possible variables can and will affect a student's classroom behavior. For example, physiological reasons such as physical illnesses may cause a behavior to occur. We are concerned, though, with environmental functions. As such, most of the functions dealt with in the schools are attentional and tangible positive and negative reinforcers. Teachers have direct access to these functions. They can stop attention from occurring for a particular behavior and can eliminate attention that evokes an escape or avoidance response. More problematic are those behaviors that serve to acquire sensory feedback. Teachers cannot get direct access to the reinforcers, so they must attempt to stop these in an indirect manner. To stop these sensory functions, specialized training is necessary. Therefore, for the purposes of this chapter, the focus is on behaviors that occur due to attention or tangible reasons. To determine what the functions of behavior are, specialized assessments must be conducted to determine what the functions of behaviors are. These assessments are called functional behavioral assessments.

Other Assumptions

Two other assumptions should be considered when conducting a functional assessment. First is an assumption that a functional assessment will lead to an intervention. If we can find out what the function of a behavior is, we are much more likely to be successful when we develop a behavior plan. Second is the assumption that when we remove the function or source of reinforcement from a behavior, the behavior will end. This assumption is basic in a behavioral interpretation of human behavior. This interpretation flows from the Law of Effect proposed by E. L. Thorndike (1905), which says that when a behavior is reinforced, the behavior will more likely occur in the future. When a behavior is not reinforced, however, the behavior will less likely occur in the future. The process of the behavior becoming less likely to occur in the future is called extinction. Therefore, if we can find the source of reinforcement and remove it, the behavior will decrease in probability in the future.

Why Are Functional Behavioral Assessments Important?

Functional behavioral assessments examine the circumstances surrounding the occurrence and nonoccurrence of an unwanted behavior. The goal of these assessments is to identify variables and events that are reliably or consistently present when the unwanted behavior occurs and does not occur. Functional behavioral assessments are considered important for two reasons. First, a functional assessment is believed to improve the quality and potential success of a behavioral intervention. Presumably, the more that is known about the behavior, the better an intervention can be designed that will fit the needs of the particular situation. Second, functional assessments are believed to lead to less aversive behavioral interventions. Interventions are considered less aversive because determining the likely reinforcers for a behavior allows the removal of the source of reinforcement, which decreases the need to use punishment or negative reinforcement (e.g., warnings) procedures.

Functional behavioral assessments are also important to know because they are required by federal law when developing a behavior plan for an individual with a disability (Yell, 1998). Because the **inclusion** movement (i.e., placing students with disabilities in the general education classroom for instruction) is a popular movement across the United States, all educators are more likely to have students with disabilities placed in their classrooms. Therefore, it is critical for all persons who work with individuals with disabilities to understand what functional assessments are and how they are conducted. As stated by Yell (1998):

> To deal with behavioral problems in a proactive manner, the 1997 amendments require that if a student with disabilities has behavioral problems (regardless of the student's disability category), the IEP [Individualized Education Program] team shall consider strategies—including positive behavioral interventions, strategies, and supports—to address these problems. In such situations a proactive behavior management plan, based on *functional behavioral assessment,* should be included in the student's IEP. Furthermore, if a student's placement is changed following a behavioral incident and the IEP does not contain a behavioral intervention plan, a *functional behavioral assessment* and a behavioral plan must be completed no later than 10 days after changing the placement. (p. 88)

Therefore, all educators should have at least a working knowledge of functional behavioral assessments. In addition, although functional behavioral assessments are required to be used in the development of a behavioral intervention plan for individuals with disabilities, these assessments should also be used for students for whom an individual intervention is needed. The **internal validity** (i.e., the results of a functional behavioral assessment lead to an effective intervention) seems to be solid. There is concern, however, about the **external validity** of functional assessments especially in school settings conducted by school personnel. (For discussion of this important issue, see Gable, 1999; Gresham, Quinn, and Restori, 1999; Nelson, Roberts, Mathur, and Rutherford, 1999; and Scott and Nelson, 1999). Essentially, the concern rests on two important issues. First, are school personnel adequately trained to conduct such assessments? At this point, the answer seems to be a general "no." This problem, however, can be overcome with behavior management classes and workshops for teachers. Second, would there be less use of functional behavioral assessments due to differences in the assumptions made in such assessments (e.g., environmentally determined) and the assumptions teachers make regarding the causes of behavior (e.g., within the student) (Scott & Nelson, 1999)? This question is more difficult to answer because it goes directly to how society generally views the causes of behavior. The overuse of stimulant medication for children who are diagnosed with attention deficit hyperactivity disorder shows how society generally views the causes of behavior (chemically, physiologically). Thus, to overcome this problem, there must be a general change in how society or at least the teaching profession explains why a student behaves in some manner. It is hoped that this book can help this transition, at least regarding the use of functional behavioral assessments.

What Are the Types of Functional Behavioral Assessments?

There are three types of functional behavioral assessments: indirect assessments, descriptive analyses, and functional analyses (see Table 10.1) (Iwata et al., 1990). Each of these assessments is described in an order moving from the least extensive assessment (indirect assessment) to the most extensive assessment (functional analysis).

TABLE 10.1   *Types of Functional Assessments*

Indirect Assessments: Subjective verbal reports of behavior under naturalistic conditions.

Examples:	Interviews, checklists, rating scales
Advantages:	Efficient, easy to use, good starting point
Disadvantages:	Reliability and validity questionable, starting point not end point

Descriptive Analyses: Quantitative direct observation of behavior under naturalistic conditions.

Examples:	A-B-C analyses, observation forms, scatter plots
Advantages:	Objective, conducted in actual setting, see behavior firsthand, may be end point
Disadvantages:	Complexity, inability to identify subtle or intermittent variables, time consuming, potential masking by irrelevant events, may not be end point

Functional Analyses: Quantitative direct observation of behavior under preselected and controlled conditions.

Examples:	Alternating treatments designs, other designs
Advantages:	Objective, high degree of control over behavior, high reliability and validity, end point
Disadvantages:	Complexity, potential insensitivity to high idiosyncratic events, prompting unwanted behavior to occur, potential risk of establishing new behavioral function

---

Indirect Assessments

Indirect assessments are those that involve gaining information from sources other than first-hand analysis of the environmental events. These assessments are usually "subjective verbal reports of the behavior under naturalistic conditions" (Iwata et al., 1990, p. 305) (i.e., reports of when the behavior occurs and what the antecedents and consequences to the behavior are). Examples of methods used to gain this information are interviews, checklists, and rating scales. These assessments have advantages over other forms of assessments in that they are efficient, easy to use, and provide a good starting point for an assessment. The difficulties with indirect assessments are that their reliability and validity are questionable (Iwata et al., 1990) and that they should not be viewed as an end point to the assessment. Information obtained from an indirect assessment should not be the only information used to develop a functional behavioral assessment. Following is a description of the types of indirect assessments.

Interviews.   **Interview** assessments are perhaps the most widely used form of functional behavioral assessment. Interview assessments seek to determine the source of reinforcement for a behavior by asking people in the student's life what they think the likely function of the unwanted behavior is (O'Neill et al., 1997). There are several types of interview assessments. Table 10.2 summarizes the information found in many interview assessments.

TABLE 10.2   *Information Contained in Many Functional Assessment Interviews*

Behaviors
1. Topography, frequency, duration, intensity
2. Response chains: behaviors that occur together

Setting Events:
3. Medications, medical or physical conditions, sleep patterns, eating routines
4. Schedule of activities: predictability, choices, staffing patterns, other students or people present, noise levels

Antecedents
5. Day of the week, time, setting, people present, activity, instructions

Consequences
6. Positive and negative reinforcers

Interventions
7. Efficiency of the behavior: effort, reinforcement schedule, immediacy of the reinforcer
8. Functional alternatives and methods of communication in student's repertoire (motoric, verbal responses, expressive or receptive language skills)
9. Methods currently used to avoid problem behaviors
10. Potential reinforcers for person: tangible, social, activity, edible
11. Past attempts to control behavior: targeted behavior(s), past program(s), length of program(s), effects of program(s)

This information can be separated into five categories: behaviors, setting events, antecedents, consequences, and interventions.

Caregivers such as teachers, parents, and instructional aides are not the only individuals who can be interviewed. The students themselves are often left out of the assessment process. Many times, students can provide information that is valuable in leading to a hypothesis of the function of the unwanted behavior. O'Neill et al. (1997) developed a student guided interview form. The information contained in such an interview is shown in Table 10.3. A critical part of the student-guided interview is targeting the behavior that got the student into trouble. Having students explain exactly what they did that resulted in the teacher's response is critical. Second, setting events should be considered with the students. Questions such as, "How did you feel before you did that?" or "Were you in a bad mood at the time and why?" could be asked. In addition, the antecedents should be considered. Questions such as, "What occurred just before you did the unwanted behavior?" "What subject were you working on?" and "Who was around you at the time?" could be asked. The consequences should also be considered through asking, "What happened when you did the unwanted behavior?" or "How did the teacher or other students react to what you did?" Finally, getting the students' opinion on what they think could improve the situation can be important. For example, if the students indicate that they did not think that the teacher respected them, additional probing into what the teacher did to result in that opinion could be done. Teachers many times do what they have always done in the class-

TABLE 10.3 *Information to Be Included in a Student-Guided Functional Assessment Interview*

Behaviors
1. The behavior(s) that got him or her into trouble at school and how intensely the behaviors occur (rate on an intensity scale)

Setting Events
2. Important events, places, or activities that are associated with the behavior (e.g., lack of sleep, illness, physical pain, hunger, trouble at home, noise or distractions, class or activities)

Antecedents
3. His or her subjects and activities and his or her teachers each class period
4. The class periods or times of day when the behaviors occur
5. Each situation that makes the behavior occur (e.g., class demands that are too hard, boring, unclear, long; teacher reprimands; peer teaching; or encouragement)

Consequences
6. Staff and student reaction(s) when he or she misbehaves

Interventions
7. What he or she thinks would improve the situation

room with students; students, however, may misinterpret an instruction presented in some manner as an indication of a lack of respect, for example. Simple changes in the manner in which instructions are presented could help improve students' behavior in the classroom. Gaining information on their views can be important. In addition, interviewing the students can also show them that their input is valued, which could result in the students being more likely to "buy into" the resulting behavior management program.

Nelson, Roberts, and Smith (1999) developed a user-friendly interview/self-report form shown in Figure 10.3. As can be seen, the information requested on the form attempts to determine the setting events, antecedents, behaviors, and consequences associated with the problem behavior.

Checklists. **Checklists** can also be used in an indirect assessment. In a checklist, caregivers such as parents or teachers check off possible antecedents and consequences the students may be exposed to when specific behaviors occur. Several checklists are available, including one described by Rolinder and Van Houten (1993). This checklist was developed for parents or other mediators to determine the precursors of problem behaviors of individuals with developmental disabilities. Checklists should contain as many antecedents and consequences as possible. Antecedents could include demands or requests made on the students, students sitting alone, students interacting with others, students engaged in academic tasks, and students interacting with adults. Consequences could include removing students from class, providing students with attention, ignoring students, and administering possible aversive stimuli such as reprimands.

INTERVIEW/SELF-REPORT FORM

Student _Ellen_   Respondent _Ms. Brown (teacher)_   Date _11_ / _18_ / ___

I. Problem Definition

1. Describe the student's target behavior(s)—primary problem behavior(s)—in objective terms.
    Ellen shouts profanities.

II. Events and Situations Related to the Occurrence and Nonoccurrence of the Target Behavior(s)

2. In what situations does/do the target behavior(s) occur?

Location	Time	Person(s)	Instructional Context
☑ In class	○ Arrival to school	☑ Teacher(s)	○ Entire group
○ Hallways	☑ Morning	○ Specialist(s)	○ Small group
○ Cafeteria	○ Lunch	○ Support staff	☑ Individual
○ Special classes	☑ Afternoon	○ Bus driver	○ Transition
○ Bus	○ Recess/break	○ Peer(s)	○ Other _____
○ Other _____	○ Other _____	○ Other _____	

Comments: _Occurs in class when given an assignment to work on independently._

3. In what situations are the student's behaviors most appropriate?

Location	Time	Person(s)	Instructional Context
○ In class	☑ Arrival to school	○ Teacher(s)	☑ Entire group
☑ Hallways	○ Morning	☑ Specialist(s)	☑ Small group
☑ Cafeteria	☑ Lunch	☑ Support staff	○ Individual
☑ Special classes	○ Afternoon	☑ Bus driver	☑ Transition
☑ Bus	☑ Recess/break	☑ Peer(s)	○ Other _____
○ Other _____	○ Other _____	○ Other _____	

Comments: _Does not occur during group instruction or nonacademic activities._

4. Are there any other internal and external events that influence the target behavior(s)?

Internal Events	External Events
○ Medication _____	○ Conflict at home _____
○ Physical health _____	○ Illegal drug use _____
☑ Academic skills _Occurs more in math class_	○ Negative peer influence (gangs, etc.) _____
○ Other _____	☑ Other _When asked to work on an_
	assignment.

Comments: _____

III. Events That Occur Prior to (Antecedents) and After (Consequences) the Target Behavior(s)

5. What typically happens prior to the student exhibiting the target behavior(s)?

○ Low levels of adult attention	☑ Presentation of activity or task	○ Under varied
○ Low levels of peer attention	○ Social interaction with adult	conditions
○ Unavailability of object/activity	○ Social interaction with peers	○ Other _____

Comments: _I ask her to work on an assignment independently._

6. What typically happens after the student exhibits the target behavior(s)?

○ Start-up request	○ Reprimand	○ Ultimatum	○ Time out
○ Ignore	○ Response cost	○ Office referral	☑ Other _Redirect_

Comments: _I redirect her and/or work with her on the assignment._

FIGURE 10.3 *Interview/self-report form.*

Source: From *Conducting Functional Behavioral Assessments in School Settings* by J. R. Nelson, M. Roberts, and D. J. Smith. Reprinted with permission from Sopris West Educational Services, Longmont, CO. 800-547-6747. (Packs of forms are available for purchase from Sopris West.)

Rating Scales.   **Rating scales** are similar to checklists except that teachers or parents can provide a level of likelihood that an antecedent or consequence would occur before or after the target behavior. As with checklists, several rating scales are available. Perhaps one of the better-known rating scales is the **Motivation Assessment Scale** (MAS) by Durand and Crimmins (1987). This 16-item rating scale requires a specific description of the unwanted behavior and a description of the setting. The items are separated into four categories of function: sensory, escape, attention, and tangible. Examples of questions in each category include the following: "Would the behavior occur continuously, over and over, if this person were left alone for long periods of time, such as several hours?" (sensory); "Does the behavior occur when *any* request is made of this person?" (escape); "Does the behavior occur whenever you stop attending to this person?" (attention); and "Does this behavior stop occurring shortly after you give this person the toy, food, or activity he or she has requested?" (tangible). The likelihood of occurrence of each of these situations is rated on a **Likert-like scale** from 0 (never) to 6 (always). The average rating per category is calculated, and a relative ranking is determined based on each average score.

The **Problem Behavior Questionnaire** (Lewis, Scott, & Sugai, 1994) is a 15-item rating scale in which the frequency with which an event is likely to be seen is rated. The range of the rating scale is "never" to "90% of the time." Examples of functions of behavior and correlated items include: "When the problem behavior occurs, do peers verbally respond to or laugh at the student?" (access to peer attention); "Does the problem behavior occur to get your attention?" (access to teacher attention); "If the student engages in the problem behavior, do peers stop interacting with the student?" (escape/avoidance peer attention); "Will the student stop the problem behavior if you stop making requests or end an academic activity?" (escape/avoid teacher attention); and "Is the problem behavior more likely to occur following unscheduled events or disruptions in classroom routines?" (setting events).

The **Functional Analysis Screening Tool** (FAST) (Iwata & DeLeon, 1996) is an 18-item rating scale. The items are correlated with four maintaining variables (five items per variable, two items overlap). It is recommended that the FAST be administered to several individuals who interact with the student frequently. An indication of "yes" or "no" is used to determine if an item statement accurately describes the student's unwanted behavior. Examples of the maintaining variables and correlated items include the following: "When the behavior occurs, do you usually try to calm the person down or distract the person with preferred activities such as leisure items or snacks?" (social reinforcement); "When the behavior occurs, do you usually give the person a 'break' from ongoing tasks?" (negative reinforcement); "Does the behavior occur at high rates regardless of what is going on around the person?" (automatic reinforcement, sensory stimulation); and "Does the behavior occur more often when the person is sick?" (automatic reinforcement, pain attenuation).

Summarizing Data.   Once an indirect assessment has been conducted, the data must be summarized in some form. The data should be summarized by determining if there are any patterns present. In other words, one must decide if consistencies in the obtained information were present. In other words, was a particular antecedent (e.g., academic instruction) usually present when the behavior (e.g., swearing) occurred, usually resulting in a particular consequence (e.g., being removed from the group)? Setting events should also be considered. For

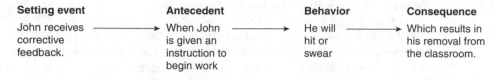

Setting event	Antecedent	Behavior	Consequence
John receives corrective feedback.	When John is given an instruction to begin work	He will hit or swear	Which results in his removal from the classroom.

FIGURE 10.4 *Summary statement for a behavioral episode.*

example, whenever the student comes to school sleepy, does he usually display a higher instance of the unwanted behavior? When conducting the analysis of the indirect assessments, look for whether or not the antecedents were part of the same stimulus class. A **stimulus class** is a class of stimuli (i.e., events that occur in the environment) that occasion the same or similar behaviors. For example, providing the student an instruction to begin her math assignment may occasion the same response from the student as requiring her to clean up a work area. Although these two events (i.e., academic requirement and cleanliness requirement) are seemingly unrelated, they nonetheless result in the same unwanted behavior. Another consideration to make is whether a set of consequences seems to result in the same outcome. For example, if the student swears, the student may be sent to the hall on one occasion but may be sent to the principal's office on another occasion. In both circumstances, the student is escaping the required work or activity.

Once antecedents, behaviors, and consequences have been identified, summary statements can be made. Figure 10.4 shows such a summary statement. Essentially, the information is placed into a four-term or three-term contingency arrangement. As shown in the figure, the setting event is corrective feedback on an assignment which results in a high probability of hitting or swearing (behavior) when the teacher provides instruction to begin work on an academic task (antecedent). The hitting or swearing (behavior) then results in being removed from the room (consequence). Now there is a possible sequence of events. This possible sequence gives information on the possible function(s) of the unwanted behavior. In the example just provided, the function of the behavior may be escape or avoidance of an academic task. This information is then used in the next step in the assessment process, descriptive analyses.

Descriptive Analyses

Descriptive analyses are considered the next level of assessment to be used before developing a behavior plan. Descriptive analyses can take several forms, such as A-B-C analyses, observation forms, and scatter plots. The main advantage of descriptive analyses is that they are more objective than indirect assessments in that they involve a direct assessment or observation of the unwanted and wanted behaviors under naturalistic conditions (Iwata et al., 1990).

A-B-C Analysis.   Figure 10.5 shows an A-B-C form. At first glance, an **A-B-C analysis** seems to be simple. A-B-C analyses, however, can be quite complex to conduct. Essentially, an A-B-C analysis involves an observer (e.g., teacher, student teacher, parent, behavior specialist, school psychologist) observing the student during normal activities. The

Antecedent	Behavior	Consequence

Antecedent: What conditions are present just before the behavior occurs.

Behavior: The student's response (what he or she does).

Consequence: What occurs immediately after the student's behavior.

FIGURE 10.5 *A-B-C analysis form.*

observations should occur when the behavior is most likely to happen. The length of the observation depends on the frequency of the target behaviors seen. This time period should be long enough to get a sample of the environmental events that lead up to and occur after the target behavior.

When conducting the observations, a narrative of events occurring just prior to (antecedents) and just after (consequences) classroom behaviors should be written. A-B-C analyses are similar to conducting an observation study in qualitative research. Their purpose is to aid in the development of hypothesis statements about the possible function(s) of the unwanted behavior. The narrative should not only include episodes of the targeted unwanted behavior(s) but also wanted behaviors. Essentially, all interactions with the student should be documented. For this narrative, the observer should develop a system of abbreviations and summaries to keep pace with the behavioral events. Narrative recordings take experience and practice so that all necessary events can be reported. These narrative events should occur over a minimum period of 3 days. We recommend that the observations occur over a period of 5 to 7 school days.

Once the observations are completed, the narrative should be reviewed. The critical aspect of any functional assessment is finding patterns in the data. Therefore, similar antecedents present before unwanted as well as wanted behaviors should be identified. For

OBSERVATION AND ANALYSIS FORM

Student Ellen   Observer Ms. Brown (teacher)   Date 11/ 18/

Target behavior(s) observed Profanities

I. Direct Observations

Start: 9:30	Setting:	Activity:
End: 10:30	Classroom	Math
Antecedent:	**Behavior:**	**Consequence:**
Get started	Profanity	Redirected
Comments:		

Start: 9:30	Setting:	Activity:
End: 10:30	Classroom	Math
Antecedent:	**Behavior:**	**Consequence:**
Get to work	Profanity	Sat with her
Comments:		

Start: 9:30	Setting:	Activity:
End: 10:30	Classroom	Math
Antecedent:	**Behavior:**	**Consequence:**
Work on your math	Profanity	Redirected helped with math
Comments:		

II. Summary

1. Identify the settings, activities, and consequences that appear to be related to the occurrence and nonoccurrence of the target behavior(s).
   Ellen shouts profanities when I give her a direction to start her math assignment.

2. Identify the events that occur prior to and after the target behavior(s).
   A direction occurs prior to the behavior at which time I redirect her and/or help her with her assignment.

3. Are they consistent with other information collected?   ☑ Consistent   ○ Inconsistent
   Comments: _____

FIGURE 10.6 *Observation and analysis form.*

Source: From *Conducting Functional Behavioral Assessments in School Settings* by J. R. Nelson, M. Roberts, and D. J. Smith. Reprinted with permission from Sopris West Educational Services, Longmont, CO. 800-547-6747. (Packs of forms are available for purchase from Sopris West.)

example, most of the time when the teacher asks the student to perform an academic task, the student swears. When the teacher requests the student to do a nonacademic task such as line up at the door, however, the student complies. Similar consequences should also be categorized together. For example, most of the time when the student is on task, the teacher does not attend to him. Whenever the student misbehaves, however, the teacher sends him to time-out. This information suggests that the student's wanted behaviors are not being reinforced and that the unwanted behaviors are resulting in the removal of the demand task for a period of time. The possible function of the behavior is escape or avoidance.

Nelson et al. (1998) present an alternative observation form. As shown in Figure 10.6, the form is a modification of the one in Figure 10.5. Nelson et al.'s. form prompts for summary statements to be made based on information gathered from the form.

Observation Forms.   **Observation forms** are also available for conducting descriptive analyses. These forms structure the observations into a checklist format somewhat similar to the narrative recording method. One of the more popular observation forms used was developed by O'Neill et al. (1997). Figure 10.7 shows an example of such a form. As shown in the figure, the behaviors of concern are written in the provided columns. There should be an operational definition of each behavior so that the person conducting the observations is sure of what to examine. The predictors are provided. In addition, information on setting events and other antecedents, such as particular people working with the student or individuals with whom the student is interacting, can be written in the provided columns. Next, the perceived functions of the behavior(s) are provided. Notice that there are two major categories provided: get/obtain (positive reinforcement) and escape/avoid (negative reinforcement). Within the get/obtain category are: attention, desired item/activity, and self-simulation. Within the escape/avoidance category are: demand/request, activity, and person. The actual consequences delivered based on the behavior(s) should be provided. Finally, the time of observation should be written on the left-hand side of the form. O'Neill et al. (1997) recommend that the observations be taken for a minimum of 3 days. As with A-B-C analysis, observations should be scheduled when the unwanted behavior is most likely to occur; the observations should be long enough to get a valid representation of the student's interaction with his or her environment.

Figure 10.8 shows a form filled out for John. There were two behaviors of concern, hitting and swearing. There were 11 episodes of these behaviors for the one day. The behaviors were not allocated to one particular teacher or time period. The behaviors occurred during either demand requests or difficult tasks. The consequence was usually a time-out. The perceived function was to escape or avoid demands or activities. Thus, time-out seemed to be functioning as a negative reinforcer. The summary statement for John is that when given demand/requests or activities to complete, he will hit and/or swear to escape the task or activity by being sent to time-out.

Scatter Plots.   Another form of assessment is the **scatter plot** devised by Touchette, MacDonald, and Langer (1985). The scatter plot enables observers to monitor targeted behaviors over an extended period of time. Figure 10.9 shows a scatter plot. As seen in the figure, the time of day is provided on the vertical axis and successive days are listed on the horizontal axis. The time of day can be divided into hour, half-hour, quarter-hour, or smaller increments, depending on what the observer wants to represent. The coding system involves three possibilities. An open box refers to a lack of target behavior. A slash through the box represents a low level of the behavior. A filled-in box represents a high level of the behavior. Whether a behavior is minor level or major level is set somewhat arbitrarily. For example, a slash could represent the behavior occurring fewer than five times during the interval. The filled-in box could represent the behavior occurring five or more times. The grouping of the slashed or filled-in boxes is an indication of when the behaviors are emitted throughout some time span. (Numbers can be placed in the boxes to give a more accurate representation of the frequency of the unwanted behaviors at various points in time.) A difficulty with the scatter plot is that environmental conditions that are related to behaviors on a time-cyclical basis can not be determined (Axelrod, 1987b). Also, the scatter plot does not determine the potential functional relationships of the unwanted behaviors, but it does lead the teacher to narrow down when an unwanted behavior is likely to occur so that a finer analysis such as an A-B-C analysis can be conducted at those times.

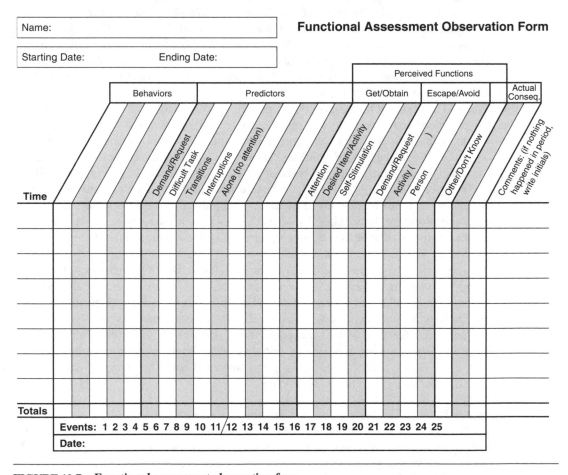

FIGURE 10.7 *Functional assessment observation form.*

For the example presented in Figure 10.9, it can be seen that the behavior tends to occur in the morning and afternoon. There is little problem behavior after 10:30 A.M. and before 1:30 P.M. Therefore, a teacher would want to determine what is occurring, who is with John, and the types of interactions going on during those times. For example, it is possible that academic tasks that are more aversive to John occur during the times of the outbursts. It is possible that a particular person such as an instructional aide is working with John during those times. Another possibility is that John is engaged in individualized seatwork at those times when the behavior is likely to occur and in cooperative learning groups when the behavior is least likely to occur. The time could also be a factor in and of itself. The outbursts tend to occur shortly after the beginning of school and about 1 to 1.5 hours before the end of school. Some setting events could be present that make John more likely to misbehave, such as getting into fights before and after school. Therefore, the scatter plot attempts to help the teacher narrow down the possibilities and also allows the teacher to focus on a more defined range of times the unwanted behavior occurs so that a more fine

Functional Assessment Observation Form

Name: John

Starting Date: 10/30/00   Ending Date: 10/30/00

Time	Behaviors: Hitting	Swearing			Predictors: Demand/Request	Difficult Task	Transitions	Interruptions	Alone (no attention)	Teacher A	Teacher B	Attention	Desired Item/Activity	Get/Obtain: Self-Stimulation	Demand/Request	Activity ( )	Person	( )	Escape/Avoid: Other/Don't Know	Time Out	Redirect	Actual Conseq.: Comments (if nothing happened in period, write initials)
9:00	1 2	2			1	2				1 2				1	2				1 2			
10:00	3 4 5	5 6			4 5	3 6				4 5	3 6			3 4	5 6				4 5 6	3		
11:00		7			7					7				7						7		
12:00																						
1:00	8				8					8				8					8			
2:00	9	10 11				9 10	11				9 10 11			9 10	11				9 11	10		
3:00																						
Totals																						

Events: 1 2 3 4 5 6 7 8 9 10 11/12 13 14 15 16 17 18 19 20 21 22 23 24 25

Date:

FIGURE 10.8 *Functional assessment observation form.*

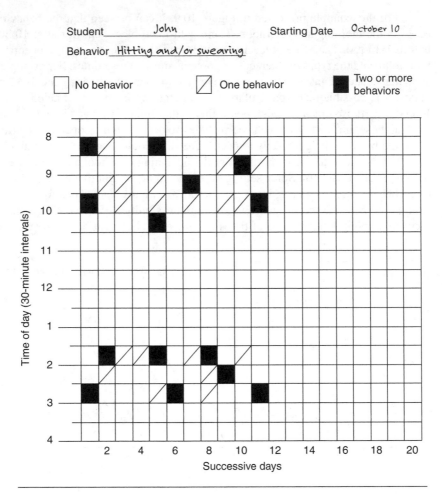

FIGURE 10.9   *Scatter plot with data.*

grained analysis can be conducted. For example, an A-B-C analysis could be conducted before 10:30 A.M. and after 1:30 P.M. to get an idea of the function of the unwanted behaviors John is exhibiting.

Summarizing Data.   Once the descriptive analyses have been conducted, the data will need to be summarized again. This summarization is similar in form to the one completed for the indirect assessment. The summary should be compared with that one to determine if the two are consistent. Frequently, they will be. At times, however, the two summaries will differ in some manner. For example, the summary presented in Figure 10.4 indicates that the setting event was receiving corrective feedback. Direct observation, however, found that corrective feedback was not a reliable predictor of the problem behavior; rather, the manner in which feedback was provided to the student was a critical setting event.

During the indirect assessment, the teacher may have identified feedback as being a setting event, but the teacher did not take into consideration that the form of that feedback may have had an effect on the behavior. Suppose that during the observation it was shown that when the teacher provided feedback by first discussing what the student did correctly (e.g., "I see that you put a lot of effort into this assignment") and then provided an effective error correction sequence (e.g., "You were on the right track in figuring out the math problems until you had to borrow. Watch how I borrow in this math problem. Let's try the next problem together. Great. Now try this one on your own"), the student was not likely to misbehave. When an ineffective error correction sequence (e.g., "You did not borrow the correct way. You knew this yesterday. Let's try again") was used, though, the behavior was much more likely to be seen when a new instruction was presented. Thus, a revised summary statement based in the descriptive analysis is presented in Figure 10.10.

Nelson et al. (1998) provide a form to help with the development of summary statements in Figure 10.11. In addition, Nelson et al. provide a summary analysis form that will help in the development of summary statements and, ultimately, in the development of behavior support plans (see Figure 10.12).

Functional Analyses

Functional analyses represent the third level of analysis of a functional assessment. Functional analyses are essentially ministudies. They allow for an experimental demonstration of the function of a target behavior. Functional analyses are defined as "quantitative direct observations of behavior under preselected and controlled conditions" (Iwata et al., 1990, p. 305). Essentially, the student is allowed to gain access to the function of the behavior. For example, a student may receive attention, escape a task, or earn a tangible item for tantrum behavior. The attempt is made to prompt the behavior to occur. If the function of the behavior is presented, the behavior rate should increase above the levels when the behavior did not receive the function for the behavior.

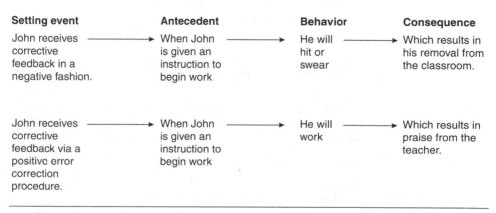

Setting event	Antecedent	Behavior	Consequence
John receives corrective feedback in a negative fashion.	When John is given an instruction to begin work	He will hit or swear	Which results in his removal from the classroom.
John receives corrective feedback via a positive error correction procedure.	When John is given an instruction to begin work	He will work	Which results in praise from the teacher.

FIGURE 10.10 *Summary statement for a behavioral episode after descriptive information is gathered.*

TEMPORAL ANALYSIS AND RANKING FORM

Student __Ellen_____   Rater ___Ms. Brown (teacher)___   Week of __11__/__18__/____

Dimension being rated: ☑ Frequency ○ Duration ○ Intensity ○ Other _____

Target behavior(s) observed _____Profanities_____

Directions: Rank the student's target behavior(s) for the designated time period.

All scales rated from 1 (low) to 10 (high)

DAY	8:30	9:30	10:30	11:30	12:30	1:30	2:30	3:30				
Mon		)))		)								
Tues		)))			)							
Wed		))))	)									
Thur		)))				)						
Fri		))										

TIME (Increments should align with distinct changes in settings/activities.)

1. In what situation(s) are the rankings of the target behavior(s) highest?

Location	Time	Person(s)	Instructional Context
☑ In class	○ Arrival to school	☑ Teacher(s)	○ Entire group
○ Hallways	☑ Morning	○ Specialist(s)	○ Small group
○ Cafeteria	○ Lunch	○ Support staff	☑ Individual
○ Special classes	○ Afternoon	○ Bus driver	○ Transition
○ Bus	○ Recess/break	○ Peer(s)	○ Other
○ Other	○ Other	○ Other	

Comments: _Profanities occur during math class and are directed toward me._

2. In what situations are the rankings of the target behaviors lowest?

Location	Time	Person(s)	Instructional Context
☑ In class	☑ Arrival to school	○ Teacher(s)	☑ Entire group
☑ Hallways	○ Morning	☑ Specialist(s)	☑ Small group
☑ Cafeteria	☑ Lunch	☑ Support staff	○ Individual
☑ Special classes	○ Afternoon	☑ Bus driver	☑ Transition
☑ Bus	☑ Recess/break	☑ Peer(s)	○ Other
○ Other	○ Other	○ Other	

Comments: _Behavior doesn't occur during group instruction/nonacademic tasks or with others._

3. Are they consistent with other information collected?   ☑ Consistent   ○ Inconsistent

Comments: _____

FIGURE 10.11 *Temporal analysis and ranking form.*

Source: From *Conducting Functional Behavioral Assessments in School Settings* by J. R. Nelson, M. Roberts, and D. J. Smith. Reprinted with permission from Sopris West Educational Services, Longmont, CO. 800-547-6747. (Packs of forms are available for purchase from Sopris West.)

SUMMARY ANALYSIS FORM

Student __Ellen_____   Date __11__/__25__/____

Staff Present __Ms. Brown (teacher)_____   _____

_____   _____

_____   _____

I. Data Collection Procedures

1. Procedures used to collect information for the functional behavioral assessment.
   ☑ Interview/Self-Report ☑ Observation ☑ Temporal Analysis/Ranking ☑ Other _reviewed math performance_

II. Events and Situations Related to the Occurrence and Nonoccurrence of the Target Behavior(s)

2. What key events appear to be related to the occurrence of the target behavior(s)?
   _Direction to complete her math assignment independently_____

3. What key events appear to be related to the nonoccurrence of the target behavior(s)?
   _Not giving a direction to work on her math assignment_____
   _Other academic tasks or instruction aside from math_____
   _Nonacademic tasks_____

4. Are there any other internal and external events that influence the target behavior(s)?
   _A direction--external_____
   _Poor math skills--internal_____

III. Events That Occur Prior to and After the Target Behavior(s)

5. What typically happens prior to the student exhibiting the target behavior(s)?
   _A direction_____

6. What typically happens after the student exhibits the target behavior(s)?
   _Redirected and/or I work with her on the assignment._____

IV. Potential Function of Target Behavior(s)

7. What is the potential function of the target behavior(s)?

○ *Access*	☑ *Escape/Avoidance*	○ *Autonomic Reinf.*	○ *Multiple*
○ Object/activity	☑ Activity	○ Comment:	○ Access
○ Adult attention	○ Adult engagement		○ Escape/avoidance
○ Peer attention	○ Peer engagement		○ Autonomic reinf.

Comments: _Uses profanity to get attention._____

FIGURE 10.12 *Summary analysis form.*

Source: From *Conducting Functional Behavioral Assessments in School Settings* by J. R. Nelson, M. Roberts, and D. J. Smith. Reprinted with permission from Sopris West Educational Services, Longmont, CO. 800-547-6747. (Packs of forms are available for purchase from Sopris West.)

As suggested by Iwata et al. (1990), the major advantage of functional analyses is that they are objective. They also provide a high degree of control over the behavior and are considered to have high reliability and validity. Functional analyses are also considered to be the end point in functional assessments. In other words, they should provide the necessary information required to determine the function of a behavior.

The downside to functional analyses is that they are somewhat complex to conduct. They take special training under the supervision of an individual who is trained to conduct such assessments (Iwata et al., 1990). Therefore, they are best conducted by individuals specifically trained in their use. Unfortunately, most school personnel do not have the training necessary to conduct functional analyses. If functional analyses need to be conducted, a behavioral specialist who has been trained to conduct them should be consulted. Fortunately, functional analyses are not usually needed. The information obtained through an indirect assessment and descriptive analysis will usually be sufficient for the development of a behavior plan. Another downside to functional analyses is that they may be insensitive to idiosyncratic events. In other words, there may be contextual factors or setting events that functional analyses cannot or do not take into consideration. Events such as an illness that made the unwanted behavior more likely to occur in the past may not be present when the functional analysis is being conducted. A further difficulty with functional analyses is that they are designed to prompt the unwanted behavior to occur. If dealing with behaviors that could cause injury, such as aggressive responses, a functional analysis may not be appropriate. Hence, only specifically trained professionals should conduct functional analyses. It may take specialized training to prompt an unwanted behavior to occur while still maintaining control over the situation. A final difficulty with functional analyses is the potential risk of establishing a new behavioral function. As will become clear later, a functional analysis requires the reinforcement of (or attempt to reinforce) the unwanted behavior. A reinforcer for an unwanted behavior that was not previously a reinforcer, however, could condition the behavior to occur for this new reinforcer. For example, suppose that a behavior is motivated by avoidance or escape. A functional analysis would require that the behavior be reinforced by allowing the individual to avoid or escape a particular stimulus. Such analysis would also require the behavior to be reinforced by attention at some other time. If the behavior was not an attention-seeking one before, it could become one now.

Overall, a functional analysis has the advantage of telling as definitively as possible what the function of a target behavior is. The major disadvantage is that not everyone is qualified to conduct such analyses.

Alternating Treatments Design.   As described in Chapter 9, an alternating treatments design (ATD) requires that several conditions be introduced in an alternating fashion. Considering that all the possible functions of a target behavior are conditions, the ATD can be used to determine the effects of these conditions on a particular behavior. Let's review the possible functions of a behavior. There are two main categories of functions: positive reinforcement and negative reinforcement. The most frequent possible positive reinforcement events in the classroom are attention, tangibles, and activities. The most frequent possible negative reinforcement event in a classroom is escape or avoidance of a demand task such as seatwork. There are a limited number of conditions that can be assessed in some manner. Therefore, the ATD provides an excellent method of comparing the effects of these conditions or possible functions. Figure 10.13 shows one possible example of a functional analysis using an ATD. When the misbehavior occurs, the student may receive attention, escape from the task, or receive a tangible item. In addition, the student may be placed alone without anyone around to see if the behavior occurs in the absence of external reinforcers. Finally, a play condition may be used whereby the student is allowed to play with toys and computers and so on as a control condition. It is not expected that the behavior would occur during the play condition because the student should be occupied. As seen in the figure, the highest rate of the target behavior occurred during the attention condition, indicating that the function of the behavior is attention seeking.

Behaviors do not always have a single function. Higher rates can be seen during two or more conditions. In such a case, several components of an intervention would need to be in place to target each function of the behavior.

Other Types of Designs. Other designs also work in a similar manner as the ATD except that rather than the conditions being randomly determined and alternated rapidly, the conditions are put into place for several sessions. Figure 10.14 shows an example of a possible functional analysis. As shown in the figure, the function of the behavior seems to be escape from a demand or task. The highest rates occurred during this time. Another example is shown in Figure 10.15. In this figure, it can be seen that high-demand tasks result in higher levels of unwanted behaviors than low-demand tasks. Therefore, the function of the behavior seemed to be the result of escaping a high-demand task.

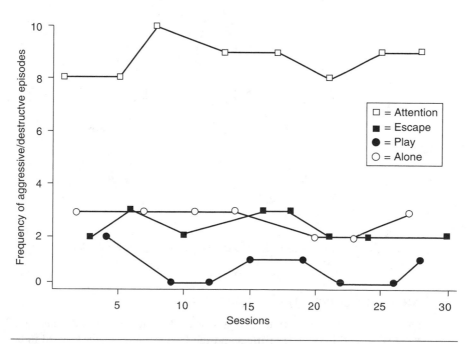

FIGURE 10.13 *Example of a functional analysis using an alternating treatments design.*

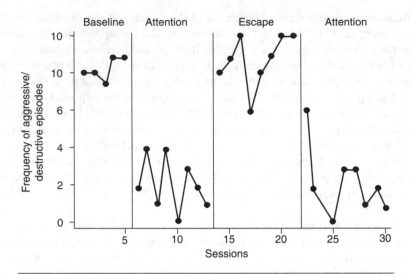

FIGURE 10.14   *Example of a functional analysis using a multitreatment design.*

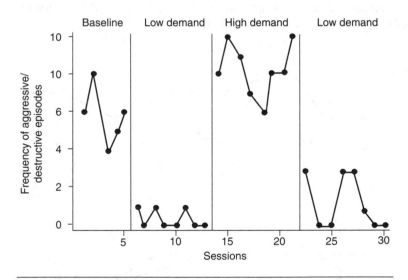

FIGURE 10.15   *Example of a functional analysis using a reversal design.*

When to Use Each Type of Assessment

There are several types of functional assessments. The type used depends to a large extent on the type used by school districts and the form of assessment learned in behavior management classes or in-service workshops. No matter what type of functional assessment is used, the type of data needed to create a behavior plan must be considered. Table 10.4

TABLE 10.4 *Decision-Making Process for Conducting Functional Behavioral Assessments*

1. Collect information through an indirect method.
   - Identify and define the target behavior.
   - Identify events and circumstances associated with the problem.
   - Determine possible function(s) of the problem behavior.
2. Collect information through a descriptive method for at least 2 to 3 days.
   - Identify and define the target behavior.
   - Identify events/circumstances associated with the problem behavior.
   - Determine possible function(s) of the problem behavior.
   - Compare with information obtained through an indirect method.
3. If function(s) is(are) apparent, go to step 5. If function is not apparent, collect additional descriptive information for 3 to 5 days.
4. If function is apparent, go to step 5. If function is not apparent, conduct a functional analysis.
5. Develop hypothesis statements about the behavior.
   - Determine the events/circumstances associated with the problem behavior.
   - Determine the likely function of the behavior.

shows a general decision-making process for conducting functional assessments that lead to an effective behavior plan. As shown in the table, collection of information through an indirect assessment method is the first activity. The first step is to identify and define the target behavior. The second step involves identifying the events or circumstances associated with the problem behavior. The final step involves the determination of the possible function(s) of the problem behavior.

Once the indirect assessment is finished, a descriptive method should be conducted. It is not recommended that a behavior plan be developed solely on the information obtained through an indirect method. The general recommendation for conducting a descriptive method of assessment is to observe for at least 3 days (O'Neill et al., 1997). The target behavior observed should be compared with the definition of the behavior based on the indirect method. For example, aggressive behavior may have been defined as any hitting, scratching, or kicking of another individual. In some cases, the behavior observed will match the definition developed earlier (e.g., aggressive episodes involved the behaviors described in the original definition). At other times, the definition may need to be revised to reflect the behavior observed (e.g., spitting was also observed and added to the definition). Finally, new behaviors not identified in the indirect assessment may need to be defined and considered (e.g., oppositional behavior also occurred throughout the day). The descriptive analysis should either verify the events that were thought to be associated with the problem behavior (e.g., the teacher reported that the behavior would usually occur when a demand was placed on the student) or result in a new event or circumstance being associated with the problem behavior (e.g., how the demand task was provided was associated with the unwanted behavior or the student was more likely to misbehave when left alone compared with when a demand task was provided). The function of the problem behavior also needs to be verified. For example, the teacher may have indicated that the likely function was escaping a task. The function, however, may be shown to be different than the function hypothesized from the indirect assessment. The teacher may have indicated that there were no obvious consequences after the unwanted behavior occurred because she ignored the student, whereas the descriptive analysis indicates that the other students were providing attention to the student.

In many cases, the function of the behavior will be apparent after the descriptive analysis. If so, hypothesis statements about the behavior can be developed. These statements describe the events or circumstances associated with the problem behavior. Once these events or circumstances are determined, the likely function of the behavior can be stated.

If the function of the behavior is not apparent through the descriptive analysis, the analysis should be extended for another 3 to 5 days. If the function of the behavior becomes apparent, hypothesis statements can be made. If the results of the descriptive analysis are inconclusive, however, a functional analysis should be conducted by a person qualified to conduct such analyses.

Some professionals in the field may feel that a functional analysis should be conducted even if a descriptive analysis provides enough information to develop a hypothesis statement. They may indicate that a functional analysis should be conducted to further validate the information received from the descriptive analysis. Another way to validate the information obtained through a descriptive analysis is to implement an intervention based on that information. Both approaches have merit. The difficulty with functional analyses, however, is that they require specialized training. Teachers or other school personnel should not conduct functional analyses unless they have received training and supervision from a competent behavior analyst who has specific training in such analyses. Therefore, to validate the information obtained through a descriptive analysis, unless someone has the requisite training and experience, an intervention should probably be introduced and its effects measured. However, we can always seek the services of a specialist to conduct a functional assessment.

How Do We Develop an Individualized Intervention?

Once the data from a functional assessment are gathered, a behavior management plan can be developed. If the behavior management plan does not flow from the functional assessment, however, the functional assessment was essentially a waste of time and resources. Thus, if developing a behavior plan, there must be commitment to conduct a functional assessment and to use the data gathered for its intended purpose.

When building a behavior support plan, several considerations must be made (O'Neill et al., 1997). First, the plan must indicate how those involved in the student's environment will change, not just how the student will change. If it is assumed that the environment influences unwanted behavior, others must be considered as part of the environment. Therefore, teachers should not only consider how the student must make different "choices"; they must look to themselves and determine how they can change to bring about a student's positive behavior.

Second, the plan should be based on the data gathered from the functional assessment. Recall that a functional assessment assumes that behaviors serve a function for the student.

In other words, there is something reinforcing the behavior. The purpose of a functional assessment is to determine the function of the behavior. If the function is determined, this information can be used to make meaningful changes in the student's environment, which in turn will result in improved behavior.

Third, the plan should be technically sound. In other words, the plan should be based on the principles and laws of human behavior, covered in Chapter 2. The plan must have support in what is known about human behavior. Also, the plan should include intervention procedures that have been shown to be effective in the research literature. There are three main areas of focus for a behavior plan. (1) We need to make the problem behaviors irrelevant. We must teach the individual skills that will lessen the need to exhibit the unwanted behavior. For example, we may at first grab an item from another person, and this grabbing is successful. Thus, the grabbing behavior is relevant to us. If we learn that we can obtain the item by asking for it, however, grabbing the item becomes irrelevant. (2) We must make the problem behaviors inefficient. Many unwanted behaviors receive reinforcement fairly immediately and continuously. To make the behavior inefficient, we need to stop the source of reinforcement from occurring. In addition, many unwanted behaviors such as tantrums require a great deal of effort to achieve a reinforcer. If we are able to provide an alternative behavior that receives reinforcement more immediately and consistently and if we provide the individual with an alternative behavior that takes less effort, the individual will display the wanted behavior instead of the unwanted behavior because the unwanted behavior becomes inefficient, especially in comparison to the alternative behavior. (3) We need to make the problem behaviors ineffective. We know that a behavior will continue to be exhibited if it is reinforced. We also know that if a behavior is not reinforced, it will cease to exist. Thus, our goal is to remove the source of reinforcement for a behavior so as to make the behavior ineffective in gaining reinforcement.

Finally, the behavior plan should be a good fit with the values and skills of the people responsible for implementation. Behavior management programs can be difficult to implement correctly. If a behavior management program is designed and the people responsible for its implementation do not agree with the plan or do not have the skills to implement it, it will fail. Therefore, before a behavior management plan is implemented, staff members or those responsible for the implementation of the plan should be encouraged to provide their input. If there are any concerns before the plan is implemented, it should be revised. It is far better to make changes before a plan is implemented than to attempt to overcome difficulties after a plan has been implemented.

Building the Plan

The summary statement shown in Figure 10.10 can be constructed to help build a behavior plan. This summary statement can be used in the diagram for use in the behavior plan (see Figure 10.16). This model, designed by O'Neill et al. (1997), provides an excellent method of developing a behavior plan. There are seven areas of concern with the diagram. First, the setting event (if any) needs to be documented. As stated before, the setting event can be anything that changes the way an individual responds to the antecedent from one moment to another, such as being tired, getting into a fight, or being punished at home.

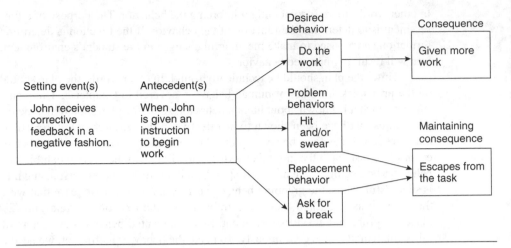

FIGURE 10.16   *Diagram to be used in behavior support plans.*

Second, the antecedent must be documented. Antecedents should be thought of in more general terms or as stimulus classes. For example, several stimuli can get a student to sit down, such as "sit down," "sit," "park it," or "relax." Although these are all possible antecedents, they may all result in the behavior being exhibited. Therefore, a general category such as "instructions to sit down" could be made. Similarly, there are several possible instructions to begin work for a variety of academic tasks. The general category would be "demand/requests for academic tasks." The antecedent or predictor for the unwanted behavior was the presentation of a demand on the student.

Once the antecedent or antecedent category has been determined, three behaviors or responses to the antecedent must be determined: desired behavior, problem behavior, and replacement behavior (third, fourth, and fifth areas of concern). The desired behavior is what the teacher wants to see. It is the behavior that well-behaved students exhibit. In the example, the desired behavior is the performance of the task. The problem behavior is the behavior that needs to be curtailed. A single behavior may not be the problem, but several behaviors may be. If several behaviors are a problem and they receive the same consequence or have the same function, the functional class should be documented by stating the behaviors in the class. In the example, there were two behaviors that seemed to occur together or for the same reason: hitting and swearing. The replacement behavior, or the behavior that can be taught to replace the unwanted behavior, should also be determined. The replacement behavior in the example is asking for a break.

The sixth area of concern is the consequence the student receives for the desired behavior. In many cases, the teacher will notice that there is a lack of reinforcement for the desired behavior. In many instances, when a student behaves appropriately the consequence is more demands. If so, the consequence for the desired behavior must be carefully planned so that the desired behavior is reinforced.

The seventh area of concern is the consequences that are maintaining the problem behavior. This information is critical and comes from the functional assessment. This area is of major concern because the consequences maintaining the problem behavior will be used to reinforce the replacement behavior. In the example, the consequence for the problem behavior is escaping the demands placed on the student. This consequence will also be used for the replacement behavior.

Once the diagram is complete, the teacher should begin to consider how the replacement behavior can be taught. The replacement behavior should make the unwanted behavior irrelevant, ineffective, and inefficient. To accomplish that, the behavior must be fairly easy for the student. The replacement behavior must be reinforced immediately and on a continuous reinforcement schedule (every time it occurs). The stimulus used as a reinforcer must function as a reinforcer. In other words, what the teacher uses to consequate the behavior must make a change in the behavior. Finally, the unwanted behavior should not receive any reinforcement. Therefore, the teacher must determine how reinforcement will be removed from the unwanted behavior. Once these considerations are made, the behavior plan can be written.

Writing the Plan

Once the diagram has been developed, the behavior plan can be written (developed by O'Neill et al., 1997). As shown in Figure 10.17, the operational definitions of the target behaviors are provided. Next, the summary statements are documented with a diagram of the three possible behavior categories (i.e., desired behavior, target behavior, replacement behavior). The diagram in Figure 10.17 shows that asking for a break is the replacement behavior for swearing.

The general approach to solving the behavior problem is presented next. A strategy for changing the setting events (if any) to prevent the problem behavior is stated. If a setting event is the use of a negative method of correction that makes the student more likely to hit or swear, change the way feedback is provided. Another example is if the behavior occurs when the student seems tired, speaking with his parents about getting him to bed earlier may be a strategy. The predictor strategies are also stated and involve methods of preventing the unwanted behavior by changing the antecedents to the task. For example, a teacher may change the way instructions are given, from a question (e.g., "Could you begin your work?") to a statement (e.g., "Please begin your work"). Another critical aspect of predictor strategies is to diagnose why a task is aversive to a student in the case of an escape- or avoidance-motivated behavior. The task may be too difficult or require too long of an on-task requirement. If the task is too difficult, stepping back into the curriculum may be appropriate. If the task requires too long of a behavior requirement, the appropriate solution may be to break the task into smaller units of time. If the problem is with attention seeking, the solution may be to provide more attention for appropriate behavior. The teaching strategies involve teaching the student how to request a break or where to go if a break is needed. The consequence strategies involve determining how the replacement behavior and the desired behavior will be reinforced. These statements should be specific so that other classroom staff can also implement the plan. Table 10.5 provides a guidance for interventions based on the function of the behavior.

The routines are also presented. The routines should indicate the manner in which the work will be provided. For example, if the student is having difficulty completing an assignment, the method of breaking the assignment into smaller units should be specified. That may involve drawing a line one-third and two-thirds of the way through the assign-

FIGURE 10.17 *Behavior support plan for John.*

Problem Behavior
1. Hitting: Any contact with the hand to another person or object with the intent to harm.
2. Swearing: Stating verbally words commonly considered (i.e., four-letter words) to be swear words.

Functional Assessment Summary Statement
When given instructions to begin working on a task after corrective feedback has been given, John will hit and/or swear. These behaviors are maintained by removing the task and sending John to time-out. Time-out allows John to escape or delay the task.

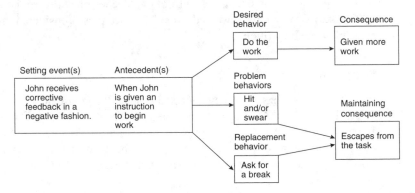

General Approach

Setting event strategies: When providing feedback, an effective error correction procedure will be used. This procedure will involve praising John for his effort, modeling the correct answer (e.g., "that word is *father*"), guiding him to the correct answer (e.g., "let's say the word together"), and having him provide the answer independently (e.g., "What word is this?").

Predictor strategies: (1) Instruct John to complete his work versus asking him to do so. (2) Although there is no indication that the work is too difficult for John, make sure to provide assignments that John can do independently (i.e., at his instructional level).

Teaching strategies: Conduct a 15-minute training session with John on how to request a break (i.e., raise hand and ask for a break when called upon) when he is feeling agitated.

Consequence strategies: (1) When John begins to work on the assignment, the teacher will praise him for getting started. When John completes the work, he will be praised for the completed work. (2) If John begins to hit or swear, the teacher will remind him to ask for a break if he thinks he needs one. Minor behaviors will be ignored. If John's behavior requires his removal, the teacher will provide a short booster training session on how to ask for a break immediately after John reenters the classroom. After the booster session, he will be instructed to complete the work he attempted to avoid.

Routines

Praise John when he begins working on his assignment and when he turns it in completed. Allow John to have a short 2-minute break when he asks for one in the prescribed fashion.

FIGURE 10.17 *Continued*

If John hits or swears, ignore minor incidents. For more serious incidents send John to time-out and have him practice appropriate asking for a break behavior upon reentering the classroom. Make sure John returns to the work that he attempted to avoid.

Monitoring and Evaluation

The observation form will be used to monitor the frequency of John's hitting and swearing behaviors. The teacher will review the data each morning prior to the start of class and at the end of the week to determine if changes in the plan are needed. The plan will formally be reviewed with John and his parents at the end of 1 month of its implementation.

ment and informing the student that when she reaches each line, a break may be taken. Also, if an unwanted behavior occurs, some appropriate response should be made by the classroom staff. The response may be simply ignoring the unwanted behavior or calling for assistance from the office. Whatever the routines are, they should be stated in specific terms so that all staff members understand what is to be done and when.

Finally, monitoring and evaluation of the plan must take place. The data must be taken to determine if the plan is having the desired effect on the unwanted and wanted behaviors. If it is shown that the intervention is not having the desired effect, the plan should be revised. It cannot be determined, however, if the plan should be revised unless data are

TABLE 10.5 *Guiding Principles for Functions for Target Behaviors*

Function	Guiding Principle
Access	
• Object/activity	• Reinforce and support the student when he or she is actively engaged with desirable objects or activities
• Attention (adult/peer)	• Provide the student attention (reinforce) when he or she is exhibiting appropriate behaviors
Escape/avoidance	
• Activity	• Reinforce and support the student to meet the performance expectation
• Social (adult/peer)	• Reinforce and support the student when he or she is engaging in desirable and important social situations
Autonomic reinforcement	• Minimize or eliminate the effects of the intrinsic factor and reinforce the student when he or she exhibits appropriate behaviors
Multiple functions	• Use the guiding principles related to the particular functions in operation

taken. Data collection is perhaps the most important aspect of a behavior plan because the data will lead the teacher to various decision points (i.e., continue with the plan as is, make minor modifications of the plan, or make a major change in the plan). Unfortunately, data collection is not frequently done when dealing with behavior problems. Effective behavior managers (i.e., effective teachers), however, use some type of feedback system to inform them of the results of their efforts. Teachers cannot effectively manage problem behavior without some form of monitoring and evaluation in place.

Implementing the Plan

Once the plan has been written, it can be implemented. The critical aspect of any behavior management plan is ongoing monitoring and evaluation. It is frustrating when a behavior management plan is implemented and is ineffective but continues to be used. If a behavior plan is not effective, the response from the teacher is simple: stop using the plan and make an adjustment. It serves no use to continue to use an ineffective behavior management program. If changes in the student's behavior are seen, continue to use the management program. In addition, once the replacement behavior has taken over for the problem behavior, the teacher should take steps to replace this behavior with the desired behavior. The way that is accomplished is to reinforce the desired behavior each and every time it is seen while putting the replacement behavior on an intermittent reinforcement schedule (see Chapter 2 for details). With adequate planning and implementation of a behavior plan, the student's behavior will change for the better.

Summary

One of the more important recent developments in the area of behavior management is the advancement in the use of functional behavioral assessments. These assessments allow for the development of behavior plans. Behavior plans developed based on the results of functional behavioral assessments are said to have a higher likelihood of being successful than behavior plans without such assessments. Before the wide use of functional behavioral assessments, school personnel would be more likely to create behavior plans (if any) by treating the topography of the behavior (i.e., what it looks like). Treating the topography of the behavior can be effective, but the information gained from a functional behavioral assessment provides information that can improve the quality of the intervention effects. Again, it should be stated that treating the behavior without conducting a functional behavioral assessment can result in improved behavior. That is what most parents and teachers do now. Determining the function of the behavior, however, can be important not only in improving the likelihood that the intervention package will be effective but also in reducing the use of punishment procedures.

When treating the topography of the behavior, there may be more reliance on punishment procedures to do so. It is known that punishment procedures result in negative side effects (see Chapter 12). Punishment procedures also do not teach an appropriate behavior but tend to suppress the unwanted behavior. With the use of functional behavioral assessments, the source of reinforcement for the misbehavior can be determined. Once this

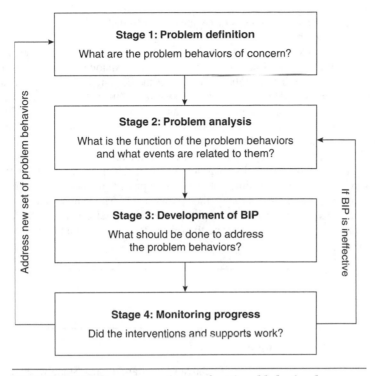

FIGURE 10.18 *Stages in conducting functional behavioral assessments and developing behavioral intervention plans.*

source of reinforcement has been identified, its removal will decrease the level of the unwanted behavior. In addition, we can also target a replacement behavior and teach the student how to behave appropriately. It is hoped that by understanding and using these assessments, the learning environment can be a much more enjoyable place for both teachers and students.

Figure 10.18 summarizes the process of conducting functional behavioral assessments and developing behavior intervention plans (Nelson et al., 1998). If teachers follow this process, their effectiveness as behavior managers should increase.

VIGNETTE • *Revisited*

Mr. Malone approached the district's behavior specialist and asked for suggestions. First, the behavior specialist made sure that there was indeed a problem. Once he was convinced that there was a problem (see Chapter 9), he told Mr. Malone that there were several steps to take to solve this problem and that Mr. Malone was going to have to change some assumptions about Katrina and her behavior. The behavior specialist indicated that labels such as "emotional disturbance" do not cause a behavior to occur or not occur. He told Mr. Malone that there is a reason to be found in the classroom for Katrina's difficulties. The behavior specialist told Mr. Malone that Katrina was either being positively reinforced by something such as attention from Mr. Malone or the other students or negatively reinforced such as by removing her from her required work to go to time-out.

The specialist told Mr. Malone that he should conduct a functional behavioral assessment to be sure of the likely cause of her behavior. He gave Mr. Malone some forms to complete. Also, he told Mr. Malone that once the "function" of the behavior was known, he should develop a behavior plan. Mr. Malone was told to make sure that the behavior plan had a summary statement that included possible setting events, antecedents, the behavior(s), and the consequences. This summary statement should show what the likely function of the behavior is. The behavior plan should also describe how to remove the function from the behavior and how to attempt to teach Katrina other ways of gaining access to the reinforcer. For example, if Katrina attempted to gain attention, Mr. Malone was told to ignore the unwanted behavior or to punish it in some way such as through a time-out and then to provide attention to Katrina when she asked for attention appropriately. Finally, the specialist told Mr. Malone that he should also consider how he was going to monitor the plan to see if it was effective. Mr. Malone told the behavior specialist that he would complete the functional assessment and get back to him on what he learned.

Discussion Questions

1. What are possible causes for misbehavior?

2. Why is knowing the assumptions of behavior important to understand when developing an effective behavior management plan? Describe each of these assumptions.

3. Why would you want to complete a functional behavioral assessment before you develop and implement a behavior management plan?

4. Of the types of functional behavioral assessments, which one is generally considered to be the most valid? What is the disadvantage of this method?

5. Of the three categories of functional behavioral assessments, which one(s) do you see as being most useable by classroom personnel? Why?

6. Why is it important to conduct and document the results of a functional behavioral assessment when working with students with disabilities?

7. If indirect assessments are considered to have questionable reliability and validity, why are they used so much by school personnel?

8. How would an intervention based on the data gathered from a functional behavioral assessment look different from one not based on such data?

9. Why are monitoring and evaluation of a behavior management plan important parts of the process?

10. How do the assumptions of the causes of unwanted behaviors differ from the traditional assumptions?

11

Managing Individualized Behavior

Increasing Desirable Behaviors

Chapter Objectives _____

After studying this chapter, you should be able to:

- Explain why teachers should target behaviors to increase rather than simply attempting to decrease behaviors.
- Illustrate how different prompting strategies can increase wanted behaviors.
- Depict the process of shaping.
- Characterize the Premack principle and the response deprivation hypothesis.
- Explain the concept of behavioral momentum.
- Describe the issues surrounding self-management.
- Illustrate correspondence training.
- Explain behavioral contracts and how they are developed.
- Depict token economy systems and how they are developed.
- Describe when it is appropriate to use different intervention procedures.
- Characterize how consequent-imposed behavior change is generalized.
- Illustrate how consequent-imposed behavior change is maintained.

VIGNETTE

MS. ARMSTRONG WAS BECOMING more and more frustrated with Juan. Juan was in Ms. Armstrong's ninth-grade social studies class and was failing due to his unwillingness to participate in class activities. Juan tended to sit in the corner of the room, and he did not interact with any of the other students. When Ms. Armstrong asked Juan to work in a group, Juan simply refused verbally or ignored her request altogether.

Exacerbating the problem was that Ms. Armstrong could not find anything to coax Juan to interact in the groups or with other students. She offered Juan points, candy, sodas, and extra time on the computer if he would just become involved in the class. None of these rewards worked. She then tried warnings such as telling him that she would send notes home to his parents, would send him to the principal, or would send him to time-out if he refused to become involved. These techniques also failed to get him to participate in any academic activity.

Ms. Armstrong was becoming increasingly concerned because Juan was at the point of no return. In other words, if Juan did not begin to put forth the required effort now, he was not going to pass the class. Therefore, Ms. Armstrong decided to bring her concerns to the "building assistance team."

The building assistance team was a group of teachers who met twice per month to problem solve students' academic and behavioral difficulties. Ms. Armstrong had heard that the team had helped other teachers with problem students, so she was anxious to talk to them about Juan.

Overview

A primary assumption used in this book with regard to effective behavior management is that students' behavior is exhibited due to things going on around them rather than something going on inside them. With this assumption made, the classroom environment must be examined to explain how and why a particular behavior occurs. Knowing that, however, is not enough to solve the problem. What steps are necessary to decrease the likelihood of the unwanted behavior and to increase the likelihood that a wanted behavior will occur in its place must be determined. Whether to change the antecedents of a misbehavior (such as changing the way instruction is provided) or to change the consequences of the behavior or some combination of both must be discussed. Some procedures used to increase the likelihood that desirable behaviors will be exhibited are examined in this chapter.

Why Should Target Behaviors Be Increased?

A very important aspect of behavior change is not only to decrease the behavior that is unwanted but also to increase a wanted behavior. Increasing a wanted behavior to take the place of the unwanted one is called the "fair-pair" rule (White & Haring, 1980). The **fair-pair rule** simply indicates that whenever there is a behavior we want to decrease, another behavior should be taught to take its place (Wolery et al., 1988). This tenet is basic to developing "positive behavior supports," a system that should be used to increase positive or wanted behaviors. A few years ago, the aim of many behavior management programs was to decrease unwanted behavior. Fortunately, today's aim is to treat an unwanted behavior as an opportunity to teach something else. Unwanted behavior can be treated as a teaching opportunity (Colvin et al., 1993).

Educators are in the business of educating our students. This education moves beyond teaching the three R's. Students must also be taught how to behave appropriately. Therefore, when unwanted behavior occurs, it is an opportunity to determine what needs to be taught. Unwanted behavior should be seen as an indication that the students have skills missing from their repertoires; these missing skills are appropriate behaviors. This approach parallels what good teachers do when students show deficits in academic areas. Good teachers not only teach academic skills; they also teach behavior skills. To do so, a teachers must be adept at using prompting and fading procedures.

How Can Prompting Strategies Be Used to Increase Desirable Behaviors?

Prompting strategies may be thought of as methods of teaching academic-related behaviors (see Chapter 7); these strategies, however, can be useful in prompting the occurrence of wanted behaviors. For example, for a student who is off task, a teacher could follow a least-to-most prompting strategy by presenting the verbal direction to begin work and waiting a predetermined time and then providing a verbal and gestural prompt to begin work. If after a time interval has passed without on-task behavior, a physical prompt such as touching the student on the shoulder could then be used (Sulzer-Azaroff & Mayer, 1991).

For the student who refuses to clean up her work area, a teacher could follow most-to-least prompting procedure, starting with a verbal-gestural-physical prompt and waiting 5 seconds; if the student begins to clean the work area, the teacher moves to a verbal-gestural prompt and waits 5 seconds; if the student begins to clean the work area, the teacher moves to a verbal prompt.

Another example of prompting involved a student who "refused" to get off of the bus when it arrived at school unless an adult would tell him that "it's time to get off the bus." A constant time delay was used to get the student to respond to the desired stimulus (i.e., when the bus stops and the other students begin to leave) and the starting stimulus (i.e., telling him to get off the bus). When the bus would stop, a 0-second time delay occurred for the first 3 days. Then, a delay of 5 seconds was provided from the time the bus stopped and the students began getting off to the prompt to the student to get off of the bus. If the student did not get off the bus during this 5-second delay, he would then be prompted to get off the bus. At some point, the student began to get off the bus before the 5 seconds elapsed. This point is called the moment of transfer, because the transfer of control from the starting prompt ("get off the bus") to the desired stimulus (bus stopping and other students getting off the bus) was beginning to occur. A progressive time delay involves first providing a 1-second time delay. After several predetermined presentations of the 1-second delay, a 2-second delay is used, and so on until the student begins to respond to the desired stimulus.

The danger in prompting methods that involve physical contact with students is that if there is resistance from the student to the physical prompt, it may not be appropriate to use the prompt. Any physical prompting procedure must be used with caution, because the risk of injury to staff and students is increased.

What Is Shaping?

The concept of shaping was described in Chapter 2 as a manner in which to teach behaviors and inadvertently increase the level of unwanted behavior. Shaping, however, can also be used as a behavior management technique. One of the most serious problems faced in today's schools is the increasing number of students who are labeled as having hyperactivity and/or attention deficits. One difficulty found with these students is that they have difficulty maintaining on-task behavior. Some students have difficulty maintaining on-task behaviors for more than 30 seconds at a time. Most teachers require some form of sustained activity or attention from students, and when students cannot for whatever reason maintain this activity or attention level for the required time, difficulties often ensue. What teachers may require is for the student to meet the requirement of a certain length of on-task behavior, or reinforcement is not provided. Unfortunately, many of these students will fail to meet the requirement set by teachers, and improvement will not occur. Therefore, some way to increase the on-task time of the student must be devised. Shaping is a method that can be beneficial to the goal of increasing on-task time. To use shaping, teachers set the initial time on-task requirement to the student's current level, such as 30 seconds. When the student is on task for 30 seconds, the student is reinforced in some manner. Once the student is able to maintain on-task behavior for 30 seconds consistently, the time is increased to 45 seconds, for example. When the student is on task for 45 seconds, the student is reinforced. Again, once the student is able to maintain on-task behavior for 45 seconds consistently, the time is again increased. Thus, the length of time the student is on task is shaped.

On-task time is not the only type of behavior for which this approach works. Another example is working with a student who is a poor speller. Feedback on the student's spelling may be provided, as done for all other students; the poor speller, however, may not ever meet the requirements for good spelling. This failure occurs with many students. When it happens, the students may experience something similar to **learned helplessness** (Seligman & Maier, 1967), which results when we continue to meet with negative consequences no matter what we do and thus we tend to give up. Students who simply stop trying may have experienced so much negative feedback for their efforts that they stop trying. Therefore, it is necessary that the student's efforts as well as overall performance receive feedback. With regard to the poor speller, the student's spelling performance can be shaped. For example, two out of ten words spelled correctly may be a good starting point for the student. When the student is able to spell 20% of her words correctly, the requirements for positive feedback could be increased to 30% of the words spelled correctly, and so on.

The critical point to understand with shaping is that the process can be used to "catch" the behavior by ensuring that it is reinforced and then gradually moving to higher response expectations. This method is preferable to setting the initial requirement for the student so high that he fails to reach the criterion. Therefore, think of positive behavior development as a progression from where the student is now to where you would ultimately like to see the behavior.

What Are the Premack Principle and the Response Deprivation Hypothesis?

It is critical to get students to display appropriate behaviors in the classroom. To get appropriate behavior to occur, teachers may need to provide some incentive to students. A time-tested method of providing students incentives is to provide them access to something that is reinforcing to them. This method can be interpreted two ways, through the Premack principle and the response deprivation hypothesis.

Premack Principle

The **Premack principle** is a concept that has been around for many years. More commonly called **"Grandma's rule"** (Cipani, 1998), the Premack principle simply says that to get a less preferred behavior to occur, reinforce it with a more preferred one. Examples include "If you eat your vegetables, you will get dessert" and "If you do your homework, you can go out to play." Technically, the Premack principle indicates that a high-probability behavior can reinforce a low-probability behavior (Premack, 1959). The relative probabilities of the behaviors are critical. Thus, if it is more likely that a child would eat vegetables than dessert, the dessert cannot be used as a reinforcer for vegetables. If doing homework is more likely than going out to play, going out to play cannot be a reinforcer for completing homework. Therefore, to use the Premack principle, one must know which behavior is more or less likely to occur than the other.

The Premack principle has been shown to be very effective in encouraging behavior to occur (Sulzer-Azaroff & Mayer, 1991). Most people over the years have known it works; it is used all the time not only with children, but also with adults. Hence, it is called Grandma's rule: Grandma knows that it works. According to some people, however, the Premack principle is a bribe, but calling it a bribe takes away from this effective method. The Premack principle, along with all reinforcement procedures, would be bribes if the purpose of the reinforcer is to achieve an advantage for the person or persons providing it (Sulzer-Azaroff & Mayer, 1991). Fortunately, ethical professionals implement reinforcement-based systems not for their own good but for the good of the student. Another difference between bribery and reinforcement is that bribery aims to promote immoral or dishonest behavior that corrupts those involved. It would be difficult to find instances in schools in which a teacher's use of reinforcement was aimed at corrupting students. A final difference between bribery and reinforcement is that reinforcement by definition comes after the behavior; bribery often comes before the act. Therefore, the ethical use of reinforcement is not bribery.

Response Deprivation Hypothesis

A question arises with the Premack principle: Can a low-probability behavior be used to reinforce a high-probability behavior? In other words, can a behavior that is less likely to occur, such as eating vegetables, be used to reinforce a more likely behavior, such as eating dessert? Can a parent get a student to play outside more so as to do homework? Theoretically, the answer to these questions may be yes. The **response deprivation hypothesis** indicates that the Premack principle is only partly correct. One can take a high-probability behavior and increase the likelihood of a low-probability behavior by reinforcing the low-probability behavior with the high one. The reason for the effectiveness of the procedure, however, may not be what was originally thought. According to the response deprivation hypothesis, the relative probabilities are not important (Sulzer-Azaroff & Mayer, 1991). It is not true that less likely behaviors can only be reinforced with high ones. In reality, more likely behaviors can be reinforced with less likely ones. The way that is done is to decrease the less likely behaviors below the baseline or normal levels (Timberlake & Allison, 1974). Children usually eat some vegetables once in a while, for example. If this level of vegetable eating is decreased below its normal level, vegetable eating will become a reinforcer.

Take a more likely classroom scenario. Suppose there is a student who sits in the corner of the room and does not interact with anyone. The goal is to get this student to be part of the student group. Nothing works, not offering extra recess time, not prompting the student back to group, not threatening a poor grade if he does not join the group. Perhaps this student does not have any reinforcers, because nothing gets the wanted behavior (sitting with the group) to occur. The Premack principle suggests finding a more likely behavior to get the student to sit with his peers, but the teacher cannot think of anything that the student finds reinforcing. The response deprivation hypothesis can help lead the way. Under this hypothesis, essentially any behavior can serve as a reinforcer as long as the student is doing the behavior at some level. Thus, the first step is to see what the student does. In this case, the student sits in a corner of the room. This behavior, then, is the potential reinforcer. The technique to try is to tell the student that if he sits with the group for some short time, such as 2 minutes, he can go back and sit alone for the rest of the period. If the student refuses to go with the group, the teacher sits next to the student. Thus, the only way the student can be left alone is by interacting with the group for a short period of time. Once the student sits with the group for 2 minutes for some criterion level (e.g., 3 consecutive days), the requirement could be increased to, say, 4 minutes. The beauty of this technique is that if the teacher is able to decrease sitting alone to below what it normally occurs, it will function as a reinforcer. If it functions as a reinforcer, the behavior it reinforces will increase in probability. Thus, interacting with the group will become more likely if sitting alone is a reinforcer. As interacting with the group becomes more and more likely, sitting alone becomes less and less likely, which in turn puts sitting alone in a more deprived state and increases its reinforcing properties. Ultimately, the hope is that reinforcing things going on in the group will reinforce being with the group, thereby overriding the reinforcement received for sitting alone. A transfer from one reinforcer (e.g., sitting alone) to another reinforcer (e.g., interacting with others) could ultimately be seen.

The response deprivation hypothesis takes away the claim that nothing reinforces this student, or "I can't find anything that reinforces this student." Yet, there is a potential problem about which teachers must be cautious: creating a deprivation state is aversive. Therefore, decreasing a behavior such as sitting alone below its normal occurrence level could result in negative side effects such as aggression. If a teacher tries to get a student to participate in a group by reinforcing participation with sitting alone, the probability of sitting alone must be decreased. If there are any signs of aggression or any other behavior that could result in injury or property damage, it should be discontinued and a behavior specialist should be consulted.

What Is Behavioral Momentum?

Behavioral momentum can be an important aspect of a behavior management procedure. It is based on the concept of response classes. **Response classes** are groups of responses that tend to occur due to the reinforcement of other behaviors (Cooper et al., 1987); that is, responses differing in topography (i.e., what they look like) grow more probable as a result of the reinforcement of another behavior (Skinner, 1969). Skinner indicated that this phenomenon allows for the survival of the species "since it would be very hard for an organism to acquire an effective repertoire if reinforcement strengthened only identical responses" (p. 131). If there are responses that are strengthened due to the reinforcement of other behaviors, they can be used to our advantage. Say we have a student who is oppositional. The student does not follow directions very well. When we provide the student an instruction to complete a task such as cleaning his work area, he usually refuses. Other directions, however, the student is likely to follow, such as coming when called. Based on the concept of response classes, we should be able to increase the likelihood of the student to complete tasks he ordinarily would refuse to do by first providing him instructions to do things he would be likely to do (Mace & Belfiore, 1990; Mace et al., 1988; Singer, Singer, & Horner, 1987). As stated by Martin and Pear (1999):

> Thus, to increase the probability that the child will follow instructions he or she normally does not follow, it is often effective to first give the child instructions that he or she is likely to follow and reinforce compliance with those instructions. If the instructions that the child is less likely to follow are then given soon after this, the chances are greatly increased that he or she will follow them. (p. 150)

What Are Self-Management Procedures?

One of the more popular behavior management methods used today is self-management training (Dalton, Martella, & Marchand-Martella, 1999). Self-management is also called self-control or self-regulation. Through **self-management procedures,** the student manages her own behavior. The way we self-manage is by engaging "in a behavior (target behavior) at one time to control the occurrence of another behavior" (Miltenberger, 2001, p. 385). This definition of self-management is different from the traditional use of the term. We typically assume that self-management or self-control lies within the individual. Statements such as "He does not have the will power to lose weight" or "She must show some self-control and begin studying more" are not unusual. Where, however, does this self-control come from? Does it come from within the individual or from somewhere else? If it comes from within, there is not much anyone can do to aid people in their self-control. If, however, self-control comes from elsewhere, such as from the learning environment, much can be done to improve the situation.

As Heward (1987) indicated, self-management or self-control comes from how we respond to the situations around us. We do not manage our own behavior independently from our learning environments but as part of these environments. Self-management or self control comes from behaving in such a way that we change our environment. This change in the environment facilitates the behavior we want to occur. Thus, self-management or self-control is a way of behaving. It is a skill we exhibit at specified times. It is a skill that we can teach. If that is true, we can begin to understand why we may not display self-control in certain situations and how we can teach self-controlled behavior for these situations.

Reasons for a Lack of Self-Control

Typically, there are two behavior categories of concern when looking at student behavior: behavioral deficiencies and behavioral excesses (Malott et al., 2000). **Behavioral deficiencies** include behaviors that do not occur enough, such as failing to complete homework or failing to get to school on time, whereas **behavioral excesses** involve behaviors that occur too often, such as talking too much or swearing. Malott et al. have determined that there are two main reasons behavioral deficiencies and excesses are present. First, the long-term outcomes (e.g., good grades) of a behavior (e.g., studying) are small though often cumulative. Second, the long-term outcomes may be too improbable, such as with stealing behavior (the overall probability of getting caught may be low). Therefore, Malott et al. indicate that for self-control to be demonstrated, the long-term consequences of desired behavior must be large or significant and must have a high probability of occurring.

Translating that conclusion into classroom practice, teachers must show students the benefits of behaving appropriately and must reinforce appropriate behavior when it occurs. For example, complying with rules is critical in the classroom. Complying with rules, however, often does not result in positive consequences, only in decreasing the probability of receiving negative consequences. If teachers can change the classroom environment in such a way that responding to rules has important long-term consequences and that these consequences are likely to come about, more appropriate behavior should be exhibited by students.

Reasons for Teaching Self-Management

Why should educators improve student self-control? Table 11.1 shows several reasons. First, acting independently is valued and expected by society. The goal for teachers is to get students to be independent, not dependent. Second, teachers may not be able to continue to implement behavior management control procedures successfully at all times. At times, teachers simply cannot watch over a disruptive student; they must attend to other students as well. Third, when students demonstrate self-managed behavior, teachers can spend more time actually teaching. If students could manage their own behaviors, our instructional time would increase and less time would be spent trying to solve management issues. Fourth,

TABLE 11.1   *Reasons for Teaching Self-Management*

- Acting independently is valued and expected by society.
- A teacher may not be able to implement external control successfully.
- When students control their own behavior, teachers can spend more time teaching important skills.
- Students learn to behave appropriately when adult supervision is not available.
- Self-management may lead to more durable changes because students are learning a strategy.
- Self-management can result in generalized responding.

when teachers are not present, students will continue to behave appropriately, which is important especially in instances when substitute teachers or others have to take over the instruction of the class. Fifth, students who are taught self-management skills may be more likely to display these skills over a longer period. Behavior can be controlled by reinforcing wanted behaviors or punishing unwanted behaviors, but that is not teaching students a strategy for use in the future. Self-management skills are strategies that students can use in the future. Finally, students who display self-managed behavior may be more likely to display such behavior in other settings, such as on the playground, on the bus, during assemblies, or in other classes.

Types of Self-Management Skills

Several self-management skills can be taught to students. These skills include goal setting, self-recording, self-monitoring, self-charting, self-evaluation, self-instruction, self-reinforcement and self-punishment, and problem solving (Martella, Marchand-Martella, & Cleanthous, 2001). These skills are described in isolation, but they are usually used in combination with one other.

Goal Setting. **Goal setting** involves the establishment of performance criteria and the identification and use of solutions to meet an established goal (Martin & Pear, 1999). Goal setting is typically set by teachers without student input. The hope of goal setting is that if students have a hand in setting their own goals, they will be more likely to try to reach these goals. Therefore, goal setting initially involves the students and teachers sitting down and determining what goals would be appropriate for students. These goals are determined mutually through discussion. In the discussion, teachers should provide rationales for the importance of setting goals and reaching them. Examples of goals and indications of why these examples are appropriate goals can be provided to students. Goals such as completing work on time, turning in homework, getting high marks on assignments, and graduating from school are examples. Teachers can also provide examples of goals that would not be appropriate, such as being the toughest student in the school, being initiated into a gang, or not attending school. Teachers can also provide examples and nonexamples of goals that are currently attainable and those that are not. For example, for someone who is failing in every subject matter, a goal of straight "A"s is probably not attainable immediately. Getting straight "A"s may be obtainable later on; a more realistic goal is passing every class with at least a "D" or "C." The student should also be taught what long-term and short-term goals are. In addition, students should be taught how long-term goals can and should be broken into several short-term goals. For example, a goal of graduating from college might be divided into passing all high-school classes, then getting "A"s or "B"s, followed by then applying to a college, and so on. Getting good grades may also need to be broken into even shorter-term goals, such as completion of each assignment (see Table 11.2).

Students should also be able to provide examples and nonexamples of appropriate goals to their teachers. Once the students have demonstrated an understanding of goals and ways to attain these goals, the goals must be set. These goals should be documented so students can refer back to them. Teachers and students should continuously monitor each goal to make sure that progress has been made.

TABLE 11.2   *Examples of Goal Setting for School Activities*

Assignment	What Do I Have to Do?	Did I Do It?	
Reading	Read pages 19 and 20 Identify the main character and the setting	____ Yes	____ No
Math	Problems 1–10 on page 20	____ Yes	____ No
Music	Follow the teacher's instructions	____ Yes	____ No
Lunch	Follow the five BIG RAM rules	____ Yes	____ No
Science	Measure and record the length of four objects	____ Yes	____ No

4 or 5 completed assignments = go home on time (3:00).

Fewer than four completed assignments = stay after school for 10 minutes (3:10)

Self-Recording.   **Self-recording** involves observing and recording one's own behavior with a prompt (Martella, Leonard, Marchand-Martella, & Agran, 1993). This prompt can be anything that evokes the recording behavior. For example, a student who has negative verbalizations (e.g., swears, makes derogatory statements) may be told by teachers to record whenever a negative verbalization is heard. Students who are frequently off task may be taught how to record whether they are on or off task whenever a bell sounds. In these examples, students were prompted to record something at a particular moment.

Due to its reactivity, self-recording has been shown to be effective in decreasing unwanted behavior. In other words, when we are prompted to record what we do or do not do, this recording usually affects our behavior in some manner. Say that we are biting our fingernails and a friend tells us to stop each time we begin to bite our nails. A step further would involve marking down each time we began to bite our nails. It is likely that nail biting would decrease. The same thing happens with students who engage in unwanted behavior. The self-recording of the behavior tends to have a reactivity effect. As with all data-collection procedures (see Chapter 9), self-recording requires the development of a data-collection form similar to that used by the teacher. Any data-collection form, however, must be simple enough for students to use. Figure 11.1 shows an example of a self-recording form, with positive and negative interactions and positive and negative comments (Sprick, 1981). Students mark each time they say something nice or something derogatory. For younger students, instead of typewritten words on a page, pictures can be used, with a positive behavior resulting in the opportunity to color in a circle (see Figure 11.2).

To teach self-recording, several steps must be completed (Martella, Leonard, et al., 1993). The first step is called preteaching. In this step, the teachers provide a rationale for self-recording. The second step involves demonstrating how the self-recording form is

FIGURE 11.1

Use the frog chart by filling in or by having a student fill in a circle whenever
he or she works hard or engages in a specific positive behavior.

FIGURE 11.2

used. This form will then be used throughout each of the remaining steps. The third step involves providing students with several examples (e.g., 10 examples) of the unwanted and wanted behaviors. Before each example is provided, the teachers name the type of example, saying "This is an unwanted behavior." The fourth step involves providing students with the examples again but having them indicate which behaviors are wanted and which are unwanted. The final step involves having the students generate a list of unwanted and wanted behaviors while labeling each behavior at the same time. The students are finished

Are you working and staying on task? (Circle yes or no.)

Monday

11:00	11:05	11:10	11:15
Yes No	Yes No	Yes No	Yes No
11:20	11:25	11:30	11:35
Yes No	Yes No	Yes No	Yes No
11:40	11:45		
Yes No	Yes No		

Tuesday

11:00	11:05	11:10	11:15
Yes No	Yes No	Yes No	Yes No
11:20	11:25	11:30	11:35
Yes No	Yes No	Yes No	Yes No
11:40	11:45		
Yes No	Yes No		

Wednesday

11:00	11:05	11:10	11:15
Yes No	Yes No	Yes No	Yes No
11:20	11:25	11:30	11:35
Yes No	Yes No	Yes No	Yes No
11:40	11:45		
Yes No	Yes No		

Thursday

11:00	11:05	11:10	11:15
Yes No	Yes No	Yes No	Yes No
11:20	11:25	11:30	11:35
Yes No	Yes No	Yes No	Yes No
11:40	11:45		
Yes No	Yes No		

Friday

11:00	11:05	11:10	11:15
Yes No	Yes No	Yes No	Yes No
11:20	11:25	11:30	11:35
Yes No	Yes No	Yes No	Yes No
11:40	11:45		
Yes No	Yes No		

FIGURE 11.3 *Self-monitoring form.*

with this preteaching when they accurately record which statement is a wanted behavior and which is an unwanted one.

Once preteaching is finished, the teachers must determine what the prompt will be, such as telling students to record a behavior when it occurs or using some signaling device such as a clock chime. Finally, teachers must monitor students' self-recording to make sure it is occurring.

Self-Monitoring.   **Self-monitoring** is similar to self-recording except that it occurs without the external prompt (Dalton et al., 1999). Thus, self-monitoring is much more difficult for students to perform because it involves a finer discrimination of when a particular behavior occurs or does not occur. For example, Dalton et al. (1999) taught two middle-school students with learning disabilities how to use a self-monitoring form to track their on-task performance in three general education classes (see Figure 11.3). Thus, the students monitored their behavior rather than simply *recorded* when it occurred. The preteaching was conducted in the same way as self-recording.

Self-Charting.   **Self-charting** involves teaching students how to graph their own behavior. It can be a great motivational technique in areas such as reading instruction. If teachers are conducting timed reading passages, the students can graph their reading rates and accuracy levels. Students can then see the progression of their reading performance over time. Goal setting can easily be combined with self-charting, with students and teachers setting a goal in reading speed and placing a data point on the graph. Students can then *see* the progression toward their goals.

Self-charting can also be used for unwanted behaviors (Martella, Leonard, et al., 1993). For example, students can take the data from a period of self-monitoring and plot the level of positive statements on a graph (as shown in Figure 11.4). Again, students get visual feedback on the level of their behavior from the graph.

Self-Evaluation.   **Self-evaluation** involves teaching students how to measure their own behavior against some specified standard (Martella et al., 2001). Students who stop trying in class may have a weakness in this skill. These students may see their performance as weak in comparison to others. On the other hand, Seligman (1995) indicates that students who think too much of their work tend to be more aggressive when provided with feedback on weak performance. Seligman indicates that students must receive accurate feedback on their performance. Students can be taught to make these evaluations themselves by providing accurate feedback on performance and/or providing them examples and nonexamples of good performance. For example, high-school students could be given an example of a well-written paper and their papers could be evaluated against this standard. Their evaluation is matched with the teacher's evaluation. Therefore, self-evaluation is taught through providing students accurate and honest feedback on their performance and by providing examples and nonexamples of some standard. The preteaching step used in self-recording and self-monitoring is an appropriate and effective way to teach self-evaluation skills.

Table 11.3 shows a self-evaluation form used by Dalton et al. (1999). As shown, students were instructed to circle "yes" or "no" to questions referring to behaviors to be exhibited before, during, and after class. In addition, each student was instructed to rate his or

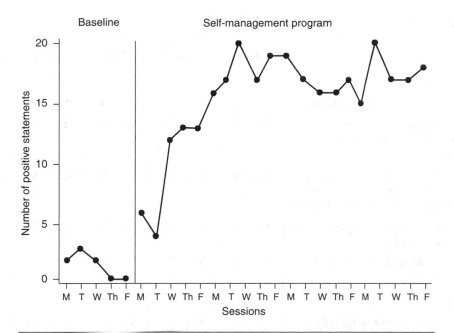

FIGURE 11.4   *Example of a self-chart.*

her overall behavior. This rating was compared with a rating provided by the teacher. Teacher ratings were operationally defined so that consistency of ratings could be ensured (see Table 11.4).

Self-Instruction.   **Self-instruction** training involves teaching individuals how to "talk themselves" through a particular set of behaviors (Martella et al., 2001). Meichenbaum and Goodman (1971) described self-instruction training and recommended a five-step sequence: (1) teachers perform task, instructing aloud while students observe; (2) students perform task while teachers instruct aloud; (3) students perform task while self-instructing aloud; (4) students perform task while whispering; and (5) students perform task while self-instructing covertly.

Research on self-instruction training shows that it can be an effective way of improving appropriate behavior (Hughes, 1991). Researchers, however, are not in agreement on the causal effects of self-instructions (see Agran & Martella, 1991, and Martella, 1994, for a review of the literature and discussion of the causal effects of self-instructions). Self-instructions may prompt or cue a behavior to occur (e.g., telling ourselves that we need to get on task may get us on task), but they may simply be a parallel behavior to the overt behavior we want to see (e.g., telling ourselves we need to get on task may be a second behavior independent of getting on task). Unfortunately, researchers have not determined which view is correct. Another problem with self-instruction research is that self-instructions may serve a causal role, but it is difficult to make this determination because the last step in self-instructional training is fading the self-instructions to covert. Therefore, it is not possible to determine if self-instructions are occurring in any direct manner.

TABLE 11.3 *Self-Evaluation Form*

Dates	Mon.	Tues.	Weds.	Thurs.	Fri.
Before Class					
1. Do I have my homework completed?	Yes No	Yes No	Yes No	Yes No	Yes No
2. Did I bring my materials (pencil, assignment log, and composition book)?	Yes No	Yes No	Yes No	Yes No	Yes No
3. Did I find out what I will be doing in class (listen to the teacher, look for the assignment, ask if I don't know)?	Yes No	Yes No	Yes No	Yes No	Yes No
4. Did I write the assignment/activity in my assignment log?	Yes No	Yes No	Yes No	Yes No	Yes No
5. Did I get started on time within 60 seconds?	Yes No	Yes No	Yes No	Yes No	Yes No
During Class					
6. Did I ask myself during the period, "Am I working?" Respond yes or no.	Yes No	Yes No	Yes No	Yes No	Yes No
After Class					
7. Did I follow the teacher's directions?	Yes No	Yes No	Yes No	Yes No	Yes No
8. Did I work on the assignment during the entire time I was given?	Yes No	Yes No	Yes No	Yes No	Yes No
9. Do I have homework tonight? If yes, write in my assignment log.	Yes No	Yes No	Yes No	Yes No	Yes No
10. Rate my behavior: (Circle the number) 1 = poor 2 = needs improvement 3 = okay 4 = good 5 = great	1 2 3 4 5	1 2 3 4 5	1 2 3 4 5	1 2 3 4 5	1 2 3 4 5
For the Teacher					
11. Please rate the student's behavior: 1 = poor 2 = needs improvement 3 = okay 4 = good 5 = great	1 2 3 4 5	1 2 3 4 5	1 2 3 4 5	1 2 3 4 5	1 2 3 4 5

TABLE 11.4 *Criteria for Teacher Ratings*

1 = student was off task for most of the period (more than 40 minutes), did not follow classroom rules, was reprimanded regarding behavior more than two times, was removed from the classroom.

2 = student worked on the assigned task, followed classroom rules for less than half the period (30 minutes or less), or was reprimanded regarding behavior two times.

3 = student worked on the assigned task, followed classroom rules for over half of the period (30 minutes or more), or was reprimanded regarding behavior two times.

4 = student worked on the assigned task, followed classroom rules, or one minor incident such as speaking without permission occurred.

5 = student worked on the assigned task, followed classroom rules, or no warnings or reprimands were needed.

Self-Reinforcement and Self-Punishment. **Self-reinforcement and self-punishment** are said to involve teaching individuals how to provide consequences for their own behavior. Self-reinforcement could be in the form of praise (e.g., I did a good job), tangible (e.g., buy a new outfit), or an activity (e.g., go to a movie) if a behavior is exhibited (Martella et al., 2001). Self-punishment usually involves self-reprimands but can also involve the removal of a potential reinforcer such as not going to a movie. The teaching of self-reinforcement and self-punishment involves having students say good things about themselves when a positive behavior is seen. For example, when students respond favorably to an instruction, the teachers could have the students tell themselves that what they did was a good thing. The teachers could also tell the students that they can go buy themselves a drink. Self-punishment works in a similar manner in that the students would be told to say to themselves that not following directions is not a good thing to do.

Self-reinforcement and self-punishment are methods that can be effective in getting wanted behaviors to occur and unwanted behaviors to not occur (Alberto & Troutman, 1999). Technically, however, there is no such thing as self-reinforcement and self-punishment as a control of behavior. As Catania (1975, 1976, 1998) points out, the true controlling variables will be found in the environment, not with what we do to consequate our own behavior. When students set up a consequence, such as going to a movie at the end of the week for studying all week, this consequence may be thought of as a self-reinforcer if the studying behavior becomes more likely in the future. Yet, there must be other consequences keeping the students from going to a movie during the week. A consequence could be the possibility of a poor grade on a test if they did not study. Therefore, although self-reinforcement and self-punishment can be important skills to teach students, it must be remembered that the teachers must set up some other contingencies to uphold these self-reinforcement or self-punishment procedures.

Problem Solving. **Problem solving** is teaching individuals how to reach a successful conclusion to a problematic situation (Martella, Agran, & Marchand-Martella, 1992). A problem is when there is no specific response to a situation and a response must be generated in some manner. Problem-solving training typically involves a four- to five-step procedure (Foxx, Martella, & Marchand-Martella, 1989). D'Zurilla and Goldfried (1971) outline one such five-step sequence. The first step involves the identification of the problem (e.g., I am getting angry). Teaching individuals to discriminate a problem situation from one that is not a problem must be achieved in this step. The second step involves defining what the problem is (e.g., another student is teasing me). This step is critical in that knowing what exactly is the problem will aid in developing a method to overcome the problem. The third step involves the generation of alternatives. This step can be achieved through brainstorming or generating as many alternatives as possible without regard to their consequences (e.g., I can hit the student, I can walk away from her, I can tell the teacher, I can leave class, I can tell her to leave me alone). The key to this step is to not make judgmental statements on the student's alternatives. The fourth step, decision making, involves considering the possible consequences—both positive and negative—of each solution (e.g., If I hit the student, she probably would leave me alone but I would get into trouble; If I tell the teacher, he will tell her to stop but I could be labeled a tattletale; If I walk away, I would avoid a confrontation but I could be seen as being afraid; If I told her to leave me alone, she may comply but she may also become more obnoxious). Once the pros and cons have been laid out, students must decide which al-

FIGURE 11.5   *Daily report card.*

Remember: 8 out of 10 "Yes" responses = 5 points

A "3" to "5" behavior rating = 5 points

If your points = 10 for the day, you get 10 minutes of free time in your study class.

You get 2 extra-credit points EACH TIME you get a "5" for behavior from your teacher.

A total of 10 points for 4 consecutive days = A candy bar or soda of your choice and the points will go toward your overall grade in the learning opportunity center (LOC) or study class.

For the teacher

Record points here:

Dates	Mon.	Tues.	Wed.	Thurs.	Fri.

ternative is likely to have the best outcome (e.g., I will tell her to leave me alone and if that does not work, I will tell the teacher). The final step involves verification. In other words, the students must be able to determine if the alternative worked. If it did, the students should be prepared to use it again. If it did not, another solution should be attempted.

The Need for Consequences

A particularly important aspect of any self-management program is arranging for consequences for the self-management skills we want to develop and maintain (Martella et al., 2001). For example, there must be some consequence for self-recording or self-instructions for them to continue. These consequences may initially come from the teacher. Dalton et al. (1999) used a daily report card to consequate appropriate classroom behavior (see Figure 11.5). Later, if the training was done correctly, the maintaining consequences will come from more natural sources, such as from other students. Therefore, simply teaching students to problem solve, self-instruct, self-reinforce, self-monitor, self-evaluate, self-record, or self-chart is not enough. Teachers must set up some system to maintain these behaviors or skills until students receive naturally maintaining contingencies from elsewhere in their environments.

What Is Correspondence Training?

Correspondence training is similar to self-management training. Self-management training, however, involves teaching individuals how to change the environment to facilitate future behavior, whereas correspondence training involves teaching students how to report on what they have done or will do accurately (Risley & Hart, 1968). When individuals report what they will do in the future, one hopes that they will be more likely to do it. Thus, reporting what we will do in the future is an aspect of self-management. Correspondence training has been researched extensively by Catania and his colleagues (e.g., Matthews, Shimoff, & Catania, 1987). Several possible relations in correspondence are important for students to learn: (1) doing what we say we will do (e.g., "I will study" and we do study), (2) accurately reporting what we have done (e.g., "I hit her" when we actually hit another student), (3) not doing what we say we will not do (e.g., "I will not write on the desk again" and we do not write on the desk), and (4) accurately reporting what we have not done (e.g., "I did not steal" when we did not steal).

Clearly, correspondence in children is a critical aspect of responsible behavior, but it may need to be explicitly taught. As shown by Matthews et al. (1987), correspondence is taught by recognizing when there is correspondence between saying and doing and reinforcing it. For example, when students say that they will complete an assignment and do so, teachers should reinforce the correspondence between what the students say and actually do. Likewise, if the students cheat on a test but accurately report that they cheated, teachers should reinforce the correspondence. Note that the behavior of cheating may still be punished by, say, giving a failing grade for the test, but the accurate reporting of the event may be reinforced by allowing the students to take an alternative form of the test with 25% of the points taken off of the top.

The critical aspect of correspondence training is to note when students are telling the truth. This aspect is critical for behavior management; working with students who do not exhibit correspondence (e.g., do not accurately report what they have done) is much more difficult because the information obtained from them is always suspect.

What Are Behavioral Contracts?

Behavioral contracts (also called contingency contracts) are popular methods of behavior management (Cooper et al., 1987; Zirpoli & Melloy, 2001). Behavioral contracts involve setting up the context under which the students will perform. The contract also sets up the context under which the teachers will perform. The behavioral contract is similar to any other contract. It spells out what each party to the contract must do to satisfy the agreement. The behavioral contract involves three main components: the task, the reward, and the task record (Cooper et al., 1987). Figure 11.6 shows an example of a behavioral contract. The task must be stated in observable terms. In other words, teachers must be able to see when the behavior occurs (e.g., getting to class on time). The task must also be accomplished in some time period (e.g., coming to class before the bell rings). Also, how much of the task is required must be documented (e.g., each day of the week).

Kabler, Dardig, and Heward (1977) (cited in Cooper et al., 1987) specify that five elements must be included in the contract. First, the reward must involve a description. In other words, what exactly the students will earn if they meet the expectations (e.g., get extra time on the computer) must be described. Asking the students what they would like to earn for the particular behavior can generate possible rewards. Note that rewards are not the same as reinforcers. If the reward does not increase the likelihood that students will perform the behavior (e.g., getting to class on time), it is not a reinforcer. If the students begin to get to class on time due to the contract, then the reward is a reinforcer. Second, the delivery of the reward must also be determined (e.g., Friday afternoon at 2:00 p.m.). Third, the contract must also specify how often the reward will be provided (e.g., every 15 minutes). Teachers must be sure that the delivery of the reward occurs after the expectations have been met and that the amount of the reward is appropriate for the task.

Fourth, a record-keeping system must be in effect. A task record could be attached to the contract, and teachers can record on it. Another system, however, is to integrate self-recording or self-monitoring into the task record. Thus, the teachers or the students mark whether or not the students have met the behavioral expectations each day. Self-recording or self-monitoring can enhance the effectiveness of the contract.

Finally, there must be an area that the teachers and students sign. Gaining the students' signature aids in getting their commitment to become involved in the contract, increasing the probability that the contract will lead to more instances of wanted behaviors.

What Are Token Economy Systems?

Token economy systems, described in detail by Ayllon and Azrin (1968), are effective in bringing about positive behaviors. We are all on token systems. If we have ever used

FIGURE 11.6 *Example of a behavioral contract.*

CONTRACT

Who: Sandy

What: Complete all work assigned

When: Every school day

How well: Sandy will complete 15 of 20 work assignments over the week and will earn one of the following: (a) lunch with Tammy on Monday. (b) 10 extra minutes of computer time before the end of school on Friday. (c) 10 extra minutes in the gym in the afternoon on Friday. (d) 10 minutes of free time before the end of school on Friday. BONUS: If Sandy completes 20 out of 20 assignments, she will receive an "Excellent Student" note sent home to her parents.

Who: Ms. Brown

What: Verify that work is completed; place a "+" for each day for each subject

When: Every school day

How much: Ms. Brown will provide one of the rewards listed. A bonus "Excellent student" note will be sent home for completion of all 20 assignments.

Sign here: _____

Date: _____

Sign here: _____

Date: _____

	Mon.	Tues.	Wed.	Thurs.	Fri.
Math					
Science					
Reading					
Social studies					

money, we have used a token system. Money is a token. A dollar by itself holds no value. The value of a dollar comes from what we can purchase with it. The things we can purchase with money are likely primary reinforcers, such as food, money, and shelter, and secondary reinforcers, such as nice clothes, fancy cars, and movies. Tokens, then, are conditioned or secondary reinforcers because they get their reinforcing value from being paired with an established reinforcer. Money is also considered to be a generalized reinforcer because it is not dependent on only one backup reinforcer such as food; if money could no longer be used to buy food, it still would be reinforcing because it can buy other things. Therefore, tokens are things that are provided contingent on some behavior that can be turned in for (or used to purchase) backup reinforcers.

TABLE 11.5   *Steps in a Token System*

1. Design a record system.
2. Select tokens.
3. Design a method of delivering the tokens immediately.
4. Set the number of tokens per behavior (specify conditions for token delivery).
5. Select backup reinforcers (things that can be purchased).
6. Set backup reinforcer prices.
7. Train staff.
8. Design the system to maintain consistency of the program.
9. Pair token delivery with positive social feedback (i.e., praise).
10. Build in a response cost system (Chapter 12).
11. Maintain a positive balance of tokens.
12. Provide access to the backup reinforcer.
13. Fade out the system.

Setting up a token system is like developing a banking system. Table 11.5 shows the steps involved in setting up a token system (Sulzer-Azaroff & Mayer, 1991). Token systems are difficult to administer effectively because they take a great deal of planning and monitoring. They also require a great deal of consistency. These systems work because the token becomes a conditioned reinforcer. Teachers can use the tokens to reinforce a wanted behavior immediately. Unwanted behaviors are ignored or punished. Token systems also bridge the time gap between the behavior and the established reinforcer. Therefore, tokens are excellent tools for immediately consequating a behavior.

The problem with token systems in the classroom is that they are artificial (Sulzer-Azaroff & Mayer, 1991). They are effective, but once they are in used in one class, there may be a lack of generalization if students transition to another class where they are not used (Cooper et al., 1987). Therefore, tokens should be used more as a last resort to gain control over unwanted behaviors, or some plan must be made to fade out the systems. Fading out token systems is important in planning for maintenance of behavior change.

Fading of token systems can be achieved in several ways (Cooper et al., 1987; Sulzer-Azaroff & Mayer, 1991). First, delay the provision of the token after the behavior has been emitted. Second, provide the token on an intermittent basis. Third, decrease the amount of tokens earned for each behavior. Fourth, increase the number of behaviors required for each token. Fifth, increase the delay between the token deliveries and the availability of the established reinforcers. Sixth, increase the prices of the established reinforcers. Finally, provide the established reinforcers on an intermittent basis.

When Should We Use These Procedures?

Selecting which behavior management system to use is important in leading to behavior change. The first step is a functional assessment of what is maintaining the unwanted behavior. Once this step has been accomplished, the most appropriate intervention method to use to bring about positive behavior change must be determined. Simply teaching a replacement behavior is not the end point. As discussed in Chapter 10, the behavior plan should replace the unwanted behavior with one that is more appropriate but receives the same reinforcer. Teachers must, however, continue to work toward the ultimate goal and at some point get the student to perform the desired behavior. Therefore, teachers need intervention methods that are aimed primarily at increasing a desired behavior. The procedures presented in this chapter attempt to do just that. Once the students have acquired the desired behavior, maintenance and generalization planning should begin.

How Is Consequence-Imposed Behavior Change Generalized?

Generalization is a critical aspect of any behavior change program. If generalization is not realized, the social validity of the management program must be questioned. Therefore, teachers and other individuals designing and implementing a behavior management program must consider it an important goal. Many of the generalization planning methods teachers and others can use to plan for generalization were originally described by Stokes and Baer (1977) and Stokes and Osnes (1989). These methods are described below.

Generalization can take two forms: response generalization and stimulus generalization (Martin & Pear, 1999).

Response Generalization

Response generalization refers to a behavior being more likely to occur in the presence of a stimulus as a result of another behavior having been reinforced and strengthened in the presence of that stimulus (Kazdin, 2001). Children who call their mothers "mom" after having been reinforced for calling them "mommy" is an example. Another example is that when students are reinforced for saying "thank you" when provided something, they may be more likely to say "thanks." Therefore, response generalization can provide an advantage in that more behaviors come about as a result of another being taught. This advantage is seen in problem-solving training when a situation may call for a certain response, such as when students are challenged to a fight by others. One student may have been taught to walk away and report the incident to a teacher. If teachers are not present or if this student is prevented from walking away, however, another response would need to be generated. In this case, the student may attempt to engage in conflict resolution by talking it out with the other students. In most problem-solving training programs, students are taught to generate several possible solutions to a problem situation. When doing so, the probability that a solution can be reached is increased. There are two general methods of programming for response generalization when increasing desirable behaviors: train sufficient response exemplars and vary the acceptable responses during training (Martin & Pear, 1999).

Training Sufficient Response Exemplars. **Training sufficient response exemplars** involves teaching students several appropriate responses to a given situation. For example, students who get frustrated when provided with difficult tasks and become verbally aggressive can request a break instead by saying, "May I take a break?" "I need help," or "I need a rest." Problem-solving teaching methods frequently teach a number of possible solutions to a problem and have been shown to promote generalization in nontraining situations (Foxx, et al., 1989; Martella el al., 1992; Marchand-Martella, & Agran, 1993).

Vary the Acceptable Responses during Training.   A similar procedure is to require different responses. For example, requiring students to wait for 5 minutes to take a break, requiring them to clean off their desk before going on a break, and/or requiring them to finish one more question before taking a break are methods of teaching a variety of responses for taking a break. This technique was used by Goetz and Baer (1973) to increase the creativity of block building of nursery school children.

Stimulus Generalization

Although response generalization is an important concept, **stimulus generalization** is usually of more concern to educators (Martin & Pear, 1999). In terms of behavior management, teachers frequently want students to behave appropriately in some particular manner, placing less emphasis on teaching them several possible acceptable ways of behaving in a situation. Stimulus generalization involves the increased probability of a response being emitted in the presence of a stimulus as a result of being reinforced in the presence of another stimulus (Kazdin, 2001). Young children calling all men "daddy" is an example of stimulus generalization. Sometimes this form of generalization can be comical. One of the authors is going bald. One morning, his 1-year-old daughter was in the living room watching a cartoon on television, and he was in the kitchen. He heard his daughter yell "Daddy" and his wife say, "Good girl, that's daddy." As it turns out, his daughter was pointing excitedly at the television, thinking she was seeing daddy. She was not seeing daddy, however, but Elmer Fudd. This example is a case of stimulus generalization. The major concern with students' behavior is that they will behave appropriately in other situations, which is a concern of stimulus generalization. There are several methods of programming for this type of generalization: teach in the target situation, program common stimuli, train sufficient stimulus exemplars, train loosely, and sequential modification of the training situation (see Stokes & Baer, 1977, and Stokes & Osnes, 1989).

Teach in the Target Situation.   Because the goal of stimulus generalization is for the behavior that is taught to be exhibited in a particular (target) setting, the best way to get the behavior to occur in that situation is to teach in that situation. For example, the best way to teach students to cross the street appropriately is not to teach it in a classroom setting but at an actual street corner, as was done by Pattavina, Bergstrom, Marchand-Martella, and Martella (1992). Similarly, if teaching students to display appropriate social skills such as asking for an item from another student without using force to gain access to the item, teachers would want to teach this skill at a time when the students really wanted something. Many times it is expected that when students are taught something in the classroom setting, they will display the taught behavior in other situations. Sometimes the behavior does not generalize to these other situations. Therefore, if there is a problem behavior and teachers attempt to decrease the likelihood of the behavior by increasing another behavior by teaching students to self-record their behavior, for example, self-recording should be taught in the actual setting in which the unwanted behavior is likely to occur.

Program Common Stimuli. **Programming common stimuli** is an important aspect of behavior management. Suppose a teacher has students who are in a more restrictive setting, such as a classroom for students with behavior difficulties. The ultimate goal is to transition them to the general education classroom once their behaviors are under control. One consideration to make is what is going on in the future environments or classrooms the students may enter. For example, if a token system is used in the classroom but the general education classroom to which the students will be transitioning does not have a token system in place, there may be difficulties in student behavior in the next classroom. Alternatively, if there is a token system in place, its use should be faded out when possible, being replaced by the management system used in the other classroom. For example, the teacher in the other classroom may extensively use rules and proximity control as the behavior management method for her students. In this case, programming common stimuli would involve fading out the system that is currently being used and moving to the system the other teacher has imposed. If the new management system is successful with the students, the likelihood of success when the students enter the other classroom is increased substantially. This technique was used by Walker and Buckley (1972) when they used the same academic materials in a general education classroom and the resource room where social and academic classroom behaviors were taught.

Training Sufficient Stimulus Exemplars. **Training sufficient stimulus exemplars** involves using as many possible examples of situations as possible. For example, if a teacher is having difficulty with students in one location such as one classroom, the management program should also be implemented in as many sites as possible, such as other classrooms, assemblies, physical education, playground, and in the cafeteria. When many situations in which the behavior management program is used are provided, there will be an increased likelihood that the wanted behaviors will occur in untrained settings, such as on a field trip. Problem-solving approaches frequently use this technique by providing as many different possible problem situations. For example, Martella, Marchand-Martella, and Agran (1993) used a problem-solving format with several stimulus exemplars to improve the adaptability (independence) of high-school students with mild disabilities.

Train Loosely. **Train loosely** has also been called incidental teaching, naturalistic teaching, nonintensive teaching, and minimal intervention (Alberto & Troutman, 1999). Training loosely involves varying the situation under which the management program is introduced. For example, have several teachers or adults in the classroom implement the program rather than one adult, vary the way instructions are provided, vary the tone of voice, or teach in noisy and quiet areas. Training loosely then aids in the generalization to other situations that may be different in some way from the one provided. Another example is for the teacher to reinforce spontaneous target behaviors, such as using statements and questions to improve academic and self-help skills as was done by Campbell and Stremel-Campbell (1982).

Sequential Modification of the Training Situation.   **Sequential modification of the training situation** involves successfully implementing the management program in one setting and then changing the management system in another setting to match that of the first setting. For example, if teachers have students who display unwanted behaviors in the classroom who are going to transition to another classroom, they may train the other teachers in the new setting to implement the management system in their classroom. Essentially, they are replicating the effects of the management program in future environments. This modification was accomplished by Dalton et al. (1999) when the self-management program they employed was sequentially applied to each of three general education classrooms.

How Is Consequence-Imposed Behavior Change Maintained?

One of the most important considerations made with regard to behavior management is how to ensure the maintenance of the behavior. **Maintenance** is defined as the endurance of a behavior after the intervention has been removed (Kazdin, 2001). Formal individualized behavior management programs should not be thought of as permanently placed procedures. Rather, they should be thought of as temporary attempts to get the behavior under control. Once the behavior is under control, the behavior management procedure should be faded out. Therefore, whether the improved behavior continues in the future without the behavior management program in place must be determined.

There are several methods of planning for the maintenance of behavior change (see Stokes & Baer, 1977, and Stokes & Osnes, 1989). Several of these methods can be placed into three categories: intermittent schedules, programming for naturally occurring contingencies, and the use of self-management procedures (Martin & Pear, 1999). (The programming methods for maintenance discussed here can also be beneficial when planning for generalization.)

Intermittent Reinforcement Schedules

As with teaching any skill, when working with behavior problems there is a need to reinforce appropriate behavior on a continuous schedule of reinforcement and not reinforce the unwanted behavior. The teaching of appropriate behaviors is critical in maintaining any behavior change that results from a behavior management program. In addition, wanted behaviors, once strengthened, should be placed on an **intermittent schedule of reinforcement.** This method of programming for maintenance is called "indiscriminable contingencies" (Cooper et al., 1987). For example, suppose that a student was out of her seat 75% of the period. The program consisted of teaching her how to monitor her own behavior with the provision of reinforcement for being in her seat throughout a 5-minute interval. At the beginning, when the student monitored her own behavior and was in her seat throughout a 5-minute span, she was reinforced. The time span was then increased from 5 minutes to 10 minutes and so on until the student was in her seat for the entire period. Once the student was able to self-monitor being in her seat throughout the period for three consecutive days, the contingencies for being in her seat were faded out. Thus, there is not reinforcement for every period completed while being in seat. A teacher could reinforce every other day for being in seat, then every third day, and so on. In this manner, the requirement of being in seat for the student is gradually increasing, but only gradually.

Schwarz and Hawkins (1970) also used indiscriminable contingencies when they improved the posture and voice loudness and decreased the face touching of a sixth-grade student by providing her with videotapes of her in-class behaviors after school. Therefore, reinforcement and feedback to the student were delayed. This delay may have made it difficult for the student to discriminate when improved performance was needed for reinforcement (Stokes & Baer, 1977). The results showed that not only did the student's behaviors improve in the training class (math), but improved behavior also generalized to another class (spelling).

Use of Naturally Occurring Reinforcers

Another tactic to program for maintenance is to get the behavior under the control of **natural reinforcers** (Sulzer-Azaroff & Mayer, 1991). Thus, not only would more and more in-seat time be required, but what should be maintaining the in-seat behavior would also be determined. In most cases, being in seat will result in the completion of more work. Thus, the attention students receive for completion of the seatwork should be natural. Teachers should increase the attention provided to the students for completed seatwork. They should move from a continuous schedule of reinforcement for seatwork completion to an intermittent one and allow for natural reinforcement to occur for the wanted behavior. With this tactic, maintaining positive behavior change is more likely.

Perhaps the most important aspect of programming for naturally occurring contingencies is changing how others respond to positive student behavior. Many students who display problem behaviors are social outcasts. These students are those who are not liked by peers or teachers. They have a long history of causing problems for other students and educational staff. Therefore, it may be difficult to interact with these students in a positive manner. It is much easier to spot unwanted behavior from these students because teachers look for their unwanted behaviors. If long-lasting behavioral change is truly wanted, other staff members must change the manner in which they interact with the students. Therefore, **positive scanning** for wanted behavior displayed by these students should take the place of negative scanning or looking for unwanted behaviors. If we as educators can attempt to make our interactions with these students positive rather than negative, we can increase the likelihood that learned positive behavior will continue. In addition, if we can change our interactions toward the students in a positive manner, the students are also more likely to do so as well.

An example is a middle-school student who displayed severe behavior problems (Martella, Leonard, et al., 1993). The teacher's main concern was with the level of negative statements the student made to other students and adults. This student displayed roughly 1.5 negative statements per minute in one class period. When he would say these negative things, the classroom staff and students would usually respond in a negative manner, such as by providing a reprimand or a "dirty look." Thus, almost all the student's interactions with others in the classroom were negative. Based on the definition of positive reinforcement, however, these "negative" interactions were positively reinforcing the student's unwanted negative statements. Once the behavior management program had been implemented, the student began to receive positive interactions with students and staff when he said something positive. The student's positive statements increased dramatically, whereas the negative statements decreased. The positive statements maintained long after the program was withdrawn, whereas the negative statements remained at zero levels. The reason the positive statements maintained after the program was withdrawn was that the staff and students changed how they interacted with the student. This new interaction was essentially a built-in maintenance procedure in which naturally maintaining contingencies (i.e., you have positive interactions with people when you are nice to them) were introduced.

The previous discussion of programming for natural contingencies involves an important concept called **behavioral traps** that involve the maintenance of a behavior by natural reinforcers after the behavior was initially developed by programmed reinforcers (Baer & Wolf, 1970; Kohler & Greenwood, 1986). In other words, students can be taught how to seek out reinforcement for positive behaviors, which should in turn "trap" or maintain the behavior.

To have a behavioral trap, one must first determine what the natural reinforcers are in the environment and then teach behaviors that will meet with those reininforcers. Another method of using behavioral traps to the educator's advantage is to teach the student specific behaviors that will prompt reinforcement. For example, individuals with developmental disabilities were taught how to avoid injuries at work (Martella et al., 1992). One part of the training was to report to the supervisor that something was done to avoid an injury (e.g., removing an object from an aisle). This step in the work safety instruction helped maintain the safe worker behavior by prompting the supervisor to praise the injury-avoiding behavior. This concept can be used in the classroom as well. For example, students who do not complete seat work very often could be taught to tell the teacher when they do complete the work. Therefore, the students prompt the teacher to reinforce the work completion.

Use of Self-Management Procedures

Self-management procedures were presented in this chapter as an intervention method. These procedures can be a part of an effective management program. They are also thought of as a way to improve the chances of maintenance because they move the control of the behavior from external agents such as teachers to the students (Cooper et al., 1987). Rather than teachers having to arrange the environment to get an appropriate behavior to occur, the students can behave in such a manner that increases the probability that appropriate behavior will occur. For example, if students are taught how to self-instruct, they may provide self-generated verbal prompts to a behavior rather than rely on teachers to provide these prompts. Thus, when the teachers no longer provide prompts for a behavior, the students may do so independently. In this way, a self-management procedure such as self-instruction may allow the behavior to be maintained by reducing students' reliance on teachers.

What Is the Planning Process for Generalization and Maintenance?

As shown, generalization and maintenance are critical aspects of a behavior management program. There are several ways of programming for generalization and maintenance, but these methods take planning. According to Cooper et al. (1987), three steps should be considered. First, all the desired behavior changes must be listed. Second, a list must be created showing all the situations, settings, and places where the wanted behaviors should occur as well as all the people with whom the wanted behaviors should occur. Finally, there must be a list of the behaviors that must be shown to those involved with the students and those who are affected by the behavior change. Behavior change must be thought of as not only changing the student behavior but also as a change in the behavior of all those working with the students. In other words, teachers must ask themselves what they must do to lead to an improvement in student behavior rather than only focusing on what students must do.

Summary

Behavior management is fairly straightforward, using techniques that have been shown to be effective through research and continuously monitoring to see if the techniques are changing the behavior (see Chapter 9). The techniques used in behavior management programs are used in all societies; when dealing with unwanted behaviors, however, the use of these typical techniques is done systematically. For example, teachers used praise for years before the effects of praise on behavior were determined. Now information on the technique to ensure that it is used in a systematic and effective manner is available.

When using behavior management procedures, there are several options. In terms of consequential procedures, there are reinforcement-based and aversive-based procedures. Ethically, teachers should begin with reinforcement-based procedures and move to procedures designed to decrease the likelihood of the unwanted behavior (see Chapter 12) only if the former has failed to bring about positive changes. Behavior change is dependent, to a large extent, on how teachers react to unwanted behaviors. It is important for teachers to understand, however, that any procedure is targeted at the behavior and not at the student. One is attempting to change a person's behavior, not the person. If this fact is kept in perspective, long-term success is more likely. The successes of any behavior management program are dependent on the application of behavior management procedures to a particular behavior. Knowledge of these procedures will only make teachers more successful in their quest to improve the classroom environment.

Once positive behaviors are taught, attention should turn to generalizing and maintaining these skills. The methods of programming for generalization and maintenance should become part of an effective behavior management plan.

VIGNETTE • *Revisited*

Ms. Armstrong presented the difficulties she was having with Juan to the building assistance team. She indicated that there was nothing that Juan would work for, in terms of a reinforcer. One member of the team told Ms. Armstrong that there was in fact something that Juan would work for, and that was not interacting with the class. This teacher told her that if she could decrease the amount of time Juan sat isolated from the class, she could use sitting alone as a reinforcer for becoming involved in the class activities. The critical aspect of this technique was decreasing the amount of time Juan isolated himself from the class. This teacher also told Ms. Armstrong that she should start small, such as requiring Juan to interact with the class for 5 minutes, and then gradually "shape" or increase this time.

Ms. Armstrong decided to give it a try. The next day, Ms. Armstrong told Juan that he could sit alone and not be bothered for the entire class period if he became involved for 5 minutes in a class activity. She also told Juan that if he refused to become involved for these 5 minutes, she would stand next to Juan while instructing the class. Wanting to be left alone, Juan agreed to become involved in the class activity. After 5 minutes he went back to the corner of the room. Once Juan was regularly involved in the 5-minute class activity, Ms. Armstrong increased the required involvement in the activity to 10 minutes. Over a period of 5 weeks, Ms. Armstrong was able to get Juan involved in all but the last 5 minutes of the class, when Juan was allowed to sit in his corner uninterrupted.

Discussion Questions

1. Why is it critical to consider increasing a wanted behavior versus simply decreasing an unwanted one?

2. How can a teacher use different prompting strategies to get wanted behaviors to occur?

3. How can shaping be used to improve a behavior that is not occurring enough, such as on-task behavior? Provide an example.

4. How are the Premack principle and response deprivation hypothesis similar? How are they different?

5. How can a teacher increase a student's appropriate responding to instructions?

6. Why is the development of self-managed behavior a desirable goal for students? What skills can be taught to help a student become more self-managed?

7. Technically, do students self-manage their behaviors independent of contingencies placed on them by the environment?

8. How can correspondence training increase the likelihood that students will accurately report what they did or follow through on what they said they will do?

9. How can token economy systems be integrated into a behavioral contract? Provide an example of such a program.

10. How can teachers plan for the generalization and maintenance of behavior change? Describe each of the methods.

12

Managing Individualized Behavior

Decreasing Undesirable Behaviors

Chapter Objectives _____

After studying this chapter, you should be able to:

- Describe the least restrictive, least intrusive, and most effective alternatives.
- Illustrate the cautions with the use of restrictive or intrusive procedures.
- Depict the informal procedures one can use to respond to unwanted behavior.
- Characterize level I behavior-reduction procedures.
- Describe level II behavior-reduction procedures.
- Explain what is meant by aversive-based procedures, including their side effects.
- Illustrate level III behavior-reduction procedures.
- Describe level IV behavior-reduction procedures.
- Explain how to decide which procedure to use.
- Characterize how consequence-imposed behavior change is generalized and maintained.

VIGNETTE

MS. JACKSON TAUGHT FOURTH GRADE. One student, Jackie, would frequently swear and have tantrums in class. Although Jackie was a slightly below average student, she did not seem to have any particular weakness in any subject, but she did seem frustrated at times with some of her assignments (both group and individual). When Jackie became frustrated, she would become angry and begin to swear until she had a tantrum. Ms. Jackson would respond to these unwanted behaviors by sending Jackie to time-out in the hallway for 5 minutes. Upon reentering the classroom, Jackie was required to become engaged in the assignment once again. Ms. Jackson found that the probability of a repeat tantrum once Jackie reentered the classroom was about 50%. Therefore, sending Jackie out of the room did not seem to be having the desired effect. Unfortunately, Ms. Jackson was not sure why these swearing and tantrum behaviors were occurring.

Ms. Jackson became concerned enough to complete a functional behavioral assessment on Jackie. She had hoped that the assessment would not only reveal why Jackie was acting this way but also lead to an appropriate and effective solution. The result of the assessment suggested that Jackie was having tantrums or swearing during difficult tasks that lasted several minutes. There did not seem to be a particular subject that was associated with the unwanted behaviors. In other words, these behaviors occurred during reading, math, and spelling. Based on this assessment, Ms. Jackson believed that the function of the behavior was to escape from a demand task.

Overview

Recall that the first step to any behavior management program is to attempt to improve students' behaviors through reinforcement procedures. Unfortunately, not all students respond favorably to these attempts. For some students, procedures to decrease the likelihood of unwanted behavior need to be implemented. The difference between procedures aimed at increasing wanted behaviors and those aimed at decreasing unwanted behaviors has to do with the focus of the intervention. The focus of the intervention of increasing wanted behavior is on the wanted behaviors. The hope is that if wanted behaviors are increased, they will take the place of unwanted behaviors. Unwanted behaviors, however, do not always go away with these attempts. Therefore, the intervention needs to focus on the unwanted behaviors themselves.

In this chapter, some of the management methods frequently used to decrease the likelihood of an inappropriate behavior being exhibited in the school setting are outlined. Be aware, however, that these procedures should not be used in isolation. The procedures discussed in Chapter 11 can and should be used in conjunction with the procedures discussed throughout this chapter. The procedures discussed will move from the least restrictive procedures to the most restrictive.

What Are the Least Restrictive, Least Intrusive, and Most Effective Alternatives?

The procedures used in behavior management place some restrictions on students and are intrusive in some manner. Ethically, however, educators must use the least restrictive and least intrusive interventions possible while still providing effective supports. Teachers must understand what restrictiveness and intrusiveness mean. In addition, they must know their professional positions on the use of different management methods as well as fully understand the rules and regulations of particular states with regard to which procedures are considered more or less restrictive and intrusive. States set guidelines as to which procedures can be used with or without formal approval and the limits placed on the use of these procedures.

Restrictiveness

Restrictiveness involves the extent to which an individual is limited access to basic human freedoms (e.g., privacy, movement, leisure) (Cooper et al., 1987). Therefore, methods that least limit this access should be used. For example, placing a student in time-out is technically considered more restrictive than providing a reprimand, physical restraint is more restrictive than time-out, and overcorrection is more restrictive than extinction.

Intrusiveness

Intrusiveness involves the extent to which behavioral interventions are obtrusive and affect a person's bodily or personal rights. Procedures associated with pain, discomfort, or social stigma are examples (Wolery et al., 1988). Thus, corporal punishment is more intrusive than time-out, reprimanding a student in front of other students is more intrusive than reprimanding her when she is alone, and placing a student in exclusionary time-out is more intrusive than using nonexclusionary time-out.

Effectiveness

Professionally, educators are obligated to use behavior management procedures that have been shown to be effective in the research literature. If teachers are going to use an individualized management system, they should be confident that it will be effective because it has been shown to be effective in the past. If a procedure has not been shown to be effective or if there is not enough information to demonstrate its effectiveness with students, the "principle of least dangerous" assumption should be used (Wolery et al., 1988). This "suggests that the strategy selected should produce the least amount of harm if the procedure is ineffective. This principle may be quite important when choosing between strategies that have not been used with a particular population, behavior problem, or setting" (Wolery et al., 1988, p. 370).

Therefore, teachers must maintain a balancing act. They must choose the least restrictive and least intrusive alternatives while using the most effective procedures. At times, the most effective interventions will be more restrictive or intrusive than other procedures. In these cases, more restrictive or intrusive interventions may be needed or some effectiveness may be sacrificed for less restrictive or intrusive interventions. Ultimately, the decision of what interventions to use will depend on what is allowed by state guidelines and what has been tried in the past (i.e., begin with the least restrictive and intrusive interventions and use more restrictive or intrusive interventions if the previous ones have failed).

Ultimately, the decision as to which behavior management procedure to use comes down to the right to effective interventions. Students have a fundamental right to receive the most effective behavior management programs available. Although the aim is to use preventative techniques and reinforcement-based systems, more restrictive and intrusive interventions may be needed.

Cautions with the Use of Restrictive or Intrusive Procedures

Lovaas and Favell (1987) discuss the need to protect students receiving restrictive or intrusive interventions. One critical aspect in protecting students' rights when using restrictive or intrusive interventions is to evaluate the efficacy of the intervention. Teachers must use the information obtained from ongoing evaluations to make decisions of the future interventions chosen. A second aspect in protecting students is to ensure adequate staff training and supervision. Restrictive or intrusive procedures can be misused and can violate the rights of students to a therapeutic environment (Van Houten et al., 1988). The better the staff training in the use of restrictive and intrusive procedures and the more extensive the supervision, the less likely that the interventions will be misused. A third concern is whether or not a functional behavioral assessment was implemented. The information obtained from such an analysis may decrease the need to resort to more restrictive and intrusive interventions in the first place. If it is determined that restrictive or intrusive interventions are required, however, this determination should result from a functional behavioral assessment. Finally, any restrictive or intrusive intervention implemented should have a scientific base. There are instances of abuse that have resulted from inappropriate application of these interventions. For example, locking a student in a closet as a time-out is not supported in the scientific community and is considered abusive. Such an intervention should not be used. Similarly, berating a student or calling a student derogatory names and terming the procedure a reprimand is not supported. Thus, the type and form of restrictive or intrusive techniques used should be shown to be effective in the scientific research literature. If the decision has been made to use restrictive or intrusive techniques, however, it is necessary to start from the least restrictive or intrusive approach before moving to more restrictive and intrusive interventions.

Conclusion

The major concern with the use of procedures meant to decrease unwanted behaviors is to use procedures that are the least restrictive and intrusive before moving to the more restrictive and intrusive methods. Therefore, procedures designed to prevent or reduce unwanted behaviors going from the least restrictive and intrusive to the most restrictive and intrusive are discussed next.

What Are Informal Procedures?

Informal procedures (also called preventative strategies) are those procedures that do not require explicit behavior management plans. That does not mean that these procedures do not take planning. A great deal of thought must be put into deciding which informal procedure to use, when to use it, and how it should be implemented. These informal procedures should be the first step in attempting to decrease unwanted behavior (Zirpoli & Melloy, 2001).

Situational Inducement

One effective method of decreasing the probability of unwanted behaviors is called situational inducement or stimulus change (Zirpoli & Melloy, 2001). **Situational inducement** involves "influencing a behavior by using situations and occasions that already exert control over the behavior" (Martin & Pear, 1999, p. 222). We have all experienced situational inducement in our interactions in society. Police substations in communities tend to decrease the likelihood of crime in those areas. Cameras visible in stores make shoplifting less likely to occur. Situational inducement can also be used to make other behaviors more likely to occur. For example, when we go into a supermarket for a high-frequency purchased item such as milk, notice that we have to go to the back of the store. The reason is that when we pass a large number of items in stores, we are more likely to buy something that we did not intend to buy initially. The items near a checkout line are also a situational inducement for buying something we may not need. When people are waiting in line, they are more likely to buy something than if they do not have to wait. Finally, go into a busy restaurant on a Friday evening and find out if there is music playing. If so, is it fast music? Music with a quick tempo tends to make people eat more quickly. Busy restaurants make more money if there is a fast turnover of customers, so inducing their customers to eat quickly is beneficial.

Situational inducement can work in the classroom to increase the likelihood of wanted behavior. Situational inducement can also be used in the classroom to decrease the likelihood of unwanted behaviors (Martin & Pear, 1999). When situational inducement procedures are used to decrease the likelihood of unwanted behaviors, they are used as an informal behavior management method. An example of situational inducement is moving a disruptive student from the back of the room to the front row. Also, moving two disruptive students away from each other is an informal management method.

Therefore, one of the first considerations in terms of decreasing the likelihood of unwanted behavior is to determine if there is an informal procedure that can be used for a student engaging in an unwanted behavior. If such an informal procedure can be used, there will be less need for a behavior management plan.

Redirection

Redirection is also an informal method of stopping a behavior. Redirection involves prompting students to do something that interferes with the unwanted behavior. Nontechnically, redirection is an attempt to get the students to take their minds off the unwanted behavior. For example, suppose that students go off task during instruction. Redirection involves telling the students that they need to get back to work. Another example involves asking students who are getting angry to talk about what they enjoy doing on weekends. Finally, students who are out of their seat could be guided back to their desk. Therefore, if a misbehavior occurs, simply prompting the students back to the task can decrease the unwanted behavior.

Chain Stopping

In Chapter 2, chaining was discussed in terms of how to teach a behavior. Behavior chains, however, can also be used to help with unwanted behaviors (Nelson & Roberts, 2000). Like wanted behaviors, unwanted behaviors occur in chains. For example, Figure 12.1 shows a possible chain of behaviors for a student who is aggressive. Several behaviors occur before the aggressive episode. If the chain of responses can be determined, the chain can possibly be broken by intervening on one of the links and preventing the aggression from occurring. This procedure is called **chain stopping.**

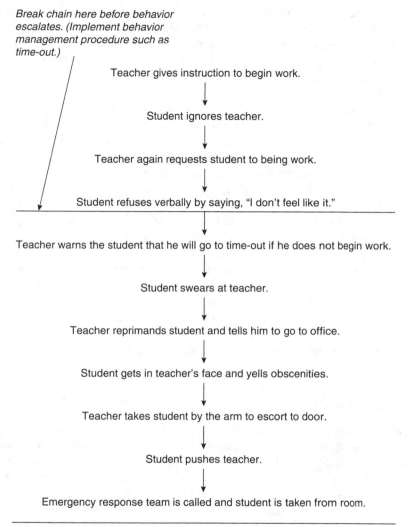

Break chain here before behavior escalates. (Implement behavior management procedure such as time-out.)

Teacher gives instruction to begin work.

Student ignores teacher.

Teacher again requests student to being work.

Student refuses verbally by saying, "I don't feel like it."

Teacher warns the student that he will go to time-out if he does not begin work.

Student swears at teacher.

Teacher reprimands student and tells him to go to office.

Student gets in teacher's face and yells obscenities.

Teacher takes student by the arm to escort to door.

Student pushes teacher.

Emergency response team is called and student is taken from room.

FIGURE 12.1   *Chain-stopping procedure for a noncompliant student.*

For example, a student had bulimia, an eating disorder. Bulimia is characterized by binge eating and purging (i.e., getting rid of the food in some manner such as vomiting). Part of the program was to define a chain of responses and then to break the chain before a binge and purge episode occurred. The behaviors or links in the chain included pacing, going to the bedroom door, opening the door a few times, going to the kitchen and back to the room a few times, going to the kitchen and opening the refrigerator, taking out food and then putting it back a few times, taking out the food and taking a bite, eating all the food (e.g., an entire jar of peanut butter), and then going to the bathroom and purging. This be-havioral chain was stopped by having the student call a friend when the pacing began. The call was enough to stop the chain. If the pacing occurred again, the student would again call the friend. (This step was only one component of the total intervention.)

Another example involves a student who engages in destructive episodes. One high-school student engaged in severe destructive episodes when he became angry. Before he became angry, he would stomp his feet. He would sit in his chair and bring his foot down to the floor lightly, like a tap at first. Then the stomping would become more pronounced and louder as he brought his foot down with more and more force as he became more agitated. Chain stopping involved going over to the student, asking him what was the matter, and attempting to diffuse the situation. Much of the time, the student was becoming frustrated with his seatwork. Therefore, the teacher provided assistance with the assignment so that the student would calm down. Chain stopping in this example prevented the problem behavior from occurring by stopping minor behaviors before they escalated into more severe behaviors.

Nelson (1996b) and Nelson and Roberts (2000) have used chain stopping with students who engaged in disruptive behavior. These authors have shown that problem behaviors early in the chain in the classroom can be predicted by these minor behaviors. Therefore, teachers should respond to the minor behaviors before the behaviors become more severe. A positive aspect of chain stopping shown by Nelson is that students are more likely to respond favorably to a behavior management intervention if the intervention occurs before the major behavior episode. Therefore, not only can the likelihood of the target behavior be decreased, but students can be more effectively taught what are appropriate and inappropriate behaviors. Chain stopping is a critical aspect of effective behavior management programs.

Proximity Control

Proximity control is a procedure often used by teachers in the classroom setting that has been shown to affect a student's behavior (Kerr & Nelson, 1998). Proximity control involves decreasing unwanted behaviors by positioning the teacher somewhere next to the student (Zirpoli & Melloy, 2001). The teacher's proximity to the student should decrease the probability of the unwanted behavior if the proximity is a signal that a negative consequence will occur if the behavior continues. In other words, proximity control is an informal method of behavior management that uses a conditioned aversive stimulus (i.e., the closeness of the teacher) to stop the behavior. How close the teacher is to the student, however, will not function as a conditioned aversive stimulus unless the close proximity has been conditioned in some manner. This conditioning could occur by following through with the management procedure in place, such as time-out from reinforcement (described later) if the behavior does not cease with a teacher's close proximity.

What Are Behavior Reduction Procedures?

Systematic behavior management procedures designed to decrease the likelihood of a problem behavior can, and in most instances should, involve the first level of restrictiveness (level I) or reinforcement-based procedures. These procedures are considered the least restrictive methods of decreasing unwanted behaviors and involve stimulus control and differential reinforcement procedures. (Other procedures discussed in Chapter 11, such as the Premack principle, self-management, and token economy systems, can also be used to reduce unwanted behavior and are considered least restrictive; these and other procedures, however, are categorized as techniques primarily aimed at increasing desirable behavior.) If level I procedures prove to be ineffective, it may be necessary to move to the next level of restrictiveness (level II), which involves extinction. The third level of restrictiveness (level III) involves the withdrawal of reinforcement for the problem behavior; these methods involve response and time-out cost. The fourth level (level IV) of management methods aimed at reducing unwanted behaviors involve the removal of an aversive stimulus if the student behaves appropriately (escape or avoidance conditions) or the presentation of aversive stimuli (reprimands, overcorrection, contingent exertion, negative practice, and physical restraint). Table 12.1 shows a hierarchy of restrictiveness. Aversive procedures should be used as a last resort because of their potential negative side effects.

Level I Procedures (Presentation of Reinforcement)

Level I procedures are the least restrictive approaches aimed at reducing unwanted behavior (Alberto & Troutman, 1999). These procedures differ from the previously described informal procedures in that they are planned and implemented in a systematic fashion. Two level I procedures—stimulus control and differential reinforcement methods—are described here.

Stimulus Control.   Stimulus control methods can be used to evoke behavior and also to stop or prevent behavior (Sulzer-Azaroff & Mayer, 1991). Stimulus control methods

---

TABLE 12.1 *Hierarchy of Interventions from Least to Most Restrictive*

Level I Procedures (Presentation of Reinforcement)
- Stimulus control
- Differential reinforcement

Level II Procedure (Removal of Source of Reinforcement)
- Extinction

Level III Procedures (Removal of Reinforcing Stimuli)
- Response cost
- Time-out

Level IV Procedures (Presentation of Aversive Stimuli)
- Escape conditioning or avoidance conditioning
- Reprimands
- Overcorrection
- Contingent exertion
- Negative practice
- Physical restraint

---

should be planned and implemented formally. In terms of producing behavior, stimulus control methods involve presenting the discriminative stimulus (S^D) and reinforcing the appropriate behavior when it occurs in its presence. For example, telling the students that it is time to work (S^D) will produce the behavior of students sitting down in their seats and then being reinforced in some manner such as being praised (if praise is a reinforcer). When teachers prevent a behavior from occurring, they *do not* present the S^D (also called the S^Δ) and do not reinforce the student in its absence. For example, if teachers did not present the instruction to get to work, they would not reinforce the student's "getting ready to do work behavior." To make sure that an S^D is in effect, teachers must be sure not to reinforce the student in the absence of the S^D. In addition, an unwanted behavior can be prevented or stopped from occurring by presenting an S^{D-} in which the stimulus presented is an indication that a behavior that is emitted in its presence will be punished. For example, providing a start-up request such as "You need to get to work" could be an S^{D-} in that not getting to work will be punished in some manner. To make sure that an S^{D-} is in effect, teachers must be consistent in providing a punisher in its presence. Thus, teachers should think of methods they can use to increase the likelihood of a behavior by reinforcing it in the presence of the discriminative stimulus (posting verbal rules on the walls). Also, teachers should decrease the likelihood of an unwanted behavior by not reinforcing a behavior in the absence of the discriminative stimulus or by punishing a behavior in the presence of a discriminative stimulus that indicates that punishment will result if the unwanted behavior is emitted in its presence (e.g., a warning).

Differential Reinforcement Procedures.   **Differential reinforcement** procedures are those used to reinforce appropriate behaviors and not to reinforce inappropriate ones (Sulzer-Azaroff & Mayer, 1991). For this reason, the approach is called differential reinforcement: behaviors are reinforced differentially. Although differential reinforcement procedures can be thought of as attempts to increase wanted behaviors, their main focus is on decreasing unwanted behaviors rather than on increasing wanted behaviors. These procedures were developed as methods of using schedules of reinforcement to decrease these unwanted behaviors in a systematic manner. They are systematic applications of reinforcement. Therefore, they are artificial. These procedures are rarely instituted for every student in a systematic manner. When a student needs an individualized behavior management program, however, teachers must become more explicit in their interventions. They can use these procedures to gain control over the unwanted behaviors and then to move to a more natural method of behavior management later. There are five differential reinforcement schedules: differential reinforcement of other (DRO) behavior, differential reinforcement of incompatible (DRI) behavior, differential reinforcement of alternative (DRA) behavior, and differential reinforcement of low-rate (DRL) behavior (see Table 12.2 for a summary of these schedules).

Differential Reinforcement of Other (DRO) Behavior.   **Differential reinforcement of other (DRO) behavior** has also been called differential reinforcement of zero rate behavior and omission training (Sulzer-Azaroff & Mayer, 1991). DROs are considered to be time-based reinforcement schedules. Reinforcement is provided if an unwanted (targeted) be-

TABLE 12.2 *Summary of Differential Reinforcement Schedules*

Schedule	Definition	Example
Differential reinforcement of other (DRO) behavior	Reinforce any behavior other than the target behavior and extinguish the target behavior.	Praise the student every 5 minutes if hitting another student does not occur and do not reinforce if hitting does occur.
Differential reinforcement of incompatible (DRI) behavior	Reinforce the opposite behavior of the targeted one and extinguish the targeted behavior.	Praise on-task and ignore off-task behavior.
Differential reinforcement of alternative (DRA) behavior	Reinforce an alternative appropriate behavior and extinguish the targeted behavior.	Allow a break for asking for one from work and ignore tantrums to get out of work.
Differential reinforcement of low-rate (DRL) behavior	Reinforce low-rate behavior and extinguish high-rate behavior.	
Spaced responding	Reinforce only if a set time occurs (IRT) between each behavior.	Answer a question if the student waits 5 minutes between questions and ignore if less than 5 minutes.
Limited responding	Reinforce if a certain number of behaviors occur or fewer within a certain time period.	Answer a question if student has asked 10 or fewer questions in hour and ignore if student asks more than 10 questions.

havior has not occurred within an established time period. For example, a DRO-5-minute schedule means that if the unwanted behavior has not occurred during a 5-minute period, the individual's lack of unwanted behavior will be reinforced. (Technically, one cannot reinforce a lack of behavior. One actually reinforces any behavior other than the targeted one). If the unwanted behavior does occur, the unwanted behavior will not be reinforced and the time is reset for another 5-minute period.

The time setting is determined by taking a baseline and calculating on average how much time elapses before each instance of an unwanted behavior. For example, if an individual displays the unwanted behavior 12 times per hour on average, the average rate of behavior is one every 5 minutes. Therefore, the time period is set at 5 minutes. Once the time has been set, the DRO is implemented. Every 5 minutes, the lack of behavior (or behaviors other than the target behaviors) is reinforced. At the end of 5 minutes, the time starts over again. If an unwanted behavior occurs during the 5 minutes, say after only 2 minutes, the 5-minute time interval starts over then (see Figure 12.2).

When the student's behavior is observed consistently over the time period, a whole-interval DRO is being used (Sulzer-Azaroff & Mayer, 1991). Once the student reliably (e.g., no unwanted behavior for 3 consecutive days) refrains from emitting the unwanted

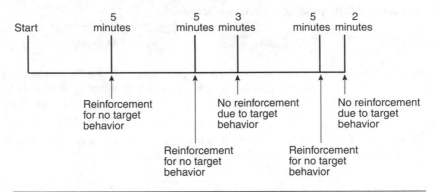

FIGURE 12.2   *Example of a DRO-5-minute schedule for an observation time of 20 minutes.*

behavior, the 5 minutes can be increased to, say, 8 minutes, then 10 minutes, then 15 minutes, and so on. Once the student reliably refrains from emitting the unwanted behavior, a momentary DRO (Repp & Deitz, 1974) can be used. With a momentary DRO, at the end of the stated time period, say 5 minutes, the teacher looks over at the student to see if the misbehavior is occurring. If not, the student's lack of behavior (or engagement in other behavior other than the target behavior) is reinforced. If the unwanted behavior is ongoing at that time, the student's unwanted behavior is not reinforced. The advantage of the momentary DRO is that the teacher does not have to observe the student's behaviors for the entire time period, only at the end of the time period.

An obstacle in the use of a DRO is knowing when to reinforce the student. In other words, a teacher must know when the time has elapsed. When observing for the entire interval, as in a whole-interval DRO, it is not difficult to keep track of the time. Once teachers move to a momentary DRO, however, they must keep track of the time somehow. Realize that a momentary DRO could result in a loss of accurate information on whether the target behavior occurred at all during each interval (Repp & Deitz, 1974). A momentary DRO should be used as a last resort to free up time to do other things such as teach or after a whole-interval DRO has been used and shown that the behavior has subsided significantly (Sulzer-Azaroff & Mayer, 1991). Therefore, some prompt must be used to inform teachers of when to observe student behavior at the end of the interval. One method uses a beeper tape, a tape that plays on a tape player and at set intervals emits a beep or some other signal.

The use of DROs have been effective across a variety of settings and for a variety of problem behaviors (Miltenberger, 2001). There is, however, one problem with the use of the DRO. The DRO does not pass the "dead man's test" (Axelrod, 1987a). The **dead man's test** refers to a lack of behavior required on the part of the student so as to be reinforced. In other words, whatever a dead man can do is not behavior. Educators are in the business of teaching skills to students. When an unwanted behavior needs to be eliminated, some replacement behavior must be increased or taught. With the DRO, no replacement behavior is taught or required. For example, if we wished to reinforce a dead man for not swearing, we would be reinforcing the person 100% of the intervals. A lack of swearing, however, is not a behavior. On the other hand, if we required a person to speak appropriately, a dead man would not be able to meet the requirements. Therefore, as silly as it might sound, one thing to consider when using any behavior management technique is whether it passes the dead man's test.

Because a DRO does not pass the dead man's test, some alteration of the procedure may be desired. For example, teachers could reinforce the lack of unwanted behavior (stated correctly, reinforce any other behavior), such as not hitting another child who wants to play with a toy, and also reinforce a specified appropriate behavior, such as sharing. Sharing can be explicitly taught and does pass the dead man's test.

Differential Reinforcement of Incompatible (DRI) Behavior. **Differential reinforcement of incompatible (DRI) behavior** is used to teach an appropriate behavior or at least make a wanted behavior more likely. With a DRI, a behavior that is topographically incompatible or opposite from the target behavior must be selected (Zirpoli & Melloy, 1997). For example, the opposite behavior of out of seat is in seat. When an opposite behavior (i.e., in seat) is increased, the other behavior (i.e., out of seat) must decrease. The way a DRI works is to first determine the behavior a teacher wishes to decrease, such as off-task behavior. This behavior must be defined operationally so that there is little doubt that the student is out of seat. An example is, "student's buttocks are higher than 2 inches above the seat of the chair or when one buttock is more than 2 inches off the chair (e.g., leaning to one side)." Once the behavior has been defined, the opposite behavior must be determined. For example, in-seat behavior may be defined as having both buttocks in the seat or lifted above the chair by less than 2 inches with both feet on the floor. Once in-seat behavior has been defined, the out-of-seat behavior is either ignored or punished (e.g., mild reprimand) and the in-seat behavior is reinforced (e.g., praised). The reinforcement is presented on a continuous schedule. Data must be taken on the occurrence of these behaviors. Once in-seat behavior is occurring at a predefined level, the use of an intermittent reinforcement schedule should be used. As the out-of-seat behavior decreases, the in-seat behavior increases. Obviously, DRIs pass the dead man's test. They have been shown to be effective in reducing unwanted behaviors in a variety of settings.

Differential Reinforcement of Alternative (DRA) Behavior. **Differential reinforcement of alternative (DRA) behavior** involves reinforcing a more appropriate form of an unwanted behavior (Martin & Pear, 1999). Individuals will engage in unwanted behaviors many times because they have a limited skill repertoire. In other words, one reason some students misbehave is that they do not have other skills to display at a particular time. Take, for example, a young child who has limited verbal skills. Suppose that this child is a year and a half old and wants a cookie. The child may go into the kitchen and begin to cry. When the parents go to the child to find out what he wants, the child gets frustrated because the parents are not sophisticated enough to understand what the child is trying to tell them. As the parents frantically search for what the child wants, the child begins to cry louder until the episode turns into a tantrum. Finally, the parents grab the cookies and ask the child if this is what he wanted. The child stops crying and smiles and reaches his hand out for a cookie. Fortunately for the parents, they have found what the child wants and are able to stop the tantrum. Unfortunately, they have just reinforced the child for the tantrum and have made it more likely to occur the next time he wants a cookie. How can this cycle be broken? The parents have taught the child that the way to get things is to tantrum. From an educational perspective, the child's tantrum can be seen as an opportunity to teach a valuable skill: communicating what we want. What are the parents to do?

As with any behavior program, the first step is to define what needs to stop; in this case, it is the tantrum. A tantrum can be defined as any whining, crying, screaming, hitting, or throwing of objects. The next step is to determine what the replacement behavior should be. In this case, an appropriate replacement behavior is asking for a cookie without having a tantrum. The child should be taught how to say something like "cookie please." When the child says "cookie please," he should be provided the cookie immediately. If the child has a tantrum, however, the tantrum is ignored. What should occur is a decrease in the tantrums because they do not receive reinforcement, and saying "cookie please" should become more likely. At first, saying "cookie please" should be reinforced on a continuous reinforcement schedule. Once the child has learned how to ask appropriately and consistently for a cookie (e.g., five consecutive appropriate requests without a tantrum), an intermittent reinforcement schedule can be used.

Another example involves a student who becomes angry and swears when provided seatwork during math. The teacher should consider what an appropriate alternative response would be for swearing. The first step is to determine the communicative intent. Based on the results of a functional assessment, the teacher may find that the communicative intent is to avoid the task for some period of time by being sent out of the classroom. Therefore, the teacher could teach the student a more appropriate method of avoiding the task rather than swearing, such as saying, "I need a break." The replacement behavior (asking for a break) serves the same purpose as the target behavior (swearing). Swearing is ignored and asking for a break is reinforced on a continuous reinforcement schedule initially and then faded to an intermittent schedule.

Obviously, DRIs and DRAs are similar in that the target behavior is ignored while a replacement behavior is reinforced. The difference is that the target behavior and the incompatible behavior cannot be emitted at the same time. With the DRA, the target behavior and the alternative behavior can be displayed at the same time. That is, the child can have a tantrum while asking for a cookie, and the student can swear when asking for a break.

Differential Reinforcement of Low-Rate (DRL) Behavior. When teachers use DROs, DRIs, and DRAs, they are looking to eliminate the unwanted behavior altogether because any level of the target behavior is not appropriate. For example, a tantrum is never appropriate. At times, however, a particular behavior is not unwanted but occurs too often. In such cases, the goal is not to eliminate the behavior but to decrease its rate of occurrence. We all have experienced this behavior at some point in our lives. Think of people who simply talk too much. They talk all the time, and you can never get a word in. Or what about the student who asks too many questions during a class? How about the friend who asks to borrow things from you all the time? These behaviors may be acceptable many times, but when they occur too often, we become irritated. To solve this problem, we would attempt to reduce their levels. There are two methods of reducing, but not totally eliminating, a behavior: spaced responding **differential reinforcement of low-rate (DRL) behavior** and limited responding DRL behavior.

A **spaced responding DRL** involves reinforcing a behavior if a certain amount of time has elapsed between responses (Ferster & Skinner, 1957). This time period between responses is called the interresponse time (IRT). For example, if there is an average of 5 minutes between a student's question, the IRT is 5 minutes. The IRT is calculated by determining the rate of response. Thus, if a student has an average of 12 questions per hour, the IRT for each question is approximately 5 minutes. Now, suppose that a student asking 12 questions per hour on average is too much. One way to decrease the number of questions per hour is to increase the IRT. If the IRT is increased to 10 minutes, there are six responses per hour. Therefore, a teacher should first determine the maximum number of questions a student could ask per hour without interrupting the instruction. Once this number is determined, say, at four questions per hour, the IRT can be determined (e.g., 15 minutes). Then, the teacher only reinforces the student (by answering a question or calling on the student when she raises her hand) if there is the required IRT (15 minutes). Thus, there must be a certain amount of time required between the previous behavior and the current one to be reinforced. If a behavior occurs before the required IRT is met (e.g., less than 15 minutes elapsing between the previous behavior and the current one), the behavior is not reinforced (e.g., question ignored).

Informally, spaced responding DRLs are used every day. For example, when a speaker asks the audience to withhold applause until all names have been called, a required IRT is being stated. If a professor says to withhold all questions until she has finished lecturing, some IRT is being required. The difference between what occurs in everyday life and a formal, spaced responding DRL is that the formal, spaced DRL is systematic. This approach will usually not occur unless more informal methods have been unsuccessful.

One possible problem with the spaced responding DRL involves setting the response time. If the required time between responses is set too far apart, the student may not meet the criterion. For example, if the student is asking questions with a 5-minute IRT, setting the required IRT at 15 minutes may not work because the student may never go 15 minutes without asking a question. If the student is not able to meet the required IRT, it should be set at a lower, obtainable level.

The **limited responding DRL** is similar in results to the spaced responding DRL but has a different approach. The limited responding DRL does not require a certain time period between each behavior. Rather, the total number of behaviors allowed are determined and reinforced (Deitz & Repp, 1973). In the previous example of a student asking too many questions, if four responses per hour are determined to be acceptable, only the first four questions are reinforced and the others are ignored. It is appropriate to tell the student that she can ask only four questions; a good approach is to teach the student how to self-monitor the number of questions asked (see self-management in Chapter 11). This approach was taken by Martella, Leonard, et al. (1993) in decreasing inappropriate verbalizations. The student was emitting up to 1.5 inappropriate verbalizations per minute (or 23 per 15-minute observation). Therefore, to decrease the number of inappropriate verbalizations, an upper number such as 16 per observation was allowed, and then the number was decreased each time the student met the criterion of having at or fewer inappropriate verbalizations during an observation period for 4 consecutive days. (In this particular case, the limited responding DRL was used to decrease the total number of inappropriate verbalizations to zero.)

Similar to the spaced responding DRL, however, is that the number of allowed behaviors must be set at a level obtainable by the student. If the number is too low, the student will likely not meet the required level. For example, if the student with inappropriate verbalizations was required to have five or fewer inappropriate verbalizations in 15 minutes, the student would be unlikely to meet the level. If the level is set too low, the teacher will notice that the student is not meeting the criterion. If that occurs, the level should be changed to an obtainable one.

Level II Procedure (Removal of Source of Reinforcement)

The **level II procedure** involves the removal of the source of reinforcement (Alberto & Troutman, 1999). This procedure is called extinction.

Extinction.   Extinction procedures can be used to decrease the likelihood of a behavior being repeated again in the future (Skinner, 1953). As indicated in Chapter 2, extinction involves the permanent removal of the source of reinforcement for a particular behavior. Therefore, based on a functional assessment, if the source of reinforcement for the behavior is determined, the removal of this reinforcement will decrease the level of the behavior.

No matter what the reinforcer is, its removal will decrease the level of the behavior. Sources of reinforcement are not always easy to remove, however. For example, suppose that the function of a behavior is negative reinforcement via the removal of the student from the classroom. The student may be reinforced in that there was something in the classroom that was aversive to the student, such as the particular task required of the student. Extinction involves the removal of the negative reinforcer by not allowing the student to escape or avoid the required task. How would that be accomplished? The choices of removal may not be all that pleasant. First, the teacher could force the student to accomplish the task through some form of prompting procedure (e.g., physically making the student go through the motions). Second, the teacher could tell the student that he cannot leave the situation until the task is accomplished. For some students, that might mean sitting in their seats for days. Third, the teacher could attempt to first punish the behavior by sending the student to the principal's office and then requiring the student to begin the task again once he comes back. This third option is the most viable of the three in that there is no physical interaction necessary, nor is there a battle of wills. The student, however, may still attempt to avoid the task each time he comes back. Also, the other students are likely to move on to another task, which puts the student behind his peers. The best options are to not allow the student to escape or avoid the task through an inappropriate behavior (extinction) and to teach an appropriate escape or avoidance response, such as asking for a break. The teacher should also determine what makes the task so aversive. Determining what makes the task aversive involves considering the skill level of the student (Are we at the correct instructional level or zone of proximal development? Is there reinforcement being provided for the task? Are the lengths of the tasks short enough to prevent fatigue?).

Another problem with the removal of reinforcement can be seen with attention-seeking behavior. The teacher may say, "I ignore the behavior, but it keeps occurring." The problem is that the attention may not be from the teacher but from the other students. Attention does not come from just the adults. If the student is being reinforced by the other students through attention, removal of this attention is difficult. The teacher may ask the other students to ignore the student, which is not very likely to occur. A second option is to get the student away from the other students when the behavior occurs; this method has been attempted and found successful by Nelson (1996b).

A final problem with extinction is that if, in the rare occurrence, the behavior is one that is receiving sensory feedback, such as with self-stimulation or self-destruction, it is very difficult to remove the source of reinforcement. Drinking behavior is an example. If a student has a drinking problem, attempting to remove the sensory stimulation that occurs from the alcohol is difficult. Extinction involves the removal of the source of the stimulation, but in many cases, that is not possible. Referring the student to experts for this particular problem behavior may be the only viable alternative. Extinction will still work for these individuals, but gaining access to the reinforcer is problematic. A second, less desirable alternative is to attempt to override the reinforcing consequences of the behavior by punishment. That is essentially what is attempted when Anabuse is used for drinking (Anabuse is a medication people take that makes an individual ill if alcohol is consumed) or when a student is sent to jail.

Overall, extinction procedures should be used if access to the source of reinforcement can be found and controlled. Also, if the extinction burst can be tolerated, extinction is a viable alternative. Caution should be used, however, because gaining access to the source of reinforcement is not always possible and we may not be able to outlive the extinction burst.

What Are Aversive-Based Procedures?

A decision practitioners must make is what type of consequence to provide for a student's behavior. Essentially, there are two choices: reinforcement and aversive-based procedures. The preferred method of behavior management is through positive reinforcement procedures (Alberto & Troutman, 1999). These procedures do not have the negative side effects that aversive procedures have (described later). If, and only if, positive reinforcement procedures prove to be ineffective, **aversive-based procedures** should be used based on the least restrictive alternative shown in Table 12.1.

Negative Side Effects

Table 2.1 showed the possible negative side effects of aversive procedures (Sulzer-Azaroff & Mayer, 1991). The first negative side effect is that the student may attempt to avoid the punisher. Recall from Chapter 2 that when an aversive stimulus (e.g., reprimand) is paired with a neutral stimulus (e.g., teacher), the neutral stimulus can take on aversive properties. If a teacher notices that the student is attempting to avoid or escape her presence, she is likely to be an aversive stimulus to the student. The second potential negative side effect is that the student may become fearful of the punisher. When aversive methods are used, emotional responses may result. One such emotional response is becoming afraid of the person providing the aversive stimulation. A third negative side effect is that aversive procedures may stop other behaviors; in other words, aversive procedures may have a generalized effect on the student's classroom performance. For example, if a teacher reprimands a student for talking out in class, the student may stop talking in class altogether. A fourth negative side effect is that the use of aversive stimuli by teachers models their use to the students. Essentially, there is a possibility that when an aversive method such as a reprimand is used, students will learn to use the same method when reacting to peer behavior they do not like. That is a main reason many experts attempt to get parents to stop spanking their children. The argument is that when we spank our children, we teach them that the way to deal with others who do something we do not like is to hit them. The same thing can occur in the classroom. Remember that teachers are critical in the learning process of students, and when teachers react a certain way to misbehavior, many students will learn from that reaction. The fifth negative side effect is that the use of punishment tends to promote negative self-esteem (Sulzer-Azaroff & Mayer, 1991). When students are exposed to aversive stimuli, they tend to feel poorly about themselves.

The last three negative side effects are perhaps the most troublesome, especially in light of the growing problem of school violence. The use of aversive procedures tends to promote aggression toward the punisher or those associated with the punisher. Technically, this reaction is called response-induced aggression. Through animal studies and studies with humans, it has been found that the use of aversive stimulation increases the likelihood of aggression. Unfortunately, educators have not taken the necessary steps to decrease the level of use of aversive stimuli in our schools and classrooms. If students become aggressive to peers or school staff, it is possible that they are reacting to aversive procedures. Acts of aggression against others are not an indication of a personal flaw of the students or an indication of mental problems. Many examples outside the research arena demonstrate this fact. Look at what happens to circus animals when they are mistreated. That is not to say that students are the same as circus animals, but, when the effects of aversives on animals can be demonstrated, educators should be concerned.

Other negative side effects to the use of aversive stimuli are that they are negatively reinforcing to the punisher and are overused. The use of aversive stimuli tends to decrease the unwanted behavior quickly. Positive reinforcement-based systems tend to take longer to work. Therefore, when aversive procedures are used, there is a rather quick decrease in the problem behavior. When the problem behavior is aversive to teachers, they will then be more likely to use the aversive procedure again when a student's behavior is irritating. Therefore, teachers get caught in a negative reinforcement trap: the more they use negative reinforcement, the less unwanted behavior they see, which increases the likelihood of using it again when they see behavior we want stopped. Unfortunately, they are reacting in the short run by using aversive stimuli; in the long run, they are likely to see other unwanted and potentially more severe behaviors due to the previously described negative side effects.

Other negative side effects listed by Sulzer-Azaroff and Mayer (1991) that are not listed in Table 2.1 include inappropriate generalization, displaying behavioral contrast, and influencing the social status of the recipient of the punishment. Inappropriate generalization can occur when the student generalizes to other situations or stimuli that were not related to the punishment. For example, if a student learns that reading is aversive due to aversive consequences placed on the student for poor performance, reading itself may become aversive. One of the authors was in a finance class in college. The professor in this class was extremely aversive and used threats and warnings to get students to perform (e.g., "Answer this question or I will give you an 'F' for your grade"). Unfortunately, finance itself became an aversive topic, which created some emotional upset when the author had to buy a house.

Displaying behavioral contrast can occur when a behavior is reduced through punishment but another behavior increases in frequency to take its place. For example, if a student is punished for climbing on a bookshelf, climbing on a chair may increase in frequency.

Finally, influencing the social status of the recipient of the punishment could decrease if that student receives continuing punishment. In other words, other students may become less likely to interact with the student who is always in trouble. On the other hand, some students may have their status enhanced if peers feel sorry for them or provide them support. If that occurs, the peer support could counteract the effects of the punishment, possibly increasing the level of unwanted behavior.

With the understanding that aversive procedures should be used only as a last resort and that their use tends to bring about negative side effects, the more popular aversive methods of behavior control are described next.

Level III Procedures (Contingent Removal of Reinforcing Stimuli)

Level III procedures involve the contingent removal of reinforcing stimuli (Alberto & Troutman, 1999). These procedures are frequently used by parents and teachers in a variety of settings. The procedures described involve response cost and time-out systems.

Response Cost.   **Response cost** systems may be used in token systems. Many of us have experienced response costs of some sort. For example, getting a parking ticket will result in a fine, and this fine is a response cost. Response costs involve the permanent removal of some portion of a reinforcer (Sulzer-Azaroff & Mayer, 1991) such as our money and can be called **negative punishment.** If a response cost system is paired with a token system, some of the tokens are taken away from the student contingent on an unwanted behavior. Unfortunately, there are three cautions with the use of such a system. First, consistency must be ensured. An adequate monetary system must be in place to track both the number of tokens earned and the number removed. Second, there must be a reserve of tokens; that is, the number of tokens removed for an unwanted behavior must not be so high that a negative balance will result. Thus, staff must determine how many tokens will be removed when a behavior occurs. If a student gets into a negative balance, the token system will probably not be successful. Finally, there is a high likelihood that the student will react against the removal of the tokens. This reaction could be in the form of aggression or an escalation of the behavior. One way to decrease this likelihood is to remove a certain number of tokens and then give some of those back to the student if the student accepts the removal appropriately. For example, if a teacher removes 10 tokens for swearing and the student gives up those tokens without a "fight," the teacher could give 3 tokens back for the acceptance of the token removal.

Time-Out.   **Time-out** is a technical procedure that involves the temporary removal of the source of reinforcement contingent on an unwanted behavior (Sulzer-Azaroff & Mayer, 1991). Time-out can be considered a negative punisher. It is critical to understand that time-out is a procedure of removing reinforcement for a behavior; it is not a location or a place. Time-out is not placing a student in the corner, out in the hall, or behind a barrier. Time-out is not putting a student in a time-out room. If time-out is thought of as a place, mistakes will be made. Mainly, teachers and other practitioners will use what they think is time-out when it does not work. As such, there are three categories of time-out, moving from the least restrictive to most restrictive: nonexclusionary, exclusionary, and seclusionary.

Nonexclusionary Time-Out.   **Nonexclusionary time-out** involves the removal of the source of reinforcement contingent on an unwanted behavior without removing the student from the group or environment (Cooper et al., 1987). An example of a nonexclusionary time-out is a sit and watch or contingent observation procedure in which the student can be part of the group but not participate (Barton, Brulle, & Repp, 1987). Missing a turn in a game for poor sportsmanship is an example. Another example is the use of a time-out ribbon (Foxx & Shapiro, 1978). In this procedure, the students wear a ribbon while behaving appropriately. Attention is provided when the ribbon is worn. If a student misbehaves, the ribbon is temporarily removed and the student is not provided attention during the time-out period. A third example would be to remove an item temporarily such as a toy, book, or game if the student is not behaving appropriately, such as when a toy is misused (Zirpoli & Melloy, 1997). If time-out is used, non-exclusionary time-out would be the choice since the student is still part of the group and does not miss out on the task or instruction.

Exclusionary Time-Out.   **Exclusionary time-out** is the form of time-out most people think of when they hear the term. Exclusionary time-out refers to the temporary removal of the student from the group or environment contingent on an unwanted behavior (Cooper et al., 1987). An example is placing the student in a corner, outside of the classroom door, behind a barrier, or in another part of the room. Exclusionary time-out is only effective if the source of reinforcement is removed. For example, if the student is in another part of the room but can still hear the other students laugh, attention may continue to reinforce the unwanted behavior. Also, if a student is in the hallway, he or she may get attention from other students in other rooms or walking in the hallway (Cooper et al., 1987).

Seclusionary Time-Out.   **Seclusionary time-out** involves the temporary removal of a student from the group or environment and isolating the student contingent on an unwanted behavior. Seclusionary time-outs are normally used in institutional settings or in special circumstances when there is a need to prevent injury to others, to the persons themselves, or to property (Zabel, 1986). There are state restrictions on the use of seclusionary time-outs. Teachers should become familiar with their state's guidelines. Therefore, teachers should not use seclusionary time-out unless there are unusual circumstances and support from administration. Seclusionary time-out should never be used as a general behavior management procedure.

How to Use Time-Out Effectively.   Several considerations should be made before time-out is used (Sulzer-Azaroff & Mayer, 1991) (see Table 12.3). First, time-out can be time based or behavior based. Time-based time-out involves removing the source of reinforcement for a set amount of time. With time-based time-out, removal from time-out is based on time, not on behavior. Behavior-based time-out involves removing the source of reinforcement until the student is calm and ready to rejoin the group. A combination of the two is to release a student from time-out after a certain time has elapsed, with the last few seconds requiring quiet behavior. For example, time-out may occur for a period of 7 minutes, with the last 15 seconds quiet. If the student is not quiet for the last 15 seconds, time-out remains in effect until the quiet behavior occurs. If a time-based time-out is used, the traditional time to use is 1 minute per year of age. Note that short-duration time-outs have been shown to be just as effective as long-duration time-outs. The advantage of short-duration time-outs is that the student is away from the group (if exclusionary time-out is used) for a shorter time.

Second, the amount of explanation to the student should be kept to a minimum, preferably fewer than 10 words. If more words are used, the student may be gaining unneeded attention. A statement such as, "John, you hit Susie, go to time-out" is preferable to a long explanation and verbal reprimand.

Third, reinforcement must be removed. If the source of reinforcement is attention from other students and time-out is used in the class, teachers may not be removing the source of reinforcement for the behavior. In such a case, an out-of-class time-out may be necessary. If the reinforcement is not removed, the procedure is not time-out.

Finally, there must be time-in. In other words, if there is not a reinforcing classroom environment, there will not be any reinforcement to remove. If a teacher uses many threats and warnings to control behavior, removal from that classroom may actually be a negative reinforcer for the student: the student escapes the negative classroom. In addition, there must be time-in once the student is allowed back in the group. In other words, teachers cannot hold grudges. Once time-out is ended, a teacher should immediately get the student back into the routine and reinforcement of the class.

TABLE 12.3 *Successful Use of Time-Out*

Removal from reinforcer for short period of time:
    Time-based time-out: 1 minute for every year of age of student
    Behavior-based time-out: Make sure behavior is appropriate before the student leaves from time-out.
    Combination: 1 minute for every year of age of student with last 15 seconds quiet
Brief explanation (fewer than 10 words before time out is given)
Removal of source of reinforcement
Immediate time-in

Why Time-Out Can Fail.   Time-out can fail for two reasons: lack of time in and not being able to remove the source of reinforcement. The first reason involves not having a reinforcing environment. If the classroom is aversive, the student may misbehave so as to escape the classroom. In such a case, time-out is not time-out. Therefore, if teachers are to use time-out, they must make sure that there are sources of reinforcement for the students in the classroom. Second, time-out can fail if the source of reinforcement is not removed. For example, a teacher placed a student in a hallway by the classroom door as a time-out. Unfortunately, the student's unwanted behavior did not improve. Knowing that removing the source of reinforcement meant that the behavior must decrease, the teacher reasoned that the student must still be getting reinforced in some manner. So, the teacher decided to monitor what was occurring in the hallway. She found that the school's principal would come by her class and ask the student why he was in the hall this time. The teacher asked the principal to ignore the student when the student was in the hallway, which the principal did. The unwanted behavior soon decreased. In this instance, what the teacher thought was time-out was not because the source of reinforcement (i.e., attention) was not removed.

Therefore, if teachers are using what they consider to be time-out and notice that it is not working, the response is fairly straightforward. Stop using the time-out procedure and try something else.

Level IV Procedures (Presentation of Aversive Stimuli)

Level IV procedures involve the presentation of aversive stimuli (Alberto & Troutman, 1999). These procedures are considered to be at the highest level of restrictiveness because they increase the probability of negative side effects to the use of aversive stimuli, such as aggressive responses on the part of the student (see Table 2.1 for negative side effects to the use of aversive stimuli). Therefore, these procedures should be used with caution and only after other procedures have been tried and failed. Six level IV procedures are described: escape conditioning and avoidance conditioning, reprimands, overcorrection, contingent exertion, negative practice, and physical restraint.

Escape Conditioning and Avoidance Conditioning.   Many behavior management systems use escape conditioning and avoidance conditioning to decrease unwanted behavior. **Escape conditioning and avoidance conditioning** involve using aversive stimuli or the threat (warning stimulus) of an aversive stimulus to get behavior to occur (Martin & Pear, 1999). Escape conditioning and avoidance conditioning involve presenting a discriminative stimulus (S^{D-}) that indicates that if a response is emitted in the presence of the stimulus, it will be punished. Escape conditioning and avoidance conditioning are negative reinforcement procedures. In escape conditioning, an ongoing aversive stimulus is removed only if the student behaves appropriately. Nagging a student until she does what the teacher wants is an example. Avoidance conditioning is when the student is conditioned to act a certain way to prevent the aversive stimulus from occurring. The student becoming compliant to avoid going to the principal's office is an example. Also, indicating to a student that if his behavior continues, he will be sent to time-out or his parents will be called is avoidance conditioning. When threats or warnings are used to get a behavior to occur, there is a hope on the part of the teacher that the threats or warnings will reduce the likelihood that some punishment procedure will need to be used. That is why some parents will

count to three to get their children to behave. The unfortunate fact about escape conditioning and avoidance conditioning is that they are effective. This finding is unfortunate because when some behavior management systems work, there is a tendency to use them again. Escape conditioning and avoidance conditioning are used in our everyday lives. Unfortunately, they can result in unwanted side effects.

One side effect is conditioning new behaviors that are unwanted, such as lying (Martin & Pear, 1999). When students lie, they are attempting to avoid the negative consequences of telling the truth. Other negative side effects are the same as those listed previously when using aversive stimuli. Therefore, teachers should be careful when using escape conditioning or avoidance conditioning. The temptation to use this type of conditioning can be great, but teachers must try not to use them so as to avoid the possible negative side effects that can result.

Reprimands. **Reprimands** are strong negative verbal stimuli such as saying, "No," Don't do that," or "That was bad" contingent on an unwanted behavior (Martin & Pear, 1999). These stimuli can be considered neutral stimuli until they are conditioned as aversive stimuli. What is called a reprimand can also be conditioned as a reinforcer if paired with other reinforcers. Reprimands are usually not considered a highly restrictive procedure because they can be considered mild aversive stimuli. They do, however, have to be conditioned as aversive stimuli by pairing certain verbal statements with an aversive stimulus. For example, if a teacher wants to condition reprimands as aversive stimuli, she must pair these stimuli with other aversive stimuli such as a firm grasp or other forms of punishment such as spankings or a loud voice. Also, many stimuli that are paired with reprimands such as the loud or angry voice must also be punishers in their own right. In addition, reprimands do involve the presentation of an aversive stimulus (i.e., negative statements). Therefore, reprimands can be considered a level IV procedure even though they can be mild.

Overcorrection. **Overcorrection** procedures have been shown to be effective methods at managing unwanted behaviors (Kazdin, 2001). These procedures were once thought to be educative in that they taught students what to do; as Foxx and Bechtel (1983) clearly indicate, however, overcorrection procedures are punishment methods aimed at decreasing unwanted behaviors. These methods are considered to be positive punishment. Therefore, because overcorrection procedures can be viewed as aversive means of control, their use should be limited. Although the use of overcorrection procedures should be limited, it is important to know what they are and how they are used because they appear every day in several contexts. There are two types of overcorrection: positive practice and restitutional.

Positive Practice Overcorrection. **Positive practice overcorrection** involves having students engage in an alternative appropriate behavior instead of an inappropriate one (Miltenberger, 2001). For example, walking in the halls is an important behavior for students because running in the hall could result in injury. If a student runs in the hall, a teacher would require the student to walk down the hall appropriately three times, for example. The premise of positive practice overcorrection is that practicing an appropriate behavior over and over again is aversive. Therefore, the future probability of running in the hall would decrease. Another example is having a student who throws a chair pick up a chair and place it under a table. The teacher then takes another chair and places it on the floor; the student must again pick it up and put it under the table, and so on, for several repetitions.

Of course, the description of positive practice overcorrection is easier said than done. Because positive practice overcorrection works based on the presentation of an aversive stimulus, negative side effects are possible. One side effect is that the student may simply refuse to go along with the request. In such a case, the teacher is left with two choices. First, the student could be allowed to refuse the instruction, which could result in future occurrences of the same refusal behavior. Second, the teacher could physically prompt the student through the task several times. The difficulty with this choice is that once the student becomes resistive, there is a probability that someone will get injured. Therefore, before teachers use positive practice overcorrection, they must determine what they would do if a student refused to follow instructions.

Restitutional Overcorrection.   **Restitutional overcorrection** involves having the student return the environment to a better state than it was before (Miltenberger, 2001). In other words, when an unwanted behavior affects the environment, the student must overcompensate for the disruption to the environment. For example, suppose that a student was writing on her desk. Restitutional overcorrection involves having the student clean off her desk with soap and water as well as all the other desks in the classroom. Another example is a student who puts chewing gum under her desk. The teacher then provides the student with a scraper and has the student scrape the gum off her desk as well as all the other desks in the classroom.

The difficulty with restitutional overcorrection is the same as with positive practice overcorrection. If a student refuses to follow the teacher's instructions, the teacher is left with two undesirable choices. Thus, before teachers decide to use restitutional overcorrection, they must make sure that they understand the potential consequences of that decision.

Contingent Exertion.   **Contingent exertion** (or exercise) was studied by Luce, Delquadri, and Hall (1980) and Luce and Hall (1981). Contingent exertion has been shown to be an effective positive punishment procedure. It has been used for several years by coaches, military officers, and teachers (Sulzer-Azaroff & Mayer, 1991). Contingent exertion refers to the practice of requiring an individual to do some physically exerting behavior as punishment for an unwanted behavior. (Whether or not contingent exertion or any other procedure is a punishment procedure will depend on how it affects the behavior.) For example, the football coach who tells a player to run five laps, the military officer who tells the recruit to do 50 push-ups, and the gym teacher who tells students to do 10 pull-ups are using contingent exertion.

Contingent exertion can be very aversive to the individual being punished. The primary problem with contingent exertion is that the student may not follow the instruction to do the exercise. As with overcorrection, the teacher is left with two unpleasant options. If the physical prompting choice is selected, the results could be unpleasant. Try to get someone to do sit-ups when they refuse to do so. Again, the use of a procedure such as contingent exercise should be used only with caution, if at all, and the possibility of student refusal should be considered.

Negative Practice.   Some individuals will confuse negative practice with overcorrection (Alberto & Troutman, 1999). **Negative practice** is similar to overcorrection except that overcorrection requires a wanted behavior to be displayed repeatedly, whereas negative practice requires the negative or unwanted behavior to be practiced repeatedly (Alberto & Troutman, 1999). In negative practice, an unwanted behavior such as throwing a chair is required over and over again. The purpose of negative practice is either to punish the unwanted behavior by requiring the repetition of behavior or to satiate individuals with the behavior (nontechnically, to get it out of their system). Negative practice has not been researched to the same extent as overcorrection. If practicing the negative behavior is aversive, however, it will be effective.

As with the previously described aversive procedures, negative practice can cause several negative side effects. Students may become resistant, and the teacher will either allow them to refuse to follow directions or will physically prompt them. Overall, negative practice is probably not worth the effort, and more positive procedures should be attempted.

Physical Restraint. **Physical restraint** is a procedure that is used to prevent students from harming themselves and others. A physical restraint should not be used as a standard behavior management procedure, only as an emergency procedure. Teachers who have not been trained in physical restraint should not attempt to restrain students (unless under dire emergencies), because untrained individuals using restraints can result in injury to the students or the teachers attempting the restraint. If teachers wish to become trained in physical restraint, they should contact their district offices for information on trainings and on district policies regarding the use of restraint.

How Do We Decide Which Procedure to Use?

Selecting which behavior management system to use is important in leading to behavior change. The first step anyone should complete is a functional assessment of what is maintaining the unwanted behavior. If the source of reinforcement can be found, this source should be removed. There are, however, negative side effects of extinction. Other behaviors must be taught so as to avoid some of these negative side effects. The decision of what and how to teach depends on the goals for the students. If there is a need for more independence, self-management procedures are a good option. If self-management procedures alone do not work, they can be combined with behavioral contracts. If self-management skills are not necessary, differential reinforcement schedules can be used to decrease unwanted behaviors and to improve the level of wanted behaviors. Token systems can also be effective in getting a behavior to occur; these systems, however, are artificial and difficult to maintain. Therefore, token systems could be used when other methods have failed or are not possible to implement.

Mild aversive techniques can be added to reinforcement-based procedures, but only mild forms such as nonexclusionary or exclusionary time-out should be used first. If reinforcement-based and mild aversive procedures fail, other procedures can be tried only as a last resort and under the permission of administrators and parents. These procedures (e.g., seclusionary time-out, overcorrection, contingent exertion) increase the likelihood that abuse and injuries could occur. Advice from behavioral specialists should be sought before these procedures are used.

How Is Consequence-Imposed Behavior Change Generalized?

The concern for generalization was discussed in Chapter 11. Whenever unwanted behaviors are decreased, another behavior to take the place of those behaviors being eliminated must also be increased (called the fair pair rule [White & Haring, 1980]). Once that is accomplished, generalization can be planned. The methods of planning generalization are the same as those described in Chapter 11.

How Is Consequence-Imposed Behavior Change Maintained?

As with generalization, the concern for maintenance was discussed in Chapter 11. Behavior change resulting from the methods described in this chapter are similar to those described there. It is critical to implement reinforcement-based methods with these methods and to place the improved behaviors on an intermittent schedule of reinforcement. Also, wanted behaviors should be moved from a more artificial reinforcement method to naturally occurring forms of reinforcement.

Summary

When teachers make the decision to develop an individualized behavior management plan, they must decide how they will approach the behavior change. They always want to complete a functional behavioral assessment first. They then must decide how to change the behavior(s) in question. They should always attempt to develop or teach skills students can use to make the unwanted behaviors unneeded. At times, however, increasing other behaviors may not be enough, and teachers may have to resort to behavior reduction strategies. If implementing behavior reduction strategies, always begin with the least restrictive and intrusive intervention, starting with informal strategies. Unfortunately, in some instances a teacher will have to move up the restrictiveness and intrusiveness scale, to aversive-based strategies.

The major concern with the use of reduction-based strategies is that teachers protect the students' right to the most effective yet least restrictive and intrusive intervention possible. Reduction procedures, however, are never used in isolation. If they are used, teachers should combine these strategies with those strategies aimed at increasing desirable behaviors described in Chapter 11. Once the unwanted behavior has decreased to acceptable levels, teachers must be concerned with maintenance and generalization. Maintenance and generalization of behavior reduction should be planned in a similar manner to that used in planning maintenance and generalization of desirable behaviors. These strategies should provide students with the types of behaviors that allow them to be successful.

VIGNETTE • *Revisited*

Based on the results of the functional assessment, Ms. Jackson knew that she had to decide on an appropriate management intervention. Therefore, she decided to teach Jackie to ask for a break when she began to feel agitated. If Jackie asked for a break without swearing or having a tantrum, she was allowed to take a 2-minute break. If Jackie swore, she was immediately redirected to the task and reminded to ask for a break in an appropriate manner. If her behavior escalated to a tantrum or if she continued to swear, she was removed from the classroom and sent to an in-school suspension room with her work. She was not allowed to come back to the room until her work was completed.

Jackie quickly learned to ask for a break. Ms. Jackson was pleased with the results of her management technique. After about 2 weeks, however, Jackie began to ask for a break about 10 times an hour. Clearly, these frequent requests were becoming as much of a problem as the tantrums. Therefore, Ms. Jackson decided to restrict the number of breaks Jackie could ask for from 10 to 8. Once Jackie was requesting a break 8 times an hour or less for 3 consecutive days, the maximum number was reduced to 6, then 4, and then to the goal of 2 per hour. Ms. Jackson thought that she had accomplished her goal of reducing Jackie's swearing and tantrums while also teaching her that she could ask for a break instead of displaying these unacceptable behaviors.

Discussion Questions

1. How should teachers balance the concern over restrictive or intrusive interventions with the need to use the most effective intervention?

2. How can teachers use informal procedures to decrease unwanted behaviors?

3. Why should teachers begin with level I procedures before moving to more restrictive or intrusive interventions?

4. How can differential reinforcement procedures be used to improve the classroom behavior of students (i.e., in what different ways can differential reinforcement be used)?

5. When would a teacher move to a level II procedure? What needs to be known before extinction can be used?

6. Why should teachers attempt to decrease the use of aversive procedures in schools?

7. How would a teacher decide on the type of time-out to use? What information must be taken into consideration?

8. How can a token economy system and response cost be combined in a behavior management program? Provide an example of such a system.

9. What needs to occur before a teacher moves to a level IV intervention? What can the teacher expect to occur?

10. Some people have indicated that overcorrection procedures are educational in nature. Is this statement true? Why or why not?

Appendix A

School Evaluation Rubric (SER)

Leadership Team to Guide the Strategic Planning Process

This category examines the school's role in effecting a leadership team that implements the strategic planning process. This process focuses on establishing positive teaching and learning environments within all systems in the school: schoolwide (i.e., all students, all staff, and all settings), nonclassroom (i.e., particular times or places where supervision is emphasized), classroom (i.e., instructional settings), and individual student support (i.e., specific supports for students who engage in chronic problem behaviors). Specifically, this category involves school's development of a **leadership team** that is capable of improving the school's:

(a) vision and organization
(b) stakeholder involvement and communication
(c) allocation of resources (human, fiscal, and time)
(d) development, implementation, and maintenance of systems to support positive teaching and learning environments
(e) continual self-assessment

Describe how the school's leadership team supports a focus on establishing positive teaching and learning environments within all systems of the school: schoolwide, classroom, nonclassroom, and individual student support.

Beginning

Leadership and decision making are in the hands of a few people and are not fully supported by the administration. Stakeholder involvement in major decisions and activities is limited or nonexistent. Data are not examined to determine the school's strengths and areas for development within the systems in the school (i.e., schoolwide, nonclassroom, classroom, and individual support systems). There is no clear language used to discuss the strategic planning process.

Developing

Leadership and decision making now include representatives of some stakeholders and are supported by the administration. The system is beginning to focus on establishing positive teaching and learning environments within some of the systems in the school (e.g., classroom system is in place but others are not). Some data are examined to determine the school's strengths and areas for development within some of the systems in the school. One language is instituted for clear discussions on the strategic planning process.

Exemplary

Leadership and decision making representing all key stakeholders are well established and are fully supported by the administration. The system works to maintain the school's focus on establishing positive teaching and learning environments within all systems of the school. The leadership team includes general and special educators, school counselor or psychologist, administrator, someone with in-depth knowledge of behavioral interventions and supports, and parent(s). Data are examined to determine the school's strengths and areas for development within all systems of the school. One language is used to discuss the strategic planning process.

SERVICE GAP ANALYSIS

Leadership Team to Guide the Strategic Planning Process

1. **Current status of system:** ☐ **Beginning** ☐ **Developing** ☐ **Exemplary**

2. **Identify attributes of the school's leadership team that are currently in place.**

Key Attributes

- ☐ Representative membership
  - Administrator
  - Grade or area
  - Parent(s)
- ☐ Behavioral capacity
- ☐ Building level status
- ☐ Support and commitment of staff (80%)
- ☐ Sustained effort
- ☐ Key part of school improvement goals

Descriptive summary of areas of improvement:

_____

_____

_____

_____

_____

3. **Develop preliminary action plan.**

Action	Timeline

1. _____

_____ _____

_____

2. _____

_____ _____

_____

3. _____

_____ _____

_____

4. _____

_____ _____

_____

Comments:

Schoolwide Organizational System

This category examines the schoolwide organizational system. The schoolwide organizational system is defined as involving all students, all staff and in all settings within a school. Specifically, this category involves:

(a) schoolwide guidelines for success
(b) strategies for teaching expectations
(c) clearly defined discipline procedures
(d) continual self-assessment

Describe the current schoolwide system in place at your school in terms of schoolwide guidelines for success, teaching, discipline, and continuous assessment.

Beginning

Schoolwide guidelines for success that provide a framework from which to create a common culture and language as well as linkages across systems are not clearly articulated. Teachers and staff are able to state guidelines for success; however, they differ from person to person. Teachers and staff do not know what behaviors they should manage and what behaviors the office should manage. There are no procedures for emergency or dangerous situations. Teachers, staff, and students are not systematically taught the schoolwide guidelines for success and discipline procedures. Assessment of the schoolwide system does not occur. There is little or no feedback given to the school staff.

Developing

Guidelines for success are articulated. Teachers and staff are able to state the guidelines for success, but do not use them or have a uniform interpretation of them. Some teachers and staff know what behaviors they should manage and what behaviors the office should manage. Options are being developed for emergency or dangerous situations. Schoolwide guidelines for success are reviewed by school staff and students, but are not taught systematically. Some assessment of the schoolwide system occurs. Some feedback is given to the school staff when needed.

Exemplary

The school has a small number (e.g., 3–5) of clearly stated guidelines for success that are linked across systems. Teachers and staff are able to state and use the guidelines for success and interpret them uniformly. Teachers and staff know what behaviors they should manage and what behaviors the office should manage. Procedures are in place to address emergency or dangerous situations. Teachers, staff, and students are systematically taught the schoolwide guidelines for success and discipline procedures. Booster training activities for students are conducted when needed (e.g., after holiday breaks). Continuous assessment of the schoolwide system is conducted. Feedback is given to school staff on a regular basis (monthly/quarterly).

SERVICE GAP ANALYSIS

Schoolwide Organizational System

1. Current status of system: ☐ **Beginning** ☐ **Developing** ☐ **Exemplary**

2. Describe the strengths and weaknesses of the schoolwide organizational system.

Key Attributes

☐ Schoolwide guidelines for success
☐ Strategies for teaching students, staff, and families
☐ Clearly defined discipline procedures
☐ Clearly defined crisis response plans (threats, actual events, classroom, and individual)
☐ Staff provided feedback on effectiveness on a regular basis

Descriptive summary of areas of improvement:

_____

_____

_____

_____

_____

3. Develop preliminary action plan.

	Action	Timeline
1.	_____	
	_____	_____
	_____	
2.	_____	
	_____	_____
	_____	
3.	_____	
	_____	_____
	_____	
4.	_____	
	_____	_____
	_____	

Comments:

Nonclassroom Organizational System

This category examines nonclassroom settings. The nonclassroom organizational system is defined as particular times or places where supervision is emphasized (e.g., hallways, cafeteria, playground, and bus). Specifically, this category involves:

(a) nonclassroom behavioral expectations
(b) strategies for teaching expectations
(c) clearly defined discipline procedures
(d) ecological arrangements
(e) continual self-assessment

Describe the current nonclassroom system in place at your school in terms of nonclassroom behavior expectations, teaching, discipline, ecological arrangements, and continuous assessment.

Beginning

There are no stated behavioral expectations for the nonclassroom settings or they are unrelated to the schoolwide ones. Only selected staff are involved in the management of student behavior in nonclassroom settings. Little or no training is provided to staff on how to actively supervise (teach students the behavioral expectations, move, scan, positively engage) students. Teachers, staff, and students are not systematically taught the behavioral expectations. Discipline procedures for nonclassroom problem behaviors may exist; however, they remain fairly ineffective. Ecological arrangements (physical arrangements and scheduling) have not been examined closely to reduce wait time, decrease the density of students, and improve safety. Assessment of the nonclassroom settings does not occur. There is little to no feedback given to the school staff.

Developing

The stated schoolwide behavioral expectations apply to nonclassroom settings. Only selected staff are involved in the management of student behavior in nonclassroom settings, but are supported by some staff (e.g., assist in supervision when needed). Some training is provided to staff on how to actively supervise students. Behavioral expectations are reviewed by school staff and students, but are not taught systematically. Some "booster" training is provided to school staff and students. Discipline procedures for nonclassroom problem behaviors exist; however, staff are not systematically taught how to use them. Ecological arrangements have been considered but not systematically examined. Some assessment of the nonclassroom settings occurs. Some feedback is given to the school staff when needed.

Exemplary

The stated schoolwide behavioral expectations (3–5) apply to nonclassroom settings. All staff are involved (to some degree) in the management of student behavior in nonclassroom settings. Training is provided to selected staff on how to actively supervise students. Teachers, staff, and students are systematically taught the nonclassroom behavioral expectations. "Booster" training is provided to school staff and students. Discipline procedures for nonclassroom problem behaviors exist, and staff are systematically taught how to use them. Ecological arrangements have been adjusted to maximize positive student behaviors. Continuous assessment of the nonclassroom settings is conducted. Feedback is given to school staff on a regular basis (monthly/quarterly).

SERVICE GAP ANALYSIS

Nonclassroom Organizational System

1. Current status of system: ☐ **Beginning** ☐ **Developing** ☐ **Exemplary**

2. Describe the strengths and weaknesses of the nonclassroom organizational system.

Key Attributes

☐ Behavioral expectations linked to schoolwide ones
☐ Involve all staff to a degree
☐ Ecological arrangements adjusted to maximize positive student behaviors
☐ Strategies for teaching behavioral expectations to students
☐ Staff receive training on active supervision and use of discipline procedures
☐ Staff provided feedback on effectiveness on a regular basis

Descriptive summary of areas of improvement:

_____

_____

_____

_____

_____

3. Develop preliminary action plan.

	Action	Timeline
1.		
2.		
3.		
4.		

Comments:

Classroom Organizational System

This category examines the classroom organizational system. The classroom organizational system is defined as instructional settings in which teacher(s) supervise and teach groups of students. Specifically, this category involves a school's:

(a) focus on instruction
(b) classroom behavioral expectations and routines
(c) clearly defined discipline procedures
(d) access to assistance
(e) continual self-assessment

Describe the current classroom system in place at your school in terms of classroom behavior expectations, teaching, discipline, and continuous assessment.

Beginning

There is not a clear curriculum focus on achieving student outcomes. There is variability across teachers in the degree to which classroom behavioral expectations and routines are established. Behavioral expectations are not linked to schoolwide ones. Little training is provided or made available to teachers on classroom management. Discipline procedures for classroom problem behaviors may exist; however, they remain fairly ineffective and there is a great deal of variability across teachers. Teachers have few, if any, opportunities for access to assistance and recommendations (observation, instruction, and coaching). Assessment of the classroom system does not occur. There is little to no feedback given to teachers.

Developing

There is a clear curriculum focus on achieving student outcomes in some areas but not others (e.g., strong focus in reading but weak in mathematics). Most teachers establish clear classroom behavioral expectations and routines; however, the behavioral expectations are not linked to the schoolwide ones. Some training is provided or made available to teachers on classroom management. Discipline procedures for classroom problem behaviors exist and are fairly effective; however, there is variability across teachers. Teachers have access to assistance and recommendations (observation, instruction, and coaching); however, it is generally ineffective or viewed as a step for special education services. Some assessment of the classroom system occurs. Some feedback is given to teachers when needed.

Exemplary

There is a clear curriculum focus on achieving student outcomes in all areas. All teachers establish clear classroom behavioral expectations and routines, and the behavioral expectations are linked to the schoolwide ones. Training is provided or made available to teachers on classroom management. Discipline procedures for classroom problem behaviors exist and are effective, and there is consistency across teachers. Teachers have access to assistance and recommendations (observation, instruction, and coaching), and it is generally effective. Continuous assessment of the classroom system is conducted. Feedback is given to teachers on a regular basis (monthly/quarterly).

SERVICE GAP ANALYSIS

Classroom Organizational System

1. Current status of system: ☐ **Beginning** ☐ **Developing** ☐ **Exemplary**

2. Describe the strengths and weaknesses of the classroom organizational system.

Key Attributes

☐ Curriculum focus on achieving student outcomes
☐ Behavioral expectations linked to schoolwide ones
☐ Consistent discipline procedures used by teachers
☐ Teachers have access to effective assistance and recommendations
☐ Teachers have access to staff development activities
☐ Teachers provided feedback on effectiveness on a regular basis

Descriptive summary of areas of improvement:

_____

_____

_____

_____

_____

3. Develop preliminary action plan.

Action	Timeline

1. _____

_____   _____

_____

2. _____

_____   _____

_____

3. _____

_____   _____

_____

4. _____

_____   _____

_____

Comments:

Individual Organizational System

This category examines the individual organizational system. The individual organizational system is defined as specific supports for students who have or are at risk of experiencing school failure. Please note that children with emotional or behavioral disorders (EBD) may not necessarily be receiving special education services. Specifically, this category involves a school's:

(a) specific prevention and intervention procedures for students at risk of school failure
(b) procedures for providing intervention and supports to students experiencing school failure
(c) continual self-assessment

Describe the current individual system in place at your school in terms of specific prevention and intervention procedures for students at risk of school failure, procedures for providing intervention and supports to students experiencing school failure, and continual self-assessment.

Beginning

The school has not developed specific prevention and intervention procedures for students at risk of school failure (e.g., one-to-one tutoring program in reading, mentor program). There is not a common solutions-oriented language (functional behavioral assessment) used by school staff to guide the development of interventions and supports for students experiencing school failure. The school does not have or it has an ineffective behavior support team to assist staff in developing, implementing, and evaluating interventions and supports for students experiencing school failure.

Developing

The school has developed some prevention and intervention procedures for students at risk of school failure, but no data have been used to guide their development and implementation. Some staff use a common solutions-oriented language to guide the development of interventions and supports for students experiencing school failure. The school has a relatively effective behavior support team to assist staff in developing, implementing, and evaluating interventions and supports for students experiencing school failure, but it is viewed as a step in the special education referral process.

Exemplary

The school has developed prevention and intervention procedures for students at risk of school failure. A data-based decision-making process has been conducted to guide the development and implementation of the procedures to ensure that they meet the specific needs of students. All staff use a common solutions-oriented language to guide the development of interventions and supports for students experiencing school failure. The school has an effective behavior support team to assist staff in developing, implementing, and evaluating interventions and supports for students experiencing school failure. The team is not necessarily viewed as a step in the special education referral process.

SERVICE GAP ANALYSIS

Individual Organizational System

1. **Current status of system:** ☐ **Beginning** ☐ **Developing** ☐ **Exemplary**

2. **Describe the strengths and weaknesses of the individual organizational system.**

Key Attributes

☐ Data-based prevention and intervention procedures for students at risk of school failure
☐ Common solutions-oriented language used by all staff
☐ Established behavioral support team (not seen as a step in the special education referral process)
☐ Simple and efficient system to access the team
☐ Use of community resources

Descriptive summary of areas of improvement:

_____

_____

_____

_____

_____

3. **Develop preliminary action plan.**

	Action	Timeline
1.	_____	
	_____	_____
	_____	
2.	_____	
	_____	_____
	_____	
3.	_____	
	_____	_____
	_____	
4.	_____	
	_____	_____
	_____	

Comments:

Academic Support System

This category examines the academic support system. The academic support system is defined as the integration of evidence-based academic skill support programs in key skill areas (i.e., language, reading, and mathematics) at the secondary level (for students who are at risk of developing learning problems) and the tertiary level (for students who are experiencing academic failure). Specifically, this category involves a school's

(a) strategies for the early identification of learning problems in language, reading, and mathematics
(b) curriculum and instruction procedures in key skill areas (e.g., code-based instruction in reading) that enhance (not replace) the primary-level ones (curriculum provided to all students)
(c) tertiary curriculum (not necessarily special education) and instruction procedures in key skill areas that enhance or replace the primary-level ones for students experiencing significant learning problems
(d) continual self-assessment

Describe the current academic support system in place at your school in terms of specific secondary- and tertiary-level curriculum and instruction procedures for students at risk of or experiencing learning problems, respectively, and continual self-assessment.

Beginning

The school has not developed specific secondary and tertiary curriculum procedures for students at risk of or experiencing learning problems, respectively. There are no early identification procedures in place to identify students in need of academic supports.

Developing

The school has developed some secondary- or tertiary-level curriculum and instruction procedures for students at risk of or experiencing learning problems, respectively. The school provides secondary and/or tertiary curriculum and instruction procedures in some areas, but they are delivered only to students formally classified as having a disability or do not address fully the need. The curriculum and instruction procedures are not connected or integrated with one another. Procedures for identifying students in need of academic supports are in place, but they are part of the special education referral process.

Exemplary

The school has developed, coordinated and integrated secondary- and tertiary-level curriculum and instruction procedures for students at risk of or experiencing learning problems, respectively. The school provides evidence-based secondary- and/or tertiary-level curriculum and instruction procedures in language, reading, and mathematics. The curriculum and instruction procedures are connected and integrated with one another to improve their effectiveness. Procedures for identifying students in need of academic supports are in place and are not necessarily part of the special education referral process.

SERVICE GAP ANALYSIS

Academic Support System

1. Current status of system: ☐ **Beginning** ☐ **Developing** ☐ **Exemplary**

2. Describe the strengths and weaknesses of the academic support system.

Key Attributes

☐ Evidence-based secondary-level curriculum and instruction procedures
☐ Evidence-based tertiary-level curriculum and instruction procedures
☐ Curriculum and instruction procedures are coordinated and integrated with one another
☐ Early identification procedures are in place

Descriptive summary of areas of improvement:

_____

_____

_____

_____

_____

3. Develop preliminary action plan.

Action	Timeline
1. _____	
_____	_____
_____	
2. _____	
_____	_____
_____	
3. _____	
_____	_____
_____	
4. _____	
_____	_____
_____	

Comments:

PLAN OF ACTION

Year: ☐ One ☐ Two

Action	Strategies	Target dates	Resources needed	Person(s) responsible	Evaluation date

Appendix B

Web Sites

Information on Behavior Analysis

Association for Behavior Analysis	http://www.wmich.edu/aba

Information on Evidence-Based Practices

Center for the Study and Prevention of Violence	http://www.Colorado.EDU/cspv/ blueprints/
U.S. Department of Education Expert Panel on Safe, Disciplined and Drug-Free Schools	http://www.ed.gov/offices/OERI/ ORAD/KAD/expert_panel/
Preventing Mental Disorders in School-Age Children: A Review of the Effectiveness of Prevention Programs	http://www.psu/edu/dept/prevention
Effective Programs and Strategies to Create Safe Schools	http://www.hamfish.org

Reports on School Violence

Youth Violence: A Report of the Surgeon General: The first Surgeon General's report on youth violence. The report includes a review of a massive body of research on where, when, and how much youth violence occurs, what causes it, and which of today's many preventive strategies are genuinely effective.	http://www.surgeongeneral.gov

Annual Reports on School Violence: Reports on school violence from the U.S. Department of Education, U.S. Department of Justice, and the National Center for Education Statistics (NCES).	http://www.ed.gov http://www.ojp.usdoj.gov http://nces.ed.gov

Reports from the National Juvenile and Criminal Justice Center

School House Hype School House Hype: Two Years Later Safe Schools and Suspension	http://www.cjcj.org/

Reports on School Shooters

The School Shooter: The Federal Bureau of Investigation document that is the result of a comprehensive 2-year study examining violence in U.S. schools. The report was assembled to develop a better understanding of adolescent violence through threat assessment, intervention, and prevention methods.	http://www.fbi.gov
Secret Service Safe School Initiative. The goal of the Safe School Initiative is to provide accurate and useful information to school administrators, educators, law enforcement professionals, and others who have protective and safety responsibilities in schools to help prevent incidents of school-based targeted violence.	http://www.ss.ojp.usdaj.gov/nij

Organizations Dealing with School Safety

Center for the Prevention of School Violence	http://www.ncsu.edu/cpsv/
Center on Juvenile and Criminal Justice	http://www.cjcj.org/
Center for the Study and Prevention of Violence	http://www.Colorado.EDU/cspv/
National Alliance for Safe Schools	http://www.safeschools.org/
National Association of School Safety and Law Enforcement Officials	http://www.nassleo.org/
National Education Association Safe Schools Home Page	http://www.nea.org/issues/safescho
National Mental Health and Education Center for Children and Families Safe School Resources	http://www.naspcenter.org/ safe_schools/safeschools.htm

National Resource Center for Safe Schools	http://www.safetyzone.org/
National School Safety and Security Services	http://www.schoolsecurity.org/
National School Safety Center	http://www.nssc1.org/

Information on Effective Reading Techniques

National Reading Panel Results	http://www.nichd.nih.gov/new/releases/nrp.cfm http://www.nationalreading panel.org

Results Noted by the American Institutes for Research

American Institutes for Research	http://www.air_dc.org
American Association of School Administrators	http://www.aasa.org/

Evidence-Based Curricular Models

Association for Direct Instruction P.O. Box 10252 Eugene, OR 97440 phone: 541-485-1293; fax: 541-683-7543	http://www.adihome.org

Success for All

Success for All Foundation 200 W. Towsontown Boulevard Baltimore, MD 21204 phone: 800-548-4998; fax: 410-324-4444 e-mail: sfainfo@successforall.net	http://www.successforall.net

High Schools That Work

Southern Regional Education Board 592 Tenth Street, N.W. Atlanta, GA 30318 phone: 404-875-9211; fax: 404-872-1477	http://www.sreb.org

Glossary

A-B design   A single-case design that combines the "A" condition or baseline/preintervention measurements with a "B" condition to determine the effectiveness of an intervention.

A-B-A-B design   A single-case design that combines the "A" condition or baseline/preintervention measurements with a "B" condition or intervention to determine the effectiveness of the intervention; the "B" condition is followed by a second "A" condition and ends with a return to the intervention "B." (See also withdrawal design.)

A-B-C analysis   Involves observing the student during normal activities when a specific behavior is most likely to happen.

Academic functional assessment   Assessment conducted to help determine the function or purpose of a student's behavior as it relates to his or her academic performance.

Academic learning time   The amount of time students spend engaged in learning activities and are being successful.

Acquisition stage   The first stage of learning; it is the entry point when learning a skill.

Alienation   Feeling estranged or different from others.

Allocated time   The amount of time a teacher or school delegates for content or subject area.

Alterable variable   Variable that affects student's school success that can be addressed by school professionals: teaching skills, quantity of teacher-to-student interactions, and the use of time.

Alternating treatments design   A single-case design in which the main purpose is to make comparisons between or among two or more conditions or interventions such as baseline and interventions or multiple interventions. Also called the multielement design.

Antecedent   A stimulus that precedes a behavior.

Antecedent prompt and fade   Providing a more intrusive prompt on initial instructional trials and then fading the prompt in a systematic manner.

Antecedent prompt and test   Prompting students during instruction and then providing them with practice or test trials after removing all prompts.

Antiseptic bounding   A quiet reflective period in which everyone disengages from a student; this period is behavior dependent, not time dependent.

Antisocial behavior   Behavior that violates socially prescribed norms or patterns of behavior.

Applied behavior analysis   A systematic, performance-based, self-evaluative technology for assessing and changing behavior.

Arbitrary consequences   Artificial stimuli that come after a behavior; used when natural consequences are not present.

Artificial reinforcer   Reinforcer that is not typically used in a particular setting, such as paying students for good behavior.

Assertive Discipline   A classroom management model that is based on the following (1) students should comply to rules; (2) students cannot be expected to determine appropriate classroom rules and follow them; (3) punishment will cause students to avoid bad behavior and engage in good classroom behavior; (4) good behavior can also be encouraged through rewards; (5) for proper classroom management, parents and school administrators must help enforce rules; and (6) better control will be demonstrated in the classroom if teachers learn to become assertive.

Assertive response style   Most effective style; rules are set and discipline procedures are used consistently with student misbehavior.

Autonomous   Independent; self-contained.

Available time   The amount of time available for instruction.

Aversive-based procedure   Used in cases in which reinforcement is not successful; connected with negative side effects.

Aversive control   Control over behavior as a result of using stimuli that evoke an escape or avoidance response contingent on a specified behavior.

Aversive stimulus Anything that evokes or occasions an escape or avoidance response; decreases the probability of a behavior when presented as a consequence.

Avoidance conditioning A negative reinforcement procedure that uses an aversive stimulus or a threat of one to get behavior to occur; a student is conditioned to act a certain way to prevent the aversive stimulus from occurring.

Avoidance response A response that allows for the removal or delay of an aversive stimulus.

B-A-B design A single case design that combines the "B" condition or intervention with an "A" condition or baseline/preintervention; the "A" condition is followed by a second "B" condition.

Backward chaining Teaching the final step in the chain until it is mastered; next teach the last and next-to-last steps together and so on.

Baseline In single-case designs, "A" refers to the baseline; the level at which the participant performs a behavior without the intervention; the repeated measurement of a behavior under natural conditions.

Behavior An act that can be clearly defined and observed.

Behavioral contract Contract that specifies in what context both the teacher and the student will perform; involves three main components: the task, the reward, and the task record.

Behavioral deficiency Behavior that does not occur enough.

Behavioral excess Behavior that occurs too often.

Behavioral intervention plan (BIP) A written document describing the environmental changes that will take place to bring about a resulting change in a wanted or an unwanted behavior.

Behavioral momentum Desired behaviors are more likely to occur if preceded by reinforcement for other behaviors; used to increase the likelihood of compliance.

Behavioral perspective A position that the environment, physiology, and culture affect behavior. Internal or covert behavior is not causal in nature, but results from the organism's interaction with the external environment. Therefore, internal behaviors can be considered dependent variables.

Behavioral support team A collaborative team composed of teachers, administrators, and support staff who possess the knowledge and competencies necessary to address complex student problems by analyzing and designing interventions and supports to improve student outcomes.

Behavioral trap The maintenance of a behavior by natural reinforcers after the behavior was initially developed by programmed reinforcers.

Big ideas The underlying concept or skill that allows for the generalization and maintenance of learned behavior.

Chaining Individual behaviors in a person's repertoire are put together to form a longer behavior.

Chain stopping Determining the chain of responses to a behavior and intervening at one of the links prior to the undesired behavior.

Changing-criterion design A single-case design that looks like an A-B design but includes "phase" lines (i.e., changes within the intervention condition); a criterion is established within each phase to reduce or increase some dependent variable in a stepwise manner.

Checklist An indirect assessment that is completed by parents or teachers by checking off possible antecedents and consequences the student may be exposed to when specific behaviors occur.

Classroom structure The seating arrangements, rules, and routines present in the classroom.

Closed social group To have no close friendships or to associate with only a single small group that excludes everyone else.

Close-ended question Respondents are asked to select their answers from among those provided.

Code of silence Inability or unwillingness to communicate concerns between staff and students.

Coercion To be compelled to do something by way of a threat or domination.

Cognitive theory A position that internal mental processes can cause external behavior to occur. Internal processes transform environmental stimuli; this transformation determines the behavior the individual will emit. Therefore, internal mental events can be considered independent variables.

Conditional threat A threat that warns that a violent act will happen unless a demand or set of demands is met.

Consequence Any stimulus that is presented or removed contingently following a particular response or behavior; things that occur just following a behavior.

Conspicuous strategies Explicit teaching strategies that ensure student mastery of skills.

Contingent exertion Exercise; refers to having a student do some physically exerting behavior as punishment for an unwanted behavior.

Continuous reinforcement schedule   Reinforcement is given for each behavior a student emits to strengthen the behavior; also called fixed ratio-1.

Control   Nonmanipulative techniques used every day that make it more likely positive behavior will continue (e.g., providing a tip to a waitress for good service).

Correspondence training   Teaching students how to report on what they have done or will do accurately.

Dead man's test   A term that refers to a lack of behavior required on the part of the individual so as to be reinforced.

Debriefing   The time when students are able to gain self-control and verbalize the inappropriate behavior in which they engaged.

Deductive criminal profiling   Interpreting forensic evidence from a crime after it has occurred to reconstruct behavior patterns and deduce offender characteristics, demographics, emotions, and motivations.

Dehumanize   Viewing others as nonpersons or as objects to be thwarted.

Deprivation   An increase in the reinforcer effectiveness of a stimulus due to a lack of that stimulus.

Descriptive analysis   A direct assessment or observation of the unwanted and wanted behaviors under naturalistic conditions.

Desists   Instructions to an individual to cease doing something.

Diagnosis and correction   Errors are identified and proper error-correction procedures are used.

Differential reinforcement   Reinforcing a behavior in the presence of one stimulus while not reinforcing in the presence of another stimulus.

Differential reinforcement of alternative behavior (DRA)   Reinforcing a behavior that is an alternative one to the target behavior.

Differential reinforcement of incompatible behavior (DRI)   Reinforcing a behavior that is opposite or incompatible with the behavior targeted for reduction.

Differential reinforcement of low-rate behavior (DRL)   A reinforcement in which the number of responses in a set time period is less than or equal to a set limit of behaviors; can be a spaced responding DRL or a limited responding DRL.

Differential reinforcement of other (DRO) behavior   A time-based reinforcement schedule in which reinforcement is provided if unwanted behavior has not occurred within an established time period; also called differential reinforcement of zero rate behavior and omission training.

Direct Instruction   A comprehensive system of instruction that focuses on active student involvement, mastery of skills, empirically validated curricula, and teacher-directed activities.

Direct threat   A threat that identifies a specific act against a specific target that is delivered in a straightforward, clear, and explicit manner.

Discipline   Training to act in accordance with rules; instruction and exercise designed to train proper conduct or action; behavior in accordance with rules of conduct; a set or system of rules and regulations.

Discriminative stimulus   An antecedent that reliably occasions a response and therefore results in reinforcement.

Duration recording   Measurement of the time a response or behavior lasts.

Effective Academic and Behavioral Intervention and Support (EABIS) program   A multilevel school-wide positive behavioral intervention and support program that provides a continuum of primary, secondary, and tertiary forms of interventions and supports for preventing problem behaviors.

Effective instructional cycle   Demonstrates how effective-teaching practices can be incorporated into daily instruction.

Engaged time   The amount of time students are on task or are actively engaged in learning activities.

Escape conditioning   A negative reinforcement procedure that uses an aversive stimulus or a threat of one to get behavior to occur; an ongoing aversive stimulus is removed only if the student emits a particular behavior.

Escape response   A response that allows for the termination of an aversive stimulus.

Establishing operation   An antecedent event or change in the environment that alters the effectiveness of the reinforcer.

Event recording   Establishes a numerical dimension of a behavior; simple tally.

Exclusionary time-out   The temporary removal of the student from the group.

Explicit   Directly stated; clearly defined and specific.

Externalize blame   To not take responsibility for own actions and fault others, events, or situations for own actions.

Externalizing behavior   Problems that are directed outwardly by the student toward the external social environment.

External validity   Asks the question, What is the generalizability of the results of a study?

Extinction   The process by which a behavior ceases to exist due to a lack of reinforcement; the permanent removal of the source of reinforcement for a behavior.

Extinction burst   A rapid increase in the frequency, duration, or intensity of the behavior.

Extrinsic reinforcer   Reinforcer that is said to occur outside of the individual's skin, such as praise, tokens, and candy.

Fact-based threat assessment   An approach to evaluate the likelihood that students will actually carry out a threat; used to make an informed judgment on how credible and serious the threat is.

Factual information   Objective information that is quantitative and collected in a systematic manner.

Fading   Transferring stimulus control from one stimulus to another stimulus.

Fair-pair rule   Increasing a wanted behavior to take the place of the unwanted behavior.

Family dynamics   Patterns of behaviors, relationships, thinking, beliefs, traditions, and family crises that make up a family.

Fixed-interval schedule of reinforcement   The reinforcement of the first response after a set time has elapsed.

Fixed-ratio schedule of reinforcement   A certain number of responses are reinforced; the last response in a series of responses is reinforced.

Forward chaining   Teaching the first step in a chain of behaviors until it is mastered; next teaching the first and second steps together until they are mastered and so on.

Four-term contingency   The addition of a setting event prior to the antecedent, behavior, and consequence in a three-term contingency.

Functional analysis   Quantitative direct observation of behavior under preselected and controlled conditions.

Functional Analysis Screening Tool   An 18-item rating scale in which a "yes" or "no" is used to determine if an item statement accurately describes the student's unwanted behavior.

Functional behavioral assessment (FBA)   Assessment that is used to determine the environmental functions of wanted and unwanted behaviors.

Gated assessment process   A series of assessments designed to screen out students with or at risk of learning problems systematically.

Generalization stage   When students use their newly learned skills in novel situations.

Ginott model   A model based on the following eight assumptions (1) students' behavior can be improved if teachers interact with them more effectively; (2) positive communication by teachers improves the self-concept of students, which produces better classroom discipline; (3) students can learn to be responsible and autonomous; (4) accepting and clarifying students' feelings will improve their classroom behavior; (5) the improper use of praise encourages dependency of students on teachers; (6) punishment encourages student misconduct; (7) insulting students causes them to rebel; and (8) promoting cooperation increases good discipline.

Glasser's model   A model based on the premise that students are in control of their own behavior and choose whether to behave appropriately or not; choices are based on the five basic needs: survival, belonging and love, freedom, fun, and power.

Goal   A broad statement of what is to be accomplished by the end of an academic term; also termed a long-term objective.

Goal setting   The establishment of performance criteria and the identification and use of solutions to meet an established goal.

Graduated guidance   Similar to the most-to-least prompting procedure except it involves more of a fluid movement from the highest level of prompt to the lowest level.

Grandma's Rule   See Premack principle.

Group-oriented contingency   Reinforcement system based on whole-group behavior.

Guided oral reading   Oral reading by the student for which the teacher provides appropriate error corrections when mistakes are made.

Guided practice   The teacher actively participates with students in learning following an initial presentation of the material; prompted practice.

High Schools That Work   A school reform model designed to raise the academic achievement of career-bound high schoolers by combining college preparatory studies with vocational studies.

History   Refers to the class's accumulation of a common set of experiences, routines, and norms that provide the foundation for the classroom environment.

Hostile response   Threats and sarcasm are used in response to student misbehavior.

Immediacy   Refers to the rapid pace of classroom events.

Implicit   Implied; not directly expressed.

Inclusion   Placing students with special needs in the general education classrooms for instruction.

Independent practice   The students complete work on their own after an 80% success rate is achieved on guided practice; examples are cooperative learning and homework.

Indirect assessment   Gaining information from sources other than a firsthand analysis of the environmental events.

Indirect threat   A threat that is vague, unclear, and ambiguous; the plan is expressed tentatively.

Individual organizational system   Specific supports for students who are at risk of or are experiencing school failure.

Inductive criminal profiling   Looking for patterns in the present data to induce possible outcomes; strategy used to predict behavior and intervene before potential offenders commit a crime.

Inequitable discipline   The use of discipline is unequally applied or staff and students perceive that it is so.

Inflexible culture   The school's culture is static, unyielding, and insensitive to the changing needs of newer students and staff.

Informal procedure   Procedure that does not require explicit behavior management plans.

Injustice collector   Student who will not forget or forgive real or perceived injustices or the persons they feel are responsible.

Instructional momentum   Students are moving quickly and successfully through the curriculum.

Intermittent schedule of reinforcement   Reinforcement is given periodically following student behaviors; consists of fixed-interval, variable-interval, fixed-ratio, and variable-ratio schedules of reinforcement.

Internalizing behavior   Problems that are directed inwardly and represent problems with self.

Internal validity   Indicates a functional relationship between the independent variable and the dependent variable; addresses the question, Did the independent variable make the difference, or was the change due to something else?

Interobserver agreement   Percentage of agreement between two or more persons concurrently observing a behavior.

Interresponse time (IRT)   The time between two responses.

Interval recording   Provides an estimate of the percentage of intervals in which a behavior occurred; involves dividing observational periods into units of time.

Intervention   A specific set of activities and associated materials developed to prevent or remediate academic or behavioral problems; systematic involvement with a student to improve his or her behavior.

Interview   An indirect assessment that seeks to determine the source of reinforcement for a behavior by asking people in the student's life what they believe is the function of the unwanted behavior.

Intrinsic reinforcer   Reinforcer that is said to occur inside the individual's skin, such as pride, interest, and self-esteem.

Intrusiveness   The extent to which behavioral interventions are obtrusive and affect a person's bodily or personal rights.

Jones model   A model that has the following three assumptions (1) children need to be controlled to behave properly, (2) teachers can achieve control through nonverbal cues and movements calculated to bring them physically closer and closer to the students, and (3) parents and administrators can be used to gain control over student behaviors.

Judicious review   Sequence and schedule of opportunities for students to apply and develop fluency with newly acquired skills.

Kounin model   A model that has the following five assumptions (1) negative or positive moves by teachers toward students radiate out and influence others; (2) students need to be controlled by their teachers; (3) control can be improved by increasing the clarity and firmness of desists; (4) teachers can improve control by displaying "withitness"; and (5) when students have been appropriately identified as problem students and when the teachers' moves are properly timed, greater control of students' behavior is possible.

Latency recording   Measurement of the length of time between the stimulus and the subsequent behavior.

Law of Effect   States that when a behavior is reinforced, the behavior is more likely to occur in the future; also, when a behavior is not reinforced, it will extinguish.

Leakage   When students reveal clues to feelings, thoughts, fantasies, attitudes, or intentions that signal an incident of targeted violence.

Learned helplessness   Results when no matter what individuals do, they are met with negative consequences, which results in a lack of an effort to escape; tendency to give up.

Least-to-most prompting   Increasing assistance when a student does not perform a behavior.

Level I procedure   The least restrictive approach aimed at reducing unwanted behavior; systematically planned and implemented.

Level II procedure   The second least restrictive approach aimed at reducing unwanted behavior; involves the removal of the source of reinforcement.

Level III procedure   The more restrictive and aversive approach that involves the contingent removal of reinforcing stimuli.

Level IV procedure   The approach with the highest level of restrictiveness; involves the use of aversive stimuli.

Likert-like scale   A scale in which one of the following is indicated: strongly agree, agree, undecided, disagree, or strongly disagree.

Limited responding DRL   Reinforcement is presented if a certain number of behaviors or fewer is emitted.

Limit setting   Communication of expectations to students through the use of body language and physical demeanor.

Logical consequences   Consequences learned through our interaction with our environment; connected in some manner with the offense.

Love and logic model   A model that rests on four basic principles: (1) students' self-concept is always a prime consideration, (2) students should always be left feeling as if they have some control, (3) an equal balance of consequences and empathy should replace punishment whenever possible, and (4) students should be required to do more thinking than the adults do.

Maintenance   The endurance of a behavior after the intervention has been removed.

Maintenance stage   Periodic practice and review of the skill to ensure that students maintain skill mastery over time.

Mastery   Performing skills at high, successful levels.

Mediated scaffolding   Adjustments to the level of instruction provided students as they move through material, enabling them to bridge the gap between current skill level and the goal of instruction.

Modeling   An instructional procedure by which demonstrations of a desired behavior are presented so as to prompt an imitative response.

Momentary time sampling   A procedure to record behavior only if it is occurring at the end of a specified time interval.

Most-to-least prompting   Progressively decreasing assistance to a student.

Motivation Assessment Scale   A 16-item rating scale developed by Durand and Crimmins; requires a specific description of the unwanted behavior and a description of the setting.

Multidimensionality   The large quantity of events and activities that occur on a continuous basis in classrooms.

Multiple-baseline design   A single-case design that involves a series of A-B designs; includes the placement of individual graphs on top of each other; can be used across participants, behaviors, or settings.

Multiple-probe design   A single-case design that is essentially a multiple-baseline design in which the measurements are not conducted frequently; overcomes the problem of using repeated measurements by probing (assessing) the behavior every so often; probes are also used in assessing generalization/transfer of maintenance of intervention effects.

Narcissism   Lacking insight into others' needs or feelings and blaming others for failures and disappointments.

Natural reinforcer   Reinforcer that is typically used in a certain environment, such as providing grades for good performance.

Negative practice   Requires the repetition of the unwanted behavior to satiate students with that behavior.

Negative punishment   The decrease in rate or future probability of a behavior that occurs when there is a removal of a reinforcing stimulus contingent on a response.

Negative reinforcement   The increase in rate or future probability of a behavior that occurs when the behavior successfully avoids or terminates contact with an aversive stimulus; requires the removal of an aversive stimulus.

Negative scanning   Looking about an area trying to find students misbehaving.

Negative traps   The provision of punishment techniques is such that negative interactions escalate.

Nonalterable variable   A variable or characteristic that cannot be changed by the school but has been found to affect school success, such as ethnicity, socioeconomic status, gender, and home background.

Nonassertive response style   Responding to undesirable behavior by placing passive demands on students without further addressing the undesirable behavior again as it is continued.

Nonclassroom organizational system   Particular times or places where supervision is emphasized in a school setting, such as hallways, cafeteria, playground, and buses.

Nonexclusionary time-out The removal of the source of reinforcement without removing the student from the group.

Nonverbal communication Gestures, body posture and body language, expression.

Objective Short-term statement designed to lead to the overall goal; also called short-term objective.

Observation form A descriptive analysis that structures the observation into a checklist format with operational definitions of each of the target behaviors.

Observer drift When observers change the way they employ the definition of behavior over the course of a study.

Observer expectations The expectations of the observers that can influence what is observed.

Open-ended question Respondents are asked to provide their own answers to questions in an essay format.

Opinion information Subjective data collected through surveys or interviews; used to direct the collection of factual information.

Overcorrection Aversive procedures aimed at decreasing unwanted behavior; two types: positive practice and restitutional.

Pacing The movement through lessons and curriculum; should be varied and fast.

Partial-interval recording A procedure used to record a behavior if it occurred at any point within a specified time interval.

Pause and punch A vocal variation that pauses before and then emphasizes a particular word.

Pecking order Certain groups of students are officially or unofficially given more prestige and respect than others.

Performance contingent Providing external reinforcers if students have met predetermined performance criteria.

Permanent product recording The teacher observes the product of a student's behavior and not the behavior itself; the most frequently used method of recording behavior in the classroom.

Personality The pattern of traits or behaviors that characterize individual students.

Phonemic awareness The skill to discriminate words as a sequence of various sounds, isolate and segment individual phonemes (sounds), blend phonemes to make whole words, and rhyme.

Phonics An approach students are taught in beginning reading acquisition that teaches sounds corresponding to specific letters or combinations of letters.

Physical restraint A procedure used to stop students from harming themselves or others; should be implemented only by those teachers trained in physical restraint.

Positive practice overcorrection Having students repeatedly engage in an alternative appropriate behavior for an inappropriate one.

Positive punishment The presentation of an aversive stimulus contingent on the occurrence of a behavior that results in a decrease in the rate or future probability of that behavior over time.

Positive reinforcement The presentation of a stimulus contingent on the occurrence of a behavior that results in an increase in the rate or future probability of that behavior over time.

Positive scanning Looking about an area for students displaying desirable behaviors.

Praise Giving positive verbal attention contingent on appropriate behavior.

Praise around technique Students surrounding a misbehaving student are praised for appropriate behavior.

Precorrection strategy Teaching students expectations, rules, and routines to prevent a misbehavior from occurring.

Preferred activity time (PAT) A time that students are allowed to engage in activities favored by them but that are still an extension of the academic content.

Premack principle States that to get a less preferred behavior to occur, we reinforce it with a more preferred one; indicates that a high-probability behavior can reinforce a low-probability behavior; also called grandma's rule.

Primary aversive stimuli Stimuli that evoke an escape or avoidance response that is not learned (e.g., pain, nauseating smells and tastes).

Primary positive reinforcer A stimulus that is a reinforcer without being learned (e.g., food, water, warmth); also called an unconditioned reinforcer.

Primed background knowledge Connection of previously acquired knowledge to the skills about to be taught.

Problem Behavior Questionnaire A 15-item rating scale in which the frequency with which an event is likely to be seen is rated.

Problem solving Can be used as a self-management procedure by which students are taught how to reach a successful outcome to a problem situation.

Proficiency stage   Follows acquisition; once students have acquired a skill, they must be able to perform the skill at a fluent or automatic level.

Profiling   Identifying students at risk for targeted violence through the use of checklists and warning guides listing characteristics and behaviors that could potentially lead to violence.

Program   A grouping of interventions designed to prevent or remediate academic or behavioral problems.

Program common stimuli   Fading the system currently being used and moving to the system another teacher has imposed.

Prompting   A method of teaching academic behaviors; can also be used to gain the occurrence of wanted behaviors.

Proximity control   Teachers or other adults stay near students to make undesirable behaviors less likely to occur.

Publicness   The public places in which all events are witnessed by a large proportion of the students.

Punishment   Presentation of an aversive stimulus or removal of a positive reinforcer as a consequence for behavior that reduces the future rate of the behavior.

Rating scale   An indirect assessment completed by parents or teachers that provides a level of likelihood that an antecedent or consequence would occur before or after the target behavior.

Reactivity   The differences in interobserver agreement that result from observers being aware that their observations will be checked.

Redirection   An informal method by which students are prompted to do something that interferes with the unwanted behavior.

Reinforcement   Presentation of a reinforcing stimulus or removal of an aversive stimulus contingent on the occurrence of a behavior resulting in an increased or maintained rate of the behavior in the future.

Reprimand   A verbal aversive stimulus used by adults to influence children's behavior by telling them their behavior is inappropriate.

Response class   A group of responses that tends to occur due to the reinforcement of other behaviors.

Response cost   The permanent removal of some portion of a reinforcer.

Response deprivation hypothesis   A decrease in less likely behaviors below the baseline or normal levels to reinforce more likely behaviors.

Response generalization   A behavior being more likely to occur in the presence of a stimulus as a result of

another behavior having been reinforced and strengthened in the presence of that stimulus.

Responsibility training   Building patterns of cooperation by getting students to behave appropriately in a voluntary manner.

Restitutional overcorrection   Having the student return the environment to a better state than it was before.

Restrictiveness   The extent to which an individual has limited access to basic human freedoms.

Reward   Something given to a student following desirable behavior that does not necessarily result in the increased future likelihood of the behavior.

Ripple effect   The tendency for primary-aged students to react to teacher's actions when those actions are aimed at other students.

Rule-governed behavior   Behavior that is controlled by verbal stimuli; also called verbally governed behavior.

Rules   Statements that contain an antecedent, behavior, and consequence; contingency-specifying stimuli.

Safe School Initiative   A collaborative partnership with the U.S. Department of Education's Safe and Drug Free Schools Program with the overall goal to provide information to educators, law enforcement professionals, and others interested in preventing incidents of targeted violence in schools.

Satiation   A decrease in the reinforcer effectiveness of a stimulus due to receiving that stimulus.

Scatter plot   A descriptive analysis that enables the observer to monitor target behaviors over an extended period.

Schedule of reinforcement   A schedule for the delivery of reinforcers for the purpose of increasing or maintaining behavior.

School evaluation rubric (SER)   A continuum of progress evaluation rubric that is integrated within a strategic planning process designed to help educators develop, implement, and maintain a schoolwide intervention and support program.

School-related violent deaths   Deaths in schools including suicides and deaths of adults or children caused by adults or children in, near, or on the way to school.

Schoolwide positive behavioral intervention and support (SWPBIS) program   The application of positive behavioral interventions and supports to achieve socially important behavior change across all school environments.

S-delta   An antecedent or stimulus that signals a lack of reinforcement for a behavior that occurs in its presence.

Seclusionary time-out The temporary removal of a student from the group to an isolated area.

Secondary aversive stimuli Stimuli that evoke an escape or avoidance response that has been learned; examples include poor grades, reprimands, and praise.

Secondary positive reinforcer A stimulus that has acquired a reinforcing function through pairing with a previously established reinforcer; those things that are learned; also called conditioned reinforcers; includes praise, money, grades, reprimands.

Self-charting A self-management procedure in which students graph their own behavior.

Self-evaluation A self-management procedure in which students measure their own behavior against some specified standard.

Self-instruction A self-management procedure in which students are taught to "talk to themselves" or engage in covert verbal responses.

Self-management procedures A variety of methods used by students to manage their own behavior.

Self-monitoring A self-management procedure in which students observe and record their own behavior without the use of a prompt.

Self-recording A self-management procedure in which students observe and record their own behavior using a prompt.

Self-reinforcement and self-punishment A self-management procedure in which students seemingly provide consequences for their own behavior.

Sequential modification of the training situation Successfully implementing the management program in one setting and then changing the management system in another setting to match that of the first.

Setting event Antecedent stimulus occurring in the environment that sets the occasion for certain behaviors; also, part of a fourth-term contingency.

Shaping A behavior change process in which a new or unfamiliar behavior is taught through reinforcing successive approximations of the behavior; progressing step by step toward a terminal objective.

Signpost The behavior that indicates that students are planning a targeted act of violence.

Simultaneity Numerous events occurring at the same time in classrooms.

Single-case experimental design An experiment in which the participant serves as his or her own control; intent is to establish a relationship between the dependent and independent variables.

Situational inducement Decreases the probability of unwanted behaviors; influencing a behavior by using situations and occasions that already exert control over the behavior.

Social learning theory A scientific approach that assumes that human behavior is determined by a person's interaction with his or her environment, which includes the physical setting, such as the home, school, and classroom, and the social surroundings, such as peers, teachers, and parents.

Spaced responding DRL Reinforcing a behavior if a certain amount of time (interresponse time) has elapsed between responses.

Specific praise Precise statements of praise in a neutral or positive tone of voice that reflect a positive response to a specific desired behavior.

Spontaneous recovery After a behavior seems to be eliminated, it returns at various times.

Stimulus class A class of stimuli that occasion the same or similar behaviors.

Stimulus control The relationship between behavior and its antecedents in which the antecedent occasions the behavior; repeated occurrences of the behavior are dependent on its being reinforced.

Stimulus generalization Involves the increased probability of a response being emitted in the presence of a stimulus as a result of being reinforced in the presence of another stimulus.

Strategic integration Integration of concepts, content, and skills that are mutually facilitative of each other or are arranged so that instruction communicates generalizations to new areas removed from the original area of instruction.

Strategy A general conceptual approach or framework for preventing or remediating academic or behavioral problems.

Success contingent Providing external reinforcers if students have met predetermined performance criteria with additional reinforcers along the way.

Success for All A school reform model developed by Slavin and Madden; comprehensive approach to restructuring schools that serve students at risk for failure.

Systematic method A method that follows a prescribed set of procedures that has been empirically validated.

Talk It Out A method used to teach the background knowledge necessary for children who are having conflicts to meet and resolve them.

Task analysis The breakdown of a task into its individual components and steps.

Task contingent Providing reinforcement to students for simply engaging in a task for some period of time without requirements on the quality of the task.

Teaching functions Classroom experiences that move students from lack of skill mastery to mastery.

Think Time Strategy Empirically validated disciplinary response used by classroom teachers and playground and lunchroom supervisors.

Threat A spoken, written, or symbolic expression of intent to do harm or to act out violently against someone or something.

Three-term contingency Made up of the antecedent, behavior, and the consequence; used to explain behavior.

Time delay Presenting the final desired stimulus and the starting stimulus at the same time. Then, a time delay is provided between the two stimuli (constant time delay), or the time delay between the two stimuli is gradually increased (progressive time delay) on subsequent learning trials.

Time-out A temporary removal of the source of reinforcement.

Token economy system A system in which tokens are provided, contingent on some behavior that can be turned in for backup reinforcers; tokens serve as secondary reinforcers.

Total task chaining *See* Whole task chaining

Training sufficient response exemplars Teaching students several appropriate responses to a given situation.

Training sufficient stimulus exemplars Using as many possible examples of situations as possible.

Train loosely Varying the situation under which the management program is introduced.

Trait A psychological characteristic of a person, including dispositions to discriminate between or among different situations similarly and to respond to them consistently despite changing stimulus conditions.

Transitions The time spent in school between subjects, classes, and breaks.

Unison oral responding All students verbally state answers simultaneously.

Unpredictability Refers to classroom events often taking unexpected turns.

Valence A student's positive or negative reaction to a lesson.

Variable-interval schedule of reinforcement Reinforcement of the first response after an average amount of time has elapsed.

Variable-ratio schedule of reinforcement Reinforcement of behaviors on a random schedule; the last response in an average number of responses will result in reinforcement.

Veiled threat A threat that strongly implies but does not explicitly threaten violence.

Wait time Allows students the opportunity to think about the answer before actually saying it.

Whole-interval recording A procedure used to record behaviors only if they occurred throughout the entire specified time interval.

Whole task chaining Teaching the entire chain of behaviors at once.

Withdrawal design Also called A-B-A design; a single-case design that combines the "A" condition or baseline/preintervention measurements with a "B" condition or intervention to determine the effectiveness of the intervention; the "B" condition is followed by a second "A" condition.

Withitness The act of teachers being aware of what is going on in the classroom; teacher skill in communicating an overall awareness of the classroom to the students.

References

Achenbach, T. M. (1991). *Manual for the teacher report form and 1991 profile*. Burlington: University of Vermont, Department of Psychiatry.

Adams, G. L., & Engelmann, S. (1996). *Research on Direct Instruction: 25 years beyond DISTAR*. Seattle, WA: Educational Achievement Systems.

Agran, M., & Martella, R. C. (1991). Teaching self-instructional skills to persons with mental retardation: A descriptive and experimental analysis. In M. Hersen, R. M. Eisler, & P. M. Miller (Eds.), *Progress in behavior modification* (Vol. 27, pp. 36–55). Newbury Park, CA: Sage.

Agron, J. (1999). Lessons learned. *American School and University, 71*, S10–S12.

Alberto, P. A., & Troutman, A. C. (1999). *Applied behavior analysis for teachers* (5th ed.). Upper Saddle River, NJ: Merrill.

American Educator. (1996). Elements of an effective disciplinary strategy. *American Educator, 19*(4), 24–27.

American Psychological Association Commission on Violence and Youth. (1993). *Violence and youth: Psychology's response* (Vol. 1). New York: Author.

Axelrod, S. (1973). Comparison of individual and group contingencies in two special classes. *Behavior Therapy, 4*, 83–90.

Axelrod, S. (1987a). Doing it without arrows: [Review of Lavigna and Donnellan's Alternative to punishment: Solving behavior problems with non-aversive strategies]. *The Behavior Analyst, 10*, 243–251.

Axelrod, S. (1987b). Functional and structural analyses of behavior: Approaches leading to reduced use of punishment procedures. *Research in Developmental Disabilities, 8*, 165–178.

Ayllon, T., & Azrin, N. (1968). *The token economy: A motivational system for therapy and rehabilitation*. New York: Appleton-Century-Crofts.

Baer, D. M., & Wolf, M. M. (1970). The entry into natural communities of reinforcement. In R. Ulrich, T. Stachnik, & J. Mabry (Eds.), *Control of human behavior* (Vol. 2, pp. 319–324). Glenview, IL: Scott, Foresman.

Bailey, J. S. (1991). Marketing behavior analysis requires different talk. *Junior of Applied Behavior Analysis, 24*, 445–448.

Barlow, D. H., & Hersen, M. (1984). *Single case experimental designs: Strategies for studying behavior change* (2nd ed.). New York: Pergamon.

Barrish, H. H., Saunders, M., & Wolf, M. M. (1969). Good Behavior Game: Effects of individual contingencies for group contingencies on disruptive behavior in a classroom. *Journal of Applied Behavior Analysis, 2*, 119–124.

Barton, L., Brulle, A., & Repp, A. C. (1987). Effects of differential scheduling of time out to reduce maladaptive responding. *Exceptional Children, 53*, 351–356.

Bates, J. E. (1976). Effects of children's nonverbal behavior upon adults. *Child Development, 47*, 1079–1088.

Berliner, D. C. (1984). The half-full glass: A review of research on teaching. In P. L. Hosford (Ed.), *Using what we know about teaching* (pp. 51–57). Alexandria, VA: Association for Supervision and Curriculum Development.

Bloom, B. S. (1980). The new direction in educational research: Alterable variables. *Phi Delta Kappan, 61*, 382–385.

Bohannon, J. N., & Marquis, A. L. (1977). Children's control of adult speech. *Child Development, 48*, 1002–1008.

Brooks, K., Schiraldi, V., & Ziedenberg, J. (2000). *School house hype: Two years later*. Washington, DC: Justice Policy Institute.

Camarata, S. M., Hughes, C. A., & Ruhl, K. L. (1988). Mild/moderately behaviorally disordered students: A population at risk for language disorders. *Language, Speech, and Hearing Services in the Schools, 19*, 191–200.

Campbell, C. R., & Stremel-Campbell, K. (1982). Programming "loose training" as a strategy to facilitate language generalization. *Journal of Applied Behavior Analysis, 15*, 295–301.

Canter, L., & Canter, M. (1976). *Assertive discipline: A take-charge approach for today's educator*. Seal Beach, CA: Canter and Associates.

Canter, L., & Canter, M. (1992). *Assertive discipline: Positive behavior management for today's classroom* (2nd ed.). Santa Monica, CA: Canter and Associates.

Carnine, D. (1994). Introduction to the mini-series: Diverse learners and prevailing, emerging, and research-based educational approaches and their tools. *School Psychology Review, 23,* 341–350.

Carnine, D., Silbert, J., & Kameenui, E. J. (1997). *Direct instruction reading* (3rd ed.). Upper Saddle River, NJ: Merrill.

Carr, E. G. (1988). Functional equivalence as a means of response generalization. In R. H. Horner, G. Dunlap, & R. L. Koegel (Eds.), *Generalization and maintenance: Life-style changes in applied settings* (pp. 221–241). Baltimore: Paul H. Brookes.

Catania, A. C. (1975). The myth of self-reinforcement. *Behaviorism, 3,* 192–199.

Catania, A. C. (1976). Self-reinforcement revisited. *Behaviorism, 4,* 157–162.

Catania, A. C. (1998). *Learning* (4th ed.). Englewood Cliffs, NJ: Prentice Hall.

Chance, P. (1992, November). The rewards of learning. *Phi Delta Kappan,* 200–207.

Chance, P. (1999). *Learning and behavior* (4th ed.). Pacific Grove, CA: Brooks/Cole.

Charles, C. M. (1996). *Building classroom discipline* (5th ed.). White Plains, NY: Longman.

Cicchetti, D., & Nurcombe, B. (Eds.). (1993). Toward a developmental perspective on conduct disorder [Special issue]. *Development and Psychopathology, 5(½).*

Cipani, E. (1998). *Classroom management for all teachers: Eleven effective plans.* Upper Saddle River, NJ: Merrill.

Clarizio, H. F. (1986). *Toward positive classroom discipline* (3rd ed.). New York: Wiley.

Clark, L. (1996). *The video SOS! Help for parents.* Bowling Green, KY: Parents Press.

Cohen, L. G., & Spenciner, L. J. (1998). *Assessment of young children.* White Plains, NY: Longman.

Colvin, G., Kameenui, E. J., & Sugai, G. (1993). Reconceptualizing behavior management and school-wide discipline in general education. *Education and Treatment of Children, 16,* 361–381.

Colvin, G., Sugai, G., & Patching, B. (1993). Precorrection: An instructional approach for managing predictable problem behaviors. *Intervention in School and Clinic, 28,* 143–150.

Cooper, J. P., Heron, T. E., & Heward, W. L. (1987). *Applied behavior analysis.* Columbus, OH: Merrill.

Crandall, J., Jacobson, J., & Sloane, H. (Eds.). (1997). *What works in education.* Cambridge, MA: Cambridge Center for Behavioral Studies.

Dalton, T., Martella, R. C., & Marchand-Martella, N. E. (1999). The effects of a self-management program in reducing off-task behavior of middle school students with disabilities. *Journal of Behavioral Education, 9,* 157–176.

Deci, E. L., & Ryan, R. M. (1985). *Intrinsic motivation and self-determination in human behavior.* New York: Plenum Press.

Deitz, S. M., & Repp, A. C. (1973). Decreasing classroom misbehavior through the use of DRL schedules of reinforcement. *Journal of Applied Behavior Analysis, 6,* 457–463.

Delaney, E. M., & Kaiser, A. P. (1997). *How to talk to kids: A summary of what we've learned.* Paper presented at the Nashville Area Association for the Education of Young Children 1997 Early Childhood Education Conference, Hendersonville, TN.

Delbert, A. N., & Harmon, A. S. (1972). *New tools for changing behavior.* Champaign, IL: Research Press.

Department of Justice. (1997). *School crime: A national crime victimization survey report.* Washington, DC: U.S. Department of Justice, Office of Justice Programs, Bureau of Justice Statistics.

Dixon, R. C. (1993). *The surefire way to better spelling.* New York: St. Martin's Press.

Donohue, E., Schiraldi, V., & Ziedenberg, J. (1998). *School house hype: School shootings and the real risks kids face in America.* Washington, DC: Justice Policy Institute.

Dorsey, M. F., Iwata, B. A., Ong, P., & McSween, T. E. (1980). Treatment of self-injuries behavior using a water mist: Initial response suppression and generalization. *Journal of Applied Behavior Analysis, 13,* 343–353.

Doyle, W. (1986). Classroom organization and management. In M. C. Wittrock (Ed.), *Handbook of research on teaching* (pp. 392–431). New York: Collier Macmillan.

Dreikurs, R. (1968). *Psychology in the classroom: A manual for teachers* (2nd ed.). New York: Harper and Row.

Dreikurs, R., Grunwald, B., & Pepper, F. (1982). *Maintaining sanity in the classroom.* New York: Harper and Row.

Dunlap, G., dePerczel, M., Clarke, S., Wilson, D., Wright, S., White, R., & Gomez, A. (1994). Choice making to promote adaptive behavior for students with emotional and behavioral challenges. *Journal of Applied Behavior Analysis, 27,* 505–518.

Durand, V. M., & Crimmins, D. B. (1987). Assessment and treatment of psychotic speech in an autistic child. *Journal of Autism and Developmental Disabilities, 17*(1), 17–28.

Dwyer, K., Osher, D., & Warger, C. (1998). *Early warning, timely response: A guide to safe schools.* Washington, DC: U.S. Department of Education.

D'Zurilla, T. J., & Goldfried, M. R. (1971). Problem solving and behavior modification. *Journal of Abnormal Psychology, 78,* 107–126.

Eber, L., & Nelson, C. M. (1997). School-based wrap-around planning: Integrating services for students with emotional and behavioral needs. *American Journal of Orthopsychiatry, 67,* 385–395.

Eggen, P., & Kauchak, D. (1997). *Educational psychology: Windows on classrooms* (3rd ed.). Upper Saddle River, NJ: Merrill.

Elam, S. E., Rose, L. C., & Gallup, A. M. (1996). The 28th annual Phi Delta Kappan/Gallup poll of the public's attitudes toward public schools. *Phi Delta Kappan, 78*(1), 41–59.

Elliott, S. N., & Gresham, F. M. (1991). *Social skills intervention guide: Practical strategies for social skills training.* Circle Pines, MN: American Guidance Service.

Engelmann, S. (1997). *Preventing failure in the primary grades.* Eugene, OR: Association for Direct Instruction.

Engelmann, S. (1999). *Student-program alignment and teaching to mastery.* Paper presented at the 25th National Direct Instruction Conference, Eugene, OR.

Evans, I. M., & Meyer, L. H. (1985). *An educative approach to behavior problems: A practical decision model for intervention with severely handicapped learners.* Baltimore: Paul H. Brookes.

Evans, I. M., Meyer, L. H., Kurkjian, J. A., & Kishi, G. S. (1988). An evaluation of behavioral interrelationships in child behavior therapy. In J. C. Witt, S. N. Elliott, & F. M. Gresham (Eds.), *Handbook of behavior therapy in education* (pp. 189–215). New York: Plenum Press.

Evertson, C. (1987). Managing classrooms: A framework for teachers. In D. Berliner & B. Rosenshine (Eds.), *Talks to teachers* (pp. 54–74). New York: Random House.

Evertson, C., & Emmer, E. (1982). Preventive classroom management. In D. Duke (Ed.), *Helping teachers manage classrooms.* Alexandria, VA: Association for Supervision and Curriculum Development.

Faggot, B. I. (1984). The consequences of problem behavior in toddler children. *Journal of Abnormal Child Psychology, 12,* 385–396.

Fay, J. (1981). *Love and logic solution: Three types of parents.* Golden, CO: Cline/Fay Love and Logic Institute.

Fay, J. (1996). *Love and logic solution: The rules of love and logic.* Golden, Co: Cline/Fay Love and Logic Institute.

Ferster, C. B., & Skinner, B. F. (1957). *Schedules of reinforcement.* New York: Appleton.

Fey, G., Nelson, J. R., & Roberts, M. L. (2000). There are plenty of ambiguity and legal ramifications to be considered if educators plan to identify students who seem inclined to commit violent acts. *The School Administrator, 57,* 10–12.

Foster-Johnson, L., & Dunlap, G. (1993). Using functional assessment to develop effective, individualized interventions for challenging behaviors. *Teaching Exceptional Children, 25*(3), 44–50.

Foxx, R. M. (1982). *Decreasing behaviors of severely retarded and autistic persons.* Champaign, IL: Research Press.

Foxx, R. M., & Bechtel, D. R. (1983). Overcorrection: A review and analysis. In S. Axelrod and J. Apsche (Eds.), *The effects of punishment on human behavior* (pp. 133–220). New York: Academic Press.

Foxx, R. M., Martella, R. C., & Marchand-Martella, N. E. (1989). The acquisition, maintenance, and generalization of problem solving skills by closed head injured adults. *Behavior Therapy, 20,* 61–76.

Foxx, R. M., & Shapiro, S. T. (1978). The time out ribbon: A nonexclusionary time out procedure. *Journal of Applied Behavior Analysis, 11,* 125–136.

Gable, R. A. (1999). Functional assessment in school settings. *Behavioral Disorders, 24,* 246–248.

Gast, D. L., & Wolery, M. (1988). Parallel treatment design: A nested single subject design for comparing instructional procedures. *Education and Treatment of Children, 11,* 270–285.

Gewirtz, J. L., & Boyd, E. F. (1977). Experiments on mother-infant interactions underlying mutual attachment acquisition: The infant conditions the mother. In T. Alloway, P. Pliner, & L. Kranes (Eds.), *Attachment behavior: Advances in the study of communication and affect* (Vol. 3, pp. 109–143). New York: Plenum Press.

Gibbs, N. (1999, May 3). The monsters next door. *Time,* 35–37.

Ginott, H. G. (1971). *Teacher and child.* New York: Macmillan.

Ginott, H. G. (1972). *Teacher and child: A book for parents and teachers.* New York: Macmillan.

Glasser, W. (1965). *Schools without failure.* Harper and Row.

Glasser, W. (1998a). *Choice theory in the classroom* (rev. ed.). New York: Harper Perennial.

Glasser, W. (1998b). *The quality school teacher: A companion volume to* The quality school (rev. ed.). New York: Harper Perennial.

Goetz, E. M., & Baer, D. M. (1973). Social control of form diversity and the emergence of new forms in children's blockbuilding. *Journal of Applied Behavior Analysis, 6,* 209–217.

Good, T. L., & Brophy, J. F. (2001). *Educational psychology: A realistic approach* (4th ed.). White Plains, NY: Longman.

Gottfredson, G. D., Gottfredson, D. C., Czeh, E. R., Canter, D., Crosse, S. B., & Hantman, H. (2000). *Final report: National study of delinquency prevention in schools.* Ellicott City, MD: Gottfredsons Associates.

Greenberg, M. T., Kusché, C., & Mihalic, S. F. (1998). *Blueprints for violence prevention, book 10: Promoting Alternative Thinking Strategies (PATHS).* Boulder, CO: Center for the Study and Prevention of Violence.

Gresham, F. M., Quinn, M. M., & Restori, A. (1999). Methodological issues in functional analysis: Generalizability to other disability groups. *Behavioral Disorders, 24,* 180–182.

Grossman, H. (1995). *Classroom behavior management in a diverse society* (2nd ed.). Mountain View, CA: Mayfield.

Hall, R. V., & Fox, R. G. (1977). Changing-criterion designs: An alternative applied behavior analysis procedure. In B. C. Etzel, J. M. LeBlanc, & D. M. Baer (Eds.), *New developments in behavioral research: Theory, method, and application* (pp. 151–166). Hillsdale, NJ: Lawrence Erlbaum.

Harris, V. W., & Sherman, J. A. (1973). A use and analysis of the "good behavior game" to reduce disruptive classroom behavior. *Journal of Applied Behavior Analysis, 6,* 405–417.

Hart, B., & Risley, T. R. (1995). *Meaningful differences in the everyday experience of young American children.* Baltimore: Paul H. Brookes.

Hawkins, R. P., & Dobes, R. W. (1977). Behavioral definitions in applied behavior analysis: Explicit or implicit. In B. C. Etzel, J. M. Leblanc, & D. M. Baer (Eds.), *New directions in behavioral research: theory, methods, and applications* (pp. 167–188). Hillsdale, NJ: Lawrence Erlbaum.

Hawkins, R. P., & Dotson, V. A. (1975). Reliability scores that delude: An Alice in Wonderland trip through misleading characteristics of interobserver agreement scores in interval recording. In E. Ramp & G. Semp (Eds.), *Behavior analysis: Areas of research and application* (pp. 359–376). Englewood Cliffs, NJ: Prentice Hall.

Hawkins, J. D., VonCleve, E., & Catalano, R. F., Jr. (1991). Reducing early childhood aggression: Results of a primary prevention program. *Journal of the American Academy of Child and Adolescent Psychiatry, 30,* 208–217.

Heward, W. L. (1987). Self-management. In J. O. Cooper, T. E. Heron, & W. L. Heward, *Applied behavior analysis* (pp. 515–549). Upper Saddle River, NJ: Merrill/Prentice Hall.

Hinshaw, S. P. (1992). Externalizing behavior problems and academic underachievement in childhood and adolescence: Causal relationships and underlying mechanisms. *Psychological Bulletin, 111,* 127–155.

Hofmeister, A., & Lubke, M. (1990). *Research into practice: Implementing effective teaching strategies.* Boston, MA: Allyn and Bacon.

Horner, R. D., & Baer, D. M. (1978). Multiple-probe technique: A variation of the multiple baseline. *Journal of Applied Behavior Analysis, 11,* 189–196.

Hughes, C. (1991). Independent performance among individuals with mental retardation: Promoting generalization through self-instruction. In M. Hersen, R. M. Eisler, & P. M. Miller (Eds.), *Progress in behavior modification* (pp. 7–35). Newbury Park, CA: Sage.

Hyman, I. A., & Perone, D. C. (1998). The other side of school violence: Educator policies and practices that may contribute to student misbehavior. *Journal of School Psychology, 36,* 7–27.

Iwata, B., & DeLeon, I. (1996). *The functional analysis screening tool.* Gainesville: University of Florida, Florida Center on Self-Injury.

Iwata, B. A., Vollmer, T. R., & Zarcone, J. R. (1990). The experimental (functional) analysis of behavior disorders: Methodology, applications, and limitations. In A. C. Repp & N. N. Singh (Eds.), *Perspectives on the use of nonaversive and aversive interventions for persons with developmental disabilities* (pp. 301–330). Sycamore, IL: Sycamore.

Jackson, P. (1968). *Life in classrooms.* New York: Holt, Rinehart, and Winston.

Johnston, J. M., & Pennypacker, H. S. (1980). *Strategies and tactics of human behavioral research.* Hillsdale, NJ: Lawrence Erlbaum.

Jones, F. H. (1987). *Positive classroom discipline.* New York: McGraw-Hill.

Jones, V. F., & Jones, L. S. (1995). *Comprehensive classroom management: Creating positive learning environments for all students* (4th ed.). Boston: Allyn and Bacon.

Kaiser, A. P., Hancock, T. B., Cai, X., Foster, E. M., & Hester, P. P. (2000). Parent-reported behavioral problems and language delays in boys and girls enrolled in Head Start classrooms. *Behavioral Disorders, 23,* 26–41.

Kameenui, E. J., & Carnine, D. W. (Eds.) (1998). *Effective teaching strategies that accommodate diverse learners.* Columbus, OH: Merrill.

Kameenui, E. J., & Simmons, D. C. (1999). Toward successful inclusion of students with disabilities: The architecture of instruction. In *An overview of materi-*

als adaptations (Vol. 1). Reston, VA: Council for Exceptional Children.

Kazdin, A. E. (1977). Artifact, bias, and complexity of assessment: The ABCs of reliability. *Journal of Applied Behavior Analysis, 10,* 141–150.

Kazdin, A. E. (1982). *Single-case research designs: Methods for clinical and applied settings.* New York: Oxford University Press.

Kazdin, A. E. (2001). *Behavior modification in applied settings* (6th ed.). Belmont, CA: Wadsworth.

Kazdin, A. E., & Hartman, D. P. (1978). The simultaneous treatment design. *Behavior Therapy, 9,* 912–922.

Kerr, M. M., & Nelson, C. M. (1998). *Strategies for managing behavior problems in the classroom* (3rd ed.). Upper Saddle River, NJ: Merrill.

Knitzer, J., Steinberg, Z., & Fleish, B. (1990). *At the schoolhouse door: An examination of programs and policies for children with behavioral and emotional problems.* New York: Bank Street College of Education.

Kohler, F. W., & Greenwood, C. R. (1986). Toward technology or generalization: The identification of natural contingencies of reinforcement. *The Behavior Analyst, 9,* 19–26.

Kohn, A. (1992, June). Rewards versus learning: A response to Paul Chance. *Phi Delta Kappan,* 783–786.

Kounin, J. (1970). *Discipline and group management in classrooms.* New York: Holt, Rinehart and Winston.

Latham, G. I. (1992). *Managing the classroom environment to facilitate effective instruction.* Logan, UT: P&T Ink.

Lewis, T., Scott, T., & Sugai, G. (1994). The problem behavior questionnaire: A teacher-based instrument to develop functional hypotheses of problem behavior in general education classrooms. *Dianostique, 19*(2/3), 103–115.

Lickona, T. (1991). *Educating for character.* New York: Bantam.

Lovaas, O. I., & Favell, J. E. (1987). Protection for clients undergoing aversive/restrictive interventions. *Education and Treatment of Children, 10,* 311–325.

Lignugaris/Kraft, B., Marchand-Martella, N. E., & Martella, R. C. (2001). Strategies for writing better goals and short-term objectives or benchmarks. *Teaching Exceptional Children, 34,* 52–58.

Luce, S. C., Delquadri, J., & Hall, R. V. (1980). Contingent exercise: A mild but powerful procedure for suppressing inappropriate verbal and aggressive behavior. *Journal of Applied Behavior Analysis, 13,* 583–594.

Luce, S. C., & Hall, R. V. (1981). Contingent exercise: A procedure used with differential reinforcement to reduce bizarre verbal behavior. *Education and Treatment of Children, 4,* 309–327.

Lynam, D. (1996). Early identification of chronic offenders: Who is the fledgling psychopath? *Psychological Bulletin, 120,* 209–234.

Mace, F. C., & Belfiore, P. (1990). Behavioral momentum in the treatment of escape-motivated stereotypy. *Journal of Applied Behavior Analysis, 23,* 507–514.

Mace, F. C., Hock, M. L., Lalli, J. S., West, B. J., Belfiore, P., Pinter, E., & Brown, D. K. (1998). Behavioral momentum in the treatment of noncompliance. *Journal of Applied Behavior Analysis, 21,* 123–141.

Mager, R. (1962). *Preparing instructional objectives.* Palo Alto, CA: Fearon.

Malott, R. W., Malott, M. E., & Trojan, E. A. (2000). *Elementary principles of behavior* (4th ed.). Upper Saddle River, NJ: Prentice Hall.

Martella, R. C. (1994). The place of the self in self-instruction. *Behaviorology, 2,* 55–61.

Martella, R. C., Agran, M., & Marchand-Martella, N. E. (1992). Problem solving to prevent accidents in supported employment. *Journal of Applied Behavior Analysis, 25,* 637–645.

Martella, R. C., Leonard, I. J., Marchand-Martella, N. E., & Agran, M. (1993). Self-monitoring negative statements. *Journal of Behavioral Education, 3,* 77–86.

Martella, R. C., Marchand-Martella, N. E., & Agran, M. (1993). Using a problem-solving strategy to teach adaptability skills to individuals with mental retardation. *Journal of Rehabilitation, 59,* 55–60.

Martella, R. C., Marchand-Martella, N. E., & Cleanthous, C. (2001). *ADHD: A comprehensive approach.* Dubuque, IA: Kendall/Hunt.

Martella, R. C., Marchand-Martella, N. E., Macfarlane, C. A., & Young, K. R. (1993). Improving the classroom behavior of a student with severe disabilities via paraprofessional training. *British Columbia Journal of Special Education, 17,* 33–44.

Martella, R. C., Marchand-Martella, N. E., Miller, T. L., Young, K. R., & Macfarlane, C. A. (1995). Teaching instructional aides and peer tutors to decrease problem behaviors in the classroom. *Teaching Exceptional Children, 27,* 53–56.

Martella, R. C., Marchand-Martella, N. E., Young, K. R., & Macfarlane, C. (1995). Determining the collateral effects of peer tutor training on a student with severe disabilities. *Behavior Modification, 19,* 170–191.

Martella, R. C., Nelson, J. R., & Marchand-Martella, N. E. (1999). *Research methods: Learning to become a critical research consumer.* Boston: Allyn and Bacon.

Martin, G., & Pear, J. (1999). *Behavior modification: What it is and how to do it* (6th ed.). Upper Saddle River, NJ: Prentice Hall.

Matthews, B. A., Shimoff, E., & Catania, A. C. (1987). Saying and doing: A contingency-space analysis. *Journal of Applied Behavior Analysis, 20,* 69–74.

Mayer, M. J., & Leone, P. E. (1999). A structural analysis of school violence and disruption: Implications for creating safer schools. *Education and Treatment of Children, 22,* 333–356.

McConough, K. M. (1989). Analysis of the expressive language characteristics of emotionally handicapped students in social interactions. *Behavior Disorders, 14,* 127–139.

McLoughlin, J. A., & Lewis, R. B. (2001). *Assessing students with special needs* (6th ed.). Upper Saddle River, NJ: Prentice-Hall.

McParland, J. M., & McDill, E. L. (1977). *Violence in schools.* Lexington, MA: Health.

Meese, R. L. (2001). *Teaching learners with mild disabilities: Integrating research and practice* (2nd ed.). Belmont, CA: Wadsworth/Thomson Learning.

Meichenbaum, G., & Goodman, J. (1971). Training impulsive children to talk to themselves: A means of developing self-control. *Journal of Abnormal Psychology, 77,* 115–126.

Michael, J. L. (1993a). *Concepts and principles of behavior analysis.* Kalamazoo, MI: Society for the Advancement of Behavior Analysis.

Michael, J. L. (1993b). Establishing operations. *Behavior Analyst, 16,* 191–206.

Millenson, J. R., & Leslie, J. C. (1979). *Principles of behavior analysis* (2nd ed.). New York: MacMillan.

Miltenberger, R. G. (2001). *Behavior modification: Principles and procedures* (2nd ed.). Belmont, CA: Wadsworth.

Moffitt, T. (1994). Adolescence-limited and life-course-persistent antisocial behavior: A developmental taxonomy. *Psychological Review, 100*(4), 674–701.

Murray, A. D. (1979). Infant crying as an elicitor of parental behavior: An examination of two models. *Psychological Bulletin, 86,* 191–215.

National Assessment of Educational Progress. (1998). *NAEP trends in academic progress.* Washington, DC: National Center for Educational Statistics.

National Education Longitudinal Study. (1998). *Confronting the odds: Students at risk and the pipeline to higher education.* Washington, DC: U.S. Department of Education.

National Research Council. (1998). *Preventing reading difficulties in young children.* Washington, DC: National Academy Press.

National School Safety Center. (1999). *Checklist of characteristics of youth who have caused school-associated violent deaths* [On-line]. Available: http://www.nssc1.org/reporter/checklist.htm

Nelson, J. R. (1996a). *Designing predictable and supportive school environments.* Spokane, WA: Cyprus Group.

Nelson, J. R. (1996b). Designing schools to meet the needs of students who exhibit disruptive behavior. *Journal of Emotional and Behavioral Disorders, 4,* 147–161.

Nelson, J. R., & Carr, B. A. (2000). *The Think Time Strategy for schools.* Denver, CO: Sopris West.

Nelson, J. R., Gutierrez-Ohrman, C., Roberts, M. L., & Smith, D. J. (2000, April). *Preventing behavioral earthquakes: A validated antecedent manipulation strategy for minor problem behaviors.* Paper presented at the 2000 National Association of School Psychologists Conference, New Orleans, LA.

Nelson, J. R., Martella, R. C., & Galand, B. (1998). The effects of teaching school expectations and establishing consistent consequences on formal office disciplinary actions. *Journal of Emotional and Behavioral Disorders, 6,* 153–161.

Nelson, J. R., Martella, R. C., & Marchand-Martella, N. E. (in press). The effects of a comprehensive school-based program for preventing disruptive behaviors. *Journal of Emotional and Behavioral Disorders.*

Nelson, J. R., & Ohlund, B. J. (1999). *School evaluation rubric (SRE).* Lincoln, NE: Center for At-Risk Children's Services.

Nelson, J. R., & Roberts, M. L. (2000). Ongoing reciprocal teacher-student interactions involving disruptive behaviors in general education classrooms. *Journal of Emotional and Behavioral Disorders, 8,* 27–38.

Nelson, J. R., Roberts, M. L., & Marshall, J. (1999). *Simple and efficient screening procedures to identify preschool age children at risk for reading disabilities.* Paper presented at the 1999 National Association of School Psychologists Conference, Las Vegas, NV.

Nelson, J. R., Roberts, M. L., Mathur, S. R., & Rutherford, R. B. (1999). Has public policy exceeded our knowledge base? A review of the functional behavioral assessment literature. *Behavioral Disorders, 24,* 169–179.

Nelson, J. R., Roberts, M., & Smith, D. J. (1999). *Conducting functional behavioral assessments in school settings: A practical guide.* Denver, CO: Sopris West.

Newcomer, P. L., & Hammill, D. D. (1997). *Test of language development.* Austin, TX: PRO-ED.

Olson, J. L., & Platt, J. M. (2000). *Teaching children and adolescents with special needs* (3rd ed). Upper Saddle River, NJ: Merrill.

Olson, L. (1999, February 17). Researchers rate whole-school reform models. *Education Week, 18,* 1, 14.

O'Neill, R. E., Horner, R. H., Albin, R. W., Sprague, J. R., Storey, K., & Newton, J. S. (1997). *Functional assessment and program development for problem behavior: A practical handbook.* Pacific Grove, CA: Brooks/Cole.

O'Toole, M. E. (2000). *The school shooter: A threat assessment perspective.* Washington, DC: Federal Bureau of Investigation.

Paine, S. C., Radicchi, J., Rosellini, L. C., Deutchman, L., & Darch, C. B. (1983). *Structuring your classroom for academic success.* Champaign, IL: Research Press.

Pattavina, S., Bergstrom, T., Marchand-Martella, N. E., & Martella, R. C. (1992). "Moving on": Learning to cross streets independently. *Teaching Exceptional Children, 25*(1), 32–35.

Patterson, G. R. (1982a). *Coercive family process: A social learning approach.* Eugene, OR: Castalia.

Patterson, G. R. (1982b). Performance models for antisocial boys. *American Psychologist, 41,* 432–444.

Patterson, G. R., Reid, J., & Dishion, J. (1992). *Antisocial boys.* Eugene, OR: Castalia.

Pierce, W. D., & Epling, W. F. (1995). *Behavior analysis and learning.* Englewood Cliffs, NJ: Prentice Hall.

Pigott, H. E., & Heggie, D. L. (1986). Interpreting the conflicting results of individual versus group contingencies in classrooms: The targeted behavior as a mediating variable. *Child and Family Behavior Therapy, 7,* 1–15.

Polloway, E. A., Patton, J. R., & Serna, L. (2001). *Strategies for teaching learners with special needs* (7th ed.). Upper Saddle River, NJ: Merrill.

Porro, B. (1996). *Talk it out: Conflict resolution in the elementary classroom.* (ERIC Document Reproduction Service No. ED 401 506)

Premack, D. (1959). Toward empirical behavioral laws: I. Positive reinforcement. *Psychological Review, 66,* 219–233.

Redmond, S. M., & Rice, M. L. (1998). The social-emotional behaviors of children with SLI: Social adaptation or social deviance? *Journal of Speech, Language, and Hearing Research, 41,* 688–700.

Reid, J. (1993). Prevention of conduct disorder before and after school entry: Relating interventions to developmental findings. *Development and Psychopathology, 5*(½), 243–262.

Reid, J. B. (1970). Reliability assessment of observation data: A possible methodological problem. *Child Development, 41,* 1143–1150.

Repp, A. C., & Deitz, S. M. (1974). Reducing aggressive and self-injurious behavior of institutionalized retarded children through reinforcement of other behaviors. *Journal of Applied Behavior Analysis, 7,* 313–325.

Risley, T. R., & Hart, B. (1968). Developing correspondence between the non-verbal and verbal behavior of preschool children. *Journal of Applied Behavior Analysis, 1,* 267–281.

Risley, T. R., & Wolf, M. M. (1972). Strategies for analyzing behavioral change over time. In J. Nesselroade & H. Reese (Eds.), *Life-span developmental psychology: Methodological issues* (pp. 175–183). New York: Academic Press.

Rogers, C., & Freiberg, H. J. (1994). *Freedom to Learn* (3rd ed.). New York: Merrill.

Rolinder, A., & Van Houten, R. (1993). The interpersonal treatment model: Teaching appropriate social inhibitions through the development of personal stimulus control by the systematic introduction of antecedent stimuli. In R. Van Houten & S. Axelrod (Eds.), *Behavior analysis and treatment.* New York: Plenum.

Rosenblatt, J. A., & Furlong, M. J. (1997). Assessing the reliability and validity of student self-reports of campus violence. *Journal of Youth and Adolescence, 26,* 187–202.

Rosenshine, B., & Stevens, R. (1986). Teaching functions. In M. C. Wittrock (Ed.), *AERA handbook of research on teaching* (3rd ed.) (pp. 376–391). New York: Macmillan.

Salvia, J., & Ysseldyke, J. E. (1995). *Assessment* (6th ed.). Boston: Houghton Mifflin.

Scheirer, M. A., & Kraut, R. E. (1979). Increasing educational achievement via self-concept change. *Review of Educational Research, 49,* 131–150.

Schloss, P. J., & Smith, M. A. (1994). *Applied behavior analysis in the classroom.* Boston: Allyn and Bacon.

Schumaker, J., & Lenz, K. (1999). Adapting language arts, social studies, and science materials for the inclusive classroom. In *Grades six through eight* (Vol. 3). Reston, VA: Council for Exceptional Children.

Schwarz, M. L., & Hawkins, R. P. (1970). Application of delayed reinforcement procedures to the behavior of an elementary school child. *Journal of Applied Behavior Analysis, 3,* 85–96.

Scott, T. M., & Nelson, C. M. (1999). Functional behavioral assessment: Implications for training and staff development. *Behavioral Disorders, 24,* 249–252.

Scott, T. M., Nelson, C. M., & Liaupsin, C. J. (2001). Effective instruction: The forgotten component in preventing school violence. *Education and Treatment of Children, 24,* 309–322.

Seligman, M. E. P., & Maier, F. F. (1967). Failure to escape traumatic shock. *Journal of Experimental Psychology, 74,* 1–9.

Seligman, M. P. (1995). *The optimistic child: A proven program to safeguard children against depression and build lifelong resilience.* Boston: Houghton Mifflin.

Sherman, L. W., Gottfredson, D. C., MacKenzie, D. L., Eck, J., Reuter, P., & Bushway, S. D. (1998). *Preventing crime; What works, what doesn't, what's promising.* Washington, DC: National Institute of Justice.

Shores, R. E., Gunter, P. L., Denny, S. L., & Jack, S. L. (1993). Classroom management strategies: Are they ecological contexts for coercion? *Behavioral Disorders, 17,* 178–190.

Shores, R. E., Jack, S. L., Gunter, P. L., Ellis, D. N., Debriere, T. J., & Wehby, J. H. (1993). Classroom interactions of children with behavior disorders. *Journal of Emotional and Behavioral Disorders, 1,* 27–39.

Shumm, J. S. (1999). Adapting reading and math materials for the inclusive classroom. In *Kindergarten through grade five* (Vol. 2). Reston, VA: Council for Exceptional Children.

Sidman, M. (1989). *Coercion and its fallout.* Boston: Authors Cooperative.

Sindelar, P. T., Rosenberg, M. S., & Wilson, R. J. (1985). An adopted alternating treatments design for instructional research. *Education and Treatment of Children, 8,* 67–76.

Singer, G. H., Singer, J. S., & Horner, R. H. (1987). Using pretask requests to increase the probability of compliance for students with severe disabilities. *Journal of the Association for Persons with Severe Disabilities, 12,* 287–291.

Skinner, B. F. (1953). *Science and human behavior.* New York: Free Press.

Skinner, B. F. (1969). *Contingencies of reinforcement: A theoretical analysis.* New York: Appleton-Century-Crofts.

Slavin, R. (1983). When does cooperative learning increase student achievement? *Psychological Bulletin, 94,* 429–445.

Slavin, R. (1995). *Cooperative learning* (2nd ed.). Needham Heights, MA: Allyn and Bacon.

Sprick, R. (1981). *The solution book: A guide to classroom discipline.* Chicago: Science Research Associates.

Stein, M., Silbert, J., & Carnine, D. (1997). *Designing effective mathematics instruction: A Direct Instruction approach* (3rd ed.). Upper Saddle River, NJ: Merrill.

Stevens, L. J., & Price, M. (1992). Meeting the challenge of educating children at risk. *Kappen, 74(1),* 18–23.

Stevens-Long, J. (1973). The effect of behavioral context on some aspects of adult disciplinary practice and affect. *Child Development, 44,* 476–484.

Stokes, T. F., & Baer, D. M. (1977). An implicit technology of generalization. *Journal of Applied Behavior Analysis, 10,* 349–367.

Stokes, T. F., & Osnes, P. G. (1989). An operant pursuit of generalization. *Behavior Therapy, 20,* 337–355.

Sugai, G., Sprague, J. R., Horner, R. H., & Walker, H. M. (1999). Preventing school violence: The use of office discipline referrals to assess and monitor school-wide discipline interventions. *Journal of Emotional and Behavioral Disorders, 8,* 65–128.

Sulzer-Azaroff, B., & Mayer, G. R. (1991). *Behavior analysis for lasting change.* Fort Worth, TX: Holt, Rinehart and Winston.

Tawney, J. W., & Gast, D. L. (1984). *Single subject research in special education.* Columbus, OH: Merrill.

Thomas, A., Chess, S., & Birch, H. G. (1968). *Temperament and behavior disorders in children.* New York: New York University Press.

Thorndike, E. L. (1905). *The elements of psychology.* New York: Seiler.

Timberlake, W., & Allison, J. (1974). Response deprivation: An empirical approach to instrumental performance. *Psychological Review, 81,* 146–164.

Touchette, P. E., MacDonald, R. F., & Langer, S. N. (1985). A scatter plot for identifying stimulus control of problem behavior. *Journal of Applied Behavior Analysis, 18,* 343–351.

Townley, A. J. (1995). Using technology to create safer schools. *NASSP Bulletin, 12,* 61–68.

Vadasay, P. F., Jenkins, J. R., Antil, L. R., Wayne, S. K., & O'Connor, R. E. (1997). The effectiveness of one-to-one tutoring by community tutors for at-risk beginning readers. *Learning Disabilities Research and Practice, 21,* 231–248.

Van Houten, R., Axelrod, S., Bailey, J. S., Favell, J. E., Foxx, R. M., Iwata, B. A., & Lovaas, O. I. (1988). The right to effective behavioral treatment. *Journal of Applied Behavior Analysis, 21,* 381–384.

Van Houten, R., & Doleys, D. (1983). Are social reprimands effective? In S. Axelrod & J. Apache (Eds.), *The effects of punishment on human behavior* (pp. 45–70). San Diego, CA: Academic Press.

Van Houten, R., Nau, P. A., MacKenzie-Keating, S. E., Sameoto, D., & Colavecchia, B. (1982). An analysis of some variables influencing the effectiveness of reprimands. *Journal of Applied Behavior Analysis, 15,* 65–83.

Vargas, E. A. (1988). Verbally-governed and event-governed behavior. *The analysis of verbal behavior, 6,* 11–22.

Vaughn, B. J., & Horner, R. H. (1997). Identifying instructional tasks that occasion problem behaviors and assessing the effects of student versus teacher choice among these tasks. *Journal of Applied Behavior Analysis, 30,* 299–312.

Vaughn, S., Moody, S. W., & Schumm, J. S. (1998). Broken promises: Reading instruction in the resource room. *Exceptional Children, 64,* 211–225.

Voeltz, L. M., & Evans, I. M. (1982). The assessment of behavioral interrelationships in child behavior therapy. *Behavioral Assessment, 4,* 131–165.

Vossekuil, B., Reddy, M., Fein, R., Borum, R., & Modzeleski, W. (2000). *U.S. S. S. Safe School Initiative: An interim report on prevention of targeted violence in schools.* Washington DC: U.S. Secret Service.

Wahler, R. G. (1975). Some structural aspects of deviant child behaviors. *Journal of Applied Behaviors Analysis, 8*(1), 27–42.

Walker, D. W., & Leister, C. (1994). Recognition of facial affect cues by adolescents with emotional and behavioral disorders. *Behavioral Disorders, 19,* 269–276.

Walker, H., Hops, H., & Fiegenbaum, E. (1976). Deviant classroom behavior as a function of combinations of social and token reinforcement and cost contingency. *Behavior Therapy, 7,* 76–88.

Walker, H., & Severson, H. (1990). *Systematic screening for behavior disorders (SSBD).* Longmont, CA: Sopris West.

Walker, H. M. (1995). *The acting-out child: Coping with classroom disruption* (2nd ed.). Longmont, CO: Sopris West.

Walker, H. M. (2000). *Current issues in the field of emotional and behavioral disorders.* Paper presented at the Annual Research Seminar Series. University of Nebraska, Lincoln.

Walker, H. M., & Buckley, N. K. (1972). Programming generalization and maintenance of treatment effects across time and across settings. *Journal of Applied Behavior Analysis, 5,* 209–224.

Walker, H. M., Colvin, G., & Ramsey, E. (1995). *Antisocial behavior in school: Strategies and best practices.* Pacific Grove, CA: Brooks/Cole.

Walker, H. M., Horner, R. H., Sugai, G., Bullis, M., Sprague, J. R., Bricker, D., & Kaufman, M. (1996). Integrated approaches to preventing antisocial behavior patterns among school-age children and youth. *Journal of Emotional and Behavioral Disorders, 4,* 194–209.

Walker, H. M., Severson, H. H., Todis, B., Block-Pedego, A., Williams, G., Barckley, M., & Haring, N. (1991). Systematic screening for behavior disorders (SSBD): Further validation, replication, and normative data. *Remedial and Special Education, 11,* 32–46.

Watkins, C. L. (1997). *Project Follow Through: A case study of contingencies influencing instructional practices of the educational establishment.* Cambridge, MA: Cambridge Center for Behavioral Studies.

White, O. R., & Haring, N. G. (1980). *Exceptional teaching* (2nd ed.). Columbus, OH: Merrill.

Witt, J., & Beck, R. (1999). *One minute academic functional assessments and interventions: "Can't" do it...or "won't" do it?* Longmont, CO: Sopris West.

Witt, J., LaFleur, L., Naquin, G., & Gilbertson, D. (1999). *Teaching effective classroom routines.* Longmont, CO: Sopris West.

Wolery, M., Bailey, D. B., & Sugai, G. M. (1988). *Effective teaching: Principles and procedures of applied behavior analysis with exceptional students.* Boston: Allyn and Bacon.

Woolfolk, A. E. (1998). *Educational psychology* (7th ed.). Needham Heights, MA: Allyn and Bacon.

Yell, M. L. (1998). *The law and special education.* Upper Saddle River, NJ: Prentice Hall.

Zabel, M. (1986). Timeout use with behaviorally disordered students. *Behavioral Disorders, 11,* 15–20.

Zirpoli, T. J., & Melloy, K. J. (2001). *Behavior management: Applications for teachers and parents* (3rd ed.). Upper Saddle River, NJ: Merrill.

Name Index

Subject Index